Machiavellian Democracy

Intensifying economic and political inequality poses a dangerous threat to the liberty of democratic citizens. Mounting evidence suggests that economic power, not popular will, determines public policy, and that elections consistently fail to keep public officials accountable to the people. John P. McCormick confronts this dire situation through a dramatic reinterpretation of Niccolò Machiavelli's political thought. Highlighting previously neglected democratic strains in Machiavelli's major writings, McCormick excavates institutions through which the common people of ancient, medieval, and Renaissance republics constrained the power of wealthy citizens and public magistrates, and he imagines how such institutions might be revived today. *Machiavellian Democracy* fundamentally reassesses one of the central figures in the Western political canon and decisively intervenes into current debates over institutional design and democratic reform. Inspired by Machiavelli's thoughts on economic class, political accountability, and popular empowerment, McCormick proposes a citizen body that excludes socioeconomic and political elites and grants randomly selected common people significant veto, legislative, and censure authority within government and over public officials.

John P. McCormick is Professor of Political Science at the University of Chicago. He was educated at Queens College, City University of New York (CUNY), and the University of Chicago. He has been a Fulbright scholar in Bremen, Germany; a Monnet Fellow at the European University Institute, Florence; and a Radcliffe Fellow at Harvard University. McCormick is the author of *Carl Schmitt's Critique of Liberalism: Against Politics as Technology* and *Weber, Habermas, and Transformations of the European State: Constitutional, Social, and Supranational Democracy*. He has published numerous articles on contemporary democratic theory, Florentine political and constitutional thought, and twentieth-century German legal, political, and social theory in scholarly journals, including *Modern Law Review*, *American Political Science Review*, and *Political Theory*.

For Annabelle

Machiavellian Democracy

JOHN P. McCORMICK

University of Chicago

CAMBRIDGE
UNIVERSITY PRESS

CAMBRIDGE UNIVERSITY PRESS
Cambridge, New York, Melbourne, Madrid, Cape Town, Singapore,
São Paulo, Delhi, Dubai, Tokyo, Mexico City

Cambridge University Press
32 Avenue of the Americas, New York, NY 10013-2473, USA

www.cambridge.org
Information on this title: www.cambridge.org/9780521530903

First published 2011

Printed in the United States of America

A catalog record for this publication is available from the British Library.

Library of Congress Cataloging in Publication data

McCormick, John P., 1966 –
Machiavellian democracy / John P. McCormick.
    p.   cm.
Includes bibliographical references and index.
ISBN 978-0-521-82390-6 (hardback) – ISBN 978-0-521-53090-3 (pbk.)
1. Machiavelli, Niccolò, 1469–1527.   2. Democracy – History – To 1500.
3. Democracy – History – 16th century.   I. Title.
JC143.M4M34   2010
321.8 – dc22   2010022940

ISBN 978-0-521-82390-6 Hardback
ISBN 978-0-521-53090-3 Paperback

Contents

Preface

A crisis of political accountability besets contemporary democracy. Mounting evidence suggests that elections, even "free and fair" ones, do not elevate to office individuals who are especially responsive to the political aspirations and expectations of their constituents. Moreover, democratic governments seem decreasingly adept at preventing society's wealthiest members from wielding excessive influence over law and policy making. Rather than facilitating popular rule, electoral democracies appear to permit and perhaps even encourage political and economic elites to enrich themselves at the public's expense and encroach upon the liberty of ordinary citizens. The inability of citizens to control the behavior of public officials and counteract the power and privilege of the wealthy poses a grave threat to the quality of political representation today; it severely debilitates conditions of liberty and equality within the republics of our age.

Inspired by the most astute analyst of republics from earlier ages, Niccolò Machiavelli, this book reconsiders constitutional measures and institutional techniques that popular governments before modern democracy devised to surveil and control political and economic elites. In order to repel the threat that such elites posed to liberty and equality, common citizens within traditional republics proposed and often enacted accountability measures far more extensive than competitive elections. Guided by Machiavelli's endorsement of such measures and his extensive analyses of the Venetian, Florentine, and, especially, Roman constitutions, I have identified the following components of a robust, extra-electoral model of elite accountability and popular empowerment: offices or assemblies that exclude the wealthiest citizens from eligibility; magistrate appointment procedures that combine lottery and election; and political trials in which the entire citizenry acts as ultimate judge over prosecutions and appeals. I name the type of popular government that incorporates such institutions "Machiavellian Democracy."

Historically, political and economic elites within republics resisted popular demands for such institutions, and the numerous philosophers and historians who served as spokesmen for aristocratic republics stridently denounced such measures. Indeed, thinkers such as Aristotle, Cicero, Guicciardini, and Madison, who preferred constitutional arrangements that in important respects insulate political and economic elites from popular control, have dominated Western political thought. Before significant numbers of European and colonial intellectuals began to champion progressive and radical democratic movements in the nineteenth century, Machiavelli was arguably the only major intellectual advocate of republics in which the people vigorously contest and constrain the behavior of political and economic elites by extra-electoral means. In this Machiavellian spirit, I conclude the book with reform proposals drawn from elite-constraining and citizen-enabling measures debated or enacted in notable ancient, medieval, and Renaissance republics – most important among them, the institution that earns Machiavelli's highest praise, the tribunes of the plebs from republican Rome. Specifically, I propose, as a thought experiment, a "People's Tribunate" to be amended to the United States Constitution.

Institutional prescriptions aside, this book accentuates the fundamentally populist – that is, citizen-empowering – and anti-elitist foundation of Machiavelli's political thought. I ultimately suggest that Machiavelli ought to be interpreted as a democrat and not a "republican" – at least not as the influential "Cambridge School" approach to intellectual history defines "republicanism" and as it depicts the illustrious Florentine secretary's relationship to it. As already mentioned, the vast majority of republics emulated and their advocates espoused aristocratic rather than democratic constitutional models. Therefore, I will argue, republicanism generally indulged, in theory and practice, far more dominance of domestic politics by socioeconomic elites than Cambridge-associated or -influenced scholars such as John Pocock, Quentin Skinner, and Philip Pettit acknowledge, and certainly more than Machiavelli's writings ever countenance. Such commentators consistently ignore or acutely underplay Machiavelli's endorsement of class-specific offices, extra-electoral modes of appointing and punishing public officials, and assemblies where common citizens broadly discuss and directly decide public policy.

On my interpretation, Machiavelli prompts us to rethink fundamentally the institutional and cultural requirements of political participation and elite accountability within popular government. Unlike republicans such as Cicero, Guicciardini, the young Madison, or later advocates of electoral democracy such as Walter Bagehot and Joseph Schumpeter, Machiavelli seeks to mitigate rather than simply exploit common citizens' general deference to socioeconomic and political elites. Indeed, liberty, according to Machiavelli, depends on institutions that respond to and even further encourage a popular disposition of distrust, bordering on animosity, toward wealthy and prominent members of the citizenry and the government.

In short, *Machiavellian Democracy* refocuses attention on the necessity of properly institutionalized class conflict for healthy domestic politics within popular governments. It revives Machiavelli's forgotten lesson that the resources of wealthy citizens and the wide discretion enjoyed by officeholders pose the principal threats to liberty in such regimes – *not* the purported ignorance, apathy, and caprice of common citizens. This book reevaluates the institutions that Machiavelli and democratic republicans thought necessary to confront these dire threats to the liberties of common citizens and their polities and it considers ways that such institutions might be revived today.

Abbreviations for Machiavelli's Writings

D *Discourses on Titus Livy's First Ten Books* (c. 1513–17).
    Niccolò Machiavelli, *Discorsi sopra la prima deca di Tito Livio*. In
        Opere I: I Primi Scritti Politici. Edited by Corrado Vivanti (Torino:
        Einaudi-Gallimard, 1997), 193–525.

DF *Discursus on Florentine Affairs* (1519–20).
    Niccolò Machiavelli, *Discursus Florentinarum rerum post mortem
        iunioris Laurentii Medicis*. In *Opere I*, 733–45.

FH *Florentine Histories* (1532).
    Niccolò Machiavelli, *Istorie Fiorentine*. Edited by Franco Gaeta
        (Milano: Feltrinelli, 1962), 68–577.

P *The Prince*, or *On Principalities* (1513).
    Niccolò Machiavelli, *Il Principe*. In *Opere I*, 114–92.

Introduction

Liberty, Inequality, and Popular Government

> The desires of free peoples are rarely pernicious to freedom.
>
> Machiavelli, *Discourses* I.4
>
> The few always behave in the mode of the few.
>
> Machiavelli, *Discourses* I.7

The political impact of economic inequality is an increasingly vexing problem in contemporary democracies, especially the United States.[1] The expectation that government will be accessible and responsive to all citizens on a relatively equal basis is an enduring hallmark of popular government. Yet democratic theorists and policy analysts today seem incapable of answering a question that was central to the life of pre–eighteenth-century republics: what institutions will prevent wealthy citizens from dominating a government that is supposed to serve the entire citizenry? Before modern democracy, the motivations and resources of the wealthy were considered among the chief threats – often, the greatest domestic threat – to the stability and liberty of popular governments.[2] Unless formally restrained, the richest citizens tended to use their power and privilege to molest the vulnerable with impunity and manipulate the workings of government for their own benefit rather than that of the general citizenry. In pursuit of these ends, wealthy individuals and families frequently subverted republican governments, maneuvering them in more narrowly oligarchic or autocratic directions, even, on occasion, going so far as to deliver them to foreign powers.[3]

On the contrary, the constitutional framers of modern republics conceptualize control of elites in politically narrow and sociologically anonymous terms: they concentrate almost exclusively on the power and influence that public officials, not wealthy citizens, might wield inappropriately. These constitutions seldom if ever explicitly guard against the likelihood that the wealthy will fill the ranks of elected magistrates disproportionately or the possibility that the former will dictate the behavior of less-wealthy citizens who do ascend to office.[4]

Consequently, it is fair to ponder whether the institutional arrangements of modern republics better realize the policy preferences of the few than those of the many. When the constitutional architects of modern republics, especially in the United States, did look beyond officeholders to consider potentially pernicious social groups, they most frequently identified citizens with less or no property – the masses, the mob, the multitude – as the principal threat to the stability of government and the liberty of fellow citizens.[5] On this view, the preeminent danger facing republics is an avariciously or fanatically motivated popular majority bent on expropriating or persecuting vulnerable minorities.[6] Although the American Framers sometimes entertained the notion that wealthy citizens could threaten liberty, they explicitly designed the U.S. Constitution to "control the government and the governed," that is, the magistrates and the majority of the people.[7]

I contend that the socioeconomic disposition of modern republicanism and the institutional choices that followed from it have deleterious implications for the workings of contemporary democracy. After all, modern popular governments are no less vulnerable than their historical antecedents to corruption, subversion, and usurpation by the wealthy.[8] Moreover, an increasing number of scholars depict election, the institutional centerpiece of modern democracy, as a less than robust means of keeping public officials accountable.[9] This state of affairs suggests that democratic accountability requires citizenries to exercise more formal, direct, and vigorous control of political *and* socioeconomic elites than has been the norm, traditionally and especially in recent decades.[10] How can average citizens deter the wealthy from exercising disproportionate influence over the common weal, and how can they dissuade public officials from behaving in ways that persistently defy the will of their constituencies and adversely affect the latter's interest? How can they effectively punish socioeconomic and political elites when both act – often collusively – in ways that threaten the liberty of citizens and the stability of popular governments?[11] Reflections on the social, intellectual, and institutional history of earlier republics suggest that the accountability crisis plaguing contemporary democracies is structural and, therefore, calls for substantive constitutional reforms.[12]

In this book, I excavate the techniques besides elections by which common citizens attempted to restrain wealthy citizens and public magistrates in prominent ancient, medieval, and Renaissance republics, and I imagine how they might be reconstructed within contemporary democracies. The political writings of Niccolò Machiavelli (1469–1527) provide the portal through which I retrieve the following forgotten or abandoned practices of elite accountability:

- Offices or assemblies empowered with veto or legislative authority that exclude the wealthiest citizens from eligibility (Chapters 3 and 4)
- Magistrate appointment procedures that combine lottery and election (Chapter 4)
- Political trials in which the entire citizenry acts as ultimate judge over prosecutions and appeals (Chapter 5)

While Machiavelli's most famous book, *The Prince*,[13] appears to instruct rulers how they might best manipulate the people, I will demonstrate, on the contrary, that his most important and perhaps most original piece of political advice is something quite different: how common people might control elites. Machiavelli's greatest work, *Discourses on Titus Livy's First Ten Books*,[14] illustrates that Machiavelli posed the question of elite accountability more sharply than any major figure in the Western political canon, including more recent and supposedly more radically egalitarian political theorists. Furthermore, I contend that even scholars, such as those affiliated with the "Cambridge School" of intellectual history, who understand Machiavelli as a "republican" (and not as a notorious enabler of tyrants), severely underestimate his efforts to establish extensive, constant, and animated modes empowering common citizens to resist domination by wealthy citizens and to discourage corruption among magistrates. Indeed, besides underestimating the place of institutions that secure elite accountability in Machiavelli's political thought, they overlook Machiavelli's insistence that republics afford common citizens the opportunity to discuss and vote directly on legislation, since widely inclusive rather than elite-dominated fora, he argued, will produce better policies for regimes characterized by a "civil way of life." Put simply, Machiavelli's political theory was more popularly participatory and empowering than was republicanism, generally, and, for that matter, than is democracy as generally conceptualized and practiced today.[15]

Machiavelli's Class Politics

Machiavelli was especially attuned to the motives and behavior of the most privileged and powerful members of republics; prominent citizens he called, interchangeably, nobles (*nobili*), aristocrats (*ottimati*), and, most generally, the great (*grandi*).[16] Machiavelli derived his opinion of society's elite from exhaustive reading of both ancient and recent histories of Mediterranean republics, as well as from his firsthand experience as a relatively lowborn public servant in the early-sixteenth-century Florentine Republic. As clearly demonstrated by the *Discourses*, Machiavelli was particularly impressed by Livy's account of social conflict, originally and continually instigated by the nobility, in the young Roman Republic.[17] More immediately, Machiavelli personally endured the especially cruel and condescending treatment of Florence's ottimati while carrying out his duties as an administrative secretary, diplomatic emissary, and militia organizer.[18]

Machiavelli frequently suffered scorn and derision due to his father's debts and alleged illegitimate birth.[19] Despite a family tradition of service in the republic's highest offices, his own relative poverty and ill-repute rendered Machiavelli ineligible for the city's chief magistracies.[20] Indeed, he owed almost entirely to the patronage of the republic's chief executive, Piero Soderini, his tenure in diplomatic, secretarial, and military posts that were usually inaccessible to individuals of low social station. The ottimati, feeling entitled to a lion's share of such positions, often lashed out at Machiavelli and frequently interfered with the effective performance of his duties: in particular, they watered down his plans to establish a citizen militia in the republic, blocked his appointments to the highest emissarial posts, and smeared him as a descendant of a bastard, as a tax debtor, and as a sexual deviant.[21]

Generalizing from his studies and experiences, Machiavelli argues that an unquenchable appetite for oppression drives the grandi's efforts to accumulate wealth, monopolize offices, and gain renown within republics (D I.5; P 9). Machiavelli suggests that wealthy and prominent citizens who are reluctant to share military command, elected office, and tenure in senatorial bodies (consultative committees, upper houses, and high courts) with average citizens are more consumed by an appetite to dominate others than they are by any desire to further the common good. Despite pretensions of noblesse oblige (D I.37) – pretensions disingenuously validated throughout history by obsequious writers (*scrittori*) (D I.58) – Machiavelli is adamant: captains, magistrates, senators, and judges desire to make others bend to their will, seek to gain elevated status within their polities, and, especially, endeavor to enrich themselves materially at the expense of the commonweal.

It must be noted that Machiavelli did not define the grandi or ottimati as a formally closed, narrowly hereditary class – his elite is not a feudal aristocracy, even if he refers to them with words such as "nobles" or "aristocrats." For instance, Machiavelli explicitly distinguishes the grandi of cities and republics from the idly rich "gentlemen" who oppress the inhabitants of countrysides from the safety of their castles (D I.55). On the contrary, Machiavelli understands the great as a class into which many newly wealthy and politically entrepreneurial commoners were constantly integrating themselves, as was the case in the Florentine Republic and the mid- to late-Roman Republic. While not as fixed as a hereditary caste of elites and despite the rather fluid upward or downward mobility of particular individuals or families, the socioeconomic class "grandi" serves as a reliable snapshot at any particular moment of those members of society who Machiavelli believes to be motivated by a desire to oppress.

Another clarification on the nature of Machiavelli's elites: Many interpreters, when addressing the issue, downplay or dismiss the material and economic aspects of Machiavelli's descriptions of the grandi's motivations and conduct.[22] The desire to oppress that Machiavelli ascribes to the grandi, they suggest, corresponds most closely with a pursuit of honor, glory, and fame. Supposedly, it has much less to do, if anything, with the acquisition of wealth or the use of material privilege to maximize political advantage. However, Machiavelli consistently emphasizes the grandi's wealth and points out the oppressive ends to which they invariably put it. For instance, the wealthiest Romans, he notes, constituted "the greater part of the nobility" (D I.37); Machiavelli identifies the ruling class of the Syracusan Republic as the senators and the rich (P 8); early in the *Discourses*, Machiavelli characterizes the grandi as those who "possess much" and who use their largesse "incorrectly and ambitiously," specifically, to oppress common citizens and undermine popular goverments (D I.5). Later in that work, he speaks in tandem of the nobility's "great ambition" and their "great avarice" (D I.40).

Most decisive, I believe, is the following judgment that Machiavelli levels in his chapter on Rome's Agrarian Laws: Machiavelli notes that, over the course of the republic's history, the nobles "always conceded honors or offices to the plebs without extraordinary scandals, but they defended property with the utmost obstinance" (D I.37). This is an earsplitting understatement. Here Machiavelli elliptically references the fateful instance when Rome's senators, seeking to protect their ever-expanding economic privilege, murdered the reformer Tiberius Gracchus in the open air of the republic's civic space. Clearly, Machiavelli understands the nobles, the aristocrats, "the great" to value material goods much more highly than they do their reputation and prestige, their honor and dignity. Indeed, they themselves openly demonstrate this fact on occasions when they are pressed vigorously with redistributive demands.

Machiavelli sharply distinguished the grandi from the rest of the citizens within republics; from the *popolo*, the plebeians or "the people."[23] Rather than desiring to oppress others, as do the grandi, the people desire primarily to avoid being oppressed by the great (D I.5; P 9). On this view, average people are inclined to seek security in their persons and for their families, to be content with whatever material goods they already possess, to avoid diminutions of relatively modest material well-being or demotions in already humble social status. The people are naturally inclined to avoid oppression, whether by suffering it themselves or inflicting it on others: in response to oligarchic oppression, the Roman plebeians peaceably secede from the city (D I.4, D I.40); in response to legislation that challenged their socioeconomic ascendance within the republic, the Roman nobles resort to electoral corruption or murder (D I.5, D I.37).

Machiavelli's notoriously cynical generalizations on the nature of "men" induce many interpreters to conclude that he attributes to all people the same passions, especially the appetites for political oppression and material acquisition.[24] However, Machiavelli's distinction between the grandi and the popolo suggests that the few and the many, respectively, are motivated by two qualitatively different appetites. As Machiavelli elaborates further: "The incorrect and ambitious conduct of those who possess much inflames in the breasts of those who do not possess so much the desire to possess more, either to avenge themselves against the former by despoiling them, or to make it possible for the latter to gain the riches and honors that they see being so badly used by the others" (D I.5). In other words, the rich do not use their largesse primarily for their own private enjoyment (let alone for public benefit) but rather to oppress poorer citizens. Moreover, the people do not naturally resent the great for possessing material advantages but rather for using such advantages against themselves, that is, to abuse less wealthy citizens.

The interaction of these two appetites – embodied by the grandi who possess much and the popolo who possess little – sets in motion the dynamics of domestic politics within popular governments. According to Machiavelli, the people, otherwise disinclined to desire material abundance, develop such a desire as a direct result of the bad example set by the grandi. The people often seek vengeance against the great by attempting to deprive them of their material advantage, or they look to defend themselves by striving to gain and deploy the wealth and power that the rich hitherto wielded inappropriately. On Machiavelli's view then, while the people certainly can be incited or provoked by oligarchic mistreatment into behavior that the grandi self-servingly characterize as "oppressive," they are, in fact, fundamentally disinclined toward domination. The people act in such a manner either to protect themselves or to exact vengeance on the grandi. Given this stark contrast between the respective appetites of the people and the grandi, Machiavelli observes that "the judgment of free peoples is rarely pernicious to liberty" (D I.4), while "the few always behave in the mode of the few" (D I.7).

Philosophers, historians, and statesmen such as Aristotle, Livy, and Cicero, whom Machiavelli deems "the writers," tended to disparage the people's capacities to deliberate and decide policy within popular governments and to exaggerate the frequency and intensity of outbursts of popular rage (e.g., D I.58).[25] These views, of course, would decisively influence the often ochlophobic constitutional prescriptions of later republican theorists such as Harrington, Montesquieu, Rousseau, and Publius, to name just the most prominent. Machiavelli, however, treats cases of popular unruliness so appalling to "the writers" as merely isolated instances – instances almost invariably justified as responses to egregious acts of oppression or usurpation on the part of the grandi (D I.28, D I.45). In fact, to Machiavelli's mind, popular indignation is an almost unequivocal good: republics best realize liberty precisely when the people respond spiritedly to domination by the grandi – especially, he suggests, when such responses become instantiated in new laws (D I.4) or result in the public execution of prominent but dangerous citizens (D III.1). Republics are doomed, Machiavelli insists, unless the people, in addition to participating substantively and directly in lawmaking (D I.18), also vigorously check the insolence of the grandi through accountability institutions such as Rome's tribunes of the plebs and popularly decided political trials (D I.5, D I.37, D III.1).[26] While the people's judgment is not always perfectly exercised in such capacities, Machiavelli argues that the people, when operating within constitutional bounds, act more wisely than do either princes or the few, when similarly constrained (D I.58). Moreover, Machiavelli will help us understand that utter "perfection" is an unrealizable standard unfairly deployed by previous writers to discredit democracies and to legitimate oligarchies.

Republics Oligarchic and Democratic

A striking exception in the long history of republican social and constitutional theory, Machiavelli's political thought was no less out of step in the Florence of his day. By advocating popularly inclusive institutional checks on the grandi, Machiavelli flouted the Venetian pretensions and aristocratic preferences of prominent Florentine republicans. Two individuals in particular typify this disposition: Bernardo Rucellai (1448–1514), the powerful patron of Machiavelli's literary circle, the Orti Oricellari, and the grandfather of one of the two young *ottimati* to whom Machiavelli dedicates the *Discourses*; and Machiavelli's young patrician interlocutor, the historian, diplomat, and eventual minister for Medici popes, Francesco Guicciardini (1483–1540). Rucellai and Guicciardini were (in differing degrees of intensity) critics and opponents of the democratic republic, or *governo largo*, founded by Friar Girolamo Savonarola after the expulsion of the Medici in 1494, a regime whose institutional centerpiece was a widely inclusive popular assembly, the Great Council. Machiavelli's patron, Soderini, eventually presided over this republic as Gonfalonier (standard-bearer) of Justice, while Machiavelli himself, as noted previously, tirelessly served it in several official capacities until its demise in 1512.

These statesmen cum humanist *literati*, Rucellai and Guicciardini, aspired to reorder Florence along the lines of Venice's oligarchic republic, or *governo stretto*, in which a senate, and the members of the upper class who invariably fill it, hold sway over the polity. In their estimation, family prominence and political experience – functional approximations for "wisdom" and "prudence" – should determine membership in the senate; and elections, tempered neither by random selection among all citizens nor by affirmative action for less privileged citizens, should determine appointments to major magistracies. Whereas ancient democracies widely distributed most public offices through lottery and medieval republics often guaranteed political positions for poorer citizens enrolled in less prosperous craft guilds,[27] Guicciardini insisted that common citizens should decide through general elections who among the "best citizens" would hold office, but generally ought not to hold office themselves.[28]

In this "electoral" and "senatorial" model of republicanism, exemplified by the kind of governo stretto preferred by Rucellai and Guicciardini, ordinary citizens possess only a limited capacity to affect the behavior or challenge the decisions of the republic's elective magistracies and chief deliberative body, the senate, both of which are dominated by a few wealthy and notable citizens. On the contrary, Machiavelli championed a reconstructed and in significant ways democratized Roman constitutional model wherein common citizens freely indict public officials and powerful citizens, exert veto power over policy, discuss and vote directly on legislation, and formally judge citizens and officials accused of political crimes. In this "tribunate" and "assembly" model of popular government – what I call Machiavellian Democracy – civic contestation is institutionalized through offices such as the tribunes of the plebs, for which the very wealthiest and most prominent citizens are ineligible, and citizen participation is facilitated in plebeian assemblies, which either exclude the most prominent citizens or at least minimize their influence.[29]

The plebeian tribunate, the centerpiece of Machiavelli's prescriptions for popular government, was an intensely controversial institution in assessments of the Roman Republic throughout the history of Western political thought. Yet, inexplicably, scholarship devoted to elaborating Machiavelli's "republicanism" virtually ignores it. Aristocratic republicans such as Guicciardini, and many more before and after him, from Cicero to Montesquieu, criticized the tribunate for opening the doors of government to upstarts, who subsequently stir up strife, sedition, and insurrection among the common people.[30] Machiavelli, on the contrary, argues that the establishment of the tribunes made the Roman constitution "nearly perfect" by facilitating the plebeians' assertion of their proper role as the "guardian" of Roman liberty (D I.3–5). As we will observe in Chapter 4, when Machiavelli proposes constitutional reforms to restore the Florentine Republic, he creates a tribunician office, the *proposti* or provosts, a magistracy that wields veto and appellate powers and excludes the republic's most prominent citizens.[31] Even commentators who understand Machiavelli to be an advocate of the people, an antagonist of the grandi, or – albeit more rarely – a democrat pure and simple largely neglect the crucial role that the Roman tribunes play in his political thought and consistently overlook his proposal to establish Florentine tribunes, the provosts, within his native city.[32]

Machiavelli against Cambridge School "Republicanism"

In fundamental ways, then, Machiavelli is an outlier in the largely conservative tradition of republican political theory, both in and out of Florence – nay, he may be that tradition's most incisive critic and steadfast adversary. In this light, highly influential scholars associated with the Cambridge School, such as Quentin Skinner and John Pocock, seriously distort Machiavelli's thought and the republican tradition itself when they force him to serve as the spokesman par excellence of "republicanism."[33] Skinner consistently speaks of the many "positive resemblances" between Machiavelli's theories and traditional Italian republicanism,[34] and he emphasizes "the remarkable extent to which Machiavelli continued to present his defence of republican values in traditional terms."[35] In particular, Skinner insists, Machiavelli's thought is almost fully consonant with that of Cicero, the paradigmatic aristocratic republican of the ancient world. Skinner duly notes, on the one hand, Machiavelli's preference for public tumult, social discord, and class conflict, and he acknowledges, on the other, Cicero's aspiration for civic tranquility conforming to the ideal of *concordia ordinum*.[36] Yet despite such stark differences, Skinner insists that "the continuities" between Machiavelli and Cicero on issues such as the common good, public interest, and civic greatness "are much more fundamental."[37]

As I demonstrate in what follows, one cannot so easily demote the issue of class division and conflict to a minor point of divergence when considering Machiavelli's place within the republican tradition. After all, it is Machiavelli's praise of tumults within Roman republican politics that leads him to endorse practices that were anathema to republicans such as Cicero in the past, Guicciardini in his own day, and, among many others, Madison in later centuries.[38] The Roman tribunate is central to Machiavelli's politics precisely because it emerged as a consequence of initial class tumult in Rome and served subsequently as a frequent instigator of further social discord.

Pocock, conversely, carefully distinguishes Machiavelli's preference for a democratic republic from, in particular, Guicciardini's more decidedly patrician predilections.[39] Nevertheless, due to a preoccupation with political contingency, with the question of the "temporal finitude" of republics, Pocock conceals the oligarchic character of modern republicanism by recasting it in a distinctly Machiavellian light – that is, by famously distilling the essence of modern, "North Atlantic" republicanism to a "Machiavellian Moment."[40] If Pocock had been concerned less with "the politics of time" and more with politics as such, he might have more accurately titled his book *The Guicciardinian Moment*.[41] After all, Guicciardini's aristocratically inflected republican paradigm wins out historically over Machiavelli's much more democratic one; Guicciardini's electoral and senatorial model and not Machiavelli's assembly-based and tribunician model serves as the constitutional template of modern representative governments.[42]

By merging with too little qualification Machiavelli's political thought and republicanism generally, Skinner, Pocock, and many scholars inspired by their work blunt the Florentine's historical originality and obscure his value for contemporary reflections on political reform and institutional innovation. It is precisely Machiavelli's *departures* from the republican tradition (a) that demonstrate how republicanism, unless reconstructed beyond all recognition, tends to reinforce rather than ameliorate the elitist aspects of contemporary representative democracy; and (b) that accentuate overlooked institutional and social alternatives available for correcting this tendency today. In particular, Machiavelli's critique of the tradition demonstrates how republicanism explicitly justified the free hand that the wealthy and public officials enjoy at the expense of the general populace within republics; and his writings advocate class-specific magistracies and popularly inclusive assemblies through which common citizens might make elites more accountable and within which common citizens might effectively deliberate and decide upon laws and policy themselves.

To catalogue criticisms that I have elaborated elsewhere, Cambridge scholars tend to emphasize inppropriately Machiavelli's conformity with traditional republicanism in the following ways: They underemphasize class conflict in Machiavelli's theory such that they generally ignore the institutional means that he prescribed for common people to render elites responsive and accountable; they associate popular agency in Machiavelli's thought exclusively with either military service or elections as opposed to more intensive and extensive participation within domestic politics; they carelessly equate his criticisms of the nobility with those of the plebeians, thereby undermining the prominent role that Machiavelli assigns to the people as "guardians of liberty";[43] they fixate on Machiavelli's abstract definitions of liberty at the expense of both his specific policy recommendations for how citizens might best achieve and maintain it, as well as his historical examples that illustrate how civic liberty operates in healthy political practice; they use Machiavelli to formulate a definition of liberty that opposes political oppression such as monarchical and imperial rule but that rather meekly addresses forms of social domination aside from slavery; and, finally, they remain largely silent on the kind of domestic domination of the people by socioeconomic and political elites that was fully consonant with republican theory and very often perpetrated in republican practice.

To be sure, Cambridge-associated scholars highlight with considerable skill certain normative advantages that republicanism offers in contrast with contemporary liberal democracy: for example, promotion of nonxenophobic patriotism, attention to the common good, emphasis on duties as opposed to rights, and the formulation of an unusually broad notion of liberty.[44] However, Cambridge interpretations for the most part overlook Machiavelli's criticisms of social domination, and they permit republicanism to be appropriated uncritically as a progressive, antihierarchical political theory. In this regard, Cambridge interpretations are helpful for neither Machiavelli studies nor democratic theory today. Indeed, such interpretations seriously undermine attempts by Cambridge scholars themselves to address the political deficiencies of contemporary liberalism and representative democracy.[45]

For example, in a rousing new afterword appended to *The Machiavellian Moment*, Pocock denounces the oligarchic tendencies of contemporary representative government.[46] Skinner, for his part, has long lamented the fact that decreased popular participation in liberal democracies has encouraged elites to encroach upon the liberty of citizens.[47] However, the republican frameworks within which the authors operate and through which they interpret Machiavelli permit them to offer very little that might constructively address the very situation that they so decry. Pocock's fixation on political contingency seems to prevent him from frankly acknowledging the institutional form that republicans most consistently recommended for dealing with political finitude: a constitutional model that circumscribes popular participation, and hence political contestation and discord, as much as possible – that is, an aristocratically dominated *governo stretto*.[48] Pocock's recent complaints against the woeful state of popular participation and elite accountability in contemporary republics would resonate more authentically if his magnum opus had better specified the attributes of "the Guicciardinian moment" in which the citizens of modern republics still live, and if it had better conceptualized how to render this protracted historical "moment" more genuinely "Machiavellian."

Alternatively, Skinner inadvertently rules out direct popular control of politics as a solution to the problem of elite dominance within contemporary politics precisely as a result of his merging of Machiavelli's political thought with that of aristocratic republicans such as Cicero. Indeed, given the strictly electoral quality of his rendering of the republican tradition, Skinner offers no alternative form of "public participation" to mere voting that can plausibly secure individual liberty and ensure elite accountability. By focusing on elections, on the neutralization of class conflict, and on institutional balance of power, among other themes, Skinner's appropriation of republicanism, despite his intentions, very much reaffirms the status quo of contemporary representative democracy. In Chapter 6, I demonstrate that, much like Skinner, republican philosopher Philip Pettit collapses Machiavelli's political theory into the aristo-cratic tradition of republicanism, a tradition from which Machiavelli worked so hard to distance himself. Moreover, I argue that Pettit's reliance on elec-toral and senatorial institutions and his rejection of tribunates and popular assemblies undermine his effort to institutionalize a robust notion of liberty appropriate for contemporary democratic republics.

Partly as a corrective to these Cambridge and Cambridge-inspired interpre-tations, I devote considerable portions of this book to Machiavelli's critical engagements with conventional, oligarchically inclined republicans. In Chap-ter 2, I explore Machiavelli's attempt to convince the young, noble dedica-tees of the *Discourses* (again, one of whom was the grandson of arch-patrician Bernardo Rucellai) to accept a governo largo: a Roman-styled republic in which the people are armed militarily with weapons and institutionally with tribunes, organized as soldiers in legions and as citizens in assemblies. Furthermore, throughout the book I contrast Machiavelli's views with those of Guicciar-dini, the young patrician who brilliantly and effectively translated traditional aristocratic preferences into novel institutional prescriptions that presage the constitutional forms of modern representative government.[49]

Indeed, I treat the writings and interactions of Machiavelli and Guicciardini, both of whom reflected at length upon the political history of their native city, as well as upon constitutional arrangements in the ancient Roman and con-temporary Venetian republics, as a fateful crossroads in the history of Western political thought. Machiavelli is often dubbed the "founder" of modern politi-cal science, modern republicanism, or "modernity" itself.[50] However, since he recommends that republics build class division and class conflict into their con-stitutions, Machiavelli's writings can be read as the most radical summation, if the last gasp, of traditional populist republicanism. Unlike Italy's principalities and oligarchic republics, the peninsula's more widely participatory and socially contestatory guild republics and *governi larghi* lacked a committed intellectual spokesman like Machiavelli – until the moment of their demise.

On the contrary, Guicciardini is the largely unacknowledged father of modern democracy understood as elective oligarchy, a cleverly reconstructed version of governo stretto: Guicciardini combined unqualified elections and wide suffrage within a framework that anticipated modern representative government and its major spokesmen, such as James Madison and Joseph Schumpeter.[51] In this model, elections allow common people to rule "indi-rectly" by determining who among the most prominent citizens exercise direct rule for specific terms of office. But it also reduces popular participation to the casting of votes, which, while sorely needed in polities where popular par-ticipation is fully absent, is a necessary but far from sufficient condition for robust democratic politics. Writing as one political epoch, presciently artic-ulated by Guicciardini, eclipsed another, vividly summarized by Machiavelli, these thinkers, read in light of each other, offer fresh yet historically grounded insights into more varied forms of popular participation and elite accountability available to republics than are usually considered viable today.[52]

Class Salience and Political Inequality

By following Machiavelli's injunction to make class conflict central to republican discourse and democratic practice, this book emphasizes a crucial difference between pre– and post–eighteenth-century constitutions. In ancient, medieval, and Renaissance republics, "the people" referred to both (a) the citizen body in its entirety and also (b) the poorest, nonwealthy, or non-elite majority of the citizenry.[53] This ambiguity is perhaps best captured by the Roman example. On the one hand, "the people" signifies the collective *res publica* of the *populus*, a unitary conception of citizenship that includes patricians *and* plebeians. On the other hand, the idea of "SPQR" (the Senate and People of Rome) reflects a binary conception of the citizenry, one in which the plebeians, set apart from the patrician elite, the nobles, or the senatorial class, separately comprise "the people."[54] The constitutions of modern republics almost invariably follow the first, unitary vision and posit the people as a homogeneous unit: the "sovereign people" is a monolithic and socioeconomically anonymous collection of individual citizens – including elites – all of whom enjoy formal equality under the law.[55]

As a result of class-anonymity and sociological "holism," modern constitutions seem less concerned with, and may be less adept at, keeping wealthy citizens from dominating politics than were traditional constitutions in which the people comprised a subset, the largest subset, of the citizenry. Machiavelli explicitly endorses class-specific institutions on the belief that they promote the class-consciousness and class-contention that animates energetic popular engagement and effective political accountability. Only with great difficulty can the people ignore, forget, or rationalize the privileges that elites enjoy at their expense and use to their disadvantage when, on the one hand, government organs reflect those differences, and, on the other, the people's own magistrates, such as the tribunes of the plebs, constantly remind them of the persistence of socioeconomic and political inequality within their polity.[56]

There are several grounds for conceptualizing class as the most basic form of social identity and difference within popular governments, even where it has *not* been formally recognized within the constitutions of such regimes. Historically, class antagonism has been a ubiquitous feature of popular governments, a feature that raises urgent normative issues concerning social and political life within such regimes. The freedom afforded more fully by popular governments than by any other regime ensures that some citizens will acquire economic and social advantages that in turn inevitably jeopardize political equality within those polities and threaten the liberty of less prosperous and entrepreneurial citizens. Among the available evidence, Aristotle's pioneering efforts in political sociology and virtually all contemporary economic research attest to this fact.[57] Since class divisions invariably undermine the moral raison d'être of regimes governed by free and equal consociates under law, traditional popular governments and their advocates sought to compensate poorer citizens politically for their lack of material resources relative to socioeconomic elites and attempted to empower them formally such that they might deliberate and decide over policy in ways that attenuated elite influence.[58]

Undoubtedly, class-specific measures that politically compensate poorer citizens for their lack of resources – affirmative action for common citizens, if you will – raise other concerns. First and foremost, the formal-institutional recognition of class division within popular governments may pose its own threat to liberty and equality. For instance, it may place sociopsychological limits on the advancement of those deemed, say, "plebeians," and conversely, it may unfairly place metaphorical targets on the backs of elites, especially the wealthy minority, in such regimes. I suggest that such concerns are too often grossly inflated. Unlike other social identities, class designations that are intended to empower poorer individuals or families do not necessarily ensnare the latter within stigmatizing categories; class designations do not, as some argue that racial and ethnic categories do,[59] fundamentally and indefinitely debilitate the social and political agency of those placed within such categories. The social mobility characteristic of most republics that I deal with in this book ensures that plebeians do not necessarily remain plebeians in perpetuity. Large numbers of poorer citizens consistently join the senatorial orders of these republics as they accumulate wealth and renown; conversely, the wealthy do not necessarily remain eternally rich and powerful in such regimes (although the precious cultural capital of a good family name may for a long time outlive, say, severely depleted fortunes or especially embarrassing public scandals). More to the point, class-specific institutions ensure that poorer citizens who do not enjoy rapid advancement in material welfare and social status enjoy compensation for their plight; these measures empower them to participate in politics on a relatively equal par with wealthy and prominent citizens.

Thus, efforts to ameliorate the political impact of class division by formally acknowledging it in a legal-constitutional manner – that is, by pursuing institutional means that permit poorer citizens to moderate *formally* the significant advantages that the wealthy enjoy *informally* – do not confine individual citizens to lifelong or generation-spanning social stigmatization and psychological debilitation. While class divisions persist within even the most vibrantly egalitarian republics (progressives hope that they persist in decreasingly obnoxious forms), individuals and families who avail themselves of the social mobility characteristic of such regimes consistently move up and down from one class to another. Furthermore, the wealthy, if they feel unfairly treated within class-conscious republics, as they so often have, may quite easily give up the designation "rich": unlike those who are coded by racial or ethnic categories, the wealthy may voluntarily cast off their identity, for instance, by giving away the preponderance of their wealth to charity or to the poor.

Class specificity also raises questions concerning the egalitarianism, economic and political, of Machiavellian Democracy. Since this model of democracy acknowledges economic inequality as a fact and seeks to instantiate it in political arrangements, doesn't it do more to entrench rather than ameliorate class divisions? Isn't it a fundamentally inegalitarian vision of democracy?

Reality, it turns out, is more subtle than appearances suggests. I will argue that Machiavelli's case for a governo largo, a widely inclusive republic, can be understood best in terms of the trepidations felt by his audience of Florentine patricians over the egalitarian threat that such regimes pose; a threat still palpable in a political culture scarred by the Ciompi Revolt (1378), a full-scale working-class revolution, that occurred a century and half before Machiavelli wrote.[60] I suggest that Machiavelli's extremely cautious discussion of the Gracchi, economic reformers who threatened the expanding economic privilege of Rome's senatorial class, suggests that Machiavelli's model of popular government is not incompatible with a politics that, in his own words, keeps "the public rich and the citizens poor" (D I.37; cf., D III.16). A close examination of Machiavelli's treatments of the Brothers Gracchus, in light of Florence's post-Ciompian backdrop, suggests that elite accountability requires economic as well as political measures to contain the "insolence" of the nobles.

I will also derive from Machiavelli's writings a pragmatic yet dynamic strategy for securing greater political equality among citizens in decidedly inequitable circumstances: Machiavelli prefers arrangements in the early history of republics where the common people are formally excluded from full political participation in the most powerful and prestigious public offices such that they more energetically and urgently use offices and assemblies reserved exclusively for themselves to secure their liberty against their more privileged fellow citizens – among other ways, by striving to gain eligibility for the highest offices from which they are initially excluded. Machiavelli's account of the Roman constitution and his proposals for reforms of the Florentine constitution suggest that the kind of participation exercised by the people in separate – even, and especially, subordinate – institutions during the early years of a polity is more efficacious than the kind they might practice when seeking offices (a) for which they are formally eligible but may never attain on a regular basis and (b) within which they are outmaneuvered by elite officeholders. The grandi, for their part, are naturally indignant over conditions that veer, however remotely, toward equality of any sort; the people, Machiavelli intimates, must be provoked into similar indignation, and are done so, with beneficial political results, by formal political inequality that, counterintuitively, inspires more substantive political equality in practice. In particular, collective memory among the people of formal inequalities from the past seems to inspire within them a sensitivity to informal inequalities that persist in the present. For instance, even after the rigid divide between plebeians and patricians was supplanted by the more fluid one between "the people" and "the nobles" in Rome, the intensity of the former division still motivated the Roman lower classes to seek more equitable standing vis-à-vis elites while living under the latter one.

Elite Accountability and Popular Participation

Before I proceed to elaborate Machiavellian Democracy in the book's main chapters, let me clarify a point on popular participation: It may appear at this juncture that my emphasis on elite accountability threatens to overwhelm considerations of wider forms of citizen participation. In other words, by focusing so extensively on control of elites, I may overlook the necessity of the kind of ground-up, self-initiated citizen activism already so sorely lacking within contemporary democracies.[61] Indeed, an emphasis on elite accountability may in fact reinforce the excessively passive quality of citizenship within contemporary electoral democracies rather than initiate a genuine corrective to this problematic trend.[62] After all, my approach may concede too easily the fact that elites will continue "to rule," while promising only that a Machiavellian remedy will ensure that they do so under greater constraints than common citizens usually impose on them. In this sense, doesn't Machiavellian Democracy necessarily place the people in a hopelessly reactive position vis-à-vis elites such that politics continues to be conducted on "the grandi's" terms? Only to a limited extent, I would argue.

Firstly, Machiavelli's writings take as their bearings the structural conditions of liberty's possibility; that is, Machiavelli's political theory addresses head on the empirical facts that any effort to establish or expand popular liberty must consider. By dedicating his two greatest works of political science, respectively, to a prince and to the ottimati, Machiavelli signals his awareness, on first principle, of the obstacles confronting the people in their efforts to secure liberty, and to exercise and enjoy it by participating in government: princely rule and oligarchic power. Machiavelli does not philosophically formulate a wholly abstract or ideal "concept" of individual or popular freedom that he then expects citizens to impose mechanically upon political reality. Instead, Machiavelli begins with basic social facts. As mentioned previously, the widespread freedom that republics afford *all* social actors, not just average people, invariably enables some citizens to amass greater material resources than others; moreover, political necessity *always* permits public officials within every regime type, even democracies, considerable prerogative in the exercise of their duties. As a result of these two facts, republics, democracies, and popular governments have eternally suffered attempts by wealthy citizens to manipulate politics to their own benefit, attempts that extend to conspiracies and coups; and even the most politically egalitarian societies, such as democratic Athens, understood that the individuals who serve as magistrates necessarily exercise potentially invidious discretionary power. This is the case no matter how much democracies or governi larghi might have attempted to control the potentially corrupting effect of such discretionary power ex ante through non-electoral means of appointment (via lottery) or ex post through threats of severe monetary or bodily punishment for bad conduct in office (via public scrutinies and political trials).

Thus, the common citizens of regimes characterized by the very highest levels of political freedom and socioeconomic equality must always confront the political influence of those who possess greater resources and the political power of those who actually hold office. In this light, elite accountability always was and always will be as much a core issue for popular government as was and is popular participation; this was the case even before post–eighteenth-century representative governments reduced virtually *all* political participation to elite accountability – elite accountability quite imperfectly secured, it must be said, through electoral politics.[63] Common citizens within *all* forms of popular government, therefore, have no choice in many circumstances but to act in a "reactive" way (since it is impossible always to act preemptively) against the behavior of socioeconomic and political elites that infringes upon public liberty. In this sense, democratic citizenship necessitates some forms of participation that are, admittedly, reactive to the motivations and conduct of elites.

Secondly, however, Machiavelli does not starkly distinguish – again, certainly not in abstract conceptual terms – practices that facilitate popular participation, on the one hand, from those that keep elites accountable, on the other. In other words, Machiavelli endorses neither a strictly "positive" or "negative" form of republican liberty, nor an exclusively "direct" or "indirect" form of popular government. Machiavelli's writings suggest, in fact, that attempts to separate participation from accountability, or what we would call positive from negative forms of liberty, exhibit either a philosophical conceit that contributes to the inefficacy of popular government or an aristocratic bias that necessarily facilitates an inflation of elite prerogative.[64] As we will observe in Chapter 3, Machiavelli clearly lauds institutional arrangements in which the people directly participate in rule, that is, where the people formally assembled deliberate over and decide laws themselves; but he also endorses indirect forms of rule, such as electoral procedures through which the people choose the chief magistrates who govern them for intermittent periods of time.

Furthermore, both the plebeian tribunate and popularly judged political trials, as Machiavelli reconstructs them from Roman constitutional history, effectively mix elements that promote both popular participation and elite accountability. Indeed, as we'll observe, both the Roman tribunes and the Florentine provosts serve as linchpins between elite accountability and popular rule: Machiavelli empowers these class-specific magistrates not only with veto authority over offices dominated by the wealthy, but he assigns them duties that explicitly link them with the functioning of popular assemblies where the people either initiate law themselves or are radically empowered to revise legislative proposals preferred by senatorial elites.

Machiavellian Democracy is characterized by class-specific, popularly empowering, and elite-constraining institutions that accomplish two tasks: they raise the class consciousness of common citizens and formally enable them to patrol more exalted citizens with a vigor that electoral politics in and of itself does not provide. Notwithstanding the conventional historical accounts that exaggerate the regularity and violence of popular outbursts against privileged and powerful citizens, for Machiavelli, average people too often exhibit a basic aversion to politics, even an inclination to class quiescence and deference, dispositions corresponding with their natural desire "not to be oppressed." The modern, socially homogeneous notion of the "sovereign people" and the establishment of class-anonymous government institutions reinforce the people's general disposition not to want to know, or do anything, about their subordinate position – just as aristocratic republicans such as Cicero, Guicciardini, and the *Federalist* Madison may have hoped. Consequently, the constitutions of post–eighteenth-century republics give wealthy citizens and public magistrates free rein to follow their natural inclinations – in Machiavelli's estimation, free rein to oppress others.

As I demonstrate in subsequent chapters, Machiavelli's constitutional analyses suggest that the apparent absence of class consciousness in modern republics is not necessarily the result of changed material conditions or the supercession of class as an objective fact. Rather, Machiavelli might attribute the contemporary absence of healthy class consciousness and class contestation to a failure on the part of modern republican constitutions to remind common people of their subordination to socioeconomic and political elites and their failure to provide the people with the proper institutional channels through which they can challenge the elite's power and privilege. The indirectness of popular participation within electoral democracy opens an expansive space within which political elites exercise dangerous discretion and into which socioeconomic elites intervene unimpeded into politics. It is this space that Machiavellian Democracy seeks to fill with broader popular participation both facilitated by ancient but seemingly novel political institutions and motivated by an acutely antihierarchical social disposition. Only through such broader popular participation will disadvantaged, marginalized, or exploited citizens bring socioeconomic and political elites more directly to account.

PART I

I

Peoples, Patricians, and the Prince

A new prince has never disarmed but rather always armed his subjects. . . . for in arming them they all become his partisans.

Machiavelli, *The Prince*, chap. 20

All the laws made in favor of freedom arise from the disunion between the popolo and the grandi.

Machiavelli, *Discourses* I.4

Machiavelli might seem a rather dubious figure from whom democrats can learn anything worthwhile about control of elites and government by the people. After all, the Florentine is notorious for advising rulers to manipulate their subjects. Indeed, many interpreters consider this to be the main point of his most famous work, *The Prince*. In the present chapter, and throughout this book, I focus primarily on Machiavelli's *Discourses*, a work largely devoted to republics and the place of popular participation and elite accountability within them. Nevertheless, it is worth noting at the outset the surprising pro-popular and anti-elitist elements evident within the former, shorter, and more infamous work explicitly devoted to principalities. I will then offer some general considerations on the respective roles of the people and the elite in Machiavelli's ideal polity, the Roman Republic.

The Prince and the People

Many readers who approach *The Prince* with justifiable skepticism often seize upon the apparent cynicism of the following observation and piece of advice: since the common people, "the vulgar," are captivated by "appearances," Machiavelli recommends that a prudent prince endeavor to exploit this disposition to his advantage (P 18). Such readers accentuate passages where Machiavelli suggests that a prince need only *appear* to be generous, merciful, honest, and pious, while he presumably may in fact *be* otherwise (P 18). They then conclude that Machiavelli's central lesson must be the following: to secure and expand his dominions, a prince must mystify the people's minds by providing circuses rather than the political equivalents of bread (cf. also P 21). Yet this interpretive approach to *The Prince* altogether neglects the other element of the people's attention, something that Machiavelli mentions in the same breath as "appearances": he declares explicitly that the people are concerned with both "appearances and outcomes." Indeed, Machiavelli devotes as much (and perhaps more) space in *The Prince* to concrete outcomes as to appearances – that is, there is as much advice about providing protection and sustenance to the people as there is concerning the plausible means by which a prince might fool or distract them (e.g., P 7, P 9, P 10).

Machiavelli even suggests that the people can differentiate and prioritize between appearances and outcomes – if, in fact, the two are fundamentally distinct: after all, outcomes themselves have appearances and all appearances are certainly not false. Machiavelli demonstrates through the examples of Cesare Borgia, Agathocles, and Hannibal, among others, that the people will forgive a prince for exhibiting qualities, such as cruelty or frugality, that are conventionally considered bad, so long as these contribute ultimately to their well-being (P 7–8, P 17). The people desire peace, security, civil courts, and retribution against those who oppress them. On these matters, Machiavelli insinuates, appearances *are* reality: since "in the world there is no one but the vulgar" – that is, no one but those concerned with appearances and outcomes – then, ultimately, appearances and outcomes are all that count (P 18). If there are many circumstances where appearances and reality converge and cannot be uncoupled, then there exist numerous matters, perhaps fundamental ones, about which the people cannot be easily deceived or manipulated. Machiavelli demonstrates, especially through his detailed account of Borgia's career, that the people must be satisfied as much by "good government" and institutions that provide political accountability as by stupefying spectacles (P 7; cf. D II.32).[1]

Cynically inclined readers should also note how Machiavelli affiliates himself directly with the people throughout *The Prince*. In the book's dedicatory letter, he ascribes to himself the perspective of a people who observe and evaluate a prince, and at other crucial junctures he emphatically affiliates himself with "the vulgar," the common people (P dedication, P 3, P 7). Indeed, while serving as advisor and minister to Piero Soderini in the 1494–1512 Florentine Republic, Machiavelli wrote to the Gonfalonier's nephew, with words that presage *The Prince* by seven years, "I am looking not through your glass [i.e., that of a young patrician], in which nothing is seen but prudence, but rather through the glass of the many, who have to judge the end of things as they are done, and not the means by which they are done."[2]

In *The Prince*, Machiavelli notoriously elevates ends over means. But the preceding statement suggests that he does so not because he wishes to subvert popular morality, but more fundamentally because the people are especially compelled to concern themselves with outcomes or ends. Both lowly public servants and the generality of the people, bereft of the vast resources enjoyed by prominent and powerful citizens, prove especially vulnerable to changes in political fortune and failed or unrealized policies. Neither can afford the luxury of fussing over means, as can members of the *ottimati*, who, when their "prudence" proves insufficient to preserve their states, seamlessly ingratiate themselves with new powers-that-be or easily avail themselves of comfortable exile.

The people's special concern with outcomes as much as, or even more than, appearances is relevant to Machiavelli's noteworthy insistence that a prince not tamper with the women and property of subjects, lest he endanger his dominion (P 19). *The Prince*, after all, offers no "ring of Gyges" with which a prince might help himself, under cover of invisibility, to the wives, daughters, land, and provisions of his subjects. There are limited means available to a prince who wishes to *seem* to refrain from such activities while actually engaging in them. Likewise, one must think through the somewhat allusive but not completely intangible implications of Machiavelli's advice that a prince militarily train and arm the people as well as live closely among them, easily accessible to them – especially, when such a people is accustomed to enjoying liberty (P 5).[3]

The range of actions available to a prince may be circumscribed in significant ways, to say the least, under such conditions: that is, in circumstances where the prince lives in intimate proximity to subjects who possess weapons, knowledge of how to use them in common, and an understanding of the difference between freedom and oppression. One need not read *The Prince* too closely to notice that a prince's reliance on the people for military strength serves simultaneously to enable and constrain his power. In any case, Machiavelli's emphasis on the considerable resources offered to a prince by "the many" also must be read in light of his views on the prince's *and* the people's timeless antagonists, "the few."

The Opposing Natures of the Popolo and the Grandi

In *The Prince*, Machiavelli advises princes to base their power on the *popolo*, the "people," rather than the *grandi*, the "great" (P 9). Every polity, Machiavelli observes, is comprised of two diverse humors: the oppressive appetite motivating the grandi, who wish to command and dominate the people; and the appetite to resist or avoid domination characteristic of the popolo, who desire only *not* to be commanded or oppressed by the grandi (cf., D I.4–5). Machiavelli observes that the people often turn to a prince seeking defense and protection from aristocratic oppression, while the great regularly elevate one of their own as a prince to serve as the vehicle of their oppressive designs on the people. However, Machiavelli is hardly indifferent to which of the two humors a prince chooses to employ as a base of power: he cautions a prince against using the grandi as a political foundation because the few perceive him to be merely one among themselves, simply a first among equals. Consequently, the grandi generally prove difficult to manage and, worse, they're inclined to dispose of a prince very readily when he displeases or disappoints them (P 9).

The people, however, will support a prince as long as he protects them from the grandi. And should they become disaffected with a prince's rule, they will tend to abandon him, rather than assassinate him, as will the grandi. Machiavelli describes the people's appetite in finite terms, while he presents the grandi's appetite as unquenchable: the people wish "only" not to be oppressed by the few, an outcome that can be achieved concretely, whereas the grandi's appetite to dominate is insatiable – there is no point at which they definitively achieve this end. Since the people's desire not to be dominated can be satisfied, and they are many, while the grandi's cannot, and they are few, Machiavelli logically reasons that a prince should build his state on the vast majority, those whose demands he can meet with relative ease.

In addition to these strategic considerations, Machiavelli also adopts a moral perspective in *The Prince* when he compares the motives of the grandi and the popolo. Machiavelli states: "One cannot with honesty or decency satisfy the great without injury to others, but one may satisfy the people in such a way, for the end of the people is more decent (*onestà*) than that of the great, since the latter want to oppress and the former want not to oppress" (P 9). The word onestà connotes, as rendered, honesty and decency, and even honor and goodness.[4] What status could such a quality hold in a work notorious for its amoral, even immoral, outlook? *The Prince* itself does not clearly convey what Machiavelli means by the people's morality, since it does not contain many examples of collective action on their part. However, the *Discourses*, as we'll observe at greater length in what follows, provides much more material with which to evaluate the people's moral capacity, their onestà.

In the *Discourses*, Machiavelli consistently entwines popular morality with civic ideals like the "common good" and "public freedom" (D I.4). For instance, he insists: "The desires of free peoples are rarely pernicious to freedom because they arise either from being oppressed or from suspicion that they may be oppressed" (D I.4). Onestà, applied in the context of this passage, suggests that the people more openly and frankly express their aspirations and intentions than do the grandi, as demonstrated in the notable episode of the Decemvirate (or the Ten), discussed more fully later in this book: when senators attempt to negotiate the end to a crisis in which tyranny has gripped the republic, the people declare that they want to burn alive both the members of the Ten and the young nobles who had abused them so egregiously during the tyranny (D I.44). The noble emissaries admonish the people for answering brutality with brutality, but then, more to the point, instruct them in the following way: the people should keep their desires to themselves until such time as they are properly positioned to satisfy them. Thus, the people prove two of Machiavelli's points in this incident: they exhibit an oppressive appetite only in response to oppression inflicted upon them; and they do so honestly, overtly, without any trace of subterfuge or guile.

The grandi, of course, are masters of concealing their intentions until opportunities arise that allow them to achieve their goals. Machiavelli fills the *Discourses* with episodes demonstrating this aptitude for concealment, starting with circumstances where the patricians showed restraint by hiding their contempt for the people only so long as the Tarquin kings were available to protect the latter (D I.3). The Roman grandi, according to Machiavelli, did not spew "the venom" they harbored in their breasts for the people until such time as the Tarquins were eliminated. Such examples substantiate Machiavelli's observations on the grandi in *The Prince*: "they are more aware and astute and allow more time to save themselves" (P 9). Moreover, as he remarks in the *Discourses*, the nobles, "possessing a great deal, can effect an alteration with greater force and greater effect" (D I.5). In Florentine parlance, the term "alteration" (*alterazione*) connotes both a change in plans and a political coup. Contrary to the professions of classical authors, then, most notably Aristotle,[5] the especially keen powers of discernment and foresight that may divide human beings into masters and slaves, elites and subjects, do not, according to Machiavelli, entitle the *aristoi* to a preeminent share in ruling. After all, the empirical evidence marshaled by Machiavelli suggests that the aristocrats rely on such qualities, and on the material advantages resulting from them, first and foremost to oppress others, to overturn regimes, and not to rule wisely or advance the common good.

In another sense, Machiavelli intimates that the people's decency or onestà entails a fundamental disinclination to injure others. The following contrast between the humors verifies this point: when the Roman people felt oppressed by the grandi and saw no recourse to relief via civic institutions such as the tribunes, they did not lash out by murdering patricians or destroying their property; rather, their first reaction was to secede peacefully from the city (D I.4, D I.40). On the contrary, when the grandi feared that they could no longer persuade, intimidate, or bribe one tribune to veto what they considered to be the radical pro-plebeian initiatives of another, they resorted to murder: as mentioned before, in a decisive incident invoked but uncelebrated by Machiavelli, senators violently and publicly cut down Tiberius Gracchus and his supporters (D III.11, D I.37; P 9).

Even more substantively, if decency or goodness means that the people are capable of superior moral judgments, the following Roman cases elaborated in the *Discourses* certainly apply. The Roman plebs wanted to share terms in consular offices with the nobles on the grounds that they were greater in number, fought the republic's wars, and protected its freedom. Yet despite the fact that they had been clamoring to wield consular authority, once eligible, in a series of elections, the plebeians elected all patricians to such positions – especially in instances when the senate stacked the slates of candidates with patently unworthy plebeians or unusually sterling patricians (D I.47–8). These elections not only validate the people's judgment at moments when they choose specific individuals to hold office, but they also underscore how indispensable for good government are the people's active challenges to elite privilege: without popular contestation of their authority, the grandi themselves, apparently, would never have put forward such excellent candidates for office from their own ranks.[6] The fact that the grandi bribe unsuitable individual plebeians to run for office is, of course, given Machiavelli's descriptions of their behavior throughout the *Discourses*, no surprise at all.

Machiavelli's praise of the people's superior judgment seems at odds with his denunciations, mentioned in the preceding, of the grandi's superior cleverness and astuteness in furthering their oppressive designs. How can those who are less clever, wanting in resources, and disinclined toward aggressive behavior rule in competition with let alone serve as watchdogs over more cunning, craven, and wealthy social actors? While I will elaborate on this at length in this book, Machiavelli's answer is fairly simple: arm the people militarily with weapons and training; and arm them constitutionally with tribunes and assemblies. Machiavelli insists that the people, led by consuls in the field and tribunes at home, bound together in legions beyond the republic's borders and in assemblies within its walls, shackled by laws and yet empowered with concrete judgment, will prove to be "wiser" than either the few or even a prince (D I.7, D I.44, D I.58). For now, it should be noted that Machiavelli contends not only that a healthy republic ought to authorize the people to choose magistrates – a point even conceded by many aristocratic republicans – but also that a republic authorize them to discuss and ultimately decide legislation in assembly and to judge political trials collectively. Moreover, the plebeian tribunate, which excludes the wealthiest and most prominent citizens, also serves to inform or remind the people of their constant oppression by the grandi, whether overt, hidden, or forgotten, and provides the concrete means through which the people endeavor to counter such oppression.

Machiavelli and the Florentine Ottimati

Machiavelli's advice that princes ought to favor the people over the grandi reappears in the *Discourses*, even though it is primarily a book on republics. He provides the Greek example of Clearchus to specify more clearly how a prince should treat the grandi and secure himself with the people (D I.16). Confirming Machiavelli's general observations on such matters in *The Prince*, Clearchus came to power through the efforts of the nobles: they brought him back from exile with the expectation that he would help them satisfy their desire to deprive the people of liberty (D I.16). But once empowered in this capacity, Clearchus switched his allegiance to the plebs and disposed of the nobles: he hacked them all to pieces, "to the extreme satisfaction of the people." Machiavelli uses this imagery repeatedly; indeed, one might think it to be his favorite recourse against elites. In at least two other places, one each in *The Prince* and the *Discourses*, he recounts with apparent approval how a group of elites is explicitly hacked to pieces (P 13) or implies that they should have been (D I.27).[7]

Machiavelli's images of dismembered elites hint at the following: If a group of self-proclaimed best men or first citizens – "aristocrats" (*aristoi*) or "optimates" (*ottimati*) – do not live up to these designations, they need to be *un*-membered, *dis*-membered, from such associations. Since the nobles are so consumed with distinction, especially with distinguishing themselves from "the multitude," Machiavelli suggests that when such distinction is no longer justified, they must themselves be rendered multitudinous – physically. The very word with which Machiavelli most generally refers to elites – grandi – means, precisely, the great or the big. Machiavelli's imagery here suggests that when they become *too* big for themselves (and everyone else), they need to be cut down to size – literally.

This gives us no small insight into Machiavelli's opinion of the patricians, the ottimati, the grandi: the elites who, over the course of his fourteen year service to the Florentine Republic, consistently harassed and obstructed the Florentine secretary. Quite understandably, Machiavelli observes and analyzes their behavior with a considerable measure of resentment, condemnation, and distrust. Three notable instances, in particular, typify Machiavelli's treatment at the hands of the Florentine grandi. In 1509, when the republic's militia, organized and partly trained by Machiavelli against fierce patrician opposition, successfully reconquered Pisa, some of Machiavelli's well-born, erstwhile opponents took the preponderance of credit for the victory: their names, not Machiavelli's, were etched in marble to commemorate the triumph.[8]

Second, when Machiavelli's patron, the republic's Gonfalonier of Justice, Soderini, nominated Machiavelli for the ambassadorship to the German Emperor, prominent patricians vetoed the appointment, asserting that more "worthy young men" from better families should represent the city. And finally, the excessively harsh treatment that Machiavelli endured when the Medici returned to power in 1512–13 is as much attributable to his social status as to his association with the republican coalition that opposed their return. After all, wealthier and more prominent individuals allied with Soderini and supportive of the *governo largo* who were also suspected of conspiracy fared much better at the hands of the restored principality.[9]

In the dedication to *The Prince*, Machiavelli famously claimed to understand the nature of individual princes from firsthand experience: he had observed the actions of kings, queens, popes, and warlords on his diplomatic missions for the republic, and he certainly experienced the less than kindly attentions of the reestablished Medici principality upon the republic's collapse.[10] On the basis of these examples, we might conclude that Machiavelli not only understands the nature of individual *princes* from firsthand experience, in addition, he may also have acquired from firsthand experience valuable insight into the nature of the few, the *great*.

Machiavelli's reports to his official superiors in the republic's magistracies plainly evidence his contempt for their arrogance and incompetence. Members of Florence's executive committees would consistently reprimand him for writing only when it pleased him and for providing too much of his own analysis rather than objective reportage that they could judge for themselves. Machiavelli's sarcastic responses are well documented.[11] Most notably, when frustrated by persistent resistance from the ottimati to his militia proposals, Machiavelli struck back with the following words: "Everyone knows that anyone who speaks of empire, kingdom, principate, [or] republic – anyone who speaks of men who command, beginning at the top and going all the way down to the leader of a gang – speaks of justice and arms. You, as regards justice, have very little, and as for arms, none at all."[12] Evidently learning that such entreaties have little effect on aristocratic audiences, Machiavelli would largely forsake speaking directly about justice to the individual princes of kingdoms and the princes plural of republics in his two greatest works of political science. As I will demonstrate in the next chapter, when addressing the young grandi to whom he dedicates the *Discourses*, he praises democratic as opposed to aristocratic republics, governi *larghi* rather than *stretti*, primarily in terms of arms and of what one does with them – namely, in terms of power.

The vivid example of Clearchus and the Heraclean nobility mentioned in the preceding, it must be noted, signifies only Machiavelli's last resort when dealing with a republic's elites. Indeed, a princely actor who subjugates or eliminates the nobility in the name of the people spells the failure and abolition of republican politics. Certainly, Machiavelli prefers republics to principalities (D II.2), even if circumstances exist where a people can enjoy greater freedom under a prince than within a corrupt republic (e.g., P 19, D I.10). But a principality is almost always a disadvantageous outcome for the nobility and on many occasions it may very well be so for the people as well. It is reminiscent of the very development that destroyed the Roman Republic, Caesarism. Much as Machiavelli might delight in revenge fantasies projected into episodes such as Clearchus's massacre of the grandi, the causes and consequences of this kind of outcome are precisely what he declares healthy republics must avoid if they are to endure rather than suffer usurpation by tyrants.

Machiavelli suggests that ungovernable and unaccountable elites can be counted among the chief attributes of unhealthy republics, of polities trending toward corruption and usurpation (e.g., D III.29).[13] One of the purposes of this book is to demonstrate how, on Machiavelli's view, popular governments can remain uncorrupt in this sense, that is, how they can control the grandi and make them more accountable to the people. What is the place of the grandi in a regime where their power is both shared with and contested by the general citizenry? How, according to Machiavelli, did the Roman Republic manage to distribute power between the people and the grandi in such a way that the former, who wish to avoid domination, controlled the latter, who ceaselessly seek to exercise it? And how can republics do so while staving off Caesarist threats for as long as or longer than Rome did? I attempt to answer these questions in Chapter 3, for any Machiavellian Democracy, any republic where the people are encouraged to contest and control the behavior of the grandi, must run the risk of elevating a Caesar to power.

Popular Passivity, the Guard of Liberty, and the Claim to Rule

Ancient wisdom recommended that republics grant wealthy and prominent citizens a decisive upper hand in ruling.[14] Machiavelli, on the contrary, promotes republics in which common citizens maintain "the guard of liberty" (D I.5), republics where the people "wield authority" (D I.53). Again, Machiavelli understands the people's oppression-averse "ambition" to differ qualitatively from the grandi's insatiable appetite for domination. Because their orientation to liberty is more trustworthy than is the grandi's, the people should serve as the ultimate arbiters of a republic's freedom: they will not use such power to oppress, but rather will act, when provoked, to defend themselves from oppression (D I.5, D I.46). However, Machiavelli suggests that the people's aversion to domination naturally inclines them toward inaction or even deference.[15] Indeed, he claims that not only do the people have less desire to usurp freedom than do elites, they also have less ability to do so (D I.5). Would logic then dictate, as Machiavelli does, that republics entrust a substantively positive political role to actors who exhibit such a passive or negative disposition? Given these defensive inclinations, how can the people actively and effectively guard a republic's liberty; how can they contain and control particularly astute and exhorbitantly wealthy actors, who themselves are motivated by an appetite for domination (P 9, D I.5)?

Contrary to Machiavelli's advice, a passive popular disposition would seem to validate the subsidiary role assigned to the people in, for instance, Guicciardini's stretto or narrow republican model and in Schumpeter's minimalist or elitist theory of democracy: the people may exhibit proficiency at selecting worthy officials and maybe even at ratifying good laws, but they should be excluded from initiating or formulating policy, or from participating politically in any proactive manner.[16] One might reasonably conclude on this basis that an optimal political arrangement is, as aristocratic republicans suggest, one in which elites actually govern but are prevented from becoming tyrants in only the most general ways by the people. This is one of the most common interpretations of elite-popular relations in Machiavelli's *Discourses*.[17]

The problem with these conclusions is that they deal with the people's appetite exclusively in the abstract, that is, without fully considering how Machiavelli describes the interactions of the people's counteroppressive appetite and the grandi's oppressive one in everyday politics. The people, after all, do not live by themselves in a petri dish. If Machiavelli's description of the two humors is correct, then the people enjoy virtually little occasion to remain passive very long within the confines of republics because they do not live free from acts of aristocratic oppression in such polities for any serious length of time. Indeed, the grandi's appetite to oppress serves as a constant spark to ignite the people's humor to live free of oppression and it often induces them to transform their natural posture of refrain to a political posture of counterattack. The crucial questions then become not so much the ramifications of people's natural, preoppressed disposition but rather their social one, that is, their actively oppressed one, and the political means they might find available to satisfy their secondary disposition.

As we will observe in the next section on the Roman Republic, princely founders and overreaching grandi give the people, respectively, weapons with which and opportunities through which they can better realize their desire not to be dominated. The people may not themselves spontaneously provide the means by which they attain, protect, and expand liberty: Machiavelli insists that the people are most powerful when "shackled by laws" and directed by "heads" (D I.58, D I.44). Without recourse to legal institutions and to entrepreneurial leadership, Machiavelli concedes that the people are "headless and thus harmless" (D I.44): they are as weak and cowardly when isolated and transfixed by their own individual fears as they are mighty when collectively empowered by laws and united under "heads" (D I.57, I.58). Princely founders organize the people in legions and assemblies (hence the indispensability of *The Prince* for the political project of the *Discourses*); the grandi provoke the people into availing themselves of these institutions such that they can create new laws that better secure their liberty and so that they can generate "heads" for themselves to counteract the grandi's oppressive behavior (D I.57). Specifically, institutions such as popular assemblies and the tribunes of the plebs enable the people to keep elites accountable without destroying the republic as a whole, and without inciting the grandi to do so themselves.

According to Machiavelli, the plebeian tribunate is the institution that serves as a "head" for the people at home: it directly checks noble machinations to oppress the people or to enlist the latter in uncivil schemes. The tribunes are directly responsive to the plebeian's concerns except in cases where the people seem especially unreasonable (e.g., D I.51). Along with Rome's popular assemblies, the tribunes make it possible for Machiavelli to claim that the Roman people both circumscribe rule by the grandi and participate in rule themselves. A not unproblematic fact for the people's liberty, however, is that the consuls, not the tribunes, function as the people's "heads" while they are engaged in combat away from the city. As I will explain later in this and in forthcoming chapters, while service in a citizen army provides the people considerable leverage in their efforts not to be oppressed by the great, the nobles nevertheless attempt to exploit their role as military heads to oppress not only Rome's enemies abroad but also Rome's own citizens on the field of battle, a strategy with serious ramifications for liberty at home.

For now, let me suggest that Machiavelli's *Discourses* demonstrates that the people are passive and deferential enough not to pose a preemptive threat to the grandi's property and status, but that when provoked with threats to their liberty, the people can react with enough spirit and virtue to punish transgressors and to deter future instances of oppression. Machiavelli suggests that, within the correct constitutional arrangements, the people are capable of lively and active defense of liberty, even if their motivations might be fundamentally passive or negative. Moreover, when empowered to discuss and decide policy within formal assemblies, usually bequeathed to the people by a regime's original "head," its founding prince, their onestà is sufficient to allow them to exercise better judgment than would ordinary "heads," namely, princes and nobles.

Going further, as we will see, Machiavelli also suggests that the popular appetite can be innovative and restorative: when vigorously responding to oppression, the people's appetite initiates creation of new laws that serve to bring a republic back to its first principles, hence substantively reforming it (e.g., D I.4, I.40, I.48, I.57, III.1). Thus, Machiavelli's analysis asks readers to ponder whether expansive, formal checking by one political actor (the people) on another political actor's (the nobility's) governing does not itself entail a form of governing; whether it is not, in itself, a substantive form of participation in rule.[18]

Machiavellian Democracy then capitalizes on ever-present moments of aristocratic oppression by seeking and putting in place institutional arrangements through which the people vigorously and effectively respond to the grandi's oppressive schemes and actions; it empowers the people to halt the grandi's insolent behavior, punish those who are especially guilty of it, and establish new laws that reset the grandi's institutional boundaries for future action (D I.40). The people's liberty requires an institutional framework through which the people consistently expose instances of aristocratic oppression and within which they can respond effectively to it. Machiavelli's account of Roman constitutional development provides the key lesson in this regard.

Arms, Class, and the Roman Constitution

Because the Roman Republic figures so centrally in Machiavelli's political thought and my engagement with it in this book, I offer here a brief overview of its constitutional features.[19] Machiavelli associates the maturation of the Roman Republic with the establishment of its three principal parts: a tamed princely power in the consuls, a somewhat chastened aristocratic power in the senate, and an insurgent popular power indirectly reflected by the tribunes of the plebs and directly embodied in the citizen assemblies. Rome's chief executives, the two consuls, were elected annually by assemblies where votes were weighted in favor of wealthier citizens. The consuls, originally drawn exclusively from the patrician class, exercised the republic's highest administrative and military duties. The possibility of popular leverage against the consuls increased when the prohibition on intermarriage between classes was lifted (445 BCE) and when plebeians were eventually permitted to serve as consuls (300 BCE).

On the notoriously complicated issue of Roman class relations, Machiavelli consistently collapses one distinction, between plebeians and patricians, with another, the distinction between the people and the nobles (the optimates, the great, etc.). In the early Roman Republic, the plebeian/patrician distinction was formal and hereditary, while the historically later people/noble distinction was largely economic and political; the latter distinction reflected the fact that newly wealthy plebeians had intermarried with patricians, secured regular tenure in the consulship, and gained admittance to the senate. Thus Machiavelli continues to use "plebeians" or "plebs," in the Roman sense of the *plebs sordida*, that is, synonymously with the people, the multitude, and such, despite the fact that, technically, many wealthy citizens from traditionally plebeian families were eventually counted among the ranks of the nobility (e.g., D I.29). Even though the nobility, comprised of both very old aristocratic families *and* very wealthy plebeians, constituted the "senatorial order" (*l'ordine senatorio*) (D I.31), Machiavelli often refers to all the members of the nobility, of the grandi, as optimates or patricians.

For Machiavelli, the senate functioned as the more or less direct institutional embodiment of the nobility. Ostensibly just a deliberative and advisory body, the senate nevertheless enjoyed substantial influence over the republic's fiscal and foreign policies. Senatorial mentoring of consuls, plus the prospect of former consuls joining the ranks of the senate, meant that this body held great sway over the republic's supreme magistrates. The two (later five and eventually ten) tribunes of the plebs, elected exclusively from plebeian ranks, were charged with popular advocacy. They reflected popular preferences, but not always directly: foreshadowing Burke's or Madison's views on representation, Machiavelli notes that the tribunes often attempted to act in the interest of the populace *against* the people's immediately expressed wishes.[20] As we will see, however, Machiavelli asserts that the most important function of the tribunes was to hold back the insolence of the grandi (D I.3, D III.11). As bearers of veto power over most of the workings of Roman government, and as the chief agents of public indictments for political crimes, the tribunes possessed the means to block policy proposals and punish magistrates and prominent citizens for violating the liberty of the citizenry or for attempting to corrupt the republic.

The Roman people participated collectively through institutions such as the centuriate assembly (*comitia centuriata*), which favored the wealthy; the tribal assembly (*comitia tributa*), in which the nobility could be outvoted; and the council of the plebs (*concilium plebis*), which very likely excluded patricians altogether. Machiavelli neither mentions nor even seems aware of the first assembly's oligarchic structure, that is, the fact that it apportioned votes on the basis of property criteria. Indeed, he suggests that the elections of consuls and the capital trials of indicted patricians conducted in this assembly were decided through majority rule or "free votes" (D I.20). In any case, over the course of the republic's history, legislative and judicial power certainly shifted from the centuriate assembly to the plebeian-dominated assemblies over which the tribunes presided.[21] Together with the deliberating assemblies, the *contiones* (*concioni*), in which citizens discussed policies but where they did not normally vote on them, these councils presumably constituted the institutional embodiment of what Machiavelli means by "the people."[22]

Of central importance to Machiavelli's understanding of the Roman constitution's development is the fact that the plebeians *earn* a full place of prominence in the Roman Republic. Neither political founders nor political philosophers had hitherto ever intentionally or explicitly granted the common people such a place. Unlike the general populace in the Spartan and Venetian republics, the Roman people actually took part in establishing their place within Rome's mixed regime. Initially, Romulus founded and the early kings maintained Rome as a monarchy (D I.1–2). But Romulus unwittingly established the conditions of possibility for a republic and also for eventual popular participation within it: he created a senate and armed the plebs (D I.9). The former advised him on policy; the latter fought his wars. To guarantee the loyalty of these armed plebeians, subsequent monarchs politically organized them within legislative assemblies. The democratic ramifications, less than fully elaborated in *The Prince*, of Machiavelli's aforementioned advice to princes to arm the people and place princely power on their shoulders becomes clearer in the context of the *Discourses*. Properly exercised princely power makes possible subsequent appropriations of it by the people: with the military means made available to them by Romulus, the Roman people actively participate in the elimination of the monarchy and the eventual creation of the tribunate (D I.6).

The civic-military organization of the plebeians by the kings thus enables the former to apply leverage against the nobles to grant them institutional safeguards on popular liberty. The tribunes were established and then restored as a result of secessions by the plebs from the city (respectively, 494 and 449 BCE). The first secession was sparked by plebeian exasperation over the massive debts they incurred during military service and the mistreatment they suffered at the hands of creditors, in particular, and patricians, generally. In the second, they withdrew in response to the tyranny of Appius Claudius and the Ten, mentioned previously. After the tribunate had been suspended during the reign of the Ten, the plebs again repaired to the outskirts of Rome, then demanded and attained the reinstitution of their own tribunician magistracy (D I.44).

Livy emphasizes the senate's fear of attack by the armed citizens in these instances of secession,[23] while Machiavelli, for his part, merely emphasizes the senate's doubts about their own ability to withstand a foreign attack without the support of the plebeian army (D I.4). Either way, the fact that the people are armed enables them to compel the patricians to grant them their own exclusive magistracy, the tribunate. Again, both examples confirm that, even when threatened, and despite being armed, the people did not automatically lash out with widespread and arbitrary violence against their oppressors. Rather, they sought the best way of avoiding continued domination – they quit the city.

At a deeper level, then, the military ordering of plebeian life instills the kind of discipline that enabled the people to withdraw from the city in these two episodes without engaging in egregious looting or excessive violence. A citizen army, even one instituted under a monarchy, inculcates in soldiers a disposition akin to that which Aristotle identified as characteristic of democratic citizenship: the disposition to rule and be ruled in turn.[24] The alternation between command and submission among soldiers of all ranks and from both classes that operates within a popular army translates readily into a civic life characterized by discipline and reciprocity.[25] It allows republics like Rome, in Machiavelli's eyes, to avail themselves of virtue wherever it resides, among both the "nobles and the ignobles" (D I.30). Republics such as Sparta, Venice, and even Florence that fail to arm the plebeians militarily or civically can never fully tap into the deep well of popular virtue.

Thus, the "accidents" to which Machiavelli attributes republican Rome's development (D I.3) are not entirely accidental: Rome evolved into a popularly inclusive republic, a governo largo, only through the efforts of princes seeking to strengthen their regimes, and then, once the kings were overthrown, from the dissension that arose between the plebs and the senate, the people and the nobles. The armed citizenry successfully leveraged greater security and more extensive participation from the grandi, already formally organized into a senate by Romulus as the plebeians' eventual negotiating adversary/partner. Left to their own devices, without being institutionally organized into a senate, the grandi abuse the people to such an extent that the latter elevate a prince to crush the nobility; or, if they manage to squelch popular resistance, the grandi resort to violent competition among themselves from which a prince inevitably emerges.[26]

In either circumstance, uncontained patrician insolence portends the end of what Machiavelli calls a "free" or "civic" way of life (D I.5, D I.7, D I.9). The existence of a senate provides an organized competitor and interlocutor for the people and minimizes inter-elite violence through the attendant norms of collegiality. But senates are far less rare in the history of republican institutions than are tribunates. In Rome, Machiavelli argues, the people, through the tribunes, held back the "insolence" of the nobles, thus more successfully preserving freedom than did any other republic (D I.3, D III.11). In short, democracies or governi larghi do not found themselves: princes found republics by instituting senates and collecting the people into legions. However, once organized, the people can exert a creative political force, as in Rome, by establishing institutions such as the tribunate and by transforming offices such as the consuls and by rearranging the balances of power among assemblies.

Thus, the logic motivating Machiavellian popular government, whether a democratic republic or governo largo, is fairly simple: arm the people militarily with weapons and collective discipline and politically with tribunes and assemblies. However, a rhetorical strategy that might successfully accomplish the following is a profoundly more complicated matter: selling this widely participatory model to powerful sociopolitical actors who are deeply suspicious of a militarily and civilly empowered people. How does one argue for such a republic when the ottimati or grandi, whose consent and cooperation are crucial for establishing any republic, are likely to resist at least one and perhaps both forms of popular empowerment? The next chapter examines the proposition that Machiavelli offers the young patricians to whom he dedicates the *Discourses*, a proposition within which Rome's superiority over Sparta and Venice figures prominently. Should these young Florentine ottimati ever find the Medici principality under which they live inconvenient – or should similarly situated young aristocrats anywhere find themselves likewise discontented with monarchical rule – there are unexpected benefits to be gained, Machiavelli seems to suggest, by making themselves more, not less, constrained by common citizens in the republic they might establish after ousting their tyrants.

A large subset of contemporary democratic theory would have one believe that the central issue at stake in democratic foundings hinges on a logical-normative question of origins: how can the authority (or force) necessary to found a democracy be justified before such action was ever legitimated democratically?[27] Fortunately, historical and empirical studies of democratic transitions suggest that this "democratic paradox" bewitching so many theorists of democracy – so much so that it has them and their conceptualized regimes figuratively chasing their tails – is largely beside the point. Democracies and governi larghi, from ancient Athens and Rome to contemporary Poland and Chile, emerge out of authoritarian regimes, whether autocratic or oligarchic.[28] The organizational and institutional choices available to democratizing forces in such regimes are always constrained by the kinds of structures within which (and against which) they operate.[29] By relying on the common people's military service or, more recently, their commodified labor, elites provide but also condition opportunities for the former to demand concessions that facilitate democratization.[30] Moreover, the legal revisibility that remains a hallmark of virtually all republics leaves open avenues through which popular governments can retrospectively correct and/or legitimate earlier political developments and choices, as well as regular and frequent opportunities for democratically legitimating future political change.[31] Democratic politics, for better or worse, is bound by neither the logical severity nor the moral purity with which "paradox" theorists evaluate it.

Keeping in mind the structural limitations constraining all transitions to popular government, I next examine the rhetorical use to which Machiavelli puts his account of Rome's transition to governo largo from autocracy and oligarchy. Machiavelli hopes that his case for Rome – a republic where the people vigorously surveilled and restrained elites; where, through the functioning of popular assemblies they arguably rule over elites; and yet where the latter still enjoyed unprecedented renown – will inspire his young aristocratic dedicatees to overthrow a principality and establish a more popularly participatory republic than the governo stretto that they, but for their intercourse with Machiavelli, would have preferred.

2

Democratic Republics and the Oppressive Appetite of Young Nobles

> When the plebs remained quiet within their bounds, the young nobles began to harm them.
>
> Machiavelli, *Discourses* I.46

> The kind of numerous and armed people necessary to achieve a great empire cannot be managed in any mode you please.
>
> Machiavelli, *Discourses* I.6

What was Machiavelli's intention in writing *The Prince*? This is one of the most anxiously posed questions in the history of political thought.[1] Was it to advise a prince, or to undo him; to encourage tyranny, or to moderate it?[2] Astute interpreters begin to answer this question by focusing on the book's dedicatee, Lorenzo de' Medici, proceeding then to read *The Prince* in light of how Lorenzo specifically, or a young prince more generally, might receive, understand, and act upon the book's advice. However, few scholars ask the same question – or ask it with comparable urgency – of Machiavelli's greatest work, *Discourses on Titus Livy's First Ten Books*. Even perceptive readers largely assume that the purpose of the *Discourses* is self-evident – to promote republics – and that its immediate audience is obvious – two young friends with republican sympathies.[3] Since Machiavelli dedicates the *Discourses* to interlocutors from his literary circle, the Orti Oricellari, who supposedly share his political predilections, the book is assumed to be a more straightforward and less rhetorically artful work than *The Prince*. In other words, one need not ponder too deeply the relationship between the book's declared audience and its content.

This chapter focuses more closely on the *Discourses'* dedicatees in order to illuminate Machiavelli's intentions regarding the extent and form of popular participation in a republic. Cosimo Rucellai and Zanobi Buondelmonti are not simply "friends" or "republicans." They are young men of considerable wealth and good name who, on the basis of lineage, education, and talent, would expect to hold positions of prominence within their polity. Defined in terms of the "appetite" that pursues and acquires such economic advantage and political privilege, and viewed from the perspective of their social subordinates, Rucellai and Buondelmonti are what Machiavelli calls *grandi*: the members of society who are driven by the "humor" to oppress. Like interpreters who detect a rhetorical strategy in *The Prince* through which Machiavelli's advice manipulates a prince into tempering or even jeopardizing his dominion over the people, I discern a similar strategy in the *Discourses* with respect to the grandi's domination of the people. Though Machiavelli dedicates neither work *to* the people, I would argue that both are very much intended *for* the people; each book is intended to alleviate the people's oppression by their two most persistently malicious political antagonists: respectively, a tyrant and the oligarchs, the one and the few.

Here, I read the first six chapters of the *Discourses* from the perspective of young ottimati such as Cosimo and Zanobi. I demonstrate that Machiavelli uses the hypothetically reconstructed Roman Republic discussed in the last chapter to moderate the behavior of the people's eternal oppressors in all regimes that are not principalities. Machiavelli convinces his audience to forsake their attachment to the aristocratic republican model exemplified by Sparta and Venice and instead to accept the Roman, popularly inclusive republican model, or as Machiavelli reconstructs it, a democratic republican model. By chapter 7 of Book I, Machiavelli no longer compares Rome with Sparta/Venice. But in the first six chapters, Machiavelli attempts to convince the grandi that the best republic is one in which they maximize the material and immaterial benefits they gain from qualified political preeminence in such regimes *and* protect themselves from the deleterious results of their own appetite for domination. Machiavelli advises the grandi, against their inclinations, natural and cultivated, to render themselves more accountable to an armed and politically empowered common citizenry. If followed, however, this advice might eventually make the grandi even more extensively and substantively accountable to the people than such young nobles might anticipate.

In these opening chapters of the *Discourses*, Machiavelli sets the parameters of a political bargain, the terms of which he hopes to maneuver his dedicatees into accepting: the grandi constrain their appetite for complete domination of the people at home, granting the latter institutions such as the tribunate and popular assemblies and practices such as public accusations, so that the people may serve as the regime's "guard of liberty." In return, the young grandi gain the opportunity for increased riches and eternal fame in two possible ways: (a) by becoming "founders," along the lines of Junius Brutus, traitors to class and family who establish institutions that fortify republics and protect the people from the grandi; and/or (b) by pursuing empire, that is, by commanding citizen-soldiers in the domination of countless others abroad. With exemplary models of founders and conquerors, Machiavelli diverts the grandi from short-term domination over their own people to long-term domination over mortality. Whether Machiavelli really anticipates or even hopes that the grandi make good on this opportunity remains an open question on this reading. Roman-style imperialism may be only one of several military options for Machiavelli – in fact, as I discuss in Chapters 3 and 4, given the decisive role that imperial expansion plays in Machiavelli's account of liberty's demise and the republic's collapse, it is perhaps not the most preferable.

A proper understanding of the dedicatees' identities, and the social significance of these identities, allows readers of the *Discourses* to adopt the appropriate perspective when confronting the book's immediate surface. By asking, first and foremost, how the work's declared audience might interpret it, the young patrician perspective of the dedicatees provides a hermeneutic key with which readers might unlock the often less than transparent significance of Machiavelli's arguments, assertions, and judgments.[4] Ultimately, I suggest that a proper understanding of Machiavelli's stated audience in the *Discourses* highlights the work's less than obvious purpose – to facilitate control of elites and popular participation within *governi larghi* or democratic republics.

In his two major works, *The Prince* and the *Discourses*, Machiavelli explicitly provides prudential reasons for favoring the people over the elite: the latter are constant threats to usurp a prince or corrupt a republic. Even when the people might be accused of too strenuously pursuing their efforts to avoid oppression by the great – that is, occasions when the great accuse the people of oppressing *them* – Machiavelli makes it a point to insist that the grandi would have subverted the republic much sooner and to a much greater extent if not challenged by the people (D I.5, D I.37). But beyond the threats that they pose to the stability of princely and republican regimes, there are, as mentioned in the previous chapter, biographical reasons for Machiavelli's animosity toward the great. Much attention has been devoted to Machiavelli's relationship with the Medici, a princely house with whose political fate Machiavelli's own career prospects and physical security were entwined and whose members alternated as antagonists and benefactors throughout Machiavelli's life. In what follows, I consider Machiavelli's less discussed but no less strained and complicated relationship with the conservative ottimati of Florence during his career as a servant of the 1494–1512 Republic. The animosity between Machiavelli and the older generation of Florentine ottimati informs our understanding of his more friendly but still far from equitable relationship with their heirs, such as Francesco Guicciardini, Francesco Vettori, and, especially, Cosimo Rucellai and Zanobi Buondelmonti.

Florentine Ottimati, Old and Young

It is now widely assumed that Machiavelli disingenuously flatters Lorenzo in the dedication of *The Prince*. After all, the Medici had recently dismissed, imprisoned, and tortured Machiavelli after the collapse of the Florentine Republic that he served for almost a decade and a half. But he's taken to be straightforwardly honest in the dedication of the *Discourses* when he flatters Buondelmonti and Rucellai. He tells them that although they are not princes, they deserve to be.

In the language of the *Discourses* (e.g., D I.12, D II.2), this primarily means that they should be leading citizens – magistrates, captains, senators – in a republic, rather than, as they presently are, the subjects, albeit rather pampered subjects, of an individual prince. Notwithstanding the perhaps unusual use of "princes" plural, this sentiment is not inconsistent with a "republican" understanding of the work, since a republic can be defined as a regime where not one but more than one person governs.[5]

Some might assume more generally that the book's specific addressees are simply private citizens, or just common people, as opposed to the exalted, royal dedicatee of *The Prince*. But this casual association of the dedicatees with "the people," and hence republicanism with popular government per se, falls prey to an undifferentiated notion of republicanism. It also bespeaks a historically uninformed understanding of who Buondelmonti and Rucellai actually were and, even more significantly, what social type they represent.[6] The *Discourses* is dedicated neither to a single prince – a prince proper – nor to the people, or even to "men *of* the people," as the word *popolani* connotes in certain contexts: Buondelmonti and Rucellai were young nobles – ottimati in the parlance of the day, grandi in Machiavelli's general usage (P 9; D I.4).[7] Both young men belonged to families with long traditions of influence and command in Florence and, more pertinently, with well-known biases against any republic that is not a *governo stretto*, that is, a polity within which only the very few, wealthiest citizens rule. And yet the interpretive literature that presents the young Rucellai and Buondelmonti as "humanists and literati," "republican sympathizers," patriots, and, overwhelmingly, just "friends" of Machiavelli generally ignores their class background and social perspective.[8]

The Rucellai and Buondelmonti families were, albeit to different degrees, opponents of the governo largo, or more widely participatory republic, that Friar Girolamo Savonarola helped establish and that Machiavelli's patron, Piero Soderini, stewarded in his ill-fated tenure as its chief executive.[9] Cosimo's grandfather, Bernardo Rucellai, in particular, admired the oligarchic Venetian regime; despised the Athenian-style citizens' assembly, the Great Council, established by Savonarola; and resented Soderini for using the Council as a populist obstacle to the aristocratic agenda of the leading ottimati. Rucellai founded the reading group named after his family gardens, the Orti Oricellari, ostensibly as a forum for humanist literati with a particular interest in the neo-platonism of Marsilio Ficino. But like other platonically inclined "academies," the Orti also served as a haven where young aristocrats aired their grievances against the purported ignorance of the popolo and the supposed oppressiveness of the popular regime under which they lived. Many of the young grandi who would participate in the overthrow of the governo largo, the ouster of Soderini, and the restoration of the Medici in 1512 were participants in the Orti Oricellari.[10]

Soderini, a member of an old patrician family, was elected to the newly created office of lifetime Gonfalonier (standard bearer) of Justice four years after Savonarola's celebrated demise.[11] While the elder Rucellai had hoped to become Gonfalonier himself, most ottimati simply assumed that a life-termed chief executive would counterbalance the Great Council, established and empowered by, to their minds, the much too democratically inclined friar. Indeed, most of them expected that Soderini would create a senate that they as a class would dominate and, furthermore, that he would perhaps even shut down the Great Council altogether. These hopes were dashed when Soderini, once elected, chose to by-pass consistent policy consultations with prominent citizens such as the Buondelmonti, Rucellai, and Salviati, to elevate "new men" such as Machiavelli to positions of responsibility and to govern in close collaboration with the Great Council.

Consequently deemed a class traitor, Soderini faced patrician obstruction and intransigence at every turn and eventually found his authority flouted, as many ottimati illegally communicated with the exiled Medici: most flagrantly, they continued to negotiate marriage alliances with "the rebel" family and attend lavish banquets hosted by the former tyrants in Rome. In the end, the grandi, particularly the youngest members of the most prominent families, conspired with the Medici to enlist Spanish forces, with papal imprimatur, to overthrow the republic and restore the family to power in Florence. While Soderini left the city as an exile, Machiavelli lost his positions and suffered imprisonment and torture when suspected of conspiring against the reinstated princes. He surely would have died in prison were it not for a general amnesty declared when Giovanni de' Medici was elected Pope Leo X in 1513.

Machiavelli's close relationship with Soderini certainly compounded his problems with Florentine ottimati such as the elder Rucellai and the influential Salviati brothers, Alamanno and Jacopo. As a close and valuable aid to Soderini, and as a "new man" recruited to public service from outside the ranks of the ottimati, Machiavelli was, to say the least, *not* considered a "friend" by this earlier generation of Florentine elites. He often suffered the scorn they could not vent directly at the Gonfalonier; they called him Soderini's "creature" and "puppet" or simply a "rogue." Unlike the Medici, the Florentine ottimati may not have resorted to physical violence against Machiavelli, but they certainly targeted him for disdain and derision and vigorously attempted to undermine his performance in whatever secretarial, emissarial, and administrative posts he managed to gain.[12]

As mentioned in the last chapter, in the most disappointing moment of Machiavelli's public career, the ottimati, insisting that the sons of better families deserved the post, scuttled his nomination as ambassador to the German emperor. Machiavelli's young aristocratic friend, Vettori, was awarded the commission instead. Not long thereafter, another young patrician acquaintance, Francesco Guicciardini, would be appointed the youngest ambassador in the republic's history when he embarked on a commission to Spain.[13] Machiavelli suffered further insult as the republic's ottimati consistently thwarted or scaled back his plans for a citizen-militia. The patricians did not want to deal with an armed populace in the city – especially one that would serve at the disposal of a life-term chief executive such as Machiavelli's boss, Soderini.

Moreover, they refused to consider, as Machiavelli hoped, militarily trans-forming into full-fledged citizens the subject population of the territories sur-rounding Florence.[14]

Yet despite good reasons for resenting and mistrusting the wealthy and the well-born, Machiavelli nurtured friendships with young members of the otti-mati, such as Vettori, Guicciardini, and also Buondelmonti and Rucellai.[15] However, "friendship" in the context of Renaissance Florence almost invari-ably entailed relations of clientage: at the time that he began the *Discourses*, the lower-born and unemployed Machiavelli was financially in debt to at least one and likely both of his dedicatees.[16] Yet, as we turn to the dedication of the *Discourses*, Machiavelli professes to reimburse Zanobi and Cosimo with intellectual rather than monetary currency: Machiavelli thanks his "friends" for having "forced" him to write what he would not have written otherwise. Apparently, excited by Machiavelli's discussions of politics and history at their reading group, the young grandi insisted that he discourse on the topic in writing. Like Plato's Socrates, Machiavelli dutifully submits to these young well-to-do friends who command him to converse with them on the matter of politics.[17] Whether Machiavelli too would provide elaborate philosophic jus-tifications for the antidemocratic prejudices of such rich young men remains, for now, an open question.

The Best or the Few?

Unlike *The Prince*, the *Discourses*, according to its dedication, was actively solicited by its dedicatees, young men who happen to be the author's social superiors and intimate friends. In this section, I will attempt both to analyze and inhabit the perspective of Machiavelli's dedicatees as they first approach the work that they commissioned. And since the young grandi to whom Machi-avelli dedicates the *Discourses* are also humanist intellectuals, members of a scholarly circle, they presumably will not scoff at a book on politics that takes a fairly academic form.[18] Embedded as they are within a context where humanist education is tied to displays and exercises of power, they might even welcome a book that presents itself as a long commentary on a classical text – a book with the full title, *Discorsi sopra la prima deca di Tito Livio*. Indeed, ottimati, whether in *or* out of power, have more time than does a prince for self-cultivation. Zanobi and Cosimo, like most members of their class, proba-bly do not expect to justify their claims to preeminence with force alone; in all likelihood, they have some pretensions about truly being "the best" citizens. Fortunately for them, both political inactivity under a principality and the polit-ical division of labor entailed by patrician rule in most republics allow young nobles the time to study and improve themselves. So the full title and scholarly form of Machiavelli's work might attract rather than discourage young grandi seeking to justify themselves through self-edification.[19]

This analysis points up the fact that grandi, when in power, unlike a prince, "collegially" share the benefits and burdens of rule among themselves. There is a name for such a regime. Nevertheless, just as "tyrant" is never mentioned in *The Prince*, the word "oligarchy" is rather scarce in the *Discourses*. In the first three chapters, Machiavelli refers to those of status, wealth, and command as aristocrats or optimates (*ottimati*), nobles (*nobili*), the few (*pochi*), the powerful (*potenti*) and, in a Roman context, the senate (*senato*). In accord with the apparently "classical mood" set by his title, his prologue and his ostensible fidelity to Polybius's famous cycle of regimes in I.2, Machiavelli seems to abide by a distinction between good and bad kinds of nobility: he distinguishes between rule by optimates and rule by merely "the few," that is, the rich.[20]

In fact, young ottimati would be quite flattered by association with the following description of their class, largely derived (but for the significant added reference to their wealth) from Polybius: Machiavelli describes them as a group who excelled all others "in generosity, greatness of spirit, riches, and nobility.... [who] governed themselves according to the laws ordered by them, placing the common utility before their own advantage;.... [who] preserved both public and private things with the highest diligence" (D I.2).[21] In the quasi-Polybian cycle of regime transformation, this truly noble class of "the powerful" are obeyed and revered by "the multitude" during the elimination of tyranny and the establishment of an aristocratic republic. But, according to Machiavelli's narrative in this early chapter, the heirs of "the powerful" in the next generation respect neither civility nor the people's property and women. As a result, a government of the best is inevitably corrupted into a regime dominated by the mere few, whose rule provokes a democratic revolution that is itself – as nobles are inclined to expect – destined to degenerate into "license."

Heartened or certainly confirmed in their expectations by Machiavelli's early rehearsing of the classical distinction between aristocracy and oligarchy, Cosimo and Zanobi might not be disturbed by mention of the Roman nobility's "insolence" toward the end of I.2. This is, after all, just one particular group of ottimati, not nobles in general, who, as Machiavelli has shown in his apparently faithful rehashing of Polybius, are basically good. However, they might be surprised that Machiavelli attributes the creation of the tribunate, a magistracy of the Roman plebs, to the insolence of the nobility rather than to the ambitions of the common people. As the writings of most aristocratic republicans make plain, the ottimati assume that the people agitate spontaneously and without provocation to seize, all or in part, a republic's political power. The dedicatees are likely more surprised that Machiavelli promises to show how conflict or disunion between the senate and the plebs made the Roman Republic "more perfect" (D I.2).

Machiavelli still refrains from offering a categorical assessment of the class to which the dedicatees belong at the start of I.3, focusing instead on humanity in general: for political purposes, Machiavelli states, it must be assumed that "all men [*uomini*] are bad," and that they are all ready to vent their malignant spirit as soon as they have a free opportunity to do so. But the immediate example of such malignant evil is the Roman senate and nobility, who concealed their hatred for the plebs during the reign of the Tarquin princes but "offended them in all the modes they could" once the monarchy was abolished. In the corresponding passages of Livy, these offensive modes include the physical abuse and forced servitude inflicted by the nobles on the plebs, who, as a result of military service, could not afford to repay their debts.[22]

The "insolence" of the grandi, and the "confusions, noises and dangers of scandals that arose" as the plebs' reacted to it, led to the creation of the tribunes by the two parties "for the security of the plebs" (D I.3). Machiavelli states that the tribunate, an office for which young nobles such as Machiavelli's dedicatees would be ineligible, was "ordered" with "much eminence and reputation" (D I.3). It is not farfetched to assume that Machiavelli's dedicatees would be familiar with the functions that the tribunes were famously empowered to perform, and from which such eminence and reputation would derive: as I discuss at greater length in Chapter 4, the tribunes could veto consular and senatorial measures; they could liberate plebs who were seized and confined, for whatever reasons, by magistrates or patricians; and their persons were sacrosanct, that is, they could not be touched physically by a noble.[23]

It is important to observe that so far Machiavelli has presented merely isolated cases of preemptively "bad" nobles. Also, we should note that the "accidents" referred to in the chapter's heading ("What Accidents Made the Tribunes of the Plebs Be Created in Rome, Which Made the Republic More Perfect") that emerged in the conflict between the plebs and senate are rather mild (confusions, noises, threat of scandal). Indeed, as mentioned previously, to establish a tribunate, the plebeians evacuated the city; they did not burn it down. Nobles are inclined to expect something much more akin to the latter in such circumstances. The most casual familiarity with classical writings, especially those on Athens, would suggest that the few are inclined to fear that they will be targeted for expropriation, ostracism, and even violence as a result of conflict with the common people.[24] Closer to home, the Florentine elite of Machiavelli's day were only a few generations removed from the Ciompi Revolt (1378), in which the city's oppressed and unenfranchised woolworkers and their plebeian allies violently seized the republic for several months.[25]

In the *Discourses*, the example of the Roman plebeians demonstrates that popular indignation need not always or even generally be expressed in ways that the grandi should fear. In I.4 and I.5, Machiavelli argues that as "wild" as tumults became in Rome, they never really resulted in harm to the Roman nobles – public shouting, street demonstrations, and popular evacuation of the city are frightening, he claims, mostly to those who only read about them (D I.5). Moreover, he later insists that the harshness with which the Athenian demos treated their prominent citizens was perhaps a justifiable response to the experience of tyranny (D I.28); and in the *Florentine Histories*, while Machiavelli criticizes the Ciompi, he nevertheless carefully catalogues their legitimate grievances against the republic's economic elite.[26] Machiavelli's compensations for classical exaggerations of the people's unruliness, his justifications of certain popular outbursts against the nobles, and his pacification of general expressions of popular indignation seem intended to reeducate Cosimo and Zanobi on the honest or decent rather than insolent or licentious nature of the people.

Educating Young Grandi about Their Appetite

Chapter 4 of the *Discourses* is devoted to the disunion or "tumults" that made Rome "free and powerful," tumults criticized by "many," that is, the unnamed classical sources that Machiavelli previously appeared to be following more or less faithfully. These authors, later termed simply "the writers" (e.g., P 14, D I.10, D I.58), adopt the nobles' perspective on republican government and pine for an orderly people, but suspect that the latter's nature inevitably inclines them to create civil discord.[27] Why, the ancient authorities ask, aren't the people sensible enough to submit quietly to rule by their betters? According to Machiavelli, however, the people themselves are *not* the cause of tumults in Rome. There are two causes of tumults, two seemingly irreconcilable appetites: "[I]n every republic are two diverse humors, that of the people and that of the great, and all the laws that are made in favor of freedom arise from their disunion" (D I.4).[28] Here is the first appearance of Machiavelli's universal category for the nobles: the grandi or "the great."

We can assume that "grandi" serves as his general category for elites on the basis of his judgment that they exist "in every republic" and by cross-referencing this passage with his description, discussed before, of the social composition of "every city" in *The Prince* (P 9).[29] Recall that Machiavelli's work on principalities argued that princely success depends on a ruler's ability to establish his authority with the correct humor of the two, while here *laws* that ensure liberty result from the free play between the great and the people.[30] In my discussion of *The Prince* in the previous chapter, I demonstrated how Machiavelli immediately identifies the substance of the grandi's indecent humor or appetite to oppress; here in the *Discourses*, he postpones such a definition until the next chapter, I.5, even if it has already been intimated by particular examples throughout the initial chapters.

It may well be that Machiavelli assumes at this point that his young dedicatees care more about their personal welfare in the hypothetical tumultuous contest between themselves and the people than about "the truth" of their own nature. Thus Machiavelli assures them with examples of the kinds of harm faced by grandi in a governo largo, examples even more specific than he proffered in his previous chapter: Machiavelli insists that exiles, fines, and capital executions were kept to an absolute minimum in tumultuous Rome and were spread out over three hundred years (D I.4). The grandi need not fear the humor of the people, now revealed to be merely the desire *not* to be oppressed. The people act rambunctiously only when they've actually been oppressed or when they have sufficient reason to be suspicious of being oppressed. In this context, Machiavelli declares "the desires of free peoples are rarely pernicious to freedom" (D I.4). Machiavelli cajoles his dedicatees further by insisting that the plebs respond only reactively or passively in most cases anyway. In accord with their nature, as discussed earlier, Machiavelli insists that the people generally *refrain* from doing something instead of *actively* doing something: in response to actual oppression, for instance, the Roman plebs exit the city or fail to enroll for military service; they do not engage in direct violent action against the grandi.

When the people feel threatened by the possibility of oppression, Machiavelli suggests that their fear can be assuaged by the testimony of a good man, a man of faith – presumably a noble – in deliberative assemblies, the *concioni*. After all, Machiavelli's terms, *"uomo da bene"* and *"uomo degno di fede,"* correspond closely with the self-attributions of Roman patricians and Florentine ottimati. While Machiavelli will later state, perhaps against actual Roman practice, that "any citizen at all" could speak in a *concione* (D III.34), hence suggesting that a noble's speech might be contested publicly by a plebeian,[31] he does not open this possibility to his young aristocratic audience at this juncture. Here Machiavelli prefers instead to concur with Cicero's seemingly authoritative judgment that the people are basically ignorant, but not *so* ignorant as to be incapable of appreciating the "truth" and of recognizing a man worthy of trust. I touched on this point in the previous chapter when discussing the moral capacities and political judgment of the people, and will reflect at length on it in subsequent chapters.

Returning to the "exiles, fines, and blood" mentioned by Machiavelli, since they should be a little more worrisome to a noble than the "confusions, noises, and scandals" mentioned initially, even if these costs are kept to a minimum, Machiavelli may suspect that they may be too exorbitantly costly for a patrician audience to accept unless the latter are guaranteed a disproportionate reward in return for their risk. (Presumably, since humors are natural phenomena, there is no possibility that young grandi such as Cosimo and Zanobi might simply choose *not* to oppress the people, or definitively refrain from giving the latter cause to worry about the prospect of oppression.) Hence, especially intriguing at this moment in I.4 is the reward that Machiavelli offers the nobles in exchange for their toleration of the people's political participation and their willingness to endure the tumults that necessarily ensue from expressions of the popular humor: republics such as Rome that permit tumults and popular participation may "avail themselves of the people in important things" (D I.4). The title of the chapter suggests that these important things pertain to "liberty" and "power." Liberty remains undefined in the chapter. Power may have something to do with empire. Rome is after all most famous for empire, and the people's involvement in military affairs mentioned in this section makes this empire possible.

Machiavelli repeats "the great" as his term for the oligarchic component "in every republic" in I.5. Etymologically, "grandi" or "the great" ought not displease the dedicatees as an appellation, affiliated as it is with grandeur (*grandiosità*) and, a word that takes on considerable import quite soon in the text, greatness (*grandezza*). It perhaps may not be as gratifying a label as "aristocrats," yet not so disparaging as "oligarchs." Traditionally, however, "grandi" is a word that had been used interchangeably with *"magnati"* or "magnates" to describe the oppressive military aristocracy that Florence's guild community defeated in the republic's early history (the wealthiest guildsmen eventually intermarried with the magnates to form Florence's contemporary commercial elite of ottimati).[32] The oppressive history of the word may inform Machiavelli's substantive definition of the "grandi" and, later in the chapter, the "nobili": Machiavelli defines the great and the nobles in terms of the appetite or humor that drives them to acquire the riches, recognition, and power that they hold and want more of – their "great desire to dominate" (D I.5). On the other hand, Machiavelli argues that the "ignobles," the people, "*only* desire not to be dominated" (emphasis added).

As opposed to classical historians and philosophers, then, Machiavelli no longer professes to define the great in terms of moral probity or meritorious accomplishment. These are the very qualities that young nobles tend to think (or pretend) that they possess and would like to develop further. These are the very qualities or pretenses that initially might have seduced the young grandi into tackling such a daunting scholarly tome as Machiavelli's *Discourses*. By chapter 5 of the work, however, they discover that they are defined simply by their appetite to make others bend to their will. They are defined as bullies. Indeed, the insolence that seemed to be incidental to the nature of the grandi earlier in the book when Machiavelli shadowed Polybius's analysis of regimes is now defined as the core of their nature when Machiavelli sets out his own political sociology.[33]

Thus, since Machiavelli's stated addressees have requisitioned this work, since they have intellectual pretensions, and since they are indeed his friends, perhaps he *can* after all be more honest about his beliefs and intentions in the *Discourses* than he is vis-à-vis his princely dedicatee in *The Prince*. Even if he must ease them along in the way I suggest here, Machiavelli does not permanently hide from his immediate audience what he thinks of them as a class or social type. What is a temporary stratagem in the *Discourses* is certainly the dominant one in *The Prince*: there Machiavelli never speaks directly on the nature of princes, instead demonstrating by example or, as he did with respect to the grandi in I.3, through generalizations about the nature of "men" (e.g., P 15, title).[34]

However, after I.3 of the *Discourses*, Machiavelli speaks more frankly about the political nature of his immediate audience, especially in I.5. We do not know whether Zanobi and Cosimo yet recognize themselves in Machiavelli's depiction of the grandi as the members of a polity who are driven by the appetite to oppress. Nonetheless, Machiavelli's straightforward presentation invites them to be honest about it rather than to be ashamed or embarrassed by it. Their oppressive nature is just a fact, a natural fact. The instruction, already in progress, is that they should obey that appetite more prudently so as to satisfy it better.

An Inconclusive Dialogue over the "Guard of Liberty"

Besides defining the respective humors of the people and the great, I.5 also deals with the "guard of freedom" and the question of which humor ought to be entrusted as this guard in a republic.[35] Before delving into this issue, it might be helpful to ponder what Machiavelli means by freedom, or "a free way of life," since he invokes it here but still does not define it. What might freedom mean to his dedicatees, Cosimo and Zanobi? We learn in this chapter that they are motivated by an appetite to oppress. What are the conditions of possibility for them to act freely, that is, with liberty, on this appetite? First, we should assume that their regime must live independent of any another regime – it cannot be a client or subject state, a satellite, or a colony. In such circumstances, the prince or princes of a foreign regime would circumscribe the extent to which the grandi could oppress their own people.

The same can be said for ottimati living under a domestic prince, who, as Machiavelli demonstrates elsewhere, cannot be secure if he allows the grandi within his domain free rein to satisfy their oppressive appetites (P 9; D I.16). Certainly, submission to the reinstalled Medici principality must frustrate the desire of these young grandi to compete freely for public offices and to exercise the supreme commands, reap the rewards, and gain the highest prestige that accompanies such magistracies. Young patricians such as our dedicatees were instrumental in restoring the Medici to power because they were dissatisfied with the governo largo founded by Savonarola, presided over by Soderini, and centered on the Great Council. Life under a principality may be superior to life within a popular government – at least before the young grandi have been educated about the latter by Machiavelli – but, given their aristocratic preferences and prejudices, it is certainly not as optimal as actually ruling an oligarchy, a governo stretto.

Therefore, the great are most "free" in the absence of imperial or princely authorities, and, in fact, this is the first component of the dedicatees' definition of a republic: an autonomous regime without a single prince. More specifically, given the inclinations of the previous generation, mentioned previously, and based, for instance, on Guicciardini's depiction of young ottimati in his political writings,[36] we can guess the following: Buondelmonti and Rucellai think of a republic as a regime in which members of the "best families" circulate political offices among themselves. They act freely vis-à-vis the people in such a regime by exercising command over the latter through these offices and by refusing to share such offices with them. The general citizenry might select who specifically among the nobility holds office at any particular time – election being, after all, an aristocratic appointment device – but the people will not exert any further control over them.[37]

Machiavelli points out in I.5 that Sparta and Venice were republics that placed the guard of liberty with the nobles; in other words, they reserved all magistracies for the grandi and entirely excluded the people from political participation. Conventional wisdom among the ottimati in Florence insisted that Sparta and, most especially, Venice were the best republics due to their tranquility and longevity.[38] Certainly, Sparta and Venice satisfy the young grandi's definition of liberty: they facilitate the young grandi's exercise of offices over the people on their own terms rather than on terms set by a foreign or domestic prince or, even, on the people's terms. This is precisely the kind of oligarchic republic that was nearly instituted in Florence when the Medici were expelled in 1494 – that is, until Savonarola and then Soderini made it more democratic in their own different ways. The ottimati only acceded to Savonarola's wish to establish a citizen assembly, the Great Council, with the expectation that a powerful senate would also be established to balance the former's power; and they opposed Soderini's retention and reliance on the Great Council's authority and, as mentioned previously, his appointing to ministerial posts ignoble "new men" such as Machiavelli.

Machiavelli concedes the longevity of Sparta's and Venice's "freedom" in I.5. But, while emphasizing his own voice ("I say"), Machiavelli argues, on normative and descriptive grounds, for granting the guard of liberty to the people, as he claims the Romans did. The people desire not to be dominated and so, "having a greater will to live free," they have less appetite to usurp or seize liberty. But if Machiavelli's argument in the previous two chapters regarding the trustworthy motives of the people has not convinced the ever-haughty, ever-suspicious grandi, Machiavelli resorts to necessity in order to persuade them: the plebs neither *want* to usurp liberty nor do they have the *ability* to do so.

Notable commentators suggest that this move effectively undermines the argument for offering liberty's guardianship to the plebs, since those who cannot usurp or seize something successfully cannot adequately guard it. But is this so? First of all, if by usurpation one means simply "overthrow," then the people *can* usurp liberty through either descent into license or resort to a Caesar. The grandi know this, and the *Discourses* bears it out at various points. In this regard, it is conceivable that the popular force that is necessary – perhaps insufficient, yet not inconsiderable – to kill all the nobles, or raise up a Caesar to keep the latter at bay, could be enlisted and ordered to defend freedom. Furthermore, since Machiavelli emphasizes that the people's desires are "rarely pernicious" to liberty, then the grandi to some extent have it in their own power to forestall the emergence of circumstances where it *is* pernicious – that is, where the people would want to usurp liberty for all. A consistent theme of the *Discourses* is that the people never attempt to usurp liberty without first being provoked to do so by patrician oppression and conspiracies (D I.28, D I.46).

Secondly, even if liberty remains undefined by Machiavelli, clearly it is not a physical object: the people could guard liberty within a republican context without being able to "seize" it, since seizing it is tantamount to extinguishing it. If they resort to either anarchy or tyranny, the people themselves lose the conditions of liberty. The grandi need to be convinced that the people are capable of calculating the following "truth": they ought never to usurp liberty (read: overthrow the nobles) when their freedom from noble oppression is greater than the limited or non-existent liberty they would gain under conditions of license or tyranny (see D I.7, D I.58, D III.8, D III.28). In light of this, it is not illogical for Machiavelli to assert that, within the confines of republican politics, "since they are not able to seize it, they do not permit others to seize it" (D I.5).

So, how do the people serve as the guardian that prevents the grandi from seizing liberty? They do so through an ensemble of pleb-enabling and noble-constraining institutions, that is, through practices and behaviors that constitute the political concessions that Machiavelli extracts from the grandi over the course of Book I of the *Discourses*, not all of which Machiavelli enumerates by chapter 5. These include examples of collective plebeian action that stop short of looting and murder, such as those mentioned previously; the institution of the tribunes; practices such as public accusations and popularly judged political trials; deliberative and legislative assemblies; eligibility to stand for and actually hold noble-dominated magistracies; and – most painfully for the grandi, as it turns out (D I.37) – claims for equitable distribution of property as well. In addition, of course, there are the ultimate threats of license and Caesarism to keep the grandi in line.

After making his personal case for Rome as the republic to be emulated, and for the people as worthy guards of liberty – a speech in which Machiavelli assumes the role of a plebeian magistrate, a tribune perhaps[39] – Machiavelli relinquishes the floor to an unnamed party, first singular, then possibly plural ("he...says," "they give as examples"). This spokesman or these spokesmen make the case against Machiavelli's Rome and in favor of an aristocratic guardianship of liberty. Although taken by a few to be Machiavelli's true opinion, the views expressed by the spokesman/spokesmen for the grandi amount to little more than the typical "aggrandizing plebs" interpretation of Roman history that was found in, for instance, Livy before and Montesquieu after Machiavelli,[40] an interpretation that was prevalent in his own day among ottimati such as Guicciardini and the elder Rucellai.

In an effort to relativize Machiavelli's arguments, the speaker or speakers contesting Roman-style governo largo and the popular guardianship of liberty assert that *both* the "powerful" *and* the plebs have aggressive ambitions; the former seek to wield "a stick" against the people and the latter are driven by a "restless spirit" to badger the nobility.[41] In fact, inverting Machiavelli's claims regarding noble and popular humors in *The Prince*, which I discussed in Chapter 1, the noble apologists here insist that the grandi's ambitions may have limits, while the people's, on the contrary, are insatiable, restless, and furious.[42] Yet those who seek perhaps too hastily to subvert Machiavelli's adoption of the popular cause in this chapter miss something terribly important about this little disputation or mini-dialogue: the noble spokesmen's claim regarding the grandi amounts to an unwitting confession; their claim against the people will be exposed as a calumny.

The spokesmen for the grandi admit in an unqualified fashion the fact that the nobles seek to hold the guard of liberty – that is, exclusive or predominant political power – as a "stick in their hand." In other words, they aspire to attain offices and honors to command and oppress others – literally and figuratively, to beat them. The noble spokesmen, who for all intents and purposes could be the two dedicatees with whom Machiavelli converses here, make no pretense of justifying a monopoly of power in the patricians' hands on the grounds that they are "the best" or that they "deserve" it.[43] Through this admission by the noble spokesman or spokesmen, Machiavelli may signal that his dedicatees have been instructed successfully in this indisputable fact of their nature: they are driven by an appetite to dominate, period. If the speech contains anything more than a self-serving justification for noble guardianship, it is the following claim that amounts to a barely veiled threat: when the grandi hold the guardianship, republics "better satisfy [the grandi's] ambitions, and having a greater part of the republic, by holding this stick in their hand, they are inclined to more contentment" (D I.5).

In other words, if given "this stick," the grandi will have their ambitions satisfied "more," but not completely; and thus they will be given cause to be "more" contented, but not necessarily fully content. With this threat, the nobles offer to disrupt a free way of life *less often* if they are given a weapon by which they can deprive other citizens of liberty. But, in their own words, there is no guarantee at all that possession of this weapon will prove sufficient to satisfy their oppressive appetite. Conversely, in Machiavelli's description of a republic where the people guard liberty, it seems as if there exists a greater possibility that liberty can be shared, that each class's definition of liberty can be partially satisfied. But there is no such possibility for anyone but the grandi to be "free" when *they* act as the guardians of liberty.[44]

The noble spokesman, who responds to Machiavelli's case for the people, of course would like to divert us from drawing this conclusion. To do so, he makes a halfhearted attempt to argue that the grandi's appetite to oppress may in fact have limits; that it may be possible to satisfy their oppressive appetite. He also slanders the desires of the people, denying that they possess the very qualities that Machiavelli attributes to them (i.e., Machiavelli's insistence that the people have *only* the desire not to be dominated). In close keeping with the aristocratic narrative of republicanism from Plato to Publius and beyond, Machiavelli's noble spokesman or spokesmen ("he" or "they," as Machiavelli addresses them) exaggerate the people's purported oppressive desires. They inflate the oppressiveness of the people to a magnitude far greater than they are willing to attribute to the nobles.

The spokespersons for the grandi even render the nobles vulnerable vis-à-vis political encroachment by the people: the spokesmen conjure up the "restless spirit of the plebs" that supposedly causes the nobles, driven to desperation, to behave even worse than they might otherwise. It is *the people* who make the nobles oppressive, not, as Machiavelli reminds us time and again, vice-versa! If the plebs are granted any authority at all, their restlessness and "fury" will always drive them to demand more, as is illustrated, they say, by Roman history. The people move in succession from one power grab to another: from demanding the establishment of the tribunes, to possession of one consular office, then to both of them; from desiring the praetors and the censors for themselves to favoring a proto-Caesar such as Marius. The noble spokesmen accuse the people of using men such as Marius as a stick, "to beat down the nobility," and hence of accelerating the destruction of the republic.[45]

Yet, if the grandi's appetite to oppress is not easily satisfied, as their spokesmen admit here, then a politically included and active people, a people charged with protecting liberty like the Roman plebeians, would be forced by necessity to escalate their attempts to contain the nobility in order to prevent the latter from seizing liberty altogether. To protect liberty, even their disproportionately lower share of it at the outset, the people will have to acquire more power at the grandi's expense. In two chapters, at the conclusion of this one, I.5, and later in I.37, after engaging in complicated evaluations of the people's ambition to protect themselves from domination versus the grandi's ambition to dominate them, Machiavelli indicts the nobles for harboring and expressing the more dangerous ambition precisely because theirs is more preemptive and provocative than is the ambition of the people.

In any case, in spite of the partisanship implied by the perspective of the plebeian magistrate that Machiavelli adopts at the start of this dispute – or perhaps because of it – Machiavelli does not decide for one side or the other, for Roman popular guardianship or Spartan/Venetian oligarchic guardianship, at the debate's conclusion. While the grandi may reveal that they want to dominate, while they might confess to harboring an oppressive humor, they will *never* admit that the people are less inclined toward oppression than they are, an admission that would logically necessitate that the nobles relinquish to the people the guardianship of liberty. Rather than make such a concession of their own free will, they dissemble, deflect, and feign vulnerability ("we're both the same; they're worse; okay, we want a stick to beat others; no, they want the stick; it is they who threaten *us* with sticks!"). Clearly, the grandi will not cede any power to the people either out of the goodness of their hearts or on the basis of sound reasoning. And while Machiavelli seems willing to leave the dispute deadlocked, he suddenly resorts to an almost unannounced criterion to break the stalemate: the prospect of empire.

Machiavelli states rather matter-of-factly that Rome is the model of an imperial republic, while Venice and Sparta are the models for self-contained republics. Therefore, the decision in favor of one or the other depends not on one's view of the respective natures of the people or the great, but ultimately on whether or not empire is a desired goal. After tossing this tiny explosive into the laps of those whom he's just maneuvered into confessing their appetite to oppress, Machiavelli promises them that he will elaborate further on this tantalizing prospect for expansive oppression in the next chapter. The people's spokesman, Machiavelli, could not settle the verbal dispute in I.5; he cannot force a conclusion on the grandi who are stronger and better-resourced than he is. A seemingly external standard, empire, must be invoked to settle the quarrel.[46]

Dialogue and speech may or may not have persuaded Adeimantus and Glaucon on the nature of justice. Yet the preceding dialogue displays Machiavelli's impotence in the art of verbally persuading his young patrician interlocutors.

To encourage Cosimo and Zanobi in the direction of a more just politics, Machiavelli of necessity resorts to the bait of greater advantage, that is, greater prospects for what they really want, oppression. In the next chapter, I.6, empire may motivate young grandi in ways that rational arguments by a plebeian spokesman or magistrate cannot. Before moving on in this vein, it must be noted that, having whet the appetite of his audience with the prospect of imperial rule, Machiavelli happens to mention, almost as an aside, the not inconsequential fact that the grandi cannot "manage" (*maneggiare*) a people enlisted in warfare simply in any "mode" the former may please (D I.6).[47]

Empire's Allure and the Discrediting of Aristocratic Republics

Of the entire *Discourses*, I.6 is one of the most closely studied chapters.[48] Many notable scholars point out the numerous problems with Machiavelli's comparison of Sparta/Venice and Rome, of self-contained and imperial republics, and raise difficult questions about his ultimate choice for imperial Rome. Sparta and Venice were not as weak as Machiavelli claims nor as free of tumult; neither were their "foundations" destroyed by their inability to keep territories gained in moments when they did attempt to expand. Moreover, his descriptions of Spartan and Venetian political institutions seem woefully flawed or at the very least seriously incomplete. As for the endorsement of Roman imperialism, in light of the rest of the *Discourses*, the decline of the republic can be attributed directly to aspects of its imperial expansion – in particular, the impoverishment of her citizen-soldiers and the prolongation of its officers' military commissions. One must also consider Machiavelli's less than favorable emphasis on Rome's elimination of liberty in virtuous cities throughout the ancient Mediterranean (D II.2–3). Many commentators, on the basis of solid evidence and serious hermeneutic efforts, conclude the following: in light of the shortcomings and inconsistencies of Machiavelli's analysis of Sparta and Venice, his unjustifiable preference for Rome is motivated primarily by his desire to unleash human appetite in an unprecedented fashion, and/or by his endorsement of the human pursuit of greatness in history. On this view, Machiavelli subordinates liberty to the necessity of acquisition and/or to a normative preference for greatness.[49]

Does this most puzzling chapter, I.6, look any different when read from the perspective of the book's young patrician dedicatees? At first blush, the chapter disappoints those who turn to it for an immediate discussion of republican imperialism: empire is mentioned in neither the chapter heading nor in the first two, rather long, paragraphs. Machiavelli obliquely refers to it in his observation that the Venetian grandi or "gentlemen" did not put the populace "to work in things in which they could seize authority" (D I.6). This refers back to the opposite kind of republic, Rome, which as mentioned in I.5 makes use of the people "in important things." In addition, empire, or lack thereof, is pertinent to Machiavelli's discussion in these passages of Sparta's resistance to growth. Rather than empire, the chapter actually continues to investigate the issue of democratic versus oligarchic republics – Rome versus Venice/Sparta – but this time from a different angle: namely, whether the "great effects" (*effetti grandi*) produced in Rome could be achieved without the controversies, tumults, and enmities between the people and the senate that occurred there.

Yet exactly what are the great effects presented to the grandi at this point? The laws that foster "liberty" mentioned earlier? Or the "power" mentioned in the title of Machiavelli's previous chapter and the empire that he invokes in that chapter's penultimate paragraph? To the frustration of the imperially curious, Machiavelli seems to be treating liberty as the great effect, mentioning both Rome's "free way of life" and Sparta/Venice, who were "free for a long while without enmities and tumults" (D I.6). But it seems strange to associate tumults with freedom by pointing out, as Machiavelli does here, that tumults caused the *ruin* of Rome's free way of life after the time of the brothers Gracchus. *This* is their great effect? The republic's decline and fall?

Machiavelli invokes the "time of" the Gracchi rather than the brothers themselves and their land reforms aimed at ameliorating economic inequality between the Roman nobility and the plebeians: Machiavelli later shows, in the midst of an apparent indictment of the Gracchi, that it was the ambition of the grandi and the avarice of the senate that made the brothers' popular appeal possible, indeed necessary, and set in motion the republic's decline (D I.37). He may reproach their method there, but he does not besmirch the Gracchan cause.[50] Yet this issue of oppression by the grandi and responses to it by the people in Rome relates directly to the issue of "great effects" without tumult in the other type of republic. How did the Venetian and Spartan grandi exclude the people politically so as to avoid tumults yet restrain themselves from oppressing them so thoroughly that the people neither revolted nor resorted to a Caesar?

Machiavelli argues that Venice and Sparta were successful noble-dominated and domestically tranquil *governi stretti* because of their small size (D I.6). Small republics may sustain themselves without extensive inclusion of the people; the proportion of nobles to commoners in such regimes remains so large as to keep the latter pacified. One might venture to say, however, that the domestic politics of Sparta and Venice appear to be fantasies from a Machiavellian standpoint: in both cities, there are nobles who do not oppress the people, either of their own volition (Venice) or as the result of a separation of the nobles from the plebs imposed by monarchical authority (Sparta). Thus, the grandi are free to govern but not to oppress the plebs in these polities. But given their fundamentally oppressive nature, as Machiavelli defines it, can the grandi really be "free" when they observe a distinction between governing and oppressing?

The people, for their part, seem to exist in what is their natural state in both cities: absent oppression by the nobles, they neither agitate against them nor, for that matter, seek any part in governing whatsoever. Machiavelli notes that Venice formed its aristocracy before a populace, in any real sense of the term, had developed there. Thus, the people never played a role in the formation of the regime, as they had in Rome, and consequently never leveraged a significant institutional role for themselves. On closer inspection, however, Machiavelli seems to identify a way of governing the people that actually is oppression, oppression that merely goes uncontested: the Venetian people apparently never experienced liberty, and hence it is not that they live free from oppression, but rather that they don't know how to contest oligarchic governance cum oppression "because nothing had been taken away from them" (D I.6). But people who have experienced a modicum of liberty under a prince-senate competition, as in early Rome, or under a governo largo, as in Florence, will not refrain from challenging grandi domination once they've lost such liberty or experience its diminution (cf., P 5). Moreover, emphasizing the connection between popular liberty and a martial citizenry, Machiavelli notes that Venice undermined social dynamism by prohibiting the people's participation in military affairs (D I.6).

Machiavelli mentions numerous factors that prevented tumults from ensuing in Sparta – insulation from foreigners, a small population, relative equality of conditions, and restrictions on growth. Unlike the Roman Republic, which was a citizen-making machine, elevating allies and former enemies to partial and even full citizenship (cf., D II.30), Sparta actively inhibited the development of a large and diverse populace by excluding foreigners, even as visitors. Two other factors that forestalled civil discord in Sparta are the role of monarchy and the status of rank. With respect to the latter, Machiavelli observes that the ranks of the city (*gradi della città*) were spread among few citizens and kept at a distance from the plebs. But what kind of rank, which entails both distinction and command, can be kept so far away from subordinates as to go unnoticed? What kind of grades, gradations, or distinctions actually matter without palpable comparison and contrast? Subordinates must observe rank – they must see it so that they can acknowledge its bearers as superior if the appetite for prestige in its holders is to be at all satisfied. Subordinates must experience rank – they must feel it, if its holder's appetite to order others about can be realized even minimally. Could the unrecognized ranks that Machiavelli locates in Sparta really satisfy the grandi?

The answer may be moot in the Spartan context where one or both kings, who were interposed "in the midst of the nobility," defended the plebs from noble-generated injuries (D I.6). Thus, the Spartan people had no cause to defend themselves actively against the nobles because the kings took it upon themselves to protect them. I would suggest that a regime with such a watered-down exercise of rank, and with a nobility that is effectively constrained by monarchical agency, is not a republic at all, but rather a principality. The upshot of all of this is, firstly, that Venice is an unrealizable republican model for grandi who wish to dominate a regime: in such circumstances, they must either establish a regime that does not yet contain a people or find a city in which the people have never enjoyed even a modicum of liberty. Secondly, Sparta is an undesirable republican model because it is a trifle too reminiscent of precisely the Medici principality to which the young patrician dedicatees already submit. In short, Machiavelli has thoroughly discredited the Florentine ottimati's two paragons of republicanism on the basis of criteria derived precisely from their own preferences.

But Machiavelli already may have diverted the attention of his audience of young grandi away from Spartan and Venetian liberty, that is, mere oppression of the people within their own republic, or at least he may have problematized it, by the introduction of empire. Having described the (unattainable and unsatisfying) liberty of the grandi in Venice and Sparta, Machiavelli suggests that Rome could have avoided tumult only if it had imitated the other two by, respectively, not arming the people and not admitting foreigners (D I.6). But in doing both, Rome strengthened the plebs by, literally, putting sticks in their hands and swelling their numbers. Had it not done so, Machiavelli avers, on the one hand, it would not have come to greatness, and, on the other, it would have been weak. These two very different claims may appeal, respectively, to two different kinds of grandi: chance-taking versus risk-averse nobles. Indeed, this passage establishes the strategy that Machiavelli pursues in the rest of the chapter: grandi who are willing to forsake some domination of their own citizens for greater oppression of others abroad (and acquisition of the greater wealth and fame that accompanies such exploits) will cede some domestic political role to the people. Grandi who still cling to a definition of liberty whereby they wholly exclude the people from politics and exercise domination over them will be made to fear that such a republic is inherently weak and hence made to live in constant danger of being annexed by another regime, an eventuality which would certainly curtail the grandi's domestic "liberty."

The latter term does not appear in the balance of the chapter, but its realization may yet be Machiavelli's main objective. He entices the grandi to compromise their notion of liberty (the monopoly on "a political way of life" at home) through appeals to the greatness or necessity of expansion and, in so doing, bargains for the people an unnamed and undefined new kind of liberty: the people assume a larger role in politics than they had been granted previously in republics. As a result, the people are empowered to protect themselves from oppression by the grandi and protect the whole regime from the collapse that domination by the grandi portends. On reflection, then, the comparison of the liberty practiced and guarded in Sparta and Venice, on the one hand, and in Rome, on the other, may have been inappropriate from the start, since they are qualitatively different in important respects. When liberty is conceived as independence from other regimes, the two models are the same; when it is conceived as the play of domestic forces, they are different in kind. Yet Machiavelli often casts the comparison as if "liberty" in both cases were equivalent, adding the element of empire to induce the grandi to tolerate a transition from the one kind of liberty to the other.

As mentioned before, interpreters often assume that the desire for domination that Machiavelli attributes to the grandi in these early chapters of the *Discourses* necessarily entails a desire for eternal fame.[51] But this is not an assumption that Machiavelli makes about either grandi in general or his noble dedicatees a priori. If it were, then the strenuous effort to elevate the Roman over the Spartan and Venetian republics would have been unnecessary. The grandi's appetite to oppress the people of their own polity is *not* in and of itself the same as the desire for worldly glory through imperial conquest. Machiavelli certainly labors to move them from the one to the other, the former to the latter, and in this chapter I have shown that much of the argument and action of the early discourses strategically serves that attempted manipulation. As the history of ancient and early-modern city-states generally shows, most grandi prefer a predominance of men of virtue (read: wealth and good name) in magistracies, defensive security over empire, and domestic stability over class conflict.[52] In other words, the grandi within most oligarchies were content with dominating their own regimes and acquiring modest renown within them. The assumption that Machiavelli is encouraging his elite to follow their most basic nature, understood as a desire for glory, is then one step removed from what is actually their more fundamental inclination. They have a humor to dominate, according to Machiavelli, *not* to be eternally famous.[53]

The desire to oppress or command has no inherent link with the desire for glory; it pertains to the pure pleasure of making others act in accord with one's own will in a way that they would not have otherwise, or of lording over someone else a privilege or status that they themselves do not possess. It does not mean, first and foremost, striving to have one's name revered eternally. Bullies do not ordinarily think about eternity (e.g., D III.1). Machiavelli's gambit is to pique such bullies' interest in domination over *mortality and time*, and offer it to them in exchange for some relinquishing of their domination over their own poorer citizens. The first six chapters of the *Discourses* induce the young grandi to include common citizens in politics so that they may be conscripted into the army, which the grandi can use to expand their regime and possibly achieve eternal fame for themselves. While ordinary nobles might require enticements to pursue eternal glory, it is Machiavelli's "founders" or would-be founders who could be said to be driven naturally by a desire for eternal glory – for them the appetite for oppression and for glory are entwined – but it is doubtful that history demonstrates or that Machiavelli assumed that this also applies to the grandi as a class.[54] In this case, Machiavelli's inspiring examples of illustrious Roman magistrates and commanders in the *Discourses* are, in this respect, prescriptive, not descriptive.

Democratic Republics: Imperial or Merely Martial?

Machiavelli's choice for Rome, his "belief," as he professes repeatedly at the climax of I.6, in the imperial republican model, rules out the possibility of a militarily strong *but* non-expansive republic. Why might we have cause to doubt his profession of faith in this respect? After all, he uses as the examples of "weak" republics, those with a "weak foundation," Sparta and Venice, republics with the greatest longevity ever recorded. Perhaps the quality of their internal liberty pales in comparison with Rome's, but their stability, longevity, and, in the Spartan case, martial virtue is incompatible with any conventional understanding of weakness. Perhaps their exploits did not rise to the level of Roman *grandezza*, but they did not lack for renown.

Machiavelli makes a rather unreserved claim about the human condition when he states that the rise and fall of worldly events necessarily requires regimes to expand or fail. This would seem to compel a republic to acquire empire by necessity. Yet Machiavelli's claim is not, in fact, as unequivocal as it first seems. At the conclusion of a highly rhetorical consideration of self-containment versus expansion, and after insisting that necessity *will* inevitably compel a republic to expand, Machiavelli concludes with the less definitive phrase: "... *if indeed* necessity brings [a republic] to expand...." (D I.6, emphasis added). This is a curiously hesitant way for Machiavelli to sum up a topic like necessity, a topic that he treats so emphatically elsewhere (e.g., D I.1).

In total, Machiavelli's endorsement of Rome over Sparta or Venice does not completely disparage the accomplishments of noble-dominated republics. He acknowledges that the latter type of republic may enjoy even greater longevity than did Rome (D I.2). Sparta lasted eight hundred years as a republic; Rome lasted only three hundred. (Indeed, Machiavelli could not have known that Venice's republic would ultimately last *twice* as long as Rome's.) But when viewed as potential vehicles by which young grandi might satisfy their appetite to oppress, Machiavelli has thoroughly discredited the Spartan and Venetian republican models. Moreover, for Machiavelli himself, I would argue, whatever might be the benefits of noble-dominated and socially harmonious republics in terms of longevity, those republics are deficient with respect to the substance of political culture, the quality of public policy, and efficacy in military affairs. These can only be achieved when antagonism between the grandi and the people ensues within a governo largo where the people are armed. Sparta, no matter how successful, was not as great as Rome because it did not enjoy as rich a civic life, nor did it acquire as much empire (D I.6). Thus, the active civic life enjoyed by Machiavelli's popularly based Rome is not a peaceful, bucolic, or tranquil arrangement of social interaction. Though he never distinguishes the two conceptually, discord seems to be good both in itself – as a preferred way of conducting public life – and as a means to better policy and military success.

But given the history of republics, most of which look more like Sparta or Venice than Rome, and based on the political prejudices of the Florentine ottimati discussed in the preceding, it is safe to assume that many grandi will *not* be seduced by the promise of imperial glory into tolerating popular inclusion and tumults "as necessary inconveniences for the greatness achieved by Rome" (D I.6). Therefore, besides the carrot (glory or greatness) and the stick (the necessity of expansion), an added element – the fear that weakness will lead to regime collapse – is required to encourage most grandi to accept such inconveniences. At the end of the chapter, Machiavelli reminds his audience of one of those inconveniences – a tribunate that enables the people to guard liberty – and he introduces public accusation, by which common citizens, but especially the tribunes, could bring other citizens to account. So besides being opposed by the plebs and their tribunes, the grandi are now encouraged to allow themselves to be indicted by and tried before the people for suspicion of usurping liberty. I discuss public accusations and popularly judged political trials at greater length in Chapter 5.

In light of these institutional prescriptions, while appetite and greatness play no small role in the *Discourses*, I would suggest that greatness and appetite are inducements that Machiavelli uses to motivate a grandi audience to pursue empire, not for its own sake, but as a mechanism that encourages greater popular participation in politics. The Roman model promises more liberty for citizens at home, but diminution of it for the citizens of other republics abroad. The Spartan/Venetian model promises virtually no liberty for most citizens at home, but it does not, for the most part, threaten republics abroad. Machiavelli is quite possibly ambivalent about both, on the one hand, maximum longevity without popular liberty, and, on the other, maximum expansion that destroys liberty elsewhere and corrupts it at home. But he explicitly endorses the Roman model that portends the latter, because it, and *not* the former model – presumably preferred by his dedicatees before reading the *Discourses* – encourages popular inclusion and empowerment.[55]

In this respect, Machiavelli's exclusion of the Swiss and the Athenians from the debate over liberty, power, and greatness in I.6 is quite curious. Machiavelli's neglect of Athens cannot be attributed simply to the fact that, as he states in I.2, it is a "simple" popular regime or democracy as opposed to a properly "mixed" republic, that is, that the Athenians did not institute a proper senate: after all, Machiavelli refers to Athens as a republic subsequently, indeed, as one of the most prosperous republics in history (D I.28, D I.58, D II.2). The Athenian republic is an example of a regime that entrusted the people with the guard of liberty and that achieved greatness and fame nearly commensurate with Rome's, and yet whose expansionary policies led to the enslavement of much of Hellas and the domestic collapse of the regime. Athens is a democratic republic that rivals Rome in greatness but that even more dramatically than Rome highlights the drawbacks of expansion.

The Swiss are an even more interesting case because Machiavelli sometimes intimates that he admires them as much as he does the Romans and, given their historical and geographic proximity, fears them more.[56] The Swiss are as powerful militarily as were the Romans, but they do not expand, or at least do not expand imperially: when their troops are not needed for domestic defense, the Swiss lease them to other regimes, such as France, which does not arm its people; and the Swiss augment themselves through enlargements of their confederation – that is, in a way that preserves or enhances the liberty of new territories rather than extinguishing it. The Swiss, who constitute a confederation of democratic republics, rival the Romans in power, but they illustrate the fact that imperial expansion is *not* necessary, even as the Swiss amplify Machiavelli's preference for military prowess derived from citizen-soldiers.

In light of these considerations, many commentators may accept too readily Machiavelli's association of the Swiss republican confederation with the ancient Etruscan ("Tuscan") one that Rome defeated (D II.4).[57] Machiavelli's examples of how the ancient French seized Lombardy from the Tuscans and how the Romans overwhelmed the latter (D II.4) may be, respectively, an ironic commentary on contemporary French-Swiss relations and an angry underscoring of the present plight of the militarily weak republics of north-central Italy. Machiavelli often remarks that the French monarchy is now the virtual puppet of the Swiss republics (e.g., D II.30); and Tuscan republicanism (under a league or a hegemonic city) is constantly undermined by the Catholic Church's alternating collusions with France, Spain, and the German Emperor to maintain and/or expand the Papal States.[58]

So why does Machiavelli fail to praise or endorse the Swiss republican-military model more openly in the *Discourses*? Quite simply, I suggest, because there is no inducement for his young patrician addressees to adopt it in practice: it promises advantages for the people and none for them. The Swiss model provides the popolo with liberty and equality without in any way compensating the grandi for this fact. Machiavelli must, on the contrary, entice them with a republican model that entails empire so as to encourage them to accept more egalitarian and participatory politics at home.[59] With the carrot of glory and the stick of necessity, Machiavelli compels his dedicatees to pursue empire, and in the process leverages a more populist domestic politics, a Machiavellian democracy, out of them. This is not to say that the grandi will cease their attempts to oppress their own citizens, both at home and out in the field, once they enlist the plebeians in the project of empire building. Machiavelli makes plain the fact that the Roman nobility will continue to try to oppress the plebs directly while they are fighting wars away from the domestic jurisdiction of the tribunes (D I.39) and indirectly by exacerbating socioeconomic inequality in the republic by pursuing empire (D I.37). I discuss the ramifications of this in Chapters 3 and 4.

Conversely, however, to what extent will the people abide by patrician direction of imperial expansion in the long run, once they've been politically empowered domestically? The grandi might be heartened by the elite manipulation of the plebeians as both citizens and soldiers that Machiavelli describes throughout the *Discourses*, but peoples might learn how to resist such manipulation precisely on the basis of Machiavelli's descriptions. Ultimately, whatever the idiosyncratic advantages or inherent deficiencies of the Swiss confederate-republican model invoked by Machiavelli, they are no more peculiar or deleterious than those that he ascribes to the Roman imperial-republican model. Therefore, I suggest, the common assumption that empire trumps liberty in the *Discourses* remains deeply problematic. Indeed, when extolling the virtues of the Roman people in a later chapter, Machiavelli praises them as lovers of *both* "the glory and the common good" of their city (D I.58). If it remains possible to separate liberty or the common good from imperial acquisition, then the model of a popularly and militarily empowered but non-imperial republic would seem to remain a viable option as well.

In sum, expanded popular participation not only improves the lot of common citizens by enabling them to contest and contain the grandi's ambition – this is liberty in practice or what Machiavelli calls a "free way of life." But the political empowerment of the plebs also helps both grandi and popolo by better ensuring the longevity of regimes, longevity endangered by the grandi's desire to oppress. Republics must not permit the grandi to oppress the people so thoroughly that they jeopardize the very regime structure that makes some satisfaction of their oppressive appetite possible. After all, in the *Discourses*, Machiavelli insists that the grandi's oppressive appetite is the most serious threat to a republic, just as he declares it to be the primary threat to a principality in *The Prince*.

Republics are usually ruined because the grandi empower a prince to help them dominate the people when laws and institutions are no longer at least partially sufficient to this end (D I.16). Or, they are ruined because the people enlist a prince to protect them from the grandi when laws and institutions no longer do so (D I.7). Either way, the fault lies with the oppressive nature of the grandi. In case they miss it, to emphasize his point to Cosimo and Zanobi about their appetite to dominate the people, Machiavelli frequently insists that *young* nobles, the "sons of Brutus" (e.g., D I.16, D I.46, D III.3), incessantly venture to satisfy their oppressive desires on more vulnerable citizens. One of Machiavelli's principal intentions as far as the dedicatees are concerned is to make them ponder whether there is more to be gained long-term as Brutuses than as his ill-fated and rightfully ill-regarded sons.

After establishing Rome as the republican model most conducive to the appetite, now refined, of his young patrician audience, Machiavelli elaborates on the following themes throughout the balance of the *Discourses*: (1) the restoration and preservation of liberty entailed by the grandi's elimination of monarchical rule; (2) the rewards of riches and fame that result from the grandi's command of an armed populace in the pursuit of empire; and (3) the prospect that the grandi will continue to hold a virtual monopoly on the chief magistracies (even if the people compete with them for such offices) and will continue to maintain a considerable influence over the policies of a republic. In brief, apropos (1) and (2), the *Discourses* suggests that tyrannicide, and the inclusion of the people in military and political affairs, increase the wealth and fame of young grandi more than does either an alliance between a prince and the grandi against the people or a simple aristocratic republic. The latter two options had been the political preferences of Florentine ottimati, who consistently colluded with various Medici princes against the popolo, or who sought to establish a narrow oligarchy, a governo stretto, in the city. In particular, Cosimo's family, the Rucellai, had close ties to the Medici, a relationship that continued during the era of the Orti; while Buondelmonti, obversely, conspired in the unsuccessful plot to overthrow the Medici in 1524, before fleeing to safety.[60]

Junius Brutus, Machiavelli reminds readers, gained immortality first for eliminating the tyranny of "princes proper," the Tarquins, in Rome, and second for sharply curtailing the incipient tyranny of young "princes plural," the sons of senators, within the republic (D I.17, D III.3). In presiding over the execution of his own sons, who had conspired to restore principality in Rome and recover their ability to oppress the plebs at their pleasure, Brutus decided that the patrimony of liberty is more valuable than progeny with a monopoly on political power. Moreover, in the course of the *Discourses*, Machiavelli establishes as exemplary the exploits of subsequent Roman magistrates and captains. Great men such as Camillus (D III.12), Scipio Africanus (D III.21), Cincinnatus (D III.24–25), Fabius Maximus (D III.49), and Manlius Torquatus (D III.34) gained far more fame than any individuals produced by the Spartan or Venetian republics. Machiavelli suggests that the ferocious participation of the plebs in war *and* politics makes possible both territorial conquest *and* glorious nobles. A popular army is the vehicle the Roman grandi ride to imperial success; and the tribunes, public accusations, and the popular assemblies are the domestic institutions that curb uncontrolled oppression by the grandi over the people – besides facilitating full participation of the people in rule, such institutions generally channel the grandi's will to dominate into something approximating salutary civic leadership (e.g., D I.3, D I.18, D I.44, D III.11).

Regarding theme (3), Machiavelli may assuage his patrician audience's fears that popular inclusion necessitates their own exclusion from places of prominence within a republic. Machiavelli shows quite explicitly how the senate, noble magistrates, and great captains manipulated the people through religion (D I.13–15), electoral deference (D I.47–8), physical appearance as opposed to reasonably persuasive words (D I.54), the prosecution of unnecessary wars (D I.37), and so on. The question is whether these examples are genuine instructions to the grandi or, so plainly stated – in the vernacular, no less – whether these provide clear guidelines for the people on how to avoid elite manipulation. To be sure, Machiavelli, as we will observe in the next chapter, also criticizes the people in the *Discourses* – although he usually focuses on occasional instances of the people's exercise of poor judgment rather than on any threat to good order that they might pose (e.g., I.44). I will attempt to gauge whether these criticisms are as severe and substantive as those he directs at the grandi – especially in light of other evaluations of the few and the many that pervade Western political thought. After all, Machiavelli's description of the Roman grandi's successful deception and manipulation of the people tends to be fairly faithful reportage from Livy; on the contrary, Machiavelli's fulsome praise of the people and apologetic approach to their mistakes are explicit departures from Livy's account. With this in mind, in the next chapter, I discuss the way in which the respective humors of the people and the grandi play themselves out within the context of Roman politics.

PART II

3

The Benefits and Limits of Popular Participation and Judgment

> I declare that a people is more prudent, more stable and judges better than a prince.
>
> Machiavelli, *Discourses* I.58

> The people, when deceived by a false notion of the good, often desires its own ruin.
>
> Machiavelli, *Discourses* I.53

Machiavelli's prescriptions for a widely inclusive and popularly empowered form of government rest on a remarkably favorable assessment of the common people's abilities, especially their capacity for political judgment. In previous chapters, I accentuated Machiavelli's arguments concerning the people's humor not to be dominated and demonstrated how these arguments undergird his case for democratic republics or *governi larghi*. In this chapter, I examine Machiavelli's arguments in favor of popular judgment and his various engagements with the serious criticisms of the people's capacities voiced by advocates of principalities or oligarchic republics. Machiavelli identifies at least three arenas in which the people exercise better judgment than do any other political actors, specifically, princes and the few: deciding political trials, appointing magistrates, and creating legislation.

Virtually every aristocratic critic of the people denies the latter authority to decide political trials, and most of them strongly advise against granting the people direct judgment over legislation. In general, such critics, when countenancing any popular participation at all, confine such participation to the appointment of magistrates through general elections. Beyond endorsing the popular election of public officials, however, Machiavelli also recommends widely participatory, substantively deliberative procedures through which the people refine their judgments over both political prosecutions and the law. In a historically unprecedented fashion, Machiavelli insists that republics permit common citizens to *initiate* proceedings pertaining to political trials, *nominate*

candidates for office, *propose* new legislation, and *discuss* among themselves
all the matters over which they will render ultimate judgment.

Popular Judgment in Historical Context

Two criticisms of the people as a political agent pervade the history of popular government: traditionally, oligarchs bent on completely excluding the
people from participation in government denounce the latter as inveterately
envious, ignorant, licentious, and prone to arbitrary displays of aggression
toward prominent citizens.[1] Alternatively, writers and statesmen who consider the common people merely unfit to exercise substantive political power
emphasize popular deference and passivity and link these qualities to a certain lack of initiative or ingenuity. The first view rejects the idea tout court
that the people are capable of sensible political judgment; the second suggests
that the people's deficient but not insignificant capacities should be exercised
in strictly circumscribed ways. As we observed in the last chapter, Machiavelli's stylized depiction of critics of the people and advocates of oligarchic
republics mixes elements of both views (e.g., D I.5). Machiavelli's insistence
on the people's fundamental desire to avoid domination somewhat neutralizes
the most extreme arguments against popular participation in politics, but the
second, more qualified set of criticisms of the people requires more sustained
engagement.[2]

Aristotle observed that some politically relevant good inhered within the
people, and that the best constitutional arrangements, despite privileging the
few in significant ways, should nevertheless include mechanisms that bring
out this good.[3] Cicero, despite an explicit preference for rule by a republic's
best men alternating terms in the supreme magistracies and then enjoying life
tenure in a senate, nevertheless consistently declared that political legitimacy
emanates from the people.[4] This Aristotelian and Ciceronian spirit resonates
in the writings of aristocratic republicans such as Guicciardini, proponents of
representative government such as Madison, and theorists of elective oligarchy
such as Schumpeter, all of whom tolerate – in fact, recommend – some inclusion
of the people in politics.[5] Specifically, they assign the people a severely limited
role, one usually confined to approving or rejecting the claims to office or the
policy proposals of particular elites.[6]

When notable constitutional theorists who were inherently suspicious of the
people's ability to reason for themselves did allow the people formal judgment
over law or policy in republican or democratic contexts, they often sought
to maximize elite influence over policy making by imposing especially narrow
restrictions on the conditions under which the people decide.[7] Unlike such
authors, Machiavelli does not grant elites alone the authority to present the
people with policy alternatives, which the people must simply acclaim or reject,
and he does not consign popular participation exclusively to occasions where
the people merely listen as their social superiors argue for and against particular
issues in advance of a popular vote on them.

On the contrary, as I demonstrate in this chapter, Machiavelli affords all citizens opportunities to initiate political proceedings by, for instance, introducing accusations against prominent citizens and proposing new laws. Moreover, he provides all citizens access to formal and informal assemblies within which they deliberatively transform their perhaps initially unconsidered opinion (*opinione*) into good judgment (*giudicio*) over laws and candidates for office.[8] Certainly, as I discuss, there is ample room in Machiavelli's theory for elites to propose policy and then attempt to persuade and even manipulate the people in the course of law and policy making. However, I suggest that those who would narrowly reduce the essence of Machiavelli's conception of popular government to such occasions of elite initiative and control grossly distort the Florentine's political thought, irresponsibly obscuring its fundamentally democratic character – both on its own terms and, especially, in light of the opinions of virtually all other authors in the history of Western political thought.

Bringing Indictments and Deciding Political Trials

While I will devote the entirety of Chapter 5 to popularly judged political trials, here I briefly discuss their place in Machiavelli's efforts to promote popular judgment. In the *Discourses*, Machiavelli recommends that republics empower the people, as the "guard of liberty," to accuse citizens, especially "powerful citizens" (*potenti cittadini*), who "sin in any manner against a free regime" (D I.7). While Machiavelli indicates that magistrates like Rome's tribunes of the plebs can most efficaciously accuse political criminals among the ranks of the great, he insists that the authority to accuse be distributed widely among the people: "every citizen within a republic should be able to accuse without any fear and without any respect" – in other words, without any fear of the *grandi*'s power or any respect for their station (D I.8).

Machiavelli further argues that, in addition to bringing indictments, all citizens, formally assembled, should decide whether to convict or exonerate those accused of political crimes: he reasons that judgments of the entire people both deter those who are tempted to threaten a republic's liberty and "crush" those who have actually harmed it (D I.7). Machiavelli concedes that a single magistrate or a small council is better than no institution at all for airing and deciding charges directed at grandi who act beyond "civil ways," but he emphatically concludes that bodies of "very many judges," like Rome's citizen and plebeian assemblies, are best suited to decide the veracity of political accusations (D I.7). Small bodies like Florence's executive committees, such as the Eight of Ward, with which Machiavelli was very familiar, are too prone to intimidation, collusion, or bias when they decide the fate of members of the *ottimati*. On the contrary, the sheer size of an assembly comprised of the entire citizenry, Machiavelli seems to suggest, (a) allows individual citizens the anonymity necessary to render judgment without worry of reprisal, and (b) overwhelms and neutralizes specific individuals or small "sects" who are motivated by partisan considerations for or against the accused (D I.7).

In the chapters of the *Discourses* devoted to accusations (D I.7–8), Machiavelli turns traditional aristocratic prejudices against the people into the very justifications for why the latter should be institutionally empowered with decisive political judgment. Consider the case of Coriolanus, who proposed that the senate starve the Roman plebs into political submission. As I'll discuss at greater length later, Machiavelli describes the negative outcomes that would have ensued if the people had violently retaliated against Coriolanus outside the senate. Machiavelli suggests that an attack by the mob, which had gathered to confront Coriolanus, would have constituted a private act on the part of particular individuals against a citizen – an arbitrarily violent and biased injury that would have provoked private reprisals by Coriolanus's partisans. This, in turn, would have sparked a civil war and portended foreign intervention that surely would have ruined the republic (D I.7). However, since the tribunes intervened and summoned Coriolanus to stand trial before the people, he faced the prospect of being "crushed through ordinary means," that is, judged by the people formally collected as a public in an assembly. Within such institutional confines, Machiavelli suggests, the people no longer act as a mass of private individuals but rather constitute a public body of legally empowered citizens.

The result for Coriolanus (who famously fled Rome rather than stand trial) would have been effectively the same whether he was torn to pieces by the people outside the senate or condemned to death by them in assembly. But, according to Machiavelli, the ramifications for the republic in each case could not have been more different. Machiavelli argues that the friends and families of a citizen who has "committed wrongs" become partisan foes of the people and enemies of the republic when they feel offended by a mob, a private party, that resorts to "extraordinary" – that is, arbitrarily violent – means. But when a prominent and powerful wrongdoer is punished through ordinary public and legal procedures, even or especially by the people, his family and friends do not subsequently become enemies of the people or partisans against the republic (D I.7).

To extrapolate a bit from Machiavelli's argument here, accused nobles, their families, and their associates find a formal decision rendered by the people constituted as a public in an assembly more palatable than they do arbitrary acts of retribution committed by the people (or some especially exercised subset of the latter) constituted as a mob for the following reasons. In the first case, the people act through law, that is, according to preestablished ground rules; a majority of citizens contribute to the judgment and decision over the accused's fate; the people consider arguments for as well as against the accused; and public officials rather than the people perform the actual execution in cases of a guilty verdict.

Put simply, a people that is empowered to decide political trials, Machiavelli suggests, cannot be compared to a violent mob;[9] rather it constitutes, on the one hand, a reliable guard against oligarchic or princely usurpations of liberty and, on the other, the surest bulwark against civil instability – not, as critics suggest, the most likely instigator of the latter. The very behavior that advocates of noble-dominated republics cite against the idea of empowering the people politically is exactly the type of conduct that can be avoided when the people are so empowered. In addition, Machiavelli shows that republics can benefit from such popular empowerment in ways that *governi stretti*, republics dominated by elites, cannot.

This logic holds in Machiavelli's discussion of calumnies, false charges spread anonymously against individuals without official hearing, concrete evidence, or witness testimony. Machiavelli concedes that the people are often susceptible to the malignant influence of calumnies, and that, consequently, they may wrongly turn against or offer favor to the targets (or even originators) of false rumors (D I.8). But appropriate institutional arrangements can mitigate this tendency: if, for instance, the Florentines had employed, as did the Romans, readily accessible and widely participatory institutions for distinguishing formal accusations from spurious rumors, the Florentine Republic would not have suffered so egregiously when calumnies were spread against prominent citizens such as Giovanni Guicciardini, Francesco Valori, and Piero Soderini (D I.7–8). Machiavelli laments the fact that the Florentine people had no formal opportunity to evaluate the claims made against these citizens and, furthermore, no official authority to punish or exonerate such targets of private parties. Absent such roles for the people in the process of political punishment, prominent citizens became increasingly indignant toward each other for spreading harmful rumors and toward the people for believing them. Machiavelli suggests that the ensuing class and factional strife eventually resulted in oligarchic coups that destroyed the Florentine Republic and elevated and then reinstalled the Medici to power.

Thus, while Machiavelli concedes that pernicious effects can and do result from the people's credulity with respect to smears and rumors, he insists that this is, in itself, no reason to shut the people out of positions of political authority. On the contrary, Machiavelli suggests that republics actually benefit when they correct this tendency by allowing the people to decide, publicly and officially, the difference between political fact and fiction. Obviously, if republics exclude the people from political power, a deluded populace can still deleteriously affect politics in an informal manner should they become stirred up by wild rumors. However, Machiavelli avers, when a republic empowers the people to distinguish rumor from fact, not only does this empowerment serve to enlighten the people, but the republic benefits from the expeditious settling of partisan disputes and the definitive punishment of political criminals.

Machiavelli acknowledges that very often misguided and vindictive popular *opinion* provokes "most of the great men" into conspiring against popular governments (D I.8); but he insists that the relative objectivity and sheer force of popular *judgment* protects the latter from the former (e.g., D I.47). After all, Machiavelli observes, it was not false public opinion that ultimately undermined the Florentine Republic, but rather the republic's failure to allow the people to transform their raw opinion into substantive judgment on Guicciardini, Valori, and Soderini – judgment that would have preempted the ensuing destructive behavior engaged in by elites. The difference between, on the one hand, the people's mere opinion, which "the writers" perhaps correctly scorn, and, on the other, the people's political judgment, which such writers unwisely seek to banish from or narrowly constrict within politics, is central to Machiavelli's account of electoral politics in a well-ordered republic.[10]

Distributing Ranks and Dignities

Recall from Chapter 1 an important episode from Livy's history of Rome that Machiavelli recounts in some depth. The plebeians felt oppressed by the patricians' monopoly over the consulship (D I.39) and thought that "men of the plebs" deserved to hold supreme authority after their extensive displays of military virtue throughout the early years of the republic (D I.47). Yet after gaining the opportunity to elect plebeians to consular office, the people judge their own candidates to be considerably weaker and less deserving than those of the nobility, and they elect only patricians to office. Machiavelli notes that while the people were of the general opinion that they should hold office with or in place of the nobles, when confronted with a concrete exercise of judgment over particular candidates, the plebeians deferred to individual excellence or experience and chose patricians. Again, while critics might scoff at the people's general opinions, Machiavelli makes it very difficult to dismiss the judgments that they render when they are disciplined by the demands of a concrete, legally binding decision.

Machiavelli makes this point even more dramatically with a peculiar example of electoral politics from the Capuan Republic. While a Carthaginian army threatens the security of Capua, *and* while severe strife between the plebs and nobility upsets the city, a certain Pacuvius Calanus holds the republic's chief magistracy (D I.47). Invoking the impending dangers of both invasion and insurrection, Pacuvius convinces Capua's senators to allow him to lock them up in their chamber. We have observed before Machiavelli's accounts of other individuals, most notably Clearchus of Heraclea, who exploit similar circumstances to seize absolute power for themselves. Yet Pacuvius, having confined the nobles to the senate house, does not slaughter them before a grateful people and establish himself prince. Instead, Pacuvius adopts an approach more conducive to maintaining republics than to instituting principalities: he raises the stakes entailed by electoral competition and establishes the people as the ultimate political judge within the republic.

With the hated senators confined to their public palace, Pacuvius convenes the people in assembly, a *concione*, thus giving the people the opportunity to eliminate the nobility in an orderly, formally legal fashion (D I.47). He invites the people to decide, on a case-by-case basis, whether or not a particular senator should be executed or exonerated. Pacuvius also suggests that the people should replace each senator who they condemn with an individual from their own ranks. After all, he declares, the people do not wish to live without government, and the people, riled up though they may be, do not dispute Pacuvius's claim.

After an initial period of silence, the people engage in a rather raucous and rowdy debate over the individual candidates for both senatorial elevation and capital execution.[11] Some of the people propose individual plebeians who might serve as senators, but others dispute the worthiness of such candidates. When lengthy deliberations do not generate agreement on any plebeians who, according to their own judgment, would be worthy of "senatorial rank," Pacuvius concludes that the people apparently think that the present government is the best available after all. If the plebeians are willing to put aside their mortal hatred for the nobles and allow the latter to continue in authority, they must, in fact, desire good government more than they desire vengeance.

Just as Machiavelli recommends, Pacuvius asks the people to come to particulars, which, within the formal confines of an assembly, they do. The people weigh the trade-offs entailed by their various desires: he sets before them several options that they presumably want and invites them to consider which in particular they prefer and to assess the costs/benefits portended by the satisfaction of their various preferences. Do the people want to govern themselves at the complete exclusion of the nobility, or do they want to benefit from the most optimal form of government viable at the moment? Do they really want to kill every single senator, or merely not be oppressed by the nobles as a class? On the latter point, Pacuvius predicts that the fear aroused in the senators by the prospect of popularly pronounced death sentences will henceforth chasten the nobility into behaving less oppressively toward the people.

One might conclude from this example, as well as the one that I discussed preceding it, that Machiavelli actually prefers government by nobles; like a good aristocratic republican or Schumpeterian democrat, he really aspires after oligarchic rule merely ratified by common citizens. He favors institutions, such as elections, and leadership, such as Pacuvius's, that facilitate noble monopolization of offices. However, elsewhere Machiavelli explicitly endorses the rise of individual plebeians to the ranks of supreme command: for instance, he writes, "It was fitting at an early hour that the plebs have hope of gaining the consulship. . . . When the hope was not enough it was fitting that this hope become reality" (D I.60). Opening the consulship to plebeians, Machiavelli suggests, allowed Rome to avail itself of virtue wherever it resided, among both "the nobles and the ignobles" (D I.30). Furthermore, Machiavelli's praise for the Roman people's judgment in appointing magistrates applies not only to consular offices, which for many years were dominated by patricians. Machiavelli includes the tribunate among the magistracies to which the Roman people consistently appointed excellent individuals: "in so many hundreds of years, in so many elections of consuls and tribunes, the people did not have to repent even four choices" (D I.58). In so doing, Machiavelli implicitly lauds both the plebeians who served as tribunes as well as those who elected them to office. In the next chapter, I explore the political ramifications for republics, such as

Rome, that maintain a distinction between offices like the consulship, for which all citizens are eligible but the nobles dominate, and those like the tribunate, which is reserved exclusively for common citizens who are not members of the senatorial order or the upper class.

The ultimate point, I suggest, of Machiavelli's Capuan example is not that common people should accede to the exclusive rule of patrician magistrates. To be sure, when aroused by oligarchic oppression, the people may need to be calmed by prudent magistrates and respected citizens (D I.13, D I.54); and, certainly, as the episodes under consideration confirm, wealthy and prominent citizens always have an advantage in elections tempered by neither class specifications nor some element of randomization. Notwithstanding the particular outcome in this instance, an outcome that in one sense clearly favors the nobility, the general and generalizable principle undergirding it is Machiavelli's affirmation of popular deliberation and final judgment. The episode validates procedurally formalized popular discussion of and judgment over the relative virtue of candidates – and ultimately over the lives of the grandi as well. An angry mob may, without reflection, proceed to destroy the senators en masse, as did the Corcyran demos (D II.2). But citizens empowered to consider the fate of the nobles through formal decision procedures – "shackled by laws," as Machiavelli writes (D I.58) – may come to altogether different conclusions.

Yet how can we understand Machiavelli to be validating popular judgment in this instance when the outcome, exoneration of the senators, seems to be a forgone conclusion? We certainly cannot attribute to the people a substantive, free choice if Pacuvius has guaranteed a single outcome a priori. But is the security of the Capuan senate really guaranteed in this instance? Pacuvius may assume that, when faced with this choice, the plebeians will defer to the grandeur of individual nobles – but surely he can't be certain. Given the intense animosity prevailing between the plebs and the grandi at the moment, the situation is rife with indeterminacy.[12] Perhaps the close proximity of an enemy army emphasized by Machiavelli is what braces the Capuan plebeians into discounting their own unseasoned abilities and into continued reliance on the expertise of incumbent senators. Absent such an external threat, it is certainly conceivable that the Capuan plebeians might decide that one, some, or many from among their ranks should replace individual nobles – if only so as to eliminate the most egregiously oppressive members of the grandi. After all, as we will observe in Chapter 5, Machiavelli certainly does *not* suggest that the grandi will always be exonerated in political trials judged by the people. I will show how Machiavelli strongly intimates that if Savonarola or Soderini had mustered the temerity to try the aristocratic enemies of Florence's governo largo in the Great Council, the assembled people would have readily condemned them to death (D I.45, D III.3, D III.30). Deference, it seems, has its limits.

Thus, legally bound, popular judgment over the lives of the grandi is not necessarily an assurance of the latter's security, let alone their tenures of office.

Again, this judgment must be decided collectively through formalized procedures, and not expressed through mob violence or even through unilateral
action by a would-be prince like Clearchus – outcomes that spell the end of a
civic way of life. Oppression may indeed temporarily blind the people to the
immorality or at least the long-term inconvenience of arbitrary violence, just
as it may allow the people to forget momentarily or underestimate the value
of good government or the necessity of government in general. But formalized procedures of judgment and decision compel the people to consider the
full ramifications of lethal force and inferior government. Furthermore, note
carefully how differently Pacuvius proceeds from the example of Clearchus.
Pacuvius combines and formalizes, on the one hand, the prospect of executing the grandi, and, on the other, popular judgment over political office; in
so doing, he creates a novel political form, an election cum capital trial. The
alternative outcomes are not, as they are for candidates seeking magistracies
in ordinary elections, either public office, on the one hand, or civilian status,
on the other. Rather, the grandi in such circumstances confront the more dire
alternatives of office or death.[13]

Returning to the more mundane realm of conventional elections, what
exactly, according to Machiavelli, are the criteria that the people employ when
selecting candidates for office? In the particular circumstances of the Capuan
example, as mentioned previously, military skill and experience would appear
to be important factors. Certainly, the Roman patricians demonstrate a profound understanding of the fact that military threats, real and fabricated, can be
used to maximize their advantages, electoral and economic, over the plebeians
(D I.13, D I.37, D I.39). Nevertheless, Machiavelli more broadly addresses "the
mode that the people follows when judging men," in other words, the factors
that the people consider when they distribute offices (D III.34).

Among the issues relevant to the people's evaluation of political candidates, Machiavelli counts family lineage, the company that a candidate keeps,
and noteworthy achievements (D III.34). In the absence of the last criterion –
actions, either private or public, that the people themselves can observe –
Machiavelli tolerates the people's reliance on the first two as guides to a candidate's worth – namely, the reputation an individual acquires from his family
legacy and/or from his associations. Machiavelli notes that the people will
appropriately adjust their assessment of an individual if concrete evidence arises
that he is not, after all, as virtuous as they had initially assumed. Facts, *actions*,
according to Machiavelli, speak louder to the people than the reputation that
initially influenced their opinions of a candidate. Among the concrete actions
that will encourage the people to elect an individual are sponsorship of laws
favorable to the common good, accusations of powerful citizens who have
committed wrongs, strict adherence to military discipline on the field of battle, and honorable displays toward one's family elders. Machiavelli concludes
that the people are "almost never deceived" when they rely on such actions in
"bestowing rank upon one of their citizens" (D III.34).[14]

As in previous examples, Machiavelli here distinguishes between the people's raw, spontaneous opinion and their considered judgment when appointing men to "the supreme ranks of the city" (D III.34). The people form appropriate judgment while participating in assemblies (*consigli*); especially, Machiavelli notes, deliberative assemblies (concioni) (D III.34). In well-ordered republics such as Rome, Machiavelli argues, the people do not "deceive themselves" into electing "inadequate men" because in such assemblies, "every citizen is permitted, in a manner that accrues to their glory, to publicize the defects of an individual such that the people will know and judge him better" (D III.34). Just as princes avail themselves of ministerial advisors, when the people advise *themselves* in assembly, Machiavelli insists, they actually err less and distribute offices better than do individual princes: "In electing magistrates, the people judge according to the surest signs ascertainable about men." Princes may have ulterior motives for permitting corrupt individuals to administer offices, while the people find the very idea of such a thing repugnant: "a people will never be persuaded into thinking that it is a good thing to elevate to office a nefarious man of corrupt ways" (D I.58).

But this "never" applies only to such a time as a republic remains uncorrupt. If we examine closely Machiavelli's remarks on how the people's capacity to choose excellent magistrates declines as Rome succumbs to corruption, we find the deleterious impact of empire to be quite prominent. Once Rome subjugated much of the globe and no longer feared external threats, Machiavelli complains that the people grew lax and began electing men who understood how to "entertain" and "bestow" favors, rather than those "who knew well how to conquer enemies" (D I.18). However, the *most* pernicious cause of this decline in the quality of magistrates is not, according to Machiavelli, an increase in frivolousness among the people but rather expanding asymmetries of power among the citizenry: no longer did the worthy (*degni*), the good (*buoni*), or the virtuous (*virtuosi*) hold office, he remarks, but increasingly only "those possessing more power."

In observations that might sound odd emanating from the pen of a supposed "might makes right" thinker, one who purportedly reduces moral *virtù* to sheer cunning and naked force, in these passages Machiavelli sharply distinguishes raw power from real virtue and declares that fear of powerful citizens prevented virtuous ones from attaining office once the Roman Republic had begun to succumb to corruption (D I.18). How did the powerful come to dominate Rome's electoral and legislative processes once its empire eliminated any genuine external threat to the republic's security? As I'll discuss later in this chapter in greater detail, Machiavelli describes how the prolongation of military commands and impoverishment of the citizen-soldiers entailed by imperial expansion enabled generals to gain excessive sway with soldiers abroad that could be put to civically detrimental use over citizens at home (D I.37, D III.24–5).

To return to Machiavelli's main point: Machiavelli argues that the many are better than the few at selecting magistrates: "A prudent man ought never to depart from popular judgments, especially concerning the distribution of ranks and dignities, for in this only does the people not deceive itself. If it does deceive itself at some time, it is so rare that the few who make such distributions will deceive themselves more often" (D I.47). The Roman populace selected better magistrates than the candidates for those offices themselves would have chosen, and certainly better than their patrician supporters would have appointed. Machiavelli's Roman examples show that the nobles could be confident that they would be granted offices by the people when they were well qualified, even when plebeians themselves were eligible for the same offices (D I.47). After all, Machiavelli demonstrates that the grandi have no humility regarding assessments of their own governing abilities: individually, patricians seldom defer to members of other patrician families when it comes to officeholding; collectively, they *never* defer to individuals who rise from the ranks of the people. Republics must force them to do so by placing the distribution of offices in the hands of an arbitrating entity like the general citizenry: in Rome, the centuriate assembly selected the consuls, and the concilium chose the tribunes.

Machiavelli claims that the people better distribute offices than do princes because they favor candidates of good reputation until the latter's deeds prove this reputation false. Solitary executives tend to fear men of good reputation as rivals and are inclined to remain stubborn about their initial decisions on such matters; on the contrary, when the people lean toward an inappropriate choice, good arguments and a trustworthy speaker can dissuade them (D III.34). Machiavelli adds that a good populace does not allow officials to get away with bad behavior just because they have performed their duties well in the past. This "what have you done lately?" attitude prevents certain potentially dangerous figures from becoming excessively insolent. Finally, Machiavelli insists that the people are inclined to give substantive rewards, even if from their own meager resources, for good service to the republic (D I.24). Thus, magistrates may be induced into good behavior by the expectation of monetary or honorific rewards from a grateful people.

In concluding his reflections on the people's judgment over the appointment of magistrates, Machiavelli advises republics to institute "modes that compel the people to descend to particulars" when they deliberate over a candidate's qualifications, procedures capable of "opening the people's eyes" with respect to the worth of individual citizens (D I.47).[15] Clearly these modes include fora where the people freely discuss and evaluate the merits of potential candidates (I.47, III.34) and where they themselves, through "free votes," select the individuals who will hold office (D I.20).[16] Establishing a mode of argument that he takes up subsequently when defending the people's cognitive capacities in general, Machiavelli suggests that whatever deficiencies in judgment over ranks and dignities the people may exhibit from time to time, the few or a prince will exercise poor judgment much more often when distributing offices themselves (D I.47, D III.34). Machiavelli concedes and, in fact, often demonstrates that the people's judgment is not perfect (e.g., D I.35), but he insists emphatically that it is nevertheless generally superior to that of both princes and oligarchs.

This "relative best" justification of the people's judgment – one decidedly *not* based on philosophically generated standards of perfection – plays a central role in the *Discourses*' most important chapter: the one that deals with the wisdom of the multitude.

Lawmaking and the People's Wisdom

In the chapter devoted to the "wisdom of the multitude," Machiavelli confronts head on the antipopular biases of "all" the historians, indeed, "all the writers" (D I.58). Traditionally, Machiavelli notes, historians and philosophers have faulted the people for inconstancy; for favoring an individual one day, and then condemning him another; for pledging allegiance to a prince one minute and then cheering for liberty the next.[17] But Machiavelli insists that the standards by which the writers judge the people are skewed: they consistently compare examples of multitudes "unshackled" by laws with those especially rare examples of law-abiding, and hence "good and wise," princes. According to Machiavelli, lawless peoples and princes both "make the errors inevitably committed by infuriated and unshackled men." In this sense, at least provisionally, peoples and princes should be faulted equally, "since all err equally when all can err without respect."[18]

The proper comparison, Machiavelli avers, is "a multitude regulated by laws," such as the Roman people, with likewise "bridled" princes, such as those who ruled ancient Egypt, Sparta, and contemporary France. From this more apposite analysis, peoples emerge not merely the equals but the superiors of princes. In *The Prince*, Machiavelli subverted the authority of "the writers" by reducing all political observers, including himself, to the station of "the vulgar" (P 3, P 7, P 18). Here in the *Discourses* Machiavelli deflates and yanks to the ground the lofty, aristocratically biased view of the writers (which the latter themselves understand to be wise and learned) by deeming it "the common opinion" (D I.58). Machiavelli hereby endeavors to refute the common opinion held by spokesmen for those exalted persons who deem themselves decidedly uncommon. In fact, Machiavelli does so in a frankly commonsensical manner; specifically, by simply comparing apples with apples and oranges with oranges: "A well-organized people that commands is just as stable, prudent and grateful as a prince, in fact, *more so* than a prince, even one considered wise; conversely, a prince unshackled by laws will be *more* ungrateful, inconstant and imprudent than a people.... [Thus] I declare that a people is more prudent, more stable and a *better judge* than a prince" (D I.58, emphases added).

Machiavelli initially hesitates to assert that the people's superiority arises from a nature that is inherently different from that of princes: at first, he suggests that the multitude and princes have different natures, then that their natures are not "diverse," and then that more "good" resides in peoples than in princes (D I.58).[19] Finally, however, Machiavelli makes the fundamental difference between the people and princes evident by describing their disparate inclinations and ensuing behaviors: the people tend to respect the laws under which they live, while princes do not; those inclined to live free of oppression uphold laws that protect them, while those who are inclined to oppress others seek to use the laws to further their reprehensible ends, and, failing that, they readily break them.

The relationship between the desire not to be dominated, on the one hand, and respect for the laws, on the other, allows Machiavelli to challenge the antipopular disposition of "all the writers," who insist that the people, like a bully, supplicates itself humbly when it must, but dominates others proudly when it can (D I.58). In retort, on the basis of Rome's example, Machiavelli asserts that a people properly ordered through laws both "commands" and "obeys" appropriately: the Roman people held rank honorably, rightfully punished those who threatened liberty, and also dutifully followed the magistrates' directives when "public safety" required it. Again, these insights recall Aristotle's depiction of democratic citizenship in principle and practice: members of the demos willingly and appropriately alternate between the exercise of rule and the experience of being ruled.

When turning to the people's legislative capacities, Machiavelli praises the people's powers of judgment even more fulsomely than recounted in the preceding: he attributes to their "universal opinion," that is, their formally enabled, collectively generated opinion, a nearly divine, "hidden virtue" – namely, an uncanny ability to foresee good and ill (D I.58). How is this popular capacity to foresee, an attribute traditionally associated with socially elevated rather than low-born members of a polity, exercised? Earlier in the *Discourses*, Machiavelli describes lawmaking in the Roman assemblies as follows:

> A tribune, or any citizen whatsoever, could propose a law to the people, against or in favor of which every citizen was entitled to speak before a decision was reached. . . . It was good that anyone who cared for the public good could propose laws, and that everyone could speak their mind on it so that the people could subsequently choose what was best (D I.18).

On Machiavelli's reading, the egalitarianism and reciprocity characteristic of Roman legislative practices contributed to the objectively beneficial results that they achieved; if all citizens were entitled to propose laws, especially those concerned with the "public good," and any citizen could speak out for or against such laws, then Roman legislative practice enlisted a more diverse array of views than could be generated by the mind of a single prince or even by the deliberation of a prudent but almost invariably homogeneous small group of elites.[20] Machiavelli's suggestion that the people gathered in assemblies recognize the truth in public speeches and make correct decisions on that basis implies that they are capable of choosing the better arguments among proposals, whether submitted by the consuls in the noble-dominated *comitia centuriata*, or by the tribunes in the *concilium plebis* and the *comitia tributa*, and those proposed by either sets of magistrates in the *contiones*.[21]

Machiavelli attributes the people's ability to discern better policies in no small part to their desire not to be dominated and to the correlation between this desire and the common good. A member of the grandi who proposes a law may have a hidden, ulterior, self-serving agenda; but once the people evaluate it, that is, openly discuss it, such a law will only be passed if they decide that it conforms to the common good. Moreover, by enabling *every citizen* to initiate legislation, Machiavelli facilitates the possibility that voices besides those of patricians will be reflected in the laws of the republic. Yet, as mentioned previously, Machiavelli laments the corruption that progressively undermined this aspect of Roman legislative practice: eventually, after successfully intimidating other citizens from speaking out, "the powerful" began to monopolize agenda setting and to pass laws that benefited only themselves (D I.18). Machiavelli remarks how, under these gradually more inequitable and oppressive circumstances, the people were increasingly "deceived or forced into deciding its own ruin" within the legislative process. Presumably better or more persistent use of citizen accusations and popularly judged political trials, which I discuss at length in Chapter 5, could have forestalled or prevented this elite cooptation of a Roman legislative process that Machiavelli claims was widely inclusive and substantively participatory while the republic maintained its vitality.

Several important discrepancies between Rome's largely timocratic and non-deliberative institutions, as best we know them, and Machiavelli's more deliberatively democratic interpretation of them accentuate his normative preference for a republic more extensively inclusive of the populace, a democratic republic that allows greater popular discussion over and control of policy formation, lawmaking, and magistrate behavior. Whether or not he was aware of them, Machiavelli never mentions the Roman practices of weighing and ordering votes in ways that favored better-propertied citizens in the centuriate assembly. Furthermore, he allows common citizens much more room for legislative initiative and greater opportunity to deliberate over the formulation of laws than did the Roman assemblies. Even important legislative assemblies that were not especially hierarchical in structure, such as the tribal assembly, still did not permit deliberation; citizens exclusively discussed laws in the less formal concioni, often days before formally deciding on them in Rome's official voting assemblies.[22]

Thus, Machiavelli's suggestion that the tribunes could propose and any citizen could speak out on laws, public policy, and political and military appointments in both legislative (the comitia and the concilium) and deliberative (the concioni) assemblies is a radical departure from Roman practice, which kept deliberation away from actual voting. More accurately, in Rome, the tribunes conducted popular deliberations in the contiones and presided over legislation in the tribal assembly and the concilium plebis (if these were in fact two different assemblies). Moreover, Machiavelli speaks as if the law, a *plebiscita*, produced by the council of the plebs, was always generally applicable throughout Rome. Actually, the plebiscita originally applied only to the plebs, since patricians had likely been excluded from the concilium; the jurisdiction of plebiscites was extended over the whole Roman population somewhat late, specifically, in 287 BCE.

However, the following is perhaps the most startling aspect of Machiavelli's account of the Roman legislative process performing at its best: elites do not unilaterally formulate policy proposals that they then submit to the people for simple acclamation or rejection without any collective discussion.[23] An aristocratic republican such as Guicciardini insisted that the people's aptitude for recognizing good arguments could only be exercised in circumstances where the people are formally excluded from full participation in government: the people sharpen their capacity to *select* appropriate policies precisely because they are cut off from *making* them.[24] Once prevented from clamorously proposing and debating policies that, on Guicciardini's view, are inevitably half-baked or viscerally motivated, the people can correctly judge fully formed and properly considered policies laid out before them by wise and prudent magistrates.

As the foregoing makes plain, Machiavelli fundamentally disagrees with Guicciardini: Machiavelli certainly grants magistrates such as the tribunes (whom Guicciardini wanted to eliminate from republican constitutions[25]) the authority to propose laws before the people, but he also insists that republics enable every member of the latter to propose and to discuss such laws, whereas, as we've seen, his young patrician interlocutor would render them simply mute.[26] In short, Machiavellian Democracy fosters expressions of popular judgment not always or necessarily mediated by magisterial discretion or blunted by nondeliberative procedures, both of which means were preferred by aristocratic republicans and later elite theorists of democracy.

None of these considerations, of course, means that elites have no role to play in Machiavelli's law-making model characterized by popular initiatives, deliberation, and decision. As Machiavelli remarks early on in the *Discourses*, when the people suffer from "false opinions," usually they can be persuaded to change their minds toward "the truth" if a "good man," a man in whom the people have "faith," speaks up to that effect in a concioni (D I.4). The phrase, "good man" (*uomo da bene*), had decidedly aristocratic connotations in Machiavelli's Florence. Likewise, one may assume that Machiavelli refers to speakers from elite ranks when he describes how the people listen to orators in the chapter on the multitude's wisdom: "in judging matters, when a people hears two orators of equal virtue who disagree, very rarely do they not support the superior opinion and fail to grasp the truth that it hears" (D I.58). He repeats near the chapter's conclusion that even a people who are veering toward licentiousness and tumultuousness may be corrected by the "words" of "a good man" (whereas "steel" is the only recourse against a power-crazed and law-defying prince).

Returning to Machiavelli's general comparison of peoples and princes, he points to the greater prosperity and empire enjoyed by republics: "cities where peoples are princes" such as Athens and Rome – that is, democracies and governi larghi – flourished once they freed themselves of monarchical rule

(D I.58). This better specifies Machiavelli's claim made elsewhere that "the common good is not observed anywhere if not in republics" (D II.2); and it indicates more precisely the kind of popular government or governo largo that he believes makes it possible for the people's children to become princes, the kind of republic that fosters familial security and increases material abundance (D II.2). Offering a correction to the skewed comparative enterprises of preceding writers and historians, Machiavelli concludes: "Considering all the disorders of peoples, and all those of princes; all the glories of peoples, and all those of princes; the people are demonstrably far superior in goodness and glory" (D I.58).

Why did all the writers treat the peoples so unfairly? Because they had no reason to fear otherwise: the writers perpetuated the bad opinion of the people prevalent in oligarchic and courtly circles, according to Machiavelli, "because everyone speaks badly of peoples freely and without fear, even while they reign" (D I.58). Republics – especially democracies and governi larghi such as, respectively, fourth-century Athens and early-sixteenth-century Florence – are the only regimes that grant their intellectual cum political critics exceedingly broad leeway to censure them; only the widest, freest regimes allow both their friendly critics and intransigent adversaries the liberty to develop philosophies and compose histories that slander them and, quite often, to provoke and participate in conspiracies against such forms of government and ways of life.[27] Writers, after all, face far fewer deleterious consequences when they accentuate the deficiencies and mistakes of the people than they do when they highlight the excesses of princes and nobles. The people express little interest in or lack any real recourse against writers who criticize them. Conversely, princes and patricians, on the one hand, patronize the *scrittori* and *literati* – cut their checks as it were – and, on the other, possess harsh means of coercion and retaliation. As a result, Machiavelli suggests, philosophers and historians tend to criticize the people gratuitously and treat elites with the utmost circumspection. For each single example of the trial of Socrates, there are thousands of incidents, largely unreported, where elites have bullied scrittori and literati into duplicity or intimidated them into silence.

In sum, Machiavelli's arguments in favor of the people's good judgment conclude that the people, within the appropriate institutional parameters (D I.35), make wiser decisions than do oligarchs or princes (D I.58). According to Machiavelli, the people successfully distinguish accusations from calumnies and truth from falsehood when they judge political criminals; they perceptively consider future benefits and ills while they discuss and formulate law; and they accurately assess the potential for corruption and virtuosity in the candidates they consider for high magistracies. Princes or the few, because of their inherent appetite for oppression, their overall disrespect for the law, and their general inclination toward corruption and collusion, conspiracy and cooptation, are incapable by themselves of effectively punishing individuals who threaten liberty, of making laws conducive to the public good, and of appointing virtuous magistrates.[28]

To repeat, the people's judgment may be best, but it remains imperfect. Machiavelli argues that the people are wiser than their rivals, that is, their choices are generally more conducive to the common good. But he is hardly oblivious to the fact that the people make bad choices on occasion, even on important occasions, and that their political antagonists, who know what's good for themselves and how to achieve it, often get the better of the people. Let us consider some questions concerning Machiavelli's argument in favor of the multitude's wisdom in light of some of his less flattering examples of its behavior.

Popular Misjudgment and Elite Persuasion (or Manipulation?)

Despite arguing in favor of the people's good judgment, Machiavelli suggests that they neither discern political reality with the utmost clarity on all occasions nor do they always confront it with requisite prudence. Indeed, they are, in particular instances, prone to duplicitous manipulation by the nobility. Sometimes, the latter used fear of the gods to frighten the people into electing patricians to office (e.g., D I.13). On another occasion, when the nobles were forced by necessity to give the plebs a stipend to march far afield and besiege towns for a long period of time, they attributed this payment to their own magnanimity (D I.51). In this instance, while the people rejoiced with misplaced gratitude to the nobles, the tribunes complained, correctly, that this policy would entail higher tax assessments for plebeians in the future.[29] We observed previously how the senate manipulated the people into letting patricians keep consular positions that the plebs claimed that they wanted for themselves by encouraging first-rate patricians or second-rate plebeians to run. In such cases, the plebs deferred to the former's excellence and recoiled in shame from the latter's unsuitability (D I.48).

Given Machiavelli's general pronouncements on the both brutal and devious character of the grandi, he provides somewhat surprising examples where individual nobles show the people what is in their best interest or what is conducive to the common good. Moreover, Machiavelli notes how, without any prompting or manipulation by the grandi, the people sometimes desire their own ruin, especially when deceived by mistaken conceptions of what is good (D I.53). For instance, the plebs wanted to move half the population of Rome to Veii as a way of maximizing the city's wealth in a more equitable manner (D I.53). Machiavelli reports that Rome's senators were willing to suffer collective death rather than accept this alternative – presumably because the plan, on the one hand, entailed a de facto redistribution of property and, on the other, would have created a city that might eventually rival Rome militarily. Yet the people were so enthusiastic about the idea that they would have obliged the nobles with death had the latter not used "as a shield" some old and esteemed citizens whom the people held in the deepest respect. Despite the animosity that the people repeatedly exhibit for the grandi as a whole (e.g., D I.4, I.47, I.48, I.58), the people held some of them, individually, in profound faith and great reverence. Clearly, according to Machiavelli, the nobles do not possess an absolute monopoly on imprudent, unfair, or dangerous intentions.

Machiavelli also demonstrates that the people may be misled not only by shortsighted notions of material gain but also by the allure of grand projects, especially audacious military enterprises (D I.53). For instance, the Roman people decried as cowardice Fabius's moderation and favored Scipio's daring during the Punic Wars. While their judgment was ultimately borne out when Scipio destroyed Carthage, along the way the people's impetuousness contributed to the infamously disastrous defeat at Cannae. Like the decision of the Athenian people to invade Sicily during the Peloponnesian War, which Machiavelli also cites here, popular support for direct engagement with Hannibal at Cannae threatened to ruin the Roman Republic. In this context, Machiavelli observes how the senate often acquiesced to overly aggressive policies favored by the people, such as the seemingly flawed one proposed by Penula (D I.53), because it feared uprisings by the people, who were always deeply suspicious of any sign of hesitation or weakness in the face of Hannibal. In other words, at times the people were capable of coercing the senate into conforming its agenda to the popular will, and not always with salutary results. These examples from both the Punic and Peloponnesian Wars serve as warnings against the alluringly dangerous plans that demagogues might propose in order to gain favor with the people. However, Scipio's ultimate victory over Carthage serves to validate the people's sound judgment – albeit, judgment that is vindicated only in the last instance.[30]

After all, for Machiavelli, the Roman defeat at Cannae does not serve exclusively as an example of popular imprudence in matters of war but also provides an occasion for him to accentuate the poor military judgment of nobles, specifically, the Carthaginian senate's fatal miscalculation in the aftermath of that battle. Machiavelli recounts how Carthage's senate rejected Hanno's prudent advice to make an advantageous peace with Rome on the strength of Hannibal's victory at Cannae (D II.27). The Carthaginian senators instead elected to prosecute the war further, resulting eventually in the city's utter destruction. Therefore, Machiavelli's invocations of the battle of Cannae and the Sicilian Expedition do not contravene his declarations in favor of popular judgment and certainly do not elevate senatorial judgment in its place. Indeed, the Carthaginian response to Cannae should remind readers that Machiavelli attributes the very first examples of military misjudgment in the *Discourses* to the aristocratic republics of Sparta and Venice (D I.6). Machiavelli notes that Sparta was "altogether ruined" by the decision to acquire an empire that it was constitutionally incapable of ruling in the wake of the Peloponnesian conflict. Similarly, aristocratic Venice "lost everything in a single day," when, at Vailà, it tried to defend with arms dominions that it had won entirely with money. Elaborating this criticism later in the work, Machiavelli claims that Venetian overestimation of its own virtue caused that devastating defeat (from which followed instances of especially contemptible Venetian cowardice) (D III.31).

As a remedy for the propensity of the people to pursue foolhardy military adventure in democratic republics, Machiavelli raises the possibility that the people themselves might pose a solution to this problem: that they themselves might deter ambitious individuals from proposing such enterprises to begin with. Machiavelli notes that when such grand enterprises collapse, the people do not blame fortune or incompetence but often the purported malice of their leaders. He emphasizes the fact that the people vigorously punish those who propose but fail to execute audacious plans, especially if the latter result in especially devastating defeats. They may imprison or kill such sponsors, irrespective of past success, as did the citizenries of Carthage and Athens – although the Florentines seem more forgiving (D I.53). Machiavelli makes little attempt to reconcile these tendencies toward retributive cruelty with the passivity and benevolence, or even the provoked or defensive ferocity, which he attributes to the people elsewhere in the *Discourses*. All such examples cannot, at first glance, be grouped together with the examples that Machiavelli uses to excuse popular vindictiveness elsewhere, that is, instances when a vengeful people has recently recovered its liberty from a tyrant or an oligarchy. However, the people's inclination, mentioned by Machiavelli, to charge individuals who have failed in such circumstances with malfeasance rather than mere incompetence suggests that the people feel betrayed and hence in some sense oppressed by citizens who would raise their expectations concerning the purported ease with which military success can be gained. Erring on the side of harshness in such circumstances, Machiavelli intimates, may not be altogether inappropriate, and if channeled institutionally into normal political practice this prospect may generally discourage irresponsible individuals from proposing such schemes in the first place.

To re-pose the central question of this section, are examples such as those just noted where the people defer to or are manipulated by the nobles, or where they pursue ruinous policies themselves, sufficient to obviate Machiavelli's arguments concerning the people's wisdom? Certainly not, since the Florentine's endorsement of the people's judgment is not based on perfectionist standards. Machiavelli insists that the people's judgment happens to be superior to that of other political actors most of the time; he never insists that the people's judgment is *always* wise or *invariably* conducive to freedom. It is worth remembering that Machiavelli's evaluative frame of reference is decidedly not informed by precepts like those generated by, say, a hypothetical oligarchy of philosopher kings (P 15). Therefore, in Machiavelli's estimation, no political actor or set thereof possesses or can possess perfect knowledge, or behaves or can behave in a manner that will escape criticism in every instance. An imaginary aristocracy of philosopher kings may be capable, in theory, of exercising *perfect* political judgment. But there is *no* such agent capable of exercising perfect political judgment in empirical reality.[31] Notwithstanding the people's mistakes, some of them spectacularly demonstrated by the likes of Plato, Xenophon, and Thucydides, Machiavelli insists that the people will generally decide in a way that produces good outcomes – that is, outcomes conducive to the common good – and they will do so far more often than will similarly empowered princely or oligarchic elites.

However, it is worth noting that Machiavelli also cites numerous episodes in which both the people *and* the nobles demonstrate their virtue in the midst of crises: esteemed senators often plead with the people *not* to follow a course ruinous for them and for republics, and the people in turn relent from their own misguided course of action in such circumstances (e.g., D I.54). Machiavelli often reinforces the argument concerning the populace's good judgment with ancient and contemporary examples where they change their mind for the better: the peoples of Rome and Florence eliminate certain institutions after wrongly blaming them for mismanaged war efforts, but both citizenries demonstrate the ability to learn by later restoring these very institutions (D I.39). Machiavelli also notes that the Roman plebs ultimately refused Spurious Cassius's cynical attempt to gain their support for his royal ambitions by distributing enemy property among them (D III.8). The plebeians also condemned Manlius Capitolinus to death for similar reasons; in fact, the people, the tribunes, and the senate all resisted powerful inducements to help him on that occasion (D III.8).

In light of such examples, an obvious danger to a republic is the possibility that rich and prominent citizens will put their resources and skills to ends that are less than civically beneficial. Nevertheless, Machiavelli observes that "a republic without reputed citizens cannot stand, nor can it be governed well in any mode" (D III.8). But precisely such reputation may serve as the genesis of tyranny. Machiavelli's proposed solution is to favor reputation earned for public goods over those earned for private goods (D III. 28). Yet it is not clear how this criterion rules out, for instance, a Julius Caesar, who gained a reputation as much for "public" goods, such as military glory and economic redistribution, as for private favors. Indeed, when Machiavelli focuses on the beneficial liberty-defending and anti-oppressive spirit of the people, he is forced to raise the specter of the more or less popularly legitimated way that the Roman Republic was eventually destroyed via Caesarism.

Machiavelli generally understands proper anti-elitist animosity to stop short of popular enlistment of either a Caesar or a foreign power to subjugate or dispose of the grandi. The Roman people never resorted to the latter but ultimately succumbed to the former. The upcoming sections are devoted to moments in the *Discourses* that foreshadow the rise of Caesar; episodes where the Roman people flirt with the possibility of abandoning institutions that secure their liberty or where they seem to go too far in contesting oppression by the grandi. The crisis associated with the Ten raises institutional questions, and controversies over the Agrarian Laws bear on socioeconomic issues. Each episode draws attention to the circumstances that established precedents for the emergence of Caesar, the usurpation of Roman liberty, and the collapse of the republic. It is important to note that the Roman people undermined their ability to foster elite accountability in each instance precisely because of their animosity for the patricians, however much the behavior of the latter justified such animosity.

Contemporary civic-culture or neorepublican critics of electoral democracy complain that popular apathy toward public affairs eventually corrodes and corrupts democratic institutions.[32] The converse problem of Caesarism should not be casually dismissed: whether or not his prognosis has been fully borne out, Tocqueville, most notably, feared that modern populaces would become so voracious in their thirst for equality that they would endorse militarily or plebiscitarily legitimated tyrants to help them attain it.[33]

The Decemvirate and the Temporary Abolition of the Tribunate

Machiavelli recounts an alarming instance when the people of Rome temporarily abandoned key institutions conducive to liberty, most notably the tribunate and the right of indicted citizens to be judged formally by the entirety of the people. Because of the "disputes and contentions" between the nobles and the people, the Romans hoped to reduce conflict by imitating the clarity of Athenian law, and they created the Ten (the Decemvirate) to codify Roman law in a similar manner (D I.40). While drafting the Twelve Tables, the Ten governed in place of both the consuls and the tribunes and formally suspended direct appeals to the people in cases of criminal indictment (D I.40). This streamlining of institutions appears to be a regression from the perspective of republican principles: it undermines the institutional diversity of mixed government as it emerged in Rome, and it hearkens back to the kind of political corruption inherent in the simple regime types famously criticized by Polybius. Such a reversion to institutional simplicity, from a classical perspective, always portends the rise of a tyranny.

Tyranny, according to Machiavelli, arises when there exists "too great a desire of the people to be free and too great a desire of the nobles to command," and when the ensuing conflict between them does not result in a situation where both "agree to make a law in favor of freedom" (D I.40). In Rome, conflicts between the humors of the senate and the people usually led to beneficial laws such as the establishment of the tribunes early in the republic and the opening of the consulate to plebeians later on. But at this point in the republic's history, as the senate persistently used religion and unnecessary wars to divert the people from demands for domestic reforms (I.13), the people started to associate, not entirely without reason, the military functions and religious trappings of the consulship with oppression itself.

While the plebs felt oppressed by the consulship, the nobles felt equally harassed by the tribunate, a magistracy designed to keep them in check and reserved for the common people exclusively. While the Ten set about reforming Rome's legal system, Appius Claudius, the committee's leader, successfully exploited the respective hatreds of the senate and the plebs for these two magistracies to suspend their operations entirely – thereby removing crucial institutional obstacles to his own power. In such manner, Appius deftly converted a special agency charged with legal reform into the "unequivocal prince of Rome" (D I.40). Machiavelli describes how Appius became the leader of the Ten through popular consent, even though he had treated the people with contempt in the past. The nobles tried to curb his growing power until they realized that it primarily victimized the plebeians rather than themselves. The senate could have eliminated the Ten, Machiavelli suggests, but instead decided to endure Appius's tyranny as long as possible in the hope of indefinitely preventing reestablishment of the tribunes. The older nobles, Machiavelli observes, were perfectly happy to see tyranny persist so long as the plebeians suffered disproportionately from abuse by Appius and by the younger nobles, whose favor the tyrant successfully cultivated.

Eventually war and Appius's crimes, especially the mortal Machiavellian sin of molesting citizens' women, proved the undoing of his tyranny. The people, having been mobilized collectively for war, were provoked into ending the tyranny and restoring the tribunate by Appius's attempt at dishonoring the daughter of Virginius, a plebeian centurian. After the second evacuation of the plebs from the city, Appius was arrested and committed suicide. Machiavelli describes how the plebeians negotiated the restoration of the tribunate and the abolition of the Ten with Horatius and Valerius, senators who had proven themselves to be relatively trustworthy in the eyes of the plebs throughout Appius's reign of terror.

Machiavelli argues that the episode of the Ten teaches the lesson that any individual elevated to authority by the people must confront some institution that makes him hesitate about becoming a criminal or tyrant or else he will in fact assume that role; the people and other political actors must always have recourse to modes of accountability provided by the consuls, tribunes, public accusations, or popular appeal (D I.40). Because the nobles and the people were consumed by such intense desires to remove each other's institutional agents, they temporarily eliminated the very buffers that prevented tyranny within the republic. With the consuls and tribunes out of the way, there was no effective way to check someone such as Appius – except through the last resort of the political leverage provided by a popular army – who would exploit the mutual animosity of the people and the nobility. Machiavelli notes how after Appius's demise each party realized that Rome's basic institutions ought not to be suspended or abandoned so readily in the future. Nevertheless, Sulla and then Caesar allowed conventional magistracies to remain in operation while they exploited the emergency powers provided to them by the office of the dictatorship, and this did little to curb their tyrannical behavior.[34] The socioeconomic circumstances that allowed these dictators to succeed where Appius, head of the Decemvirate, had failed come to the fore in Machiavelli's account of the controversy over Rome's Agrarian Laws.

The Agrarian Laws and the Roman Republic's Collapse

Through several of the preceding examples, Machiavelli effectively demonstrates the following: neither do the people always behave so passively, nor are their desires always so invariably benign, as a superficial reading of

The Prince and the *Discourses* might suggest. This raises several questions. Again, do these examples repudiate Machiavelli's ascription of a benignly passive disposition to the people? Or are these examples merely isolated manifestations of the people's defensively passive posture necessarily turned excessively ferocious? Complicating matters is the fact that Machiavelli shows, on several occasions, how difficult it is to distinguish between aggressiveness that is appropriately defensive from that which is dangerously offensive (e.g., D I.5). Does the people's appetite not to be dominated by the grandi result in behavior that eventually goes too far? As advocates of aristocratic republics always insist, does it necessarily lead to Caesarism and the downfall of free regimes?

Recall from the previous chapter how, through the voice of a patrician spokesman, Machiavelli denounces the plebeians' "furious" attraction to men, such as Gaius Marius, willing to beat down the nobility, thus paving the way for Caesar (D I.5). In the same discourse, Machiavelli notes an episode in which two plebeian magistrates, Marcus Menenius and Marcus Fulvius (respectively, dictator and master of the horse), were empowered by the people to investigate the nobility's efforts to corrupt consular elections (D I.5). Clearly, the Roman people were *not* satisfied with simple freedom *from* oppression; or rather, it is nearly impossible to guarantee this "negative" freedom from noble domination without some "positive" freedom exercised through public offices.[35] The plebeians sought to use the power of the tribunate, the consulship, and even, it turns out, the dictatorship to constrain the oppressive behavior of the grandi. Furthermore, as Machiavelli points out, the very highest political offices proved insufficient in protecting the plebeians from oppression: Machiavelli's chapter on the Agrarian Laws (D I.37) demonstrates that the plebs also recognized that liberty required them to share in the vast wealth controlled by the nobility. The Gracchi, Tiberius and Gaius Gracchus, emerged as champions of the plebeian's quest for economic parity and became the very embodiments of the nobility's fear of populist "tyrants" intent on usurping senatorial authority.

The plebeians had demanded and numerous tribunes had tried to pass agrarian reforms since the earliest days of the republic. From the very beginning, the patricians had been putting into their own "custodial care" public lands and territories acquired from conquered enemies that in principle belonged to the entire commonwealth. When the people and the tribunes sought legal redress, Machiavelli claims that the senate responded by sending armies *even farther* afield to seize provinces that the plebs would not covet, or at least that they could not plausibly afford to make profitable (D I.37). This senatorial strategy increased the likelihood that such spoils would remain the exclusive preserve of the nobility. Through such self-enriching policies, the nobles aggravated the republic's social and political problems; they not only perpetuated conditions of economic inequality, but they also made military commanders inordinately powerful (III.24).

These two developments are intertwined in Machiavelli's account: senatorially driven acquisition of territory farther away from Rome, and then from the Italian peninsula, necessitated the prolongation of military commands (D III.24). Consequently, many fewer officers received military experience, compelling the republic's reliance on a smaller and smaller cadre of commanders. Simultaneously, Rome's citizen-soldiers were becoming economically dependent on the generals with whom they lived for years at a time away from the city. Indeed, while senators sent armies greater distances from Rome, they encouraged their clients among the creditors to foreclose leases on plebeian lands and to render the latter more profitable by hiring slaves rather than citizens to work them.[36] Before long, commanders-cum-tyrants began to use their extended commissions to cultivate personal loyalty from the soldiers, who were increasingly impoverished by the foreclosures back home. Military officers, who had become more like warlords, and not the republic itself, began to take responsibility and credit for the soldiers' material sustenance, hence earning their ultimate loyalty.[37] Moreover, with fewer and fewer citizens gaining experience in governing and command, the overall civic-military culture of the republic suffered: the alternation between ruling and being ruled was no longer the average experience of Rome's citizen-soldiers; instead, they became habituated to being ruled as such and placated with plunder as compensation for this civically depreciating state of affairs.[38]

The brothers Gracchus devoted their terms as tribunes to attempts at resolving this emerging economic, military, and civic crisis through a revival of the Agrarian Laws (133 BCE). These laws angered the nobles by limiting the amount of public land any citizen could hold and by distributing among the plebs lands seized from vanquished enemies. As Machiavelli puts it, this legislation enraged the senate, for it sought to take from them property they already controlled and denied them access to the means of getting more (D I.37, III.24–5). Machiavelli emphasizes that the controversies and scandals that arose over the Agrarian Laws led to a cycle of disorders that ultimately destroyed the republic: civil conflicts between the plebeians and the nobility encouraged recourse to "private remedies" (presumably the murder of Tiberius Gracchus by senators), which led to the establishment of armed party heads (Marius for the people, Sulla for the nobles) and ultimately to far more blood letting and violence than is healthy for a well-ordered republic (D I.37). The nobles initially gained the upper hand by brutally quashing the Gracchi and by condoning Sulla's bloody, extended dictatorship; but the precedent was established for a popular champion such as Caesar, in turn, to emerge as tyrant. In light of these circumstances – complicated by any measure – who, the nobility or the plebs, in Machiavelli's view, was really responsible for laying the groundwork of Caesarism and the collapse of the republic?

At the start of the chapter on the Agrarian Laws, Machiavelli reiterates the very charges leveled by the patrician critics of the people during the debate he stages in I.5: ambition and greed, power and gain, *not* the necessity of self-defense, motivated the people to contest the nobility's authority during the struggle over the Agrarian Laws (D I.37). Yet, lest one think that Machiavelli definitively condemns the people through such statements, he concludes the chapter by insisting that the nobility caused the Agrarian Laws crisis, and hence that *they* are responsible for whatever decline the crisis set in motion (D I.37). The ambition and greed of the nobles needed to be checked and in fact would have brought Rome down much sooner if the people had not sought to halt them – not only through tribunician authority and then access to the consulship, but also through redistributive programs precisely like the Agrarian Laws. As Machiavelli emphatically declares, "well-ordered republics must keep the public rich and citizens poor" (D I.37; cf., D III.16).[39] According to Machiavelli, it was the oppressively avaricious behavior of the grandi that provoked the people into supporting the Gracchi and made necessary measures such as the Agrarian Laws.

Therefore, Machiavelli invites us to understand popular ferocity as the righteous indignation of a normally passive people who have been violated, abused, and threatened. The people's aggressive behavior is revealed to be a legitimate and indeed necessary response to the prideful and greedy nature of elites: "so enormous is the ambition of the great that it soon brings that city to ruin if it is not beaten down in a city by *various ways and various modes*" (D I.37, emphasis added). In other words, the nobles' ambition is far more damaging to a republic than that of the plebs, and the latter need more than one means, such as access to office, to hold back the insolence of the great. "If the contention over the Agrarian laws took three hundred years to make Rome servile," Machiavelli observes, "it would perhaps have been led into servitude much sooner if the plebs had not always checked the ambition of the nobles, both with this law and with its other appetites" (I.37). Machiavelli indicates here and elsewhere that the senate's self-aggrandizing economic-military strategies led to Caesarism more directly than did the people's inclination to worship "one man" who exhibited the ability and willingness to beat down the nobles.

In the episodes devoted to the Decemvirate and the Agrarian Laws, instances that presage the collapse of the Roman Republic, both the people and the nobles behave poorly. But Machiavelli suggests that there is one possession of which the grandi undoubtedly deserve a greater share than the people: namely, blame for the republic's demise.

Returning to themes that I explored in earlier sections of this chapter, while unprecedented in its overall force within the aristocratically biased history of Western political thought, Machiavelli's case for the validity and even superiority of the people's judgment nevertheless combines elements put forward, albeit more hesitantly, by other notable authors. For instance, Aristotle first ventured to suggest that the people could make good decisions on the basis of social diversity: a multitude expressing a wide array of views can choose good outcomes in much the same way that a meal combining a mixture of different ingredients, even ingredients varying in quality, may taste better than one comprised exclusively of a single rare, delicious one (cf., D I.18).[40] Condorcet emphasized the epistemic value of collective decisions: when the people's individual judgments are aggregated, the majority's decision is more likely to be correct than would be that of any particular person within the group (cf., D I.7–8; I.57).[41] Finally, Locke surmised that political experience contributes to the people's superior judgment in assessing the legitimacy of government: because the people experience oppression in a unique, direct way, they understand freedom in a manner that eludes elites and thus the former and not the latter should serve as its ultimate arbiter (cf., D I.4–6; I.58).[42]

On this last point, we've observed Machiavelli claim baldly that the grandi move more swiftly than do the people, that they are quicker on their feet than the latter; nobles foresee more immediately what means will attain their ends and they possess the material resources to fund such means in order to secure what they want (P 9, D I.5). Unfortunately, what they want is usually not, as are the desires of the people, conducive to the common good of a republic. This poses a peculiar problem: while Machiavelli extols the people's powers of foresight (D I.58), they clearly cannot foresee what is beneficial or deleterious for the common utility as quickly as the grandi foresee what is in their own interest.

The constitution of a Machiavellian Democracy, therefore, must ensure that the people's elongated learning curve is permitted to yield beneficial knowledge over time, and furthermore it must provide the means for eventually enacting legal or institutional changes on the basis of that knowledge.[43] The republic must survive the grandi's victories over the popolo in specific battles so that the people, and therefore the republic, can win the domestic war. Again, Machiavelli clearly shows how the people lose skirmishes over consular elections: the senate uses religious belief, military adventures, and electoral corruption to dissuade the people from elevating plebeians to the highest magistracies. But eventually the people see through such tactics (D I.39) and, with Machiavelli's explicit approval, gain a share in the consulship (D I.60).

The civic war that the people never win, in Rome at least, is the contest over economic inequality: they lose many minor engagements as the senate consistently fabricates military conflicts that postpone consideration of the Agrarian Laws until some later date (D I.13, D I.37, D I.39). By the time that the Gracchi actually enacted such legislation, the nobility had amassed from the fruits of empire such economic power, and the citizen-soldiery had been reduced to such egregious poverty and abject servility, that no successful recourse short of a wholesale refounding of the republic is available to potential reformers.[44] The senate may win two notable battles in causing the death of each Gracchus brother (and many of their supporters). But the Roman Republic as a whole is destined to lose this war: the senate loses its authority and the people their liberty. While the senate's economic and political choices spelled doom for that particular republic, Machiavelli's reflections on Rome raise the possibility that future citizenries might learn from this example and better constrain the senatorial orders of their own republics.

4

Elections, Lotteries, and Class-Specific Institutions

> The tribunes were ordered with such eminence and reputation that they mediated between the plebs and the senate, and halted the insolence of the nobles.
>
> Machiavelli, *Discourses* I.3

> In my opinion, the office of the tribunes did the Romans more harm than good.
>
> Guicciardini, *Dialogue*, Book II

The constitutions of modern republics attempt to keep public officials accountable and responsive in three principal ways: through the reward/sanction scheme of election and prospective reelection; the institutional counterposition of functionally separated powers; and, in extreme cases, the threat of removal through impeachment procedures conducted by other public officials. All citizens are formally eligible to hold office in such schemes, and the category "elite" applies technically only to those who do. These constitutions posit a sociologically anonymous political subject, "the sovereign people," out of which political elites are made and unmade through general elections.

These institutional arrangements and the principles underlying them would strike many adherents of premodern popular government as odd, unjust, and dangerous. From their viewpoint, if wealthy citizens are free to stand for all magistracies, if they can participate in every public council, and if unqualified election is the only device that determines officeholding or assembly attendance, the wealthy would hold distinct and persistent political advantages over poorer citizens. The rich would simply overwhelm the political process. After all, wealth enables such citizens to cultivate greater reputation, a more distinctive appearance, and better public-speaking skills such that voters almost inevitably choose them in electoral contests.[1] In addition, financial resources allow the wealthy to fund, groom, and/or bribe nonwealthy candidates to serve their interests at the expense of broader constituencies. Put simply, election is a magistrate selection method that directly and indirectly favors the wealthy and keeps political offices from being distributed widely among citizens of all socioeconomic backgrounds.

Ancient democracies assumed that law and public policy would not serve the common good unless large numbers of nonwealthy citizens participated in government by holding office themselves. Wealthy citizens, despite habitually florid promises to the contrary, were expected to pursue their own interests and not those of the general populace upon ascension to office – a danger obviously exacerbated in electoral systems where the wealthy monopolize offices. To avoid the "aristocratic effect" of election,[2] ancient democracies assigned most magistracies by citizenwide lotteries or "sortitions" and observed frequent rotation in office.[3] In keeping with the egalitarian aspirations and distrust of oligarchy characteristic of such regimes, lotteries conducted over the fairly wide portion of the citizenry who were willing to serve in office minimized the chances that wealthy and notable citizens would govern in a manner highly disproportionate to their actual numbers within the population. Sortition guaranteed that offices would be distributed in a fairly random fashion among all classes of citizens.[4] Moreover, regular and frequent turnover of officeholders ensured that wealthy magistrates could deploy their greater financial resources neither to ensconce themselves in office nor to influence or determine the appointment of like-minded or similarly interested successors.

As straightforward sortition became increasingly rare in Mediterranean popular governments, Italian peninsular republics attempted to ameliorate the aristocratic effect of elections and ensure wider distribution of offices in two alternate ways: by establishing class-specific eligibility stipulations for certain offices and/or by combining election with lottery-like randomization measures. The first part of this chapter focuses on the first strategy, more favored by Machiavelli, and typified by the tribunes of the plebs in Rome. Later sections of the chapter examine the second strategy, practiced by various incarnations of the Florentine Republic when appointing officials (priors) to its chief executive committee, the *Signoria* (or Priorate), an approach that Francesco Guicciardini, Machiavelli's young patrician interlocutor in early-sixteenth-century Florence, analyzed and severely criticized.

Class-Specific Magistrates – the Tribunes of the Plebs

As we observed in previous chapters, Machiavelli's *Discourses* reconstructs the history and constitution of the ancient Roman Republic, reviving and revising it as a model for present and future popular governments. Machiavelli was especially concerned with the ambition and behavior of the wealthiest and most powerful segments of a republic, the *grandi*, whose unquenchable appetite to oppress motivates them to acquire the socioeconomic and political advantages they enjoy in such regimes (D I.5; P 9). In the Roman context, the grandi were the republic's wealthy nobility who constituted the senate and monopolized terms in Rome's major magistracies – especially the consulship, its annually elected, two-member chief executive. I have emphasized that

Machiavelli, standing virtually alone in the history of intellectual reflection on republics, favors Roman institutions and practices that excluded wealthy and prominent citizens, that operated as much as possible beyond their influence or that directly opposed their power and privilege.

For holding back the "insolence" of the Roman grandi, the "ambition" of the nobility, Machiavelli bestows his highest praise on the common people's magistrates, the tribunes of the plebs (D I.3, D I.39, D I.50, D III.11).[5] According to Machiavelli, the grandi's insolence, and the appetite for domination that it reflects, are threats to the liberty of every citizen and to the stability of all republics: the grandi will eventually raise up a prince or enlist a foreign power to further their inexhaustible efforts to oppress the people, or the latter will resort to such measures themselves as protection or in retaliation to persistent aristocratic abuse. The tribunate's "great and necessary power" in acting on behalf of Rome's plebeians or poorer citizens earns it Machiavelli's admiration as the domestic, internally directed institution above all others that facilitated Rome's unprecedented success at attaining liberty and glory (D I.3, D III.11). As I discussed earlier, a popular army – another, albeit more indirect, means of elite accountability – is the externally directed institution that Machiavelli endorses as a prerequisite for the freedom and security of republics.

Over the course of Roman history, as many as ten plebeians would serve as tribunes for one-year terms. The plebeians elected the tribunes in their assembly, the *concilium plebis*, which may have been the tribal assembly, the *comitia tributa*, convened in the absence of patrician citizens.[6] Though the tribunate was an elected office, the plebs selected tribunes from their own ranks, and this class-specificity minimized election's aristocratic effect.[7] The wealthiest or most notable citizens among the plebs were certainly most likely to become tribunes on a fairly consistent basis, but these notable plebeians were generally not the very richest and most prominent citizens in the republic as a whole.[8] Much to the annoyance of the patricians, the plebeians would sometimes reelect to consecutive terms tribunes who were especially successful at thwarting the nobility's oppressive designs. Yet Machiavelli judges this practice to be less pernicious than the senate's efforts to extend the terms of consuls so as to send armies farther away from Rome (D III.24).

As mentioned earlier, Machiavelli's accounts of the tribunate's creation and restoration during episodes of plebeian secession give credence to his view of the reactive quality of popular behavior, conduct that he initially contrasts with aggressively proactive noble behavior (D I.40, D I.44). In this spirit, the powers of the tribunes, generated and revived during these episodes, were, in many ways, powers of response rather than of initiation. The tribunes could veto most official acts through the *intercessio* – in particular, policies favored by the noble-dominated senate and about to be enacted by their agents, the consuls. The bodies of tribunes were "sacrosanct," that is, patricians could not touch them physically; in fact, the plebeians pledged to kill any patricians who violated their bodily integrity. Relatedly, the tribunes wielded a power, the *auxilium*, akin to *habeas corpus*, by which they could demand the release of individual plebeians who had been seized for failing to pay debts or for any reason whatever by nobles or magistrates. These characteristics reflect, in Machiavelli's words, the "eminence" and "reputation" enjoyed by the tribunes; these functions, which Machiavelli sums up in terms of efforts to "halt" the nobility's "insolence," suggest action directed *against*, or significant recourse *from*, aggressive behavior or political encroachment by the nobles or magistrates (D I.3).[9]

Nevertheless, as noted previously, over the course of Machiavelli's account, the disposition of the tribunicianly empowered people transforms from initial passivity to aggressive indignation as the people suffer continued abuse by the nobles and senate and increasingly avail themselves of the procedural avenues of protection afforded by the tribunate. Indeed, the less than exclusively reactive quality of the tribunes and the people is already evident when Machiavelli explicitly emphasizes the following proactive tasks entrusted to the tribunate: the tribunes' authority to indict and prosecute magistrates and prominent citizens suspected of political crimes (D I.7–8); and to propose laws before and conduct discussion among the people collected in assembly (D I.18). Historical evidence confirms that the people availed themselves of tribunician authority in these capacities to prosecute ex-consuls for having levied troops in an oppressive manner and to pass legislation permitting citizens to vote via secret ballot.[10] As I've already concluded, the people and their plebeian magistrates must act in more than a merely passive and reactive manner if they are to contain and control wily and well-resourced social actors identified first and foremost by an insolent humor to oppress others. They must impose more than simply negative constraints on the elites who rule; they must do much more than simply refrain from engaging in rule themselves. Through the tribunes and in their assemblies, Machiavelli demonstrates unequivocally that the plebeians participate in rule.[11]

According to Machiavelli, the tribunes did not only protect the plebeians and facilitate their part in the republic's "administration" (D I.4); they also served as mediators between the nobles and the people (D I.3) – and, indeed, also as mediators among the nobles themselves (D I.50, D III.8). For instance, when senators or consuls could not reach agreement, they were known to consult with the tribunes. Thus, the people arbitrated potential conflicts among elites at two levels: not only by selecting magistrates and deciding political trials themselves in assembly but also by having their own agents actively mediate conflict among elites while the latter served in office. Moreover, the tribunes served as agents of magistrate accountability in a system, unlike contemporary democracy, in which the prospect of immediate reelection was not an inducement to good behavior.[12] The consuls, like most magistrates, were elected for one-year, nonrenewable terms and could stand for reelection only some years after the end of their term. Through public accusations, the tribunes could punish consuls for poor conduct in office once their term was over, even if consuls could not be removed from office during their tenure (except by the dictator under the direst circumstances).[13]

To be sure, the expectation that former magistrates would become senators upon the termination of their service induced a certain degree of good behavior among officeholders – but good behavior presumably assessed according to the nobility's criteria, especially once the patrician-dominated institution of the censors was established to scrutinize and validate senatorial tenure (D I.49, D III.1, D III.49). The promise of being accepted by and the hope of getting along with prospective senatorial colleagues must have inclined magistrates toward behavior pleasing to that set of actors. (This is no doubt one of the reasons that the Roman people considered the consuls to be the agents of the nobility and sought to have plebs elect the consuls by simple majority vote and to serve as consuls themselves.) In addition, reputation for good behavior in office was important if former magistrates wanted to be considered for prominent positions in the future, such as the dictatorship, or for additional terms in the consulship.

Senate–tribune relations are a more complicated and more important issue for Machiavelli: since the tribunate did not begin as an official, curule magistracy, there was no expectation that former tribunes would enter the senate when their terms were over. One might argue that this tended to discourage their collusion with the nobles. The opening of the senate to former tribunes roughly coincided with the growing power of the concilium, an assembly in which the plebeians as a whole were exerting considerable influence over the republic. We might speculate that these developments offset each other, such that the tribunes were not coopted to a significant extent by the nobility once they were eligible to enroll in the senate, since they still had to take heed of the considerable emerging potency of the popular assemblies.[14]

How were the tribunes, as opposed to consuls and senators, made accountable to the plebeians and to the republic as a whole? No institution is beyond potential misuse, Machiavelli insists, and no political actor should be able to direct or obstruct the workings of government unilaterally (D.III.11, D I.51). Thus, in cases where the tribunes became "insolent and formidable to the nobility and to all of Rome," that is, also to the plebeians themselves, Machiavelli cites how the nobility successfully "tempered" their behavior: they coerced, corrupted, or convinced one tribune to veto the actions of any colleagues who were pursuing antipatrician or civically dangerous legislative agendas (D III.11). Machiavelli need not mention something that would be obvious to anyone with cursory knowledge of Roman history: Tiberius Gracchus circumvented senatorial attempts to cultivate, intimidate, or bribe a fellow tribune into vetoing Gracchus's agrarian reforms by successfully appealing his colleague's veto to the people. He thereby called forth the nobility's ultimate recourse in protecting their political and material advantage: assassination (cf., P 9).

There is another noteworthy aspect of Machiavelli's account of patrician use of the tribunate's collegial veto: perhaps surprisingly, the supposed arch-cynic Machiavelli lists the "love of the common good" inhering in particular tribunes to be one of the factors that nobles exploit when encouraging tribunes to veto a colleague's initiative (D III.11). This statement undermines a serious charge frequently leveled against the tribunes by Roman optimates and still hurled by many contemporary interpreters of Machiavelli's *Discourses*: specifically, the claim that the tribunes are merely wannabe grandi – individuals with an appetite to oppress – who happen to emerge from the ranks of plebeians; or, more crudely, that the tribunes are merely out for themselves and have no desire to advance the cause of plebeian citizens.[15] Machiavelli makes perfectly clear his view on this matter when he states that the tribunes supported first and foremost initiatives that to the best of their knowledge benefited the people – and if such policies also harmed the nobles, that is, restrained their efforts to oppress the people, so much the better: "The tribunes of the plebs were always inclined to propose what they thought benefited the people, and the more such things opposed the nobles the more did [the tribunes] propose them..." (D III.8). In any case, Machiavelli is insistent that no one institution, not even one such as the tribunate that in some significant sense embodies the people's desire not to be dominated, should operate beyond veto or appeal in his model of popular government, even if these institutional checks inevitably open possible avenues for further patrician intrigue (D I.51).

Generally, how effective were the tribunes at protecting the plebeians from patrician oppression? Very effective, Machiavelli suggests, but not perfectly so. Machiavelli writes repeatedly that the tribunes successfully helped hold back the insolence of the nobility (D I.3, D III.11). Indeed, so successful were the tribunes at shielding the plebeians from domination at home that the senate was willing to subordinate itself to Appius Claudius's tyranny rather than see the tribunate reinstated (D I.40). Machiavelli also notes the following with respect to the senate's military agenda: "since the nobles could not punish the plebs once defended by tribunician authority within Rome, they desired to lead it beyond Rome under the consuls so as to crush it where it had no support" (D I.39). Besides noting the avarice, discussed previously, that motivated the senate to send troops farther from Rome, Machiavelli emphasizes its desire to oppress the people directly in their persons while away from the city on the field of battle.

As we observed in the last chapter, when the tribunes sought to curtail the nobility's exacerbation of economic inequality through the Agrarian Laws, the senate sent troops farther and farther away from Italy to maximize its economic advantages (D I.37). In the preceding cited passage, Machiavelli notes that, because the tribunes successfully defended the people's bodily integrity and legal entitlements within the city, the nobles sought to lead them outside its walls in order to inflict harm on them there. The tribunes, a domestic political institution, could halt physical oppression and violations of the citizen's rights only at home, not abroad. In light of these observations, we can begin to observe the following: since the nobility's appetites for direct subordination of the people and for material gain were insatiable, they were destined to destroy the republic through the imperial expansion that was gratifying these appetites; the tribunes could only delay this destined destruction. If tribunes such as the Gracchi ultimately failed to address the increasing economic inequality that was socially and militarily undermining the republic, Machiavelli suggests that the tribunes' consistent lobbying for agrarian reform and for other forms of political redress throughout the history of the republic slowed rapacious senatorial self-aggrandizement to such an extent that the senate did not ruin the republic as rapidly as it otherwise would have.

Thus, if we step back and analyze the success of the tribunes at halting the insolence of the grandi, and therefore at preserving Rome's freedom, we must conclude that its success, although "great and necessary" (D III.11), is ultimately incomplete and temporary. Republics without tribunes, Machiavelli suggests, succumb either to military defeat, due to their inability to arm the people (e.g., Sparta and Venice), or to fairly immediate princely usurpation, due to their inability to prevent the grandi from visiting harm upon the *popolo* (e.g., Syracuse and Heraclea). Tribunician republics (which admittedly constitute an "n" of only one in the history of popular government) achieve military success and forestall immediate domestic domination by the nobles and hence hinder fairly rapid collapse. However, the empire won by Rome's military success allowed the grandi to indirectly reimport domination of the plebs back into the domestic life of the republic in a form against which the tribunes had little recourse and the result of which was ultimately princely usurpation on a larger scale, Caesarism. In addition to tribunes, then, what a tribunician republic requires to preserve its liberty and longevity is the external presence of other tribunician republics capable of containing its own imperial expansion.

After all, Machiavelli wrote not for one particular republic, but rather for republics in general. One could imagine that a single tribunate republic might hope to maintain its liberty indefinitely – indeed, perhaps perpetually (D III.1) – by confronting equally virtuous tribunate republics abroad that serve to halt its expansion and thereby prevent the emergence of the following threats to the common good: gratuitous oppression of the plebs, economic aggrandizement of the nobility, and inflation of military commanders' authority.

The Conundrum of Class in the Roman Assemblies

As noted before, the Roman assemblies in Machiavelli's account function more like the Athenian *ekklesia* than the centuriate assembly of historical fact because (1) one-man-one-vote, majority rule obtains within them and (2) wide public deliberation and not just voting characterize their proceedings. Machiavelli seems to acknowledge some distinction between the *comitia centuriata* and the concilium plebis. He calls the former the *comizi consolari* (D I.14) or simply the *comizi* (D II.28), and he describes it as the assembly that elected magistrates with consular authority. Alternately, Machiavelli seems to refer explicitly to the concilium when he juxtaposes the *publico consiglio* to the senate (D III.30), and he probably namelessly makes reference to it when he cites the assembly in which tribunes proposed the laws that are subsequently discussed and voted on by the people (D I.18).[16]

Why do I assume that Machiavelli is either oblivious to the historical reality of weighted voting for the wealthy in the centuriate assembly or that he explicitly rejects this characteristic when he prescriptively reconstructs the Roman assemblies for his own purposes? As observed in previous chapters, Machiavelli establishes a rather sharp contrast between the popolo and grandi in Rome, the many and the elite (D I.5), a distinction that corresponds fairly closely – indeed, identically, in his account – with a plebeian versus patrician divide. The episodes discussed on several occasions, where Machiavelli recounts how the plebeians elect all patricians to consular office even though the former had been made eligible for it (D I.47–8), make sense only if the lower classes have the opportunity, via majority rule, to determine outcomes in this assembly.

In other words, unless plebeians have it within their power, by sheer force of numbers and without obstructionist property provisions that inflate the voting prowess of patricians or the wealthy, to elect one of their own to the office, the example is less than useful to Machiavelli. If the nobility possesses a majority of votes on the basis of property qualifications, then these instances would not illustrate the fact that the people deferred to excellence when they "come to particulars" at the decisive moment of election; rather, it would demonstrate that they were simply out-voted plutocratically by the patricians. Recall that Machiavelli also makes a point of praising the Roman people – that is, the people identified with the plebeians – for consistently electing, via "free votes" (D I.20, D I.58), the best candidates to offices throughout the life of the republic. This praise would be misplaced if the electoral system were weighted in Machiavelli's model such that the grandi could effectively elect whomever they liked through ballot-counting procedures that seldom or never reached poorer citizens, as often happened in the actual centuriate assembly.

It is worth reiterating the following: One of the lessons reinforced by these episodes where the nobles prevail in elections for which all citizens are eligible is the necessity of plebeian-specific magistracies, such as the tribunate, if a republic is to achieve political equality in any meaningful sense. General eligibility for an office, under conditions of even the widest suffrage conceivable, will most often result in the election of wealthy and prominent citizens – even without the special weighting of rich voters favored by, for instance, Rousseau.[17] As noted, plebeian citizens may have successfully gained access to the consulship in Rome, but the aristocratic effect of election ensures that wealthy and prominent nobles would enjoy a persistent advantage in generally wide electoral contests. Hence, the necessity of tribunes of the plebs and/or, as will be discussed, elections tempered by an element of randomization.

Another ambiguity concerning Machiavelli's account of Roman assemblies is whether or not his concilium, his plebeian-dominated assembly, actually excludes patricians. Recall what he writes of the assembly over which the tribunes presided: "A tribune, or any citizen whatsoever, could propose a law to the people, against or in favor of which every citizen was entitled to speak before reaching a decision" (D I.18). The sentence is vague in the following respect: does the "any citizen whatsoever" mentioned pertain exclusively to the plebeians participating in the concilium, as would have been the case historically? Or, does it apply literally to *any* citizen such that this description must include patricians? If the latter, then this statement implies that they too participate in the concilium.

Or, for that matter, does Machiavelli's sentence refer to any one assembly in particular? It could very well be that Machiavelli is suggesting that the tribunes and plebeian citizens propose laws in the concilium, on the one hand, while "any citizen," including patricians, can propose laws in the centuriate assembly, on the other. Perhaps the discussion and disputes over laws take place *not* in the plebeian-specific environment of the concilium, but rather in the informal assemblies reserved for public deliberation, the *contiones* or *concioni*, which Machiavelli frequently invokes (D I.4–5, D III.34) but does not mention explicitly here. However, if it is, in fact, the concilium of the plebs that Machiavelli describes in this instance, it is unlikely to include patricians for this reason: since social antagonists in Machiavelli's Rome are even *more* class-conscious than were their actual historical antecedents (if that's possible), it is hard to believe that the proud and insolent grandi, patricians, or *ottimati* would have deigned to participate in an assembly presided over by "tribunes of the plebs."[18]

Thankfully, Machiavelli is much clearer on the place of deliberation in his reconstruction of Rome's assemblies. As noted in the previous chapter, Machiavelli insists – contra Francesco Guicciardini in his own day, and Rousseau centuries later – that public deliberation should occur in close proximity to voting. Historically, the presiding magistrates of deliberative assemblies or concioni, whether a tribune, a consul, or a lower curule magistrate, had the discretion to recognize whomever they liked as speakers, a practice that invariably favored prominent individuals. But Machiavelli insists that anyone entitled to *attend* an assembly – from a senator in the senate to a plebeian in a concione – must be entitled to *speak* within it (D I.18, D I.58). This was a controversial recommendation in Machiavelli's own time, as prevailing wisdom, typified by Guicciardini's writings, insisted that popular assemblies were best reserved for ratifying or rejecting, *not* for initiating or deliberating over, policy proposals.

In short, while Machiavelli presents a somewhat confusing account of Roman assemblies, he certainly provides a genuine voice for common citizens in most of them. The patricians and the wealthy constitute the senate; all citizens attend the comizi, which, in Machiavelli's version, favors the rich through the aristocratic effect of elections (but does not doubly favor them by weighing votes according to wealth); and the plebeians attend their own assembly, the consilium or publico consiglio, presided over by their own magistrates, the tribunes, an assembly that generates real laws, the plebiscites. Every citizen who is eligible to attend these particular assemblies enjoys free speech within them, just as all citizens generally do in the informal concioni. The proceedings of no Machiavellian assembly are formally and disproportionately weighted toward wealth as is, most notably, Rousseau's appropriation of actual Roman practice. Alternately, plebeians and the poor, on the one hand, and patricians and the wealthy, on the other, may be excluded from a particular assembly, but no one is treated inequitably within any specific assembly.

Rousseau may insist that each citizen must be eligible for every assembly but, in a manner largely ignored by scholars who appropriate his political philosophy for radically democratic or republican political agendas,[19] he also recommends that citizens of large republics be organized hierarchically, that is, according to wealth, within them.[20] Machiavelli, conversely, advises republics to maintain separate assemblies for citizens of different social classes. Rousseau's theory of assemblies is egalitarian in principle, but not in practice; Machiavelli's is explicitly inegalitarian in a way that, counterintuitively, may produce more egalitarian outcomes – or at least results that are more intensely contestatory of power and privilege. For Machiavelli, a republic, a mixed regime, must be *mixed* in an appropriate way; that is, there must be institutions monopolized separately by wealthy *and* poorer citizens. The former cannot dominate all of them, either overtly or covertly, if every kind of citizen is to exercise and enjoy the liberty promised by a free or civic way of life.

Two Polities, One Republic?

Quite strikingly, then, Machiavelli's reconstruction of the Roman Republic is a tale of two cities: within the one republic, there is, on the one hand, a poorer, popular polity that shadows, on the other, an elite, wealthier one. The former serves as the latter's mirror, its negative image: the grandi deliberate policy in the senate, the plebs in the concilium (and both in the concioni). The senate influences the consuls to enact laws that it favors; when necessary, the people press the tribunes to veto such legislation. The consuls wield the power of life and death, but the tribunes deliver plebeians from just such a threat. One might argue that the formal *separation* of these two polities within one republic allows the less dangerous one, the plebeian polity that wants only to avoid domination, to patrol the one that Machiavelli explicitly claims is more dangerous, the aristocratic polity that seeks perpetual oppression over others. Indeed, Roman patricians often voiced consternation over the two polities that comprised their republic on precisely these grounds.[21]

There were echoes of this "two-polities-in-one" scenario in medieval Florence and throughout the other Italian republics of the thirteenth century: as the people, organized in occupational guilds, gained confidence and engaged in political and even armed conflict with their cities' traditional aristocracies, the *magnati* or grandi, they set up alternative institutions within the communes. Alongside the legislative and executive institutions dominated by the magnates, such as the Council of the Commune and the *Podestà*, in Florence and elsewhere the guild-organized people established the councils of the popolo and the office of the people's *Capitano*.[22] The offices of the Podestà and Capitano were filled by esteemed foreigners invited to Florence to dispense justice impartially among classes and families, with dubious results, according to Machiavelli.[23]

The grandi and popolo both competed to be priors within the Signoria, as I'll discuss in greater detail later in this chapter, just as their Roman counterparts competed over terms in the consulship once the plebeians realized that the tribunate was a necessary but not sufficient guard of their liberty against the patricians (D I.37, D I.47).

However, general election did not determine seats in Florence's Signoria or Priorate; class-specification – or more precisely, occupational-specification and randomization – characterized the appointment process. At its most widely and substantively participatory (1343–8 and, especially, 1378–82), the republic went so far as to reserve two of the six seats in the Signoria for members of each of the three sets of politically recognized guilds: in descending order of wealth and status, the major, minor, and *minuti* guilds. Without such quotas for middling and lower guildsmen, the rich *popolani* of the major guilds and the patrician magnates (when permitted to enroll in the upper guilds) would have consistently dominated offices in the Priorate.[24] In the more progressive schemes, the heads of each of the twenty-three guilds nominated members of their rank and file whose names were then submitted, along with those nominated by sitting magistrates and ward officials, into bags (*borse*). Out of the latter were drawn the number of names conforming with the number of open seats in the Signoria and also satisfying the equal distribution requirement across higher, middling, and lower guilds.

Unlike citizenwide general elections, or even ward-based ones demarcated by neighborhood, this procedure ensured that lower tradesmen, artisans, and shopkeepers had a relatively equal chance of holding office with bankers and owners of large-scale production: guild-specific nominations preceded a lottery, the results of which met corporate quotas. Offices were distributed more widely among citizens, certainly more widely than they would have been distributed in a general election: all the guilds supplied nominations and seats were allotted according to classes of guilds. On the one hand, the Florentine method differed from the general lottery characteristic of Athenian democracy: in Florence, the minority of wealthy citizens was guaranteed positions disproportionate to their number of the population due to the reservation of seats for members of the upper guilds. On the other hand, unlike the general elections of modern democracy, the Florentine guild/randomization model ensured that citizens besides the most wealthy would hold office. Successive waves of oligarchic or princely alterations undermined and then destroyed the guild basis of the early Florentine republics,[25] but its corporate character or class-specificity is very close to what Machiavelli attempts to revive through the tribunate in his neo-Roman model: socioeconomic specificity in political institutions better ensures participation by common citizens in government than do class-anonymous institutions and formally wide, general eligibility for office.

However, Machiavelli clearly favors Roman constitutional arrangements over Florentine ones, since the latter proved less stable and less conducive to military prowess. As Machiavelli suggests in the *Florentine Histories*, the people and nobles in Florence had available only limited institutional means to minimize the abusive behavior visited upon the former by the latter – Florence lacked both a senate and a tribunate. Consequently, the people, when faced with what Machiavelli describes as consistent recidivist oppression by the nobility, found themselves compelled to disenfranchise the nobles completely. In response, the latter made themselves appear "popular" by enrolling in trade guilds and by abandoning positions of military leadership, from which, as in Rome, even plebeians benefit and learn.[26]

Not surprisingly, then, Machiavelli's neo-Roman proposal for noble- and popolo-specific institutions in the *Discourses* avoids two major errors committed by popular republics in the history of Florence: on the one hand, losing the support of lesser guildsmen or the *sottoposti* (resident laborers and taxpayers not formally organized into guilds); and, on the other, as mentioned previously, making outright enemies of the magnate class above the guilds. As for the first mistake, Machiavelli's lifelong campaign for a citizen militia, drawn not only from the residents of Florence but also from inhabitants of the surrounding countryside, if enacted, would have ensured the loyalty of the popolo minuti and the sottoposti and swelled the numbers of citizens available to the city as soldiers, taxpayers, and potential magistrates. A popular army would have integrated a greatly expanded and widely inclusive Florentine citizenry into the politics of the republic, but, as mentioned before, the plan was less than wholeheartedly adopted in Machiavelli's own time due to aristocratic resistance. Machiavelli's plans were consistently thwarted or scaled back by the republic's ottimati, who did not want to deal with an armed populace in the city – especially one that would serve at the disposal of a lifetime chief executive such as Machiavelli's boss, Gonfalonier of Justice Piero Soderini. Moreover, they refused to consider the population of the territory surrounding Florence, the *contado*, as anything but subjects, certainly not as potential fellow citizens.[27]

As for the enmity of the Florentine magnates or grandi, the Florentine popolo disenfranchised them in an effort to halt their incessant acts of physical violence and political intimidation against common citizens.[28] This course of action rendered Florentine popular government perpetually unstable as the disenfranchised magnates were always eager to (a) aid an external enemy against the city in the hopes of reassuming their political prominence; or (b) coopt or collude with members of the "major," wealthier guilds, especially those engaged in banking and finance, to shut out the lower guilds of merchants and artisans and undermine the republic.[29] Machiavelli's model ensures the grandi of their place within a republic: it maintains a senate and initially permits an aristocratic monopoly over military command.

Moreover, Machiavellian Democracy allows socially mobile upper popolo to integrate into the nobility without causing the demise of republican forms, rather than, as in Florence, encouraging the aristocracy to give up its military prowess as it attempts to integrate downward into the guilds embodying the wealthiest commercial strata of the popolo (FH III.1). Indeed, by Machiavelli's own time, the Florentine ottimati or grandi effectively fused old magnate families and newer, upper-guild popolani. In short, Machiavelli's emendations of the Florentine model demonstrate his belief that if republics are to endure, the grandi must be granted a prominent place lest they perpetrate oligarchic or princely coups. However, Machiavelli's neo-Roman model also includes magistracies not easily corrupted by both the traditional nobility and the recently "ennobled" popolani, offices that check the power and privilege of these combined groups. In his reconstructed Roman Republic, Machiavelli calls these magistrates tribunes of the plebs; in his reformed Florentine Republic, he calls them provosts.

Machiavelli's Florentine Tribunes

When Machiavelli proposes a constitution for a revived Florentine Republic, he very subtly – indeed, almost surreptitiously – incorporates tribune-like offices, the provosts (*proposti*), into his plan. Machiavelli wrote the "Discursus on Florentine Affairs" (1519–20)[30] in response to Giovanni de'Medici's (Pope Leo's) solicitations for advice on converting Florence from a de facto principality to a genuine republic, since the leading Medici, now Church prelates, will leave behind them no legitimate heirs to serve as princes of Florence. The audience of Machiavelli's reform proposal – Pope Leo, his cousin Giulio de' Medici (eventually Pope Clement VII), and their "*amici*" – would undoubtedly reject out of hand any overt plea for a tribunate, a citizen army, and a popular assembly as expansive and powerful as the Great Council of the 1494–1513 republic (DF 737). After all, the Medici and their "friends" had been steadily making staunch enemies out of the Florentine people since resuming rule within the city (DF 735).[31]

In good Venetian rather than Roman fashion, then, Machiavelli's proposal seems to entrench the power of a life-termed executive committee and a senate of ottimati, and it apparently renders impotent the revived popular assembly that Machiavelli includes in the proposal. However, Machiavelli will empower his provosts, drawn from the ranks of common citizens exclusively and rotated by lot into the Signoria and the senatorial council, to delay the decisions of such bodies and appeal them to the Great Council. In this way, Machiavelli's proposal leaves ample room for the Great Council, through the provosts, to constrain the actions of the upper organs dominated by Florence's socioeconomic elite and become the dominant institution of the republic. Unfortunately, the manner in which Machiavelli presents the provosts may have been too subtle and understated for commentators on the "Discursus": most scholarly interpreters simply ignore them.[32]

While Machiavelli introduces the provosts, agents of the common people, discretely and gradually in the "Discursus," he makes explicit the need to satisfy the grandi's appetite for command. Machiavelli begins by professing to offer Leo a republic that is neither so *stretto* as "the republic of ottimati" that prevailed in the oligarchic era between the Ciompi Revolt and the Medici Principate, nor so *largo* as the 1494–1512 republic so hated by the ottimati (DF 733–4). Under the latter republic, Machiavelli concedes, prominent patricians (famously, Bernardo Rucellai and Alamanno Salviati) resented having to share seats in the priorate with "men of low status" (*uomini abietti*) (DF 733). To avoid this situation, which provoked such ottimati to undermine the regime or withhold their support from it, Machiavelli proposes a Signoria of sixty-five life-tenured citizens, likely to be men of Rucellai's and Alamanno's stature. He hopes that a highly exclusive Signoria will at least partly satisfy such individuals of "haughty spirit," powerful citizens who "think they deserve precedence before all others" (DF 738).[33] Machiavelli would divide this signorial class into two sets of thirty-two signors, each set containing the names of the individuals eligible to serve as priors in alternating years. The Gonfalonier of Justice, who would serve a two- or three-year term as head of state, would also emerge from the names making up this signorial class. Thus, at any particular moment, the Signoria, according to this plan, would be constituted by eight priors from among the set of thirty-two, who would serve for three months at a time alongside the Gonfalonier, who would be filling as much as a three-year term.

Below this nine-membered executive committee, Machiavelli proposes the "Council of the Select": a senatorial body of two-hundred, life-tenured members. Comprised mostly of upper guildsmen, rich popolani who did not qualify for the more exalted signorial posts, the "Select" council or "the Two Hundred" is intended by Machiavelli to satisfy the ambitions of the "middling" citizens within the regime (DF 740). Leo himself, according to Machiavelli, would determine the initial composition of these bodies. This gives the Pope such a secure hold over "the republic" that he might actually consider entertaining Machiavelli's next proposition: reinstituting the Great Council as the assembly reserved for the "generality" or "universality" of the people (DF 740–1). Machiavelli suggests that initially Leo may want to set the Great Council's membership at a manageable six hundred citizens before expanding it to a full membership of one thousand. (Machiavelli never broaches the possibility of restoring the Council to its original, incredibly large size of over three thousand citizens.) Further, Machiavelli blatantly advises Leo to allow his amici, his "friends" (i.e., his relatives, clients, and henchmen), to determine, in secret, the results of any elections in the Council conducted during the Pope's lifetime (DF 741).

However, Machiavelli is adamant that if Leo does not reinstitute the Great Council, the people will never be satisfied, and an enemy will emerge to reestablish it, resulting in the Pope's "displeasure" and his amici's "destruction and ruin" (DF 741). However much of a sham the proceedings of the Great Council may be during the remainder of Leo's life, Machiavelli insists that after the Pope's death, the Great Council and *not* Leo's "amici" must be the heart and soul of the republic: the Great Council, not the Pope's allies and clients, will select replacement members of the Signoria and the Two Hundred, as well as elect all the other officers of the republic. In fact, he implies that after Leo's death, the pontiff's memory and glory better rests with the generality of the people than with his "friends" among the ottimati – a theme that rises to a crescendo toward the essay's conclusion (DF 741–2, DF 745). The Pope should actually consider shifting his alliance from the few to the many if he wants to be remembered as a great reformer – indeed, an illustrious refounder – of the republic. In the context of such advice, Machiavelli is ready to introduce his Florentine tribunate, a magistracy through which the Great Council might eventually take precedence over the two initially "higher," or more powerful, executive and senatorial institutions of the republic, and, hence perhaps become the vehicle through which the generality of the people will gain ascendance over the citizens of middling and exalted rank sitting in life-tenured magistracies.

As if almost an afterthought to an already complete constitutional order founded on the personal appointment and election of elite citizens, Machiavelli introduces the office of the provosts: a lottery-determined magistracy reserved for common citizens, which, like the tribunate in Rome, Machiavelli claims, will make this republic more perfect (DF 741). Machiavelli establishes the provosts as a subset of sixteen "Gonfaloniers of the Companies of the People," an office originally associated with the popular militia during the guilds' armed struggle with the magnates in the early Florentine republics (DF 742). These Gonfaloniers of the Companies eventually evolved into one of the Signoria's formal advisory bodies. Machiavelli leaves open whether his reconstructed popular Gonfaloniers will be selected each year by city ward, by the guilds, by the Great Council, or by Leo himself as long as he lives. But Machiavelli insists that these popular magistrates, however they are appointed, must *not* belong to the signorial class; the grandi, citizens eligible to hold life-terms in the Signoria, must be excluded from its ranks (DF 742). Furthermore, Machiavelli declares that common citizens who serve as provosts must be prohibited from gaining rapid reappointment "such that the magistracy will be spread more widely throughout the city" (DF 742). Lottery will determine which of the popular Gonfaloniers will serve short, week- or month-long terms as provosts, attending the proceedings of the Signoria, sitting in on sessions of the Select Council, and participating as full voting members in the Great Council.

It first appears as if the provosts are merely nonvoting "witnesses" to the proceedings of the two upper assemblies comprised of their social superiors. But Machiavelli soon insists that neither the Signoria nor the Select Council should be permitted to convene without provosts present (DF 742). Moreover, the provosts can delay enactment of decisions made by these bodies and appeal them to their more broadly popular, immediately subordinate councils.[34] Machiavelli explains neither why provosts must be designated from among the Gonfaloniers of the Companies of the People by lottery nor why their terms in any particular body may be as short as a week. A plausible reason is that sortition prevents the ottimati in the upper councils from gaining advance knowledge of exactly which popular Gonfaloniers will be convocating with them as provosts, thereby thwarting any attempts on their part to corrupt or intimidate the provosts beforehand (cf., FH IV.17). Moreover, the provosts' short terms guard against political cooptation while they serve among the ottimati in the Signoria and senatorial Select Council. Machiavelli clearly expresses a desire that as many nonsignorial citizens as possible take part in this office, which effectively serves as the people's eyes and ears in both the republic's executive committee and senatorial council and that explicitly wields veto or referral power over the policies proposed within them.

In two important respects, then, Machiavelli's Florentine provosts can be understood as an improvement over the Roman tribunes. As Machiavelli himself acknowledges, the tribunes could be bribed or intimidated by the nobility, and as Livy's history makes plain, the most prominent citizens among the plebeians were consistently elected to the tribunate. Machiavelli, however, designs the office of the provosts so that, on the one hand, they may perform their duties free as far as possible from the influence of the ottimati, and, on the other, so that as many common citizens as possible serve in the office. While the provosts clearly function as popular agents of elite accountability, they also provide common citizens with an invaluable political education: the popular Gonfaloniers/provosts allow a wide array of political amateurs to watch and observe in close quarters the deliberations and decisions of the most powerful and prominent citizens of the republic.[35]

Machiavelli writes: "It is not good if magistrates lack somebody to observe them and make them refrain from actions that are not good" (DF 742). He clearly expects that popular surveilling of magistrate behavior and that vetoing/ appealing of elite policy making in his proposal will be particularly intense since Florence's common citizens, as in the early Roman Republic, initially will be closed off formally from the highest signorial offices – offices for which they traditionally had been eligible. However, in taking from common citizens offices that they previously exercised at a disadvantage when sitting alongside the ottimati, Machiavelli now reserves for them *exclusively* offices possibly more potent. A persistent problem with the Florentine guild-based model for assigning seats in the Signoria was not only, as Machiavelli states explicitly, that the ottimati resented sharing office with lower guildsmen, but also that the former could readily intimidate, cajole, or corrupt the latter within the confines of the Signoria. In the Roman Republic, the tribunate functioned as the plebeian answer to magistracies from which plebeians were formally excluded initially and which they then obtained only with great difficulty – the tribunes, in effect, were counterconsuls. Similarly, in Machiavelli's reformed Florentine Republic, the provosts are, in effect, counterpriors; the popular Gonfaloniership functions as a "counter-Signoria."[36] This new popular magistracy of the provosts, "resembling" but in practice positioned against the office taken away from the people, will be, according to Machiavelli, "greater, more honorable and more useful to the republic" than was a Signoria nominally open to all citizens (DF 743).

Provoking the people by excluding them from the most powerful magistracies and providing them a subordinate magistracy that is nevertheless theirs exclusively is Machiavelli's way of better empowering the people, both psychologically and institutionally, to make elites accountable. On the one hand, common citizens will no longer suffer from the delusion that they are effectively exercising the higher offices that they regularly attain but within which they are marginalized. On the other, they will not be overwhelmed by the ottimati within the new magistracies created for them alone; the manner in which they are appointed and the short terms they enjoy protect them from cooptation, coercion, and corruption by the ottimati. Letting a wider number of plebeian citizens than ascended to the Roman tribunate use offices reserved exclusively for themselves in efforts to check oppression by the grandi and, perhaps eventually, to reattain offices from which they are now formally excluded better empowers them than would formal eligibility for all offices generally.

Machiavelli insists that Pope Leo's friends among the ottimati, those who will "sit in the primary governmental seats," need not fear the loss of their property from this proposed constitution – in fact, Machiavelli declares, it is still in reality a *monarchy* during Leo's lifetime (DF 743–4). Yet this proposal leaves ample room for the popular Gonfaloniers/provosts, and through them, the Great Council, to constrain the actions and even to control the behavior of the Gonfalonier of Justice, the Signoria, and the senate once this Medici Pope dies (since he will, given the nature of his office, leave it without a princely successor). In the relationship between the provosts and the Great Council, we can observe how closely aligned, for Machiavelli, elite accountability, a supposedly negative function, is with popular rule, an explicitly positive one. By enabling non-elite citizens to appeal all policy proposals of elite magistrates to the Great Council, Machiavelli provides a path through which the latter may become the dominant institution, and its members – common citizens – the dominant force in the republic.

Machiavelli states quite candidly that the "generality of the citizens" will expect more allotments of power, "little by little," to fall into their hands over time (DF 744). Conceivably these expansions of power include enlarging the size of the Great Council and constricting those of the aristocratic bodies, not to mention altering the distribution of political authority between them. The plebeian-based Gonfaloniers of the Companies of the People, and the lot-determined subset of them, the provosts, are the vehicles that will deliver these increases in power to the people assembled in the Great Council. A subtext of Machiavelli's memorandum is that a popular government without effective class-specific institutions such as the provosts is barely a republic; such a government is, basically, a naked oligarchy.

Mixing Lottery and Election

As the first theorist to reconcile the aristocratic effect of elections with wide suffrage, Guicciardini deserves to be recognized as the intellectual forefather of modern representative government.[37] A Florentine patrician who served his city as a statesman and historian, Guicciardini first fully articulated the intuition that so troubled ancient democrats and that James Madison would later systematize as one of the fundamental principles of modern constitutionalism: elections produce virtually the same aristocratic effect whether or not voters are formally separated from an electable elite.[38] General elections, especially if conducted in a large population or over a wide territory, tend to elevate the most virtuous, prudent, just (read: wealthy and prominent) citizens to office.[39] In his mature political work, the *Dialogue on the Government of Florence*, Guicciardini endorsed a system in which the general citizenry, more or less excluded from holding office, was granted full power to choose which "virtuous" individuals would hold political magistracies for relatively short terms in office. Despite being one of them, Guicciardini did not trust elite citizens, the Florentine ottimati, to distribute offices among themselves, but he resented and feared the demands of Florence's "jealous" and "ignorant" common citizens to hold the republic's highest offices themselves.[40] On his way to these conclusions about election, however, Guicciardini critically analyzed the mixing of sortition and election characteristic of Florentine politics in his youth, an analysis from which we may draw contemporary lessons. Before engaging his analysis directly, allow me to provide some further background on Florentine electoral politics.

The many different constitutions that Florence observed from the thirteenth through much of the fifteenth centuries attempted to neutralize antagonisms corresponding with external alliances, family rivalries, and the like.[41] But class conflict between the ottimati, members of families with wealth and a good name, and the popolo was a consistently intense form of competition playing itself out in the struggle for office. The ottimati preferred a stretto or narrow regime in which a few prominent citizens from patrician families (magnati) or wealthy guilds (*popolano grasso*) rotated magistracies of long duration under short reeligibility stipulations. The people, lower guildsmen, and workers not organized in guilds (popolo minuti or sottoposti), desired a governo largo, a more widely participatory regime in which many more citizens held office due to relaxed property and residency requirements, shorter terms, and stricter limits on reappointment. In the early republic, the debate seldom focused on the lottery/election question; most of the parties agreed on sortition as the final mode of appointment to the major magistracies. Rather, conflict ensued most intensely over the composition of the committees that scrutinized citizens for eligibility to hold office; the severity or laxness of the criteria they employed; and the extent to which positions in office would be reserved for less wealthy citizens from lower guilds.[42]

Magistrates could be appointed in a number of ways: from a simple lottery for the lowest offices to a multistage lot/election combination for the highest magistracies in the republic, as well as alternative formats of varying complexity residing in-between these two extremes. Most often, the process for appointing seats in the Signoria functioned in this way: the names of all citizens whose taxes were paid and whose families had participated in governing the city going back several generations were placed in a bag (*borsa*), and the number of names corresponding with the number of open positions would be pulled at random. The ottimati preferred members of "the best families" to serve repeatedly as priors, while the popolo preferred to distribute magistracies more widely to "a stream of new and largely unknown guildsmen."[43] Ottimati tended to lobby for the incumbent executive committee of the city, the Signoria's six to eight priors, to determine which particular names met these qualifications and, secondly, for a shorter *divieto*, the span of time for which a former magistrate was ineligible to hold office again. On the other hand, the popolo would generally push for the heads of the major trade guilds to determine eligibility and request a much longer divieto.[44] After all, members of the ottimati served more often in the Signoria and therefore could bring greater pressure to bear on sitting priors, while the broader popolo had more direct influence on the annually elected "consuls" of the guilds to which they belonged.

The ottimati consolidated power in the wake of the failed proto-proletarian rebellion, the Ciompi Revolt, and by undermining a widely participatory republic that included members of the lower guilds (1378–81). During this period, the so-called Albizzi Oligarchy (1381–1434), the wealthiest families determined the personnel of the nominators or scrutinizers (*accoppiatori*), who, in turn, vigorously vetted the names placed in the bags of office, sometimes by imposing strict property requirements and cumbersome "grandfather" stipulations, but mostly by judging the individual's patronage links to the ruling clique. Under the de facto Medici principate of the fifteenth century (1434–94), the Medici family controlled appointments in a similar way through friendly scrutinizers and an extraordinary council, the *balìa*, which was supposedly acclaimed by and acting on behalf of the whole people. In both of these circumstances, the nominators would load the bags such that only the names of individuals who were pleasing to the oligarchs or the first family would be most likely to emerge. Thus, under both of these dubiously "republican" scenarios, a veneer of "popular government" could obtain while outcomes that tended toward oligarchy or autocracy were in fact predetermined. While the number of citizen office-holders expanded during these regimes, the policy independence of the offices held was reduced by the excessive authority wielded by the leading families.

Writing during the republic established under the influence of Friar Girolamo Savonarola after the expulsion of the Medici in 1494, the young Guicciardini discusses election and lottery as means of nominating and appointing magistrates within a legitimate rather than a sham republic. In both his *History of Florence* (c. 1508)[45] and "*Discorso* on Bringing Order to Popular Government" (1512),[46] Guicciardini seems content with lot as a method that draws a group of nominators from among the approximately 3,400 citizens collected in Florence's popularly inclusive Great Council.[47] However, these works begin to reveal Guicciardini's preference for election over lot in the final appointment of magistrates. In the *Discorso*, Guicciardini suggests that the appointment process for the republic's top committees – the Signoria, the Ten of War, and the Eight of Ward – be reformed as follows: the names agreed upon and submitted by the lot-determined nominators should be voted on in the Great Council, and those who win a majority may then either be voted upon again *or* submitted to sortition as the way finally to determine who will fill open positions.[48]

In this scheme, the lot-election combination is fairly complex: lottery ensures that nominators will be chosen at random and hence cannot be expected to harbor preconceived biases toward the kind of candidates they eventually name. The presumably diverse set of candidates that results from this nomination process is then submitted to election, such that Guicciardini likely expects the most wealthy or notable individuals to have an advantage. Having incorporated both democratic and aristocratic elements into the appointment process through the use of lottery and election up to this point, Guicciardini is ambivalent in the final stage about whether to use the democratic or aristocratic method to make the actual appointments. But once Guicciardini comes to observe how a method that combines lot and election actually works in reality, he becomes much more skeptical of lottery and more enthusiastic about election as the decisive mode of selecting magistrates.

In the *History of Florence*, when Guicciardini discusses Florence's constitutional innovations of 1497–9,[49] he reports that the move from election to lot at the definitive stage of magistrate appointment expanded the effectual pool of possible officeholders from two hundred members of the best families to a much wider, much less "suitable" segment of the citizenry.[50] Taking into account Guicciardini's aristocratic prejudices, we might question whether the newly appointed magistrates really were unworthy.[51] More importantly, the episode suggests that election *used in tandem with lot* – especially when lot serves as the ultimate technique of appointment – can produce much more equitable and less oligarchic effects than election used by itself or as the final means of selection. On the basis of Guicciardini's own account, it appears that when election serves a nominating function in advance of lot as the definitive mode of selection, the electorate is much less biased toward "distinction."

Although a requirement that nominees gain an initial 50 percent vote of approval ensures against the emergence of candidates who would be completely unacceptable to the ottimati,[52] the citizenry assembled in the Council enjoyed the opportunity to vote at the nomination stage for a group of candidates with a wide range of personal qualities, social backgrounds, and political opinions. We may conclude that the option to vote for more than one candidate somewhat neutralizes the impact of qualities such as wealth and notability upon the electorate when citizens know that they are leaving the ultimate "choice" of magistrate to chance, that is, to the outcome of a lottery. In other words, something less than the "aristocratic effect" prevails when, on the one hand, elections produce a slate of candidates wider than, say, two individuals, or, on the other, when they winnow down a large slate to something like half a dozen candidates who will gain office eventually on the basis of lot.

His critical stance in the *History* notwithstanding, Guicciardini's relative openness in the "Discorso," mentioned previously, either to election or to lot as the decisive means by which individuals enter the Signoria, may be explained by his lifelong campaign to establish a proper senate in Florence. Like many Florentine ottimati, Guicciardini attributed the longevity and stability of Venice's "mixed constitution" to the preeminence of the senate over the Doge and the Great Council – that is, of the Venetian constitution's "noble" element over its "kingly" and "popular" components.[53] Once a senate would be established in Florence, Guicciardini proposed to transfer to such a body most of the powers wielded in contemporary practice by the Signoria, the Great Council, and, at that time, the republic's life-tenured chief executive, the Gonfalonier of Justice. In other words, Guicciardini may not mind employing lot to constitute political bodies that he hopes eventually to emasculate. Perhaps not surprisingly, then, lot plays *no* role in determining the composition of his proposed two hundred member senate. More than half of the senate would, in Guicciardini's plan, by-pass the Council's central function of directly or indirectly appointing all magistrates. Although the Great Council would regularly elect 80 citizens to *finite* terms as senators, in Guicciardini's plan as many as 120 former magistrates and ambassadors would immediately assume *lifetime* membership in the senate without a Council vote.[54]

A possible rationale for legitimating such appointments, unstated by Guicciardini, is that the Council had already "approved" or "selected" these individuals when it originally elected them to serve in the Signoria, on other government committees, or as ambassadors. But a more cynical reader might interpret the proposal as doubly oligarchic: the rotating members of the senate are "aristocratically" elected; they are *not* assigned seats through a method incorporating even a small element of sortition, the democratic method of appointment. Moreover, these elected members of the senate are themselves outnumbered, in Guicciardini's scheme, by a grandfathered-in, permanent set of notables. The Great Council would play, however, some limited role in replacing permanent members of the senate once they die or retire, according to Guicciardini's plan. By majority vote, the Great Council would choose one of three replacement candidates who had been scrutinized by the senate and nominated by that body on the basis of an internal two-thirds vote.[55]

In addition, Guicciardini's hypothetical senate plays a decisive role in his recommendations for reforming the appointment of the lifetime Gonfalonier of Justice. The first citizen to hold this office – at the time of Guicciardini's writing, Piero Soderini – had been elected directly by the Great Council in 1502 and proved to be a great disappointment to the ottimati. They hoped that a patrician such as Soderini would help them regain some of the leverage that the "best citizens" had been denied under the post-1494 Savonarolan governo largo. But, as mentioned earlier, Soderini resisted ottimati influence as best he could; he elevated "new men" such as Machiavelli to important posts and ruled in tandem with the Great Council. In Guicciardini's proposal, the ottimati might ensure the appointment of a more friendly chief executive in the future: in the same manner that the senate would replace its own permanent members, it would propose to the Great Council three candidates for Gonfalonier of Justice who received two-thirds of the vote within this "upper house," one of whom the Great Council would elect to the chief magistracy with the most votes above 51 percent.[56] This elucidates one of the ways in which Guicciardini envisioned the establishment of a senate to serve the interest of the ottimati.

In Chapter 7, I abstract away from the details of Florentine constitutional arrangements circa 1494–9, and Guicciardini's proposed improvements of them circa 1512, to formulate a typology of republics that evaluates their prospects for keeping economic elites from dominating political magistracies. I conclude the present section by emphasizing the fact, noted by Guicciardini with considerable consternation, that an element of randomization in the magistrate selection process offsets the elite-enabling bias of elections. The constitutional reforms in 1497 Florence, described earlier in this chapter and analyzed by Guicciardini, suggest that a popular government need not adopt wholesale the general scheme of lottery associated with Athenian democracy in order to minimize the advantages enjoyed by wealthy and notable citizens when it distributes offices.

Let us now review the logic of Machiavelli's revival and endorsement of Rome's class-specific institutions: the organs dominated by wealthy citizens, the senate and consuls, enjoyed great agenda-setting and proactive authority. However, plebeian institutions, such as the tribunes and the popular assemblies, granted common people similar power, and also provided them with negative authority over aristocratic conduct sufficient to channel it in liberty-preserving ways. One might conclude on this basis, especially with the hindsight provided by Western history since Machiavelli's day, that either a more intimate mixing of the two quasi-separate polities *or* that the establishment of a single, sociologically anonymous constitutional framework would only allow the grandi to overwhelm the people in a fairly unchallenged fashion.

In fact, in his commentary on Machiavelli's *Discourses*, Guicciardini criticizes Rome and frowns at Machiavelli's praise of it on precisely such grounds: if only the Roman patricians had allowed the plebs the formal right to stand for offices such as the consulate from the beginning; then the plebeians would have pursued these offices rarely and reluctantly, and they certainly never would have agitated for the creation of their own magistracy, the tribunate.[57] General eligibility for office, according to Guicciardini, would have left the Roman grandi with a virtually uncontested monopoly over all the magistracies and left the patricians free from the meddlesome instigation of plebeian magistrates such as the tribunes. Such a scenario, however, according to Machiavelli, can never facilitate the free way of life; it provides no institutional means by which common citizens can actively contest and contain the oppressive behavior of the wealthy, directly control the actions of magistrates on their own, and immediately influence policy making. In Machiavelli's model, the people arguably require separate deliberative institutions so that they might form their opinions independently of the wealthy and choose officials from among their own ranks. Furthermore, they need popularly accessible means of directly blocking or immediately sanctioning the actions of public magistrates, such as the veto and, as we will see in the next chapter, public accusations and popularly decided political trials.

It cannot be overstated how difficult it is to sell the grandi on the establishment of a tribunate or some functional equivalent thereof. This aristocratic bias against the tribunes is evident in the ranting of Quintus in Cicero's dialogue *On the Laws* and in Montesquieu's interpretation of Roman history; moreover, it is sustained in the thought of the patricians without titles who founded the American Republic.[58] As the history of Italian republics makes plain, common citizens fairly regularly managed to leverage and negotiate for magistrate selection methods mixing sortition and election. Council seats and even whole legislative assemblies reserved exclusively for poorer citizens were not unusual in premodern republics. But a popular magistracy, a quasi-executive office, for which the wealthiest and well-born are as a rule ineligible, is a rare occurrence indeed in the history of republican constitutions. Yet Machiavelli considers such institutions, like his provosts, modeled on the Roman tribunate, indispensable to a free regime. Popular government requires, almost paradoxically, both the participation and loyalty of the grandi *and* the establishment of an institution that they inherently detest.

5

Political Trials and "the Free Way of Life"

> Men are kept better and less ambitious longer through fear of punishment.
>
> Machiavelli, *Discourses*, I.29
>
> In Rome, the people ordinarily wielded authority over the blood of fellow citizens.
>
> Machiavelli, *Discourses*, I.49

Freedom is the sine qua non of popular government. Political actors and political philosophers dating back as far as Pericles and Aristotle convincingly attest to this fact.[1] Yet the freedom so prevalent in *governi larghi* or democracies, ancient and modern, often allows citizens with considerable material resources and the cultural capital of family and personal reputation to enjoy these advantages at the expense of less privileged citizens. Obviously, if "liberty" is to be more than an empty slogan or an ideology permitting haves to oppress have-nots, common citizens must live unmolested *and* unthreatened by fellow citizens of whatever rank.[2] Such liberty is, however, notoriously difficult to achieve and maintain: ordinary citizens intimidated by the prospect of retaliation by those with greater economic, political, or social wherewithal will not readily accuse, indict, or convict abusive and self-aggrandizing members of the privileged classes. How can the common people, in addition to well-intentioned but perhaps vulnerable public officials, confidently take steps that protect genuine freedom for all citizens? Absent political institutions that allow them to do so safely and without disrupting public order, "republican liberty" signifies nothing but the freedom of wolves among lambs.

Machiavelli and Guicciardini, two of history's greatest analysts of republican government and a "free and civic way of life," understood the difficulty and emphasized the necessity of keeping prominent citizens from overstepping their bounds. This chapter analyzes their considerations on criminal proceedings designed to keep privileged citizens and public magistrates accountable for their political conduct – procedures intended to protect the freedom of all citizens in popular governments. Conspiracies plagued the

Florentine Republic (1494–1512) that the young patrician Guicciardini served as ambassador and that the lower-born, if more experienced, Machiavelli served as chancery secretary, diplomatic emissary, and military advisor. On several notable occasions, prominent citizens attempted to establish an oligarchy, a *governo stretto*, or to reinstall the Medici principality in order to diminish drastically or eliminate completely the expanded authority that common citizens enjoyed under the popular government, the *governo largo*, founded by Friar Girolamo Savonarola. Machiavelli and Guicciardini agree that the republic's responses to political crimes failed to deter would-be usurpers or punish active plotters, and both criticize the arbitrariness that sometimes characterized the political trials that the republic in fact managed to conduct.

In this chapter, I analyze Machiavelli's and Guicciardini's proposals for political indictments, trials, and appeals. Guicciardini, who provides extensive details of Florence's experience with potential coups and political trials, places accusations and final appeals firmly in the hands of a few "wise" public officials, thus anticipating the citizen-excluding "impeachment" provisions of most modern republican constitutions. Looking back to the Roman Republic, Machiavelli recommends that popular governments avail themselves of more widely inclusive institutions and of the entire citizenry's judgment when prosecuting political crimes, an approach largely abandoned by modern republics. In my estimation, Machiavelli's prescriptions prove superior to Guicciardini's because they guarantee *both* of the following: (1) wealthy and prominent citizens will not be harassed incessantly or convicted arbitrarily through political prosecutions accessible to common citizens, but (2) such elites will be punished swiftly and surely when they actively engage in conspiracies – especially plots aimed at undermining popular governments and replacing them with naked oligarchies or princely tyrannies. Guicciardini's model, on the contrary, is likely to secure only the first of these results.

Furthermore, while notable scholars emphasize the scapegoat effect of Machiavelli's recommendations for political trials (the discrediting of whistle-blowers through aristocratic smear campaigns or the narrowing of popular attention on a single convicted patrician that leaves the rest of the senatorial class unassailed), my analysis demonstrates that Machiavelli permits and often encourages the prosecution and execution of indeterminate but decidedly plural numbers of privileged citizens intent on subverting republics and usurping popular liberty.

Political Accusations in Machiavelli's Rome

As discussed in Chapter 3, according to Machiavelli, any Roman citizen could publicly accuse magistrates of corruption, treachery, or malfeasance, and could even indict prominent private citizens on more amorphous charges such as wielding excessive political influence. Such an accusation would prompt a hearing in an informal deliberative assembly, a *concione*, or a trial in one of the official voting assemblies (a *comitia* or the *concilium plebis*), where the accused would be fined, exiled, or sentenced to death. As in democratic Athens, the people could punish magistrates and citizens for political plans or proposals, not just for concrete actions.[3] Machiavelli emphasizes that the tribunes of the plebs, given their authority with the people and against the *grandi*, most effectively compelled patrician citizens or public magistrates to account for their behavior in the popular assemblies and to submit their fate to the people's judgment (D I.7).

Machiavelli especially admires the Roman practice of committing the final decision over capital execution in political trials to the judgment of the people. Capital cases were tried before the more oligarchically organized *comitia centuriata* and, eventually, the more popular concilium. It is quite apparent in Machiavelli's primary source, Livy's histories, that capital cases are especially sensitive in republics, such as Rome, with a high level of class conflict: the people are inclined to interpret a death sentence against one of their own as an act of class oppression by the nobility, who monopolize most positions in the government. The people need the opportunity to overturn or reduce such sentences, and in Rome they could do so in a variety of ways. Capital sentences pursued or rendered by consuls, the centuriate assembly, and even, after the fact, by a dictator might be overridden or commuted to exile by invocation of the *provocatio* or "appeal to the people" on the part of the convicted and/or by the decision of the concilium plebis.[4] One of Machiavelli's objectives, as we'll observe, is to convince the *ottimati* that it is in *their* interest to be judged by the whole people, as well.

Recall Machiavelli's arguments in favor of public accusations and popularly judged political trials: he treats them as direct forms of citizen participation, as institutionalized practices that render all citizens, but especially public magistrates and members of prominent families, accountable (D I.7); and he lists them among the best instruments available to the "guardian of freedom," which, in governi larghi, he identifies as the generality of the people (D I.5, D I.7). Machiavelli argues that formal and popularly accessible accusation procedures punish those who deserve it, deter others who might consider committing such offenses in the future, and prevent the escalation of factional violence that too often results from unofficial and arbitrary punishments in such cases (D I.7).

In light of the class rivalry underlying all polities (D I.4), Machiavelli argues that accusations provide a regulatory benefit beyond deterrence and punishment of individual magistrates and ottimati: accusations provide an outlet for the ordinary venting of social "humors" that are generated by class antagonism. A republic will be ruined if the inevitable conflict between the grandi, who above all desire to oppress others, and the people, who above all desire not to be dominated, manifests itself extraordinarily, that is, illegally or extra-institutionally. Machiavelli is adamant that the "alternating humors" of the people and the grandi should be ordered through, among other modes and orders, ordinary laws governing public accusations and political trials (D I.7). This is not to discount the important functions of public accountability that popularly inclusive political accusations and trials serve in a popular government.[5] In mixed republics such as Rome, where wealthy citizens dominated specific institutions such as the senate and the consulship through appointment or election, officials were not automatically inclined to accommodate the interests of the general or poorer portion of the populace. In a context where all citizens aspire to enjoy "the free way of life," this scenario necessitates additional means of ensuring the government's responsiveness and accountability to the common people; public accusation of magistrates is one such means, as is, for instance, the plebeian-specific office of the tribunes, which functioned like an ombudsman for the lower classes.

Moreover, in the context of Italian peninsular republics such as Rome and Florence, the possibility of reappointment after holding office was postponed for fairly long intervals of time; the *divieto* that a magistrate and members of his immediate family had to wait for re-eligibility could last as long as three years. Without the impending threat of failure to be reelected, accusations were a fairly immediate and effective way of holding magistrates to account for their behavior. However, the two accountability devices – immediate eligibility for reelection and popularly inclusive accusations/political trials – need not be mutually exclusive. There is no reason to think that magistrates who enjoy reappointment possibilities within electoral or representative republics would not be made more responsive and accountable by the additional threat of conviction in popularly judged political trials.

Political Trials in Rome versus Florence

As the primary illustration of the utility of citizen accusations and public trials, Machiavelli discusses the first popular judgment against a patrician adversary of the people: the magistrate, senator, and general Coriolanus, who was and remains renowned for his prideful disdain of Rome's plebeians. Recall from Chapter 3 that Coriolanus proposed withholding stores of food during a famine to compel the plebs into forsaking the tribunate (D I.7). Before the people could physically retaliate against him outside the senate, the tribunes intervened, publicly accusing Coriolanus and initiating formal proceedings that required him to stand judgment before the people in assembly.[6] Were it not for this intervention and subsequent trial (that Coriolanus faced in absentia), Machiavelli suggests that the plebs would have killed him immediately, "in a tumult," on the senate steps. The public accusation and promise of a trial before the people helped defuse a potential civil war, as Coriolanus's murder would have set in motion a disastrous chain of events resulting in excessively bloody class conflict (D I.7). Machiavelli argues that when ambitious and powerful citizens are "crushed ordinarily" – that is, when they are legally convicted and punished by "public forces and orders" rather than assassinated on the street or assaulted in their homes – then vengeance-seeking friends and families will rarely enlist private or foreign forces, always anathema to a "free way of life," to sustain the disputes indefinitely (D I.7).

Machiavelli laments that, unlike Rome, his own republic of Florence afforded "the multitude" no way to "vent its animus ordinarily" against an individual (D I.7); in other words, the people could not formally accuse, pass judgment on, and punish prominent citizens. In Florence, such matters were handled by small committees, such as the Eight of Ward, which dealt with public safety, or the *Signoria*, the republic's chief executive board. And while citizens convicted of political crimes in these small councils enjoyed the legal right of appeal to the entire citizenry collected in the Great Council, observance of this provision, as we will see, was inconsistent. Machiavelli contrasts Florence with Rome to illustrate the point that the deciding and appellate bodies in political cases must be large and diverse, even so large as to encompass the whole populace (D I.7). The Romans, Machiavelli reports approvingly, ordinarily placed "the authority to shed fellow citizens's blood" in the hands of the people gathered in assembly (D I.49).

Because small trial and appellate bodies are susceptible to intimidation, corruption, or self-interested behavior (D I.49), Machiavelli suggests that committees such as the Eight, usually comprised of ottimati, are less useful to republics than larger assemblies, such as Florence's Great Council (which contained 3,400 of Florence's citizens), or than the people "ordinarily" gathered, that is, formally assembled as a whole (D I.49). In this context, Machiavelli makes a declaration perhaps emblematic of his theory of popular government overall: such bodies are ineffective because "the few always behave in the mode of the few" (D I.7). Small councils either voice the interests of the most influential citizens or prove too cowardly or vulnerable to undertake punitive measures against the latter. Later, repeating these criticisms of the Eight in Florence, Machiavelli asserts that "the few were always ministers of the few and the most powerful" (D I.49). As a result, Florence simply could not render fair and objective judgments in political cases.

Machiavelli points out that even an aristocratic republic such as Venice, the republican paragon for ottimati in Machiavelli's audience,[7] avails itself of larger bodies to "hold powerful men in check" (D I.49). Even the oligarchic Venetians know, as Machiavelli observes, that small councils alone "might not be enough to punish the powerful, although they had the authority for it" (D I.49). Due to their numbers and anonymity, individual members of large bodies of judgment, most effectively bodies such as Rome's vast assemblies, needn't fear retribution from offended friends and partisans of convicted individuals.

The case of Francesco Valori exemplifies, for Machiavelli, the inadequacy of Florentine arrangements. After the Medici's expulsion and the republic's reestablishment, Machiavelli reports that Valori rose to the rank of something "like a prince of the city" (D I.7). Consequently, Valori aroused sufficient suspicion of his designs and envy of his stature that competing sects of partisans formed to oppose or to support him. Machiavelli asserts that Valori "had no fear except of extraordinary modes," meaning that the ordinary committees charged with checking overweening citizens, the Eight and the Signoria, were too much under Valori's sway to move against him or to allow his opponents to do so (D I.7). Without legal means by which the people could ordinarily "vent their animus" against Valori and judge the extent to which he posed a genuine threat to "a civil way of life," Francesco's opponents took up private arms (D I.7). As usually happens with extraordinary, as opposed to ordinary, measures, Machiavelli recounts that not just Valori, but many others, particularly "nobles," were harmed in the ensuing sectarian violence (D I.7). Had Valori been formally charged by his enemies and officially judged by the people, only he, if convicted, would have suffered harm.

Machiavelli uses a Florentine example even closer to his heart, that of his patron, Gonfalonier Piero Soderini, (a) to reiterate the necessity of political trials before "very many judges," (b) to emphasize the perniciousness of enlisting foreign powers to settle internal political scores, and (c) to accentuate the distinction between accusations and calumnies (D I.8). Machiavelli insists that when Soderini, the republic's chief executive for life, was suspected of exhibiting excessive ambition and abusing his power, his detractors should have been able to level charges to a body larger than the Eight, that is, to a council that neither Soderini nor his adversaries could decisively influence or control (D I.7). Machiavelli insists that if the people of Florence themselves had been able to judge Soderini, either he would have been punished for inappropriate conduct or his enemies would have been sanctioned for pressing false charges, for hurling calumnies.

In either case, Machiavelli insists, the Gonfalonier's adversaries would not have summoned the Spanish army in 1512, an event that led to the ouster of Soderini, the restoration of the Medici principate, and the demise of the republic – not to mention the sacking and torture of Machiavelli and the termination of his political career. There is, for Machiavelli, an inverse relationship between the availability of appeal to a large and diverse domestic body and the likelihood of appeal to an arbitrating foreign power. Unlike Florence's social antagonists, who enjoyed recourse to only deeply imperfect institutions, Machiavelli observes that neither the senate nor the plebs in Rome, despite the considerable animosity between them, ever availed themselves of foreign forces (D I.7).

Calumnies and the People as "Very Many Judges"

Machiavelli insists that republics need not worry that accusations will be made casually so long as accusers fear being indicted themselves should their charges be exposed as frivolous. Again, Machiavelli distinguishes accusations, corroborated by facts and witnesses and directed to legal authorities, from calumnies, anonymous and unsubstantiated charges that are whispered in piazzas, loggias, and back rooms (D I.8). While accusations deter, punish, and quell social discord, calumnies encourage bad behavior, obscure the identity of wrongdoers, distract citizens and magistrates from the real issues at hand, and generally exacerbate partisan strife. Machiavelli suggests that a republic may discourage calumnies in the following way: if the entire citizenry decides that an accusation

is false, the calumniator should face a punishment similar to that which threatened the original accused. In Soderini's case, if the Great Council had been
the final arbiter of accusations and calumnies, his adversaries would not have
acted against him casually lest the people punish *them* for exhibiting excessive
ambition.

It should be noted that both Guicciardini and Machiavelli knew firsthand
the abusive ends to which excessive, spurious, and partisanly motivated denunciations could be put. Throughout his service to the republic, Machiavelli was
the constant target of anonymous charges, almost invariably originating with
Sodernini's adversaries among the ottimati, charges aimed at removing the
Gonfalonier's "puppet" *(mannerino)* from secretarial, military, or diplomatic
posts or inhibiting him from discharging his responsibilities in them.[8] Machiavelli was denounced on various occasions as the descendant of a bastard, for
failing to pay debts and taxes, and for committing sodomy with a mistress.[9]
To Machiavelli's greatest disappointment, in response to a patrician smear
campaign, Soderini withdrew support for his trusted aid's appointment as
ambassador to the German Emperor.[10] The ottimati charged that Machiavelli
was unworthy of the office and insisted that his young noble friend, Francesco
Vettori, be appointed and sent along instead. As for Guicciardini, when the
Florentine Republic was restored after fifteen years of Medici reascendance
in 1527, he was called to account for his administrative, ambassadorial, and
military service to the tyrants.[11] The republican authorities accused him of
corruption and treason, fining and exiling him, arguably with excessive zeal.
Guicciardini even gestured to the possibility that this popular government,
to his mind, run amok would unjustly condemn him to death, as other such
regimes had executed Socrates and Bernardo del Nero (who is discussed in
greater detail later in this chapter).

Guicciardini's experience seems to confirm a steadfast patrician prejudice
against popularly accessible accusations and citizenwide juries. Both Guicciardini and Machiavelli recognize that ottimati prefer to be tried before and offer
appeals to small bodies of their peers rather than before larger ones comprised
of the people whom they consider "ignorant" and "envious."[12] Machiavelli's
declared audience of the *Discourses*, the young Florentine ottimati Cosimo
Rucellai and Zanobi Buondelmonti, would no doubt share such a view. In
order to persuade persons of that class and disposition, Machiavelli uses the
famous Roman case of Manlius Capitolinus to suggest that the people can
judge patricians objectively even when the people themselves are a party to the
controversy at hand (D I.8).

Intensely jealous of the glory that Furius Camillus gained after defeating the
Gauls, and resentful of the senate's refusal to honor him as much as it had
honored Camillus, Manlius spread rumors to foment popular unrest against
the senate: he claimed that the senate was hoarding war booty to exacerbate the
plebs' economic burdens (D I.8). The senate appointed a dictator to confront
Manlius and quell the imminent popular insurrection. When Manlius could not
substantiate his claim during public interrogation by the dictator, the plebeians

forsook their antipatrician anger and abandoned their support of Manlius, their erstwhile champion. This example suggests that the people can indeed focus on the substantive facts of a political trial rather than adhere in a partisan fashion to their own cause and to their own advocates. The Manlius episode also demonstrates that while calumnies can serve demagogues who cynically and illegitimately exploit the people's prejudices against the grandi, accusations always serve the republic as a whole. Had Manlius's charges, from the very beginning, been made publicly, through official channels and supported by witnesses, the senate would not have been compelled to resort to the ultimate measure, the appointment of a dictator, to address them.

As mentioned briefly in Chapter 3, Machiavelli also refers to the more recent Florentine example of Giovanni Guicciardini, an ancestor of Francesco, to emphasize this point further (D I.8). A military commissioner for the republic, the earlier Guicciardini was calumniated among the people to the effect that he had accepted a bribe from the Lucchese not to attack their city. If Guicciardini could have directly appealed to the people formally collected in assembly, rather than to a foreign arbitrator such as the People's Captain, Machiavelli argues that the Florentine nobles would not have taken up his cause so fanatically – a development that furthered the collapse of that republic (D I.8). In the *Florentine Histories*, Machiavelli portrays this as an instance where the Medici smeared someone so as to accelerate their rise to power. At first, Machiavelli suggests that the people *spontaneously* blamed Guicciardini for a failed policy that was their own foolhardy initiative, but he then reveals that the Medici hatched the plan to take Lucca, only to blame Giovanni for it via rumors upon the plan's collapse. The consolidation of patrician support behind Guicciardini precipitates the conflict with the Medici from which Cosimo emerged as first citizen of the republic, "father of the city" and, effectively, prince.[13] A formal public hearing of the issue would have prevented or at least postponed Medici ascendance and the collapse of the Albizzean republic.

The Giovanni Guicciardini episode in the *Discourses* suggests that despite class animosity, the general public will give a noble (a) a fairer hearing within the formal procedures of a political trial than in the murky dens and alleyways that echo calumnies, and (b) a fairer hearing than will a magistrate, even one acting in the name of the people, and, especially, an imported foreigner. Machiavelli consistently criticizes the Florentine Republic for being insufficiently equipped to accommodate civic necessities, using it as the constant foil for Rome's greatness in this and other regards: Florentine politics is too susceptible to calumnies, does not facilitate popular judgment of accusations, and too frequently invites foreign powers to settle domestic disputes.

For Machiavelli, the imperative of efficiency is no argument for recourse to small, elite-dominated bodies or foreign powers in lieu of public accusations and popular political trials. In Rome, if the hearing of accusations or capital appeals proved to be too slow for especially pressing cases, the consuls and senate appointed a dictator to handle the matter but never enlisted a foreigner.[14] For Machiavelli, time constraints may be factored into the initiation of

popularly inclusive political trials: the latter need not be adhered to so firmly as
to risk the general security of the republic, but neither should expediency pose
as a pretext for unilateral foreign intervention.[15] Machiavelli relentlessly criticizes earlier Florentine republics for putting political prosecutions and appeals
in the hands of purportedly objective foreigners (e.g., the *Podestà*, the People's
Capitano, the pope, the king of France). In reality, like small committees comprised of elites, foreigners are too easily influenced and corrupted by particular
factions within the city or prone to act in their own interests (D I.49).

Along with the effort to make ottimati more amenable to popular judgments in political cases, Machiavelli attempts to show them that the people's
own magistrates, the tribunes, will not simply prosecute the patricians incessantly on behalf of their plebeian constituency. In an instance where the people
perhaps overreacted against the patricians after Appius and the Decemvirate
had quashed popular liberty and established a temporary tyranny in Rome,
the tribunes imposed a one-year moratorium on accusations against the grandi
(D I.45). In other words, Machiavelli suggests that the ottimati need fear neither
a structural disadvantage in political trials where the people are judges nor perpetual persecution through accusations by plebeian magistrates. Nevertheless,
grandi will have to think twice about oppressing the people and threatening
their liberty in regimes where such institutions do in fact exist.

Post–eighteenth-century framers of republican constitutions dispense with
the practice of accusations because they believe it tends toward demagogic or
factional excesses. Obstructionist interests, they supposed, could level accusations at strategic moments to prevent particular policies from taking shape or
being enforced for the benefit of the general public. Moreover, charges that
may never be definitively proven as either accusations or calumnies might still
serve to smear or damage a public official, especially if the person(s) dissem-
inating disparaging information cannot be identified and called to account.
Machiavelli suggests that severely punishing those who level false charges and
allowing the citizenry as a whole to decide the veracity of charges strongly discourage but, of course, cannot completely eliminate such behavior. In fact, in a
chapter before those devoted to accusations and calumnies, Machiavelli treats
an instance where the Roman nobles undermine reform efforts conducted on
behalf of the Roman people by a plebeian dictator, Marcus Menenius, and
his plebeian master of horse, Marcus Fulvius (D I.5). The senate so effectively
smears the integrity of the dictator that he resigns his office, even though he is
exonerated of corruption by trial in a popular assembly.[16]

Practical Prescriptions for Reforming Political Trials in Florence

Both Machiavelli and Guicciardini were afforded opportunities to put their
reflections on political trials into practice while composing reform proposals
for the constitution of Florence. Guicciardini is of the same mind as Machiavelli
regarding the difficulty of punishing influential citizens who have committed
political crimes: "When some noble or powerful man is guilty, the magistrates

often lack the courage to punish him, knowing that someday they or their interests might be in the hands of the brothers or relatives of the accused. At times they even have reason to fear violence against their person."[17] But Guicciardini's prescriptions for addressing this problem are very different from Machiavelli's.

We observed in the last chapter that Guicciardini, in his "*Discorso* on Bringing Order to Popular Government," composed just before the collapse of the 1494–1512 republic, establishes a powerful senate as the centerpiece of his constitutional proposal. Guicciardini assigns to this proposed senate the task of trying the republic's chief executive should he be indicted of a crime: a member of the Signoria – *not* just any citizen at large, as in Machiavelli's neo-Roman recommendations – could denounce the Gonfalonier to the senate and request a particular punishment, including censure, fine, removal, and even death. But that particular prior could launch only one accusation per term in the Signoria, to prevent him from becoming a persistent nuisance to the chief magistrate. A two-thirds vote in the senate would decide the Gonfalonier's guilt or innocence and the appropriateness of the proposed penalty.[18] Notably, Guicciardini's proposal affords the Florentine citizenry assembled in the Great Council no role in the Gonfalonier's trial, conviction, or acquittal.

Guicciardini proposes an ad hoc tribunal, or *quarantìa*, as the trial forum for other citizens who are accused of political crimes. Any citizen may initiate such a procedure with an accusation. Once someone accuses a private citizen or public magistrate, either anonymously or with personal attribution, to one of the other magistrates, the latter must call a quarantìa before which the accused or his or her proxy must appear. At this point, the accuser must come forward as a witness, and the tribunal must provide a written decision within one month.[19] If the sentence is death, an appeal is handled in the same way as the Gonfalonier's trial before the senate, mentioned previously – but, again, the appeal is *not* directed to the republic's most populous assembly, the Great Council. Therefore, in Guicciardini's constitutional scheme, common citizens have the right to accuse magistrates below the Gonfalonier of Justice and to denounce other citizens, but *not* the right to serve en masse as the body of judgment or to participate in any formal appellate capacity. For lesser punishments, Guicciardini suggests that some smaller portion of the senate, thirty to fifty senators selected by lot, decide the appeal by a two-thirds vote.[20]

Guicciardini concurs with Machiavelli's criticisms of the republic's small committees and their failure to punish prominent men for misbehavior: "One can count a thousand who have been left unpunished by the courts, or punished lightly, for each one who was punished excessively."[21] But Guicciardini insists that a judgment rendered by the citizenry collected in Florence's Great Council is no solution to the problem of excessively light or severe sentences: "A remedy, superfluous though it may be, against this last danger would be to allow appeals to be brought before the Council for sentences in political matters brought against citizens. But this does not please me, because these things must be determined with gravity and mature judgment."[22] Expressing a view diametrically opposed to Machiavelli's, Guicciardini remarks that the Great Council is not "an adequate judge" of appeals because the "naturally suspicious people" are too "full of ignorance and animosity toward great and excellent men."[23] Machiavelli would strictly qualify this assessment by asserting that popular animosity will not lead to the conviction of men who can prove that they have not been engaged in oligarchic or autocratic plots against the people's liberty and the republic's security. But when these "great and excellent men" are, in fact, engaged in such machinations, they will be prosecuted, tried, and executed by and before the people, perhaps with great animosity but certainly not on the basis of "ignorance."

Moreover, Guicciardini thinks that it is too "difficult to obtain acquittals" in the Great Council, which served, at Savonarola's insistence and with Machiavelli's approval (D I.45), as the appellate forum for capital cases in the post-1494 republic: the required two-thirds majority vote and the prestige of convictions rendered by the Signoria and backed by the Gonfalonier, in Guicciardini's estimation, pose an unreasonably high threshold for condemned citizens to overcome.[24] Thus, as a reflection of Guicciardini's general distrust of the people under almost any circumstance (perhaps influenced by his forbearer Giovanni's experience with calumnies, recounted by Machiavelli and discussed earlier), and as a reaction to the inefficacy of the "right" of appeal in his own day, Guicciardini's reforms place the appeals process for all political crimes under the control of a patrician-dominated council only slightly larger than the small body that rendered the initial judgment. Guicciardini hopes that such reforms will lead to the punishment of "crimes committed in office," and will "deter evil men from grasping for private or public goods" without, at the same time, unnecessarily or unjustly constraining the behavior of the best citizens whose ambition, he insists, is useful to a republic.[25]

Guicciardini's proposals obviously stand in marked contrast to Machiavelli's emphasis on broadly public accusations and popularly judged political trials and appeals. However, in a departure from his arguments in his *Discourses*, in the "Discursus on Florentine Affairs" Machiavelli makes serious concessions toward Guicciardini's position and to traditional Florentine practices (DF 733–45). Responding to a general solicitation from Medici prelates for constitutional proposals aimed at converting Florence from a principality back to a republic, Machiavelli is noticeably mindful of the vulnerability that the Medici's "friends" among the ottimati would feel toward a revived popular government (DF 735).[26] If Machiavelli has any hope of seeing his republican plan adopted, he must assure Pope Leo that the institutions he proposes guarantee "his *amici*'s security" (DF 737). Not surprisingly, then, in this context Machiavelli treats the issues of public accusation, political trials, and popular appeals with great sensitivity. Were these to fall immediately into popular hands amid the general Florentine dissatisfaction with the Medici circa 1525, one can imagine that Leo and his amici would be the first targets of a prosecutorially re-empowered Florentine people. After all, in the *Discourses*, Machiavelli observes how intensely the people seek vengeance against the former agents of their servility (D I.16);

and in *The Prince*, he emphasizes the animosity expressed by republics toward their former oppressors: "in republics there is more vitality, greater hatred, and more desire for vengeance, which will never permit them to allow the memory of their former liberty to rest" (P 5).

Therefore, Machiavelli's proposal leaves in place the Medici principality's small collegial bodies, the Eight of Defense and the *balìa*, that serve as the fora for judging public offenses – small councils very similar to the committees that, in the *Discourses*, Machiavelli criticizes for inefficacious punishment of political criminals. While he still insists on a "broad" appellate body, the one he proposes in the "Discursus" does *not* contain the "very many judges" seated in the Great Council he would like to see reopened (scaled down, in this context, from the original 3,400 to between 600 or 1,000 citizens). Rather, Machiavelli proposes a court drawn from, on the one hand, the narrow list of citizens he makes eligible for the Signoria, and, on the other, the members of the best families and the richest guilds seated in his proposed senate, the Council of the Select; that is, approximately 264 of the city's most prominent citizens would serve as the jury pool that would ultimately judge political offenses (DF 743). With Pope Leo's permission, convictions by the Eight or the *balìa* can be appealed to this Court of Appeals, comprised of thirty names drawn by lot from the 264 – a far cry, to be sure, from the *populus Romanus* collected as appellate judges in their assemblies. But, as we observed in the last chapter, Machiavelli raises the possibility and even implies the probability that the reestablished Great Council will recover most of its former political prerogatives over time and, in fact, add others (DF 742, 744). One would expect the judgment and punishment of those who undertake, in Machiavelli's words, "actions that are not good" to fall into this category (DF 742).

Coriolanus, Manlius, and the Necessity of Capital Punishment

As we observed both earlier in this chapter and previously in Chapter 3, Machiavelli sets out his basic ideas on indictments and political trials in the early chapters of the *Discourses* devoted to accusations and calumnies (D I.7–8): he insists that prominent citizens ought to be crushed when they threaten a republic's civil or free way of life. They should be punished by legal rather than extralegal means because the latter only perpetuate extraordinary acts of violence that harm many more individuals than just the guilty parties. Moreover, extralegal punishments encourage the families and friends of harmed citizens to invite foreign powers to invade the republic, inevitably ruining it. The legal bodies assigned the function of deciding political accusations should be larger than Florence's executive committees; if possible, they should be as large as the Roman assemblies of all the plebeians (the concilium) or of the entire citizenry (the comitia centuriata). Accusations must be supported by evidence; if the latter proves unconvincing to the people, then the accuser will be deemed a calumniator, who must then suffer a punishment as harsh as the one looming over the person they recently accused.

But each of the cases discussed in these chapters (Coriolanus, Manlius, Valori, and Soderini) is more complicated than Machiavelli initially indicates. As he elaborates at later junctures of the *Discourses*, each case suggests much more about the proper functioning of accusations and political trials within a popular government.

One of the lessons that Machiavelli's young patrician audience might have learned from the Coriolanus episode in I.7 is that plebeian-specific accusation procedures (administered through the tribunes) and popularly inclusive political trials might actually save their lives. After all, Coriolanus would have been killed by the angry people whom he was scheming to oppress if not for these institutions. But matters are not that simple. Even if Machiavelli generally discusses the possibility of "execution" in the vicinity of the Coriolanus example, his last word on the proud senator in this chapter conveys only that he was "summoned" to appear before the people. Later, Machiavelli affirms that Coriolanus actually fled Rome (D I.29). Livy reports what is well known: Coriolanus returned from exile with an enemy army that, but for the intercessions of his mother, wife, and children, would have destroyed Rome.[27] This puts a different twist on Machiavelli's claim that a republic must fear that an offended party, either the convicted himself or his friends or relatives, will enlist foreign forces – the worst of all possible outcomes, according to Machiavelli, for a republic.

The problem posed by exiles who return to threaten a regime seems to imply that offenders such as Coriolanus should be executed rather than exiled or permitted to flee. Indeed, Machiavelli reinforces this intimation when he discusses Cosimo de' Medici's return from exile, a return that ended a republic and inaugurated a principality: the mistake committed by his opponents was not necessarily moving against him, but rather expelling instead of eliminating him in the first place (D I.33). These are the first indications that, Machiavelli's aristocratic dedicatees and their prejudices notwithstanding, his ultimate objective concerning political trials may not be, first and foremost, the preservation of patrician lives, but, in certain instances, quite the contrary.

Death, after all, is the only appropriate reward for usurpers of liberty, the most powerful deterrent to those with an unquenchable appetite to dominate, and the best insurance against repeat offenses by the previously convicted. Machiavelli asserts that, at base, usurpers of the law are always motivated by envy (D III.30). Manlius envied Camillus's public triumphs; Coriolanus envied the plebeian's new, exclusive magistracy, the tribunate; and, as Machiavelli suggests, Brutus's sons, who sought to overthrow the fledgling Roman Republic, envied the freedom enjoyed by the people after the expulsion of the Tarquin kings (D I.16). All these "possessions" acquired by others appear to young nobles as instruments of their own servitude (D I.16). According to Machiavelli, such envy can be confronted successfully only with lethal force: "To conquer this envy, there is no remedy other than the death of those who have it" (D III.30); and further, "there is no remedy [for usurpation] more powerful, nor more valid, more secure, and more necessary, than to kill the sons of Brutus" (D I.16).[28] A new regime, especially, Machiavelli avers, will benefit from a political trial that concludes with the "memorable execution" of usurpers, and in the case of a "newly emerged" republic or a "free state," this means the execution of conspirators against the people's liberty.

Prominent interpreters take Machiavelli's early chapters on accusations to be the summation of his theory on political trials, and conclude on this basis that Machiavelli hopes to preserve as many noble lives as possible.[29] Yet, if one takes into account Machiavelli's discussion of political trials later in the work, it becomes clear that Machiavelli advocates the execution of conspirators plural, not singular; conspirators whom Machiavelli represents allegorically as the "sons of Brutus" (D III.3). Ultimately, Machiavelli is neither reluctant to witness members of the grandi executed, nor is he determined to keep the number of executed patricians to one individual scapegoat in the hopes of preserving the authority of the senatorial class as a whole. While he reserves the option of wiping out the ottimati as a class for only the direst circumstances, Machiavelli does leave open the possibility of executing a large number of them if this will serve the purpose of deterring bad behavior among this class's survivors for some significant length of time. It is in this context that one should read Machiavelli's declaration: "Men are kept better and less ambitious longer through fear of punishment" (D I.29).

Perhaps to prevent scaring off his young patrician audience, Machiavelli, in his early chapters on accusations, calumnies, and political trials, neither trumpets the necessity of executing prominent citizens convicted of political crimes nor reveals how many such executions may be, in fact, necessary to protect public liberty. For instance, he concludes the chapter on calumnies by mentioning that Manlius Capitolinus was merely imprisoned by the dictator who exposed him as a fraud (D I.8). Only later does he explain how Manlius, after his conviction by the people, "was without any respect for his merits thrown headlong from the Capitol that before, with so much glory for himself, he had saved" (D I.24). In light of his audience, Machiavelli initially underplays the necessity of lethal violence directed toward patricians and, in fact, early on invokes such examples only as negative outcomes. Recall how Machiavelli makes the case for public accusations and popularly inclusive political trials by emphasizing, absent such institutions, how many other "nobles" were killed in the frenzy surrounding Valori's murder (D I.7). However, the need to kill the usurpers of freedom – perhaps numerous "sons of Brutus" – requires a much more extensive argument in favor of popularly judged political trials and appeals than Machiavelli proffered in the early chapters of the *Discourses*'s first book.

We observed in Chapter 3 how Machiavelli recapitulates traditional arguments against the inconstancy of the people's opinions: "the multitude is often observed to have condemned someone to death, and then wept for the same and greatly desired him, as the Roman people did for Manlius Capitolinus" (D I.58). As a rejoinder, Machiavelli insists that peoples are no more inconstant than princes; in fact, "a multitude regulated by laws" is perhaps the wisest judge of all, one less prone than others to either abject servility or overbearing arrogance (D I.58). For Machiavelli, the fact that the Roman people shed tears for Manlius after it had condemned him to death is not a sign of inconstancy but merely an indication of its astute judgment of a valiant warrior who had helped to save the city from the Gauls and a political leader who had addressed their economic plight, even if he did so excessively in the end: "If the Roman people desired Manlius Capitolinus after he was dead, it is no marvel; for it desired his virtues, which had been such that the memory of them brought compassion to everyone" (D I.58). Machiavelli does not wish the following to escape the notice of ottimati: the people condemned a noble with so much "virtue of spirit and body," even though he favored them, because they recognized that he was consumed with an "ugly greed for rule" (D III.8), which is the natural outgrowth of the humor to oppress, more generally.

But the ottimati should not be displeased that the people decided against such a man, even if he originated from patrician stock, because he posed a threat to the senatorial order as well. The people can serve as defenders of the latter when they act to preserve the liberty of the republic as a whole, despite the people's love for a champion and their animosity toward the patricians: "The people of Rome, very desirous of its own utility and a lover of things that went against the nobility, did many favors to Manlius. Nonetheless, as the tribunes summoned him and delivered his case to the judgment of the people, *formerly his defender but now become his judge*, they, without any respect, condemned him to death" (D III.8, emphasis added). The political status quo offers benefits, most notably liberty, that can be enjoyed by the people and the patricians, the senate and the tribunes alike, benefits that the people will defend when empowered as ultimate judge – so long as the patricians do not upset mutually beneficial conditions by attempting to satisfy their humor to oppress too gratuitously.

Indeed, as discussed before, one enduring aspect of republican government that is problematic for political accountability but reassuring for ottimati who subject themselves to the judgment of the people is deference: the people do not generally fear or suspect prominent citizens individually, even if they hate the grandi as a class (D I.47). Rather, the people tend to express gratitude to such persons for their service to the republic and are inclined to reward them for it with honors and offices (D I.29, D III.34). For this reason, political trials that actually enlist the entire people's judgment will rarely if ever execute as many citizens as do Sullan proscriptions, Stalinist purges, or Robespierrian terror campaigns. Coriolanus and, more problematically, Appius Claudius (D I.40–2) represent exceptional cases: patricians whose arrogance and abusive behavior toward the people are so egregious as to arouse especially intense popular ire. In the normal course of events, most grandi attempt to satisfy their oppressive humor against the people less extravagantly than did these individuals. However, political trials where the patricians, individually or in groups, are frequently indicted for corruption and usurpation, and where the whole citizenry is empowered as a "hangman's jury," may constantly serve to remind the people of the grandi's oppressive appetite. Such trials can bring to light on a regular basis conduct that the grandi prefer to keep hidden, and if these trials do not always deter them from engaging in such behavior, they will at least punish them for doing so.

Valori, Savonarola, and the Cost of Unjust or Botched Political Trials

Machiavelli's account of Francesco Valori's fate in the chapter on accusations (D I.7) barely scratches the surface of facts surrounding this case and its implications for political trials and republican liberty. Here I'll enlist Guicciardini's *History of Florence* to supply details of the circumstances pertinent to Valori's fall, highlighting the fact that his political fortunes were tied to those of Savonarola and that he flubbed the opportunity to make use of popular support against the Florentine ottimati. Again, when Guicciardini was writing, appeals of death sentences for political crimes were directed to the Great Council in its entirety.[30] After the Medici were expelled in 1494, as Savonarola guided the reestablishment of the Florentine Republic, he insisted on two constitutional features that aroused fierce opposition from the ottimati. Firstly, he instituted as the focal point of the republic a Great Council containing virtually all of Florence's citizens, nearly 3,400 – an assembly that passed the laws and appointed magistrates. Secondly, he insisted that the Great Council, via a two-thirds vote, be given the authority to commute death sentences for political crimes.[31] As Machiavelli describes it, Savonarola "had a law made so that one could appeal to the people from sentences pronounced by the Eight and the Signoria in state cases" (D I.45). Valori, although descended from an old, prominent, and wealthy Florentine family, became the leader of Savonarola's populist party, a defender of the Great Council and an antagonist of the most oligarchically and autocratically inclined ottimati.[32] The latter included important members of the following revered families: the Capponi, Nerli, Martelli, Pazzi, Vespucci, Strozzi, Ridolfi, Tornabuoni, Pucci, Cambi, and Rucellai.[33]

In an infamous case discussed by both Guicciardini and Machiavelli, five of these anti-Savonarolan ottimati were condemned to death in 1497 for planning to overthrow the republic and reinstall the Medici (D I.7, D I.45).[34] The Savonarolans denied them the opportunity for an appeal before the Great Council and summarily executed the conspirators. On the one hand, Machiavelli emphasizes Savonarola's failure to insist that they be allowed a popular appeal because their interests were opposed to his. On the other hand, Guicciardini explains at length how Savonarola's main ally, Valori, under the pretext of state security, blocked the appeal because of an intense personal-political rivalry with one of the convicted. Of the "Medici Five," Bernardo del Nero might have been spared by the Council: Bernardo, a popular and respected citizen who rose from low birth to wealth and political prominence through Medici patronage and his own considerable talents, merely knew of the plot while he served as Gonfalonier (not yet a lifetime office), but, despite his own antipathy toward the governo largo, did not actively participate in the proposed coup.[35] Guicciardini argues that Valori recognized in del Nero the only rival to his authority among the aristocratic faction, and rather than risk a popular commutation of his death sentence, even if the people upheld the convictions of the other Mediceans, Valori demanded the immediate execution of all five.[36]

Shortly thereafter, in retaliation, a mob comprised of the dead Mediceans' relatives (especially the Pitti, Ridolfi, and Tornabuoni families) and well-armed young nobles murdered Valori and his wife, among others, with considerable popular support. During the assault, Valori requested safe passage to the Palazzo della Signoria and the observance of due legal procedures, but he was stabbed to death en route to his hearing.[37] For his part, Machiavelli suggests that the denial of the Medici Five's appeal eroded Savonarola's own domestic support among the people and led to his demise (D I.45). Savonarola did not speak out on behalf of the law that he authored and fought for – a law that empowered the people – simply because such non-observance benefited his party, and thus no one came to his defense when he was arrested and tortured by the ottimati and executed at the instigation of his longtime antagonist, Pope Alexander VI.

When discussing this case, Machiavelli speaks, just as he did in the chapters on accusation and calumny, in strict procedural terms: "If the appeal was useful it ought to have been observed; if it was not useful, [Savonarola] ought not to have had it passed" (D I.45). But in what sense is Machiavelli a strict proceduralist in this context? Early in Book I, Machiavelli appears to be nonpartisanly objective when discussing Florentine examples and ancient Roman episodes. Machiavelli seems to care only that political trials convict the guilty, punish false accusers, and maintain public order, no matter who the players are, whether an overweening senator or a plebeian champion, or whatever their ideological sympathies. But this nonpartisan façade begins to fade as Machiavelli discusses these cases in greater depth later in the *Discourses*. After all, the enemies of Savonarola and Valori, especially the Salviati, Ridolfi, and Rucellai families, would before long be the enemies of Soderini and Machiavelli during their service to the very same republic. Even members of the Valori and Buondelmonti families, who formerly had been staunch Medici opponents, began to favor the return of the tyrants rather than endure the governo largo, to their minds, dominated by class traitor Soderini, "new men" such as Machiavelli, and the unworthy rabble collected in the Great Council.[38] Thus, a certain tension is palpable in Machiavelli's narrative and analysis of these cases. Does Machiavelli admonish Savonarola and Valori for behaving hypocritically over the appeal of the Medici Five, or for behaving imprudently, in fact, stupidly?

To be sure, there are many respects in which Savonarola's and Machiavelli's politics do not coincide, especially regarding religion, particularly the role of the Christian Church in the affairs of Italy. From this standpoint, well represented in the scholarly literature, it seems obvious that the split of spiritual and temporal power between Savonarola and Valori is not conducive to the elimination of the enemies of the Florentine governo largo. Savonarola, after all, was not free to speak out on the law of appeal or instruct his supporters how to behave because he was under papal interdict at the time and could not preach publicly (D III.30). And, in the end, Valori needed more legitimacy than could be provided by the Friar's ultimately ephemeral religious charisma. Machiavelli must be alluding to this deficiency when he remarks that Valori was only "like" a prince of the republic (D I.7): he could not successfully and safely eliminate a rival such as del Nero, and he depended too much on Savonarola, who himself relied too much on religious authority provided ultimately by Rome. But there are other important respects in which Soderini and Machiavelli are Valori's and Savonarola's heirs in the post-1494 republic. Specifically, like their predecessors, they uphold the authority of the Great Council, struggle with Medicean conspiracies, and try to maintain the Gonfalonier as the "prince of the city" without converting Florence into an actual principality. I take this up further in the next section, but would like to establish some preliminary lines of analysis here.

When Machiavelli discusses usurpers of new laws, he declares that an individual becomes "glorious without scandal" when he can eliminate such usurpers "ordinarily," that is, legally (D III.30). He also adds that if such a figure is not sufficiently fortunate to have usurpers of their new orders eliminated "ordinarily," they must nevertheless resort to "anything," presumably extraordinary action, which will help to dispose of them successfully. Machiavelli elevates Moses as the chief example of this approach and mentions in the same context the unsuccessful examples of Savonarola and Soderini. The latter two, he claims, "knew this necessity very well," but could not carry it out as did Moses (D III. 30). Savonarola, as a cleric, had even less "authority" to eliminate usurpers than a magistrate or even a private citizen would have had, and, presumably, due to his excommunication and the papal ban on his preaching, he could not make clear to his followers, several of whom did in fact possess the authority of magistrates, exactly what needed to be done (D III.30).

But exactly what kind of action that eliminates usurpers is Machiavelli talking about here? In his discourses on accusations and calumnies, didn't Machiavelli insist that usurpers of a republic's state and liberty must be handled ordinarily, legally, lest disaster ensue for all persons involved and the regime itself? Machiavelli denounces arbitrary mob violence, private recourse, and foreign forces, all principal forms of extraordinary means, in such cases. And doesn't he criticize, on the one hand, Savonarola for silently condoning the elimination of usurpers through the non-observance of a law, and, on the other, the Florentine constitution for allowing Valori's adversaries no ordinary, legal means of opposing him? Machiavelli seems to be implying here that to be like Brutus or Moses, the two should have resorted to extraordinary means to eliminate the enemies of the orders they established when founding the new republic. However, Machiavelli stops just short of this conclusion. In fact, he suggests something quite different.

According to Machiavelli, any means deployed to eliminate usurpers of new orders that formally enlist the people in the effort cannot be deemed "extraordinary"; such means are always "ordinary" (D I.16). In Machiavelli's definition, the "extraordinary ways" of securing a new regime are those adopted by founders or princes who "have the multitude as enemies," *not* those who have made "the people friendly" (D I.16). The latter group would include Brutus, who took up "the governing of a multitude" by the "way of freedom," that is, as the founder or prince of a republic. Such founders who suffer "the few as enemies" but enjoy the people as friends by definition do not resort to extraordinary means when defending their regime against usurpers (D I.16). In light of this, the problem with Savonarola and Valori in Machiavelli's view is *not* that they failed to take up extraordinary measures against the patrician enemies of the republic, but rather that they did not fully avail themselves of the ordinary ones at their disposal as popularly favored princes of a republic. In fact, with Machiavelli's retrospective advice, Savonarola and Valori, and later Soderini, could have improved upon the examples of Moses and Brutus, who operated, respectively, unilaterally and within a small tribunal: the would-be republican princes could have formally enlisted the people assembled in Florence's Great Council to participate in the punishment of liberty's usurpers.

Savonarola and Valori misplayed the one decisive advantage that they held over their adversaries, the favor of the people, one that would have allowed them to observe the laws of the republic and still emerge victorious against the ottimati. Machiavelli implies that Savonarola and Valori should have followed the ordinary orders – that is, observed the law of appeal – with confidence that the Five would lose their appeal in the Great Council if the Friar or Francesco made the best possible case against them. In Guicciardini's account of the episode, this would not have been difficult to accomplish given popular prejudices against the ottimati and the Medici at the time. Of course, Guicciardini also insists that Valori was not willing to proceed in this manner because he feared that his rival, Bernardo del Nero, might have been spared. But this ambiguity only confirms Machiavelli's assessment that accusation and trial procedures, more widely accessible and firmly established than what existed in Florence, would have deterred Valori's overreaching and actually would have better served his own position. Because Valori would have known that his enemies could have leveled accusations against *him* for executing an innocent man and would have had the ability to pursue a case against *him* in the Great Council (that is, outside of the small councils that he dominated), Valori likely would have settled for the elimination of four of the five conspirators via the people's verdict. But this leader of the populist faction did not fully understand or genuinely believe in the utility, let alone the *onestà*, of popular judgment.[39]

Observance of the law of popular appeal would have strengthened the popular regime and Valori's own place within it.[40] As savior of the governo largo, Valori's reputation among the people would have been enhanced; as sympathizer of the republic's enemies, del Nero's reputation, even if he had been spared by the Great Council, would have declined. The main conspirators would have been dead, other would-be traitors deterred for the time being, and Valori's and Savonarola's enemies among the ottimati would have been left without viable options, ordinary *or* extraordinary. However, emboldened by his sway over the committees that tried political cases in Florence, Valori committed perhaps the only two mistakes that could have undermined the Savonarolan republic and brought himself down: he angered the people both by usurping their legal authority as the final arbiter of appeals and by executing a respected man who was guilty of something less than the people might have deemed a capital crime. Valori and Savonarola, ostensible champions of the Great Council, denied the people the appellate judgment that they previously insisted was the people's exclusive right to pronounce. If Valori had observed the proper procedures when prosecuting the Medici Five, the people would have readily absolved him had the ottimati subsequently submitted retaliatory charges against him. Instead, the families of the executed traitors easily enlisted the people, now an angry mob, as accomplices in Valori's murder. And if Savonarola had come forward as a defender of both his own laws and the people's formal judgment, he would not have been successfully branded a self-interested hypocrite, and the people might not have left him naked unto his enemies. In sum, Valori and Savonarola should have been sufficiently astute to realize that their popular support would have carried the day in the Great Council and that their prominence within the republic would have been assured – even if del Nero had survived. We cannot judge for sure whether Savonarola and Valori actually were hypocrites; Machiavelli clearly thinks that they were fools.

Soderini (and Machiavelli) and the Need to Kill "the Sons of Piero"

Returning to the other Florentine figure, Piero Soderini, who could not, as did Brutus and Moses, fend off usurpers of new laws: according to his former underling, Niccolò Machiavelli, Soderini understood the grave threat posed by usurpers but not how to deal with it appropriately. Soderini, Machiavelli complained, believed that time, goodness, good fortune, and favors would minimize the threat of usurpers (D III.30). He thought that his success in becoming the republic's first (and only) Gonfalonier for Life – in other words, the good luck and favor that his election represented – would allow him "to overcome as many as were opposed to him through envy without any scandal, violence and tumult" (D III.30). But Soderini's "patience and goodness" were no match for the "appetite that inhered within the sons of Brutus for returning to another government," that is, more accurately, the "sons of Piero": figuratively, the insolent young members of Soderini's own class, the young ottimati who felt better served by the Medici principality or a governo stretto headed by that family than by a republic with the Great Council at its center (D III.3).[41] They could not be placated by kindness and gifts, "for malignity does not find a gift that appeases it," and time would not diminish their appetite for oppression (D III.30). In Machiavellian terms, they *envied* the institutional embodiment of an empowered people, the Great Council, and a life-term magistracy possessed by a traitor to the patrician class, Soderini.

Machiavelli asserts that Soderini recognized that the Mediceans had to be neutralized if the republic was to survive, but he does not elaborate on the statement that "fate and the ambition of those who struck him gave him opportunity to eliminate them" (D III.3). Guicciardini is more specific here. During Soderini's tenure, the Medici, exiled in Rome, warmly and lavishly received and entertained an increasing number of disgruntled ottimati visiting from Florence, including members and clients of the Rucellai and the Buondelmonti families. Much as this vexed Soderini, he never sought to punish with sufficient energy these patricians for consorting with the former tyrants of the city.[42] During this time, a scandal erupted when the Medici encouraged the marriage of one of their female relatives to a young member of the Florentine ottimati, Filippo Strozzi. Soderini was furious at this insolence bordering on treason and sought to punish the youth.[43] But he did so with such coolness, hesitation, and lack of focus that the young noble got off with a fine and temporary exile. It is not hard to imagine that Machiavelli would have liked Soderini to exploit these circumstances to try to purge from the republic as many of the pro-Medici ottimati as possible; after all, they despised not only the Gonfalonier and the Great Council, but the former's *mannerino*, Niccolò, as well. Guicciardini emphasizes Soderini's sway with both the Great Council and the republic's other collegial bodies, such that they would have convicted and rejected the appeals of anyone who the Gonfalonier prosecuted with vigor, especially those who were exposed as enemies of the Council and advocates of Medici restoration.[44]

However, Machiavelli recounts conversations between Soderini and his friends (presumably including Machiavelli himself)[45] in which the Gonfalonier confesses that he didn't want "to strike his opponents vigorously" and "beat down" his adversaries by resorting to "extraordinary authority," thus disrupting both civil equality and the rule of law (D III.3). The Gonfalonier apparently did not heed his attendant's advice that one can eliminate the usurpers of a popular government without resorting to extraordinary means by enlisting the people as the ultimate judge in such efforts – or else, his assistant, Machiavelli, had not yet come to this conclusion himself. Soderini feared that if he purged the republic of the pro-Medici ottimati, the people would never again trust a lifetime chief executive and would consequently reform the magistracy in a deleterious way after his tenure (D III.3).

Soderini, Machiavelli suggests, needed only to preside over a single case, such as the trial where Brutus participated in the prosecution of his pro-Tarquin sons and then witnessed their execution, to save the republic in a manner that eventually would be excused and discouraged as a precedent: "Since [Soderini's] works and his intention had to be judged by the end, he should have believed that if fortune and life had stayed with him, everyone could certify that what had to be done served the safety of the fatherland and not his own ambition; and he could have arranged things such that a successor of his would not be able to do for evil what he had done for good" (D III.3). Permitting or even encouraging the families and partisans of the Medicean grandi whom Soderini had executed, in turn, to accuse the Gonfalonier and prosecute *him* before the Great Council for severity, ambition, and corruption might have been one such "arrangement" preventing future evil.

Recall how earlier Machiavelli suggested that, with the proper institutions in place, Soderini's patrician enemies could have accused the Gonfalonier before the people, and, whether or not he was convicted, the civil strife that led to the Spanish invasion and the Medici restoration could have been avoided (D I.7). We now begin to realize that this invasion/restoration scenario is precisely the outcome that the ottimati wanted, in any event. Thus, given Soderini's popularity, accusations against the Gonfalonier in the Great Council would likely have been converted into calumnies that led to the punishment of the very ottimati who leveled them. Machiavelli, in the end, is *not* neutral on the question of who should be convicted: much more deserving of punishment were the ottimati, who wanted either a Venetian-styled oligarchy or a restored Medici principate; *not* his patron, the defender of the governo largo. This sentiment bubbles beneath the surface as Machiavelli considers other options open to the ottimati in tempering what they considered to be Soderini's excessive influence vis-à-vis the Great Council.

Machiavelli suggests that the grandi could have undercut the Gonfalonier's source of power by doing as he did in "favoring the collectivity," that is, the people, and stealing his reputation as "a lover of the freedom of the city" (D I.52). Certainly, the people would have benefited even further in the domestic politics of the governo largo if both the Soderinians *and* the ottimati competed for their favor. But, as Machiavelli knew well from the scorn they heaped upon him as a "new man" and a "rogue,"[46] and as Guicciardini documents so vividly in his history, the Florentine ottimati were much too arrogant and insolent to reconcile themselves to the Great Council and thus to show favor to the people. Instead, they resorted to means that Machiavelli rightly identifies as the cause of the republic's ruin: they conspired to win the favor of the exiled Medici and facilitated the invasion of Spanish forces to oust Soderini and reinstate, at first, an oligarchy, and then, a principality (D I.52).

On the contrary, Machiavelli asserts that Soderini himself could *not* undercut his adversaries' authority by adopting their own methods – that is, by consorting with the Medici himself – because this would have cost him both his popular support and left him as vulnerable as Valori and Savonarola found themselves after they had abandoned the people (D I.52). Nevertheless, the Gonfalonier lost his power and the republic for the same reason that Valori and Savonarola wound up dead: all three underestimated and underplayed the great advantage of enjoying the favor of the people, formally collected in assembly, against the ottimati. By enlisting the Medici, as far as Machiavelli is concerned, the ottimati adopted the surest route to tyranny. He uses the example of Cicero and the Roman nobles who promoted Octavian against Mark Antony to emphasize the following point: when seeking the favor of a tyrant rather than the people, even in the effort to defend patrician prominence and senatorial privilege in a republic, one precipitates the complete collapse of the republic and the utter "destruction of the party of the aristocrats" (D I.52).

As a result of this strategy, Rome suffered the elevation of Octavian as Emperor Augustus, and Florence gained in the Medici restoration not the return of "first citizens" but, eventually, the establishment of the Duchy of Tuscany. Roman optimates, such as Cicero, may have wished to restore the authority of the senate, and the ottimati, such as Bernardo Rucellai, may have wanted the Medici to preside over a "government of the few." But both helped to usher in a tyranny of the one. The only strategy that would have saved the Florentine Republic in 1512, preserved Soderini's administration, and kept Machiavelli employed is the same one that would have maintained Valori and Savonarola as quasi-princes of the governo largo fifteen years earlier: the accusation, trial, and capital conviction of the leadership of the pro-Medici ottimati, and, when the conspirators appealed, the vindication of that conviction by the people collected in the Great Council.

Thus, rather than preserve the patrician class by scapegoating and executing only one of its numbers, in both these cases Machiavelli actually advocates the trial and execution of some undetermined number of grandi. This number may perhaps stop short of the complete "destruction" of the aristocratic party, but Machiavelli is clear that often the life of much more than one young noble with an unquenchable appetite to oppress and an unseemly desire to rule is the price that must be paid for the preservation of a popular government's free way of life.

It should be noted that Machiavelli justifies popular judgment in his fully elaborated discussion of the Manlius, Valori/Savonarola and Soderini cases on somewhat different grounds than he did in his early discourses devoted to accusations and calumnies (D I.7–8) and, especially, in the discourses that extol the people's excellence at making laws and distributing offices (D I.58). In the previous discussions, Machiavelli argued that popular judgment yields optimal outcomes, or better outcomes than would be yielded by the decisions of other political actors, such as the one or the few. In the later discussions, however, Machiavelli insinuates that whatever the people, formally gathered in assembly, decide is, by definition, "ordinary," that is, not "extraordinary" in the sense of being arbitrary, extralegal, or even incorrect. In other words, Machiavelli seems to assert, either implicitly or explicitly, that there exists no external standard by which one might evaluate whether the people's decision in a political trial is good or bad. More important than the content of the judgment – that is, the genuine guilt or innocence of the accused person evaluated objectively – is the identity of the judge. Apparently, what matters most to Machiavelli in these cases are (1) the fact that the people decide – that is, the people are incapable of making a bad, incorrect, or extraordinary decision; and (2) the expedient effects resulting from popularly judged political trials – that is, these trials efficiently eliminate the aristocratic enemies of republics, and they do so without provoking particularly intense partisan retaliation.[47]

Moreover, in Machiavelli's fully elaborated account of political trials, the people do not seem quite as objective or even deferential as they appeared in earlier accounts: the people's prejudices against the ottimati, in fact, do incline them to decide against the latter when plebeian champions or populist magistrates accuse "the sons of Brutus" of conspiring against the republic. However, this prejudice does not necessarily guarantee that the people will *invariably* convict aristocratic enemies of the republic such that the latter should accelerate treasonous or oppressive schemes against republics. As I've tried to make clear, Machiavelli's insistence on enlisting the people in the prosecution of political criminals doesn't mean that prominent citizens must desperately fear incessant indictment, conviction, or execution by the combined efforts of the people and pro-plebeian magistrates – the Florentine example of Bernardo del Nero and, as mentioned before, the Roman example of the tribune-initiated moratorium on patrician prosecutions bear this out. The people would have exonerated the former and did in fact abide by the latter. One may infer that republican freedom requires that the grandi generally feel wary of political punishment but only intermittently *terrified* by it (see D III.1).[48] What should keep the ottimati from overthrowing a republic is their ability to try plebeian magistrates before the people and the expectation that when they find themselves on trial, the people will not automatically find them guilty. Moreover, the indeterminacy over the people's resentment of or their deference toward the grandi, and their inclination to judge objectively when formally empowered with decision-making authority, should, as Machiavelli suggests in his discussion of Soderini, keep plebeian leaders and patrician class traitors in the magistracies from using popularly judged political trials for merely tyrannical ends.

Both Guicciardini and Machiavelli recognize that the greater freedom of action enjoyed by both political *and* socioeconomic elites in republics than in, say, principalities (where, according to republican ideology, only one individual is truly "free") is a threat to the liberty of other citizens and to the stability of the regime itself. This is not to suggest by any means that ottimati invariably choose republics over principalities: as Machiavelli notes and as we've observed quite clearly, the "sons of Brutus/Piero" will attempt pro-monarchical coups when they think that a prince better facilitates their oppression of the people than do republican arrangements (which, in any case, they understand in narrowly oligarchic terms) (D I.16, D III.3; P 9).[49]

But this is where the agreement ends. Machiavelli disapproves of the exclusion of the general citizenry from censure, impeachment, or removal proceedings directed at suspect public officials and prominent private citizens. For Machiavelli, leaving such matters only to political colleagues and rivals in government, as Guicciardini recommends and modern republics do, is a greater invitation to corruption than is the practice of putting the ultimate judgment in such cases to the people formally assembled. Guicciardini and his eighteenth-century constitutionalist heirs, most notably the American founders, overcompensate in an ochlophobic manner for the purportedly arbitrary and excessive use of exile, ostracism, and public punishment in ancient popular governments: they both tighten the legal procedures of political trials *and* exclude the general citizenry from them. Machiavelli, on the other hand, offers a model for punishing prominent citizens and public magistrates that is both grounded in the rule of law *and* inclusive of common citizens.

According to Machiavelli, the lack of legally established and broadly popular accusation, trial, and appellate procedures in Florence was one of the chief causes of the republic's instability. With such procedures, he avers, Florence could have avoided both the bloodletting of prominent citizens in the wake of the Medici Five execution and the enlistment of the Spanish army during the ouster of Soderini and the return of the Medici. Early in the *Discourses*, Machiavelli suggests that if the ottimati had enjoyed recourse to appropriate accusation procedures, Valori, Savonarola, and Soderini would have been either punished or acquitted individually, without factional violence or the fall of the republic ensuing. The Eight of Ward and the Signoria, ineffective in these instances, were bodies too small to hear such cases, to judge these individuals properly, or to be trusted to refer convictions to the people upon appeal. Machiavelli suggests that a body as large as the entire citizenry should serve as both the initial judge *and* the appellate forum in political cases. If the magistrates or smaller collegial assemblies perform the first function, matters may never get to the people to perform the second one. To be sure, an institution such as the tribunate might pressure magistrates to ensure that the people always make the final decision in such cases (D III.11) – but, much to Machiavelli's exasperation, Florence lacked such an intermediary between the magistracies and the people.

Elsewhere in the *Discourses*, Machiavelli suggests that wide, popularly inclusive bodies are in fact powerful weapons of popular magistrates and the citizens at large against members of the ottimati who scheme to narrow the people's liberty or overthrow governi larghi. Rather than simply protecting the senatorial class as a whole by focusing popular animus on one lone patrician and making the people forget the structural advantages that the patrician class maintains over them, public accusations and popular political trials may in fact intensify class consciousness and punish large numbers of the grandi in defense of a republic's free and civic way of life. When accusations, as well as trial and appellate fora, remain the preserve of the few, as they do in most modern constitutions, plebeian leaders and progressive magistrates are too easily calumniated and smeared, and popular governments become increasingly vulnerable to conspiracies and incremental coups on the part of the oligarchs.

PART III

6

Republicanism and Democracy

> In Rome, a tribune, or any citizen, could propose laws, on which every citizen could speak . . . so that ultimately the people might choose what was best.
>
> Machiavelli, *Discourses* I.18

> The people are too ignorant to discuss important matters freely and ably in assembly. . . . Magistrates alone should choose speakers and topics.
>
> Guicciardini, *Considerations* I.2

Democrats should worry when philosophers employ the language of "republicanism." When philosophers espouse purportedly objective principles, such as the common good, the rule of law, depoliticization – that is, normative standards that they claim will make democracy operate more justly – democrats should be very worried indeed. History teaches that this discourse of republicanism – of a common good not fully achievable through extensive popular participation and ultimate majority judgment – enjoys a rather dubious legacy. Republicanism, historically, often prompted aristocratic coups against popular governments or justified oligarchic consolidation once more democratic regimes had been overthrown. On principle, neither of these outcomes is necessarily problematic for contemporary adherents of republicanism; after all, as I discuss in what follows, they value popular participation much less than they do policy outcomes that supposedly benefit the populace at large or track the common good. Minimal or, at best, indirect authorization and distended contestation of elite governance by common citizens, they suppose, is sufficient to promote and protect the people's liberty.

Looking back over time, dominant strands of "republican" theory and practice – from Aristotle to Guicciardini to Madison, from Sparta to Venice to the American Founding – have empowered economic and political elites over common citizens and insulated the former from the latter's reach. Indeed, the major spokesmen for Roman and Florentine "republicanism," Cicero and Bruni, respectively, sought to enhance the consolidation of elite control of their republic's politics or legitimated such consolidation after the fact.[1] On the one hand, classical republicanism assigned to aristocratically dominated offices and councils, especially senatorial bodies, preeminent authority over institutions reserved for poorer citizens. On the other, modern republicanism primarily permits the populace at large to select via general election the particular – usually wealthy and notable – individuals who will rule over them as magistrates. (Of course, classical republicans also favored electoral means of appointing magistrates over methods that enlisted elements of randomization; and modern republicans often rely extensively on senatorial institutions, such as high courts and upper legislative houses.) Put bluntly, republicanism has always justified serious constraining or constriction of democracy or *governo largo*; in both the old and new forms of *governo stretto*, the few are granted ascendance over a still politically "included" but subordinated many.

Machiavelli, as demonstrated in previous chapters, conceived of popular participation more broadly and sought to constrain elites more tightly than did proponents of either of these forms of republicanism. His political theory is simply more popularly empowering and anti-elitist than what generally passes under the name of republican theory today. Machiavelli is certainly no political idealist or democratic naïf: he concedes that socioeconomic elites will wield significant political power within even the most democratically inclined constitutional arrangements. However, Machiavelli's theory of popular government differs significantly from the aristocratic advocates of governo stretto who preceded him (e.g., Aristotle and Cicero), from those who dominated the political discourse of his milieu (i.e., Bruni and Guicciardini), as well as from the strictly electoral or minimalist democratic theorists (e.g., Madison and Schumpeter) who shaped our understandings of post–eighteenth-century republics.

In the first section of this chapter, I show how the minimizing or narrowing of popular participation advocated by philosophical republicans of the past, such as Cicero, Bruni, and Guicciardini, led to political outcomes that did not track the common good as perceived or avowed by most citizens within their republics. In the short run, the sharp curtailing of popular participation in such contexts served only the interests of the elites consequently empowered to act on behalf of the people; and, in the long run, popular marginalization and elite empowerment invariably led to the collapse of the regimes served by these vaunted republican philosopher-statesmen. In subsequent sections, I highlight significant affinities shared by exponents of traditional republicanism and the work of the most prominent and intellectually formidable philosopher who advances "republicanism" today, Philip Pettit. I draw upon Machiavelli to argue, contra republicans traditional and contemporary, that the people themselves are much more likely than the few to make decisions conducive to the common good within republics, and that therefore political democracy that empowers the people to deliberate over and decide policy themselves is preferable on normative and empirical grounds to philosophical republicanism that narrowly empowers elected representatives and even neutral or "depoliticized" experts to decide on behalf of the people.[2]

Philosophical Republicanism from a Historical Perspective

John Dunn recently reminds us of an essential point made by Moses Finley decades ago: Western philosophy emerged in hostile response to democratic politics and society.[3] Dunn and Finley highlight the enormous overlap between the oligarchic and philosophic critiques of Athens, an overlap best exemplified by Plato's and, to a lesser extent, Aristotle's writings. The critique of Athenian democracy is inextricably bound to the moral and philosophical projects of both authors, and is quite pertinent to their endorsements of the oligarchies and tyrannies that usurped or supplanted rule by the demos in Athens and other Greek democracies during their lifetimes.

The writings of Italian authors associated more directly with "republicanism" as such are just as antidemocratic and oligarchically inclined, and can also be situated in close proximity to subversions or usurpations of popular governments: I refer specifically here to the philosopher-statesmen Marcus Tullius Cicero, Leonardo Bruni, and Francesco Guicciardini. Cicero insisted that the senate secure a monopoly over policy making within the Roman Republic: he openly advocated manipulation of plebeian magistrates such as the tribunes, public rather than secret ballots, and the influence of patrons over clients to ensure the compliance of common citizens with the senate's will. For Cicero, the common good is best served when the republic's wisest and most virtuous men, collected in the senate, deliberate over and decide policy. The people's participation should be confined to little more than deciding, via elections for major magistracies, which individuals eventually become senators, and to acclaiming as law policies made by the republic's best men.[4]

Did Cicero's aristocratic republicanism, which sought to neutralize the republic's plebeian-empowering institutions, the tribunes and the popular assemblies, serve the common good in Rome? This would be hard to argue. Cicero and fellow senators opposed attempts by the *populares* to address the economic-military crisis that was destroying the republic.[5] As recounted in Chapter 3, Roman citizen-soldiers were gradually forced into worsening poverty as senators and their clients refused to share public lands with them; in fact, they even refused to employ poor citizens to work such lands, opting to hire much cheaper slave labor instead. The more the people clamored for land redistribution, the more the senate advocated the conquest of ever more distant lands. They did so hoping to acquire territory that only nobles, and not plebeians, could afford to make profitable. As a result of such policies, citizen-soldiers began to live for ever-longer periods of time with their commanders away from Rome, and thus became economically dependent on their generals, individuals to whom, instead of the republic, they now pledged their loyalty. These circumstances, of course, culminated in the civil wars among Rome's military commanders that cost Cicero his life and the republic its liberty.[6]

In a similar vein, Bruni, whom Hans Baron famously identified as the founder of Florentine civic republicanism, served as intellectual spokesman for the oligarchy that replaced generations of popular rule exercised through guild corporatism in the Florentine Republic.[7] Bruni celebrated, in classical philosophical terms, practices of popular "participation" that, in fact, had been quite recently denuded of any significance by the oligarchy headed by the Albizzi family.[8] After subverting guild-republican institutions, the Albizzeans opened the magistracies of Florentine government to a wider number of citizens than ever before; *but* they reserved all consequential decisions to themselves. The Florentine patricians deliberated and decided public policy in consultative sessions (compiled in the *Consulte e Practiche*), and then more or less dictated it to the magistrates for implementation.[9] Did this dramatic narrowing of Florence's decision-making procedures produce better public policy than Florence's more popularly participatory regimes? Hardly. The leading citizens could not successfully resolve conflicts among themselves, and they corrupted the civic culture of common citizens through clientage to such an extent that circumstances were ripe for the Medici family to emerge as tyrants of the city.[10]

Finally, as mentioned before, Guicciardini crystallized the aspirations of wealthy and notable citizens within republics and served as a crucial if unrecognized conduit between the republicanisms of Cicero and James Madison.[11] After the Medici's expulsion in 1494, Florence reinstated popular government: a governo largo characterized by a large, Athenian-style citizen assembly and, eventually, by magistrate appointment procedures that mixed lottery and election. In protest, Guicciardini proposed simple election as the proper mode of appointing magistrates and the establishment of a senate, where policy would be more substantively discussed and better decided than in the Great Council. Such reforms, he claimed, would allow the most wise, prudent, and virtuous men, rather than the variable, ignorant, and jealous multitude, to decide what is best for the city.[12] We don't know whether Guicciardini's proposal to reform Florence as an electoral-senatorial republic would have resulted in a government that better realized the common good than did the governo largo; when many of his wealthy friends and relatives did not win such reforms, they summoned the Spanish army, abolished the Great Council, and placed the republic once again in Medici hands.

In addition to these vivid instances of domestic social domination, republican philosopher-statesmen justified domination by particular republics over other regimes, including other republics.[13] Cicero celebrated Rome's multi-continental empire and Bruni justified Florence's smaller-scale hegemony over Tuscany. In light of the pervasiveness of domination, both domestic and foreign, in the theory and practice of republicanism, nondomination – central to the contemporary republican revival – without *much more* qualification, seems a rather peculiar principle to derive from this political tradition.[14] Furthermore, if one were to enlist Machiavelli in a more careful and progressively constructive reformulation of republican theory, one would have to take into account the following: unlike conventional republican theorists, he was dismayed by the kinds of social domination characteristic of the domestic politics of republics mentioned previously, and he promoted decidedly unconventional institutional measures to address it; moreover, as I discussed in Chapter 2, he endorsed, ostensibly at least, in a manner even more enthusiastic than other republican theorists, the kind of imperial domination mentioned here.[15] In light of these reflections on the principle and practice of traditional republicanism, I now engage the work of Philip Pettit, the most philosophically sophisticated of the many thinkers attempting to revive republicanism as a just and viable political program today.

Between Republicanism and Democracy

In the path-breaking books *Republicanism* and *A Theory of Freedom*, Pettit formulates a philosophically systematic theory of republican liberty that he hopes will impact contemporary politics: freedom as nondomination.[16] In these and subsequent writings,[17] Pettit also proposes institutional reforms through which liberty as nondomination might be more fully realized and contemporary democracy might be substantively enhanced.[18] Pettit derives this theory of freedom from an interpretation of the history of Anglo-European political thought that sharply, perhaps too sharply, distinguishes liberal from republican conceptions of freedom.[19] The former tradition, Pettit avers, exclusively upholds the principle of freedom as non-interference; that is, liberalism seeks to free individuals from direct forms of *interference* – from actual constraints, physical impediments, and so on. Republicanism, on the contrary, upholds the broader, more robust normative standard of freedom from *domination*. Classical liberalism defines liberty only in terms of the absence of *actual* interference, and so it ignores the forms of dependence or subordination that living with the *threat* of arbitrary intervention entails for individuals and polities.[20]

For Pettit, "domination" obtains in circumstances where individuals suffer subordination whether or not some other agent actually intervenes in their lives at any particular moment; the mere threat, either implicit or explicit, of arbitrary interference by another is sufficient to warrant the attribution of domination to such a relationship, whether social or political. Pettit defines as "arbitrary" any interference that does not comport with the perceived or expressed interest of individuals; he catalogues instances of arbitrary interference by private parties over other such parties under the term *dominium*; and he lists governmental actions that violate the "common avowable interests" of individuals under the category *imperium*.[21]

I suggest that Pettit's account of liberty as nondomination posits two goals that actually conflict with each other: on the one hand, he takes great pains to situate liberty as nondomination within "the broad republican tradition," while, on the other, he suggests that his theory of freedom is best secured by practices that he associates with "democracy, electoral and contestatory," an institutional ensemble that Pettit promotes as a superior alternative to democracy as conventionally practiced and understood. I argue that the first effort seriously undermines the second; in fact, I demonstrate that Pettit's committed adherence to republicanism compels him to endorse some of the aspects of contemporary "democratic" politics that are least friendly to liberty, conceived in Pettit's own terms.

Machiavelli and Negative Liberty

Through various iterations of his theory of republicanism, Pettit freely expresses suspicion of both popular judgment and majoritarian politics. Unlike, for instance, Athenian democrats, Roman *populares*, and Florentine guildsmen, Pettit ascribes no superior moral status, no particular *onestà*, to wide and efficacious popular participation. As Pettit describes the intellectual legacy to which he adheres: "the writers who identify with the broad republican tradition of thinking take liberty to be defined by a status in which the evils associated with interference are avoided rather than by access to the instruments of democratic control, participatory or representative."[22] Following Quentin Skinner in certain important respects here, Pettit credits Machiavelli with shaping a republican tradition that focused on "avoiding interference rather than on achieving participation";[23] moreover, he places Machiavelli alongside Cicero, Harrington, Sydney, and Montesquieu as an author who does not embrace a "positive concept of liberty," who does not associate freedom with "a self-determining democracy," and who does not, first and foremost, prioritize "participation."[24]

Pettit thereby includes Machiavelli among republican writers who value liberty negatively as nondomination, *and* who minimize or even reject extra-electoral and collectively active means by which citizens might actually attain such liberty.[25] In line with Skinner, and others,[26] Pettit emphasizes passages in which Machiavelli describes the desire of common people to be left free from arbitrary interference in their persons and property, as well as from the *fear* that they might be so interfered with.[27] There is more than a small element of truth in such claims. Unfortunately, however, the fixation on the abstract "concept" of liberty in Machiavelli that motivates these claims allows Pettit to underestimate, quite dramatically, the participatory means that the Florentine deems necessary for the popular attainment, maintenance, and expansion of this liberty, and therefore to render much too sharply the distinction between negative and positive facets of Machiavelli's description of liberty in practice.

By ascribing to the people a desire not to be dominated, Machiavelli prioritizes as more just and decent their desire to be free, that is, their desire to live free of domination. At the same time, the Florentine justifies and encourages the people's active contestation of elites lest their own liberty be threatened or eliminated. It might be said that Machiavelli's theory legitimizes the people's "natural" disposition of passivity while also justifying an "unnatural" or learned active political posture. Conversely, Machiavelli's assertion that the elites' appetite to dominate is insatiable, whether or not this can be demonstrated in every case, necessitates the extra-electoral safeguards against them, such as the class-specific offices and popularly judged political trials that I discussed in previous chapters, as well as participation that is not only active but also antagonistic.

As we have observed throughout this book, Machiavelli prescribes popular participation in the following forms: competing for office with the *grandi*; establishing class-specific advocacy institutions; opening processes of appeals;

creating opportunities for the condemnation of officials and powerful individuals; directly deliberating and deciding over legislation and political trials in assembly; and sharing in the republic's wealth and honors. As I'll discuss further in this chapter, by focusing narrowly on elections, and by largely ignoring these more intensive and extensive participatory practices, Pettit, like Skinner, inappropriately casts Machiavelli's notion of liberty as strictly "negative." Moreover, Pettit, wittingly or not, elevates the aristocratic preferences of republican philosopher-statesmen, such as Cicero, to the status of "republicanism" itself, while ignoring the aspirations of the much more democratically participatory tradition of plebeian or guild republicanism.

Election and Contestation

Pettit defines republican liberty in light of the "common avowable interests" of citizens, that is, the interests that citizens recognize as being shared in common with each other.[28] But, in line with his interpretation of the republican tradition, the means of participation that Pettit endorses by which citizens avow or express those interests are, in fact, quite narrow. Pettit agrees with Aristotle, Cicero, Bruni, Guicciardini, and Madison that collective participation should not extend much beyond the people's choice of the specific individuals who will hold office. Participation need not transcend the politics of election. For instance, Pettit favorably invokes the English republicans Richard Price and Joseph Priestly, who confine participation to, respectively, "choosing representatives" and "voting."[29] As Pettit remarks in *Republicanism*: "Electoral standing gives the collective people the power of an indirect author in relation to governmental laws and decisions. They may not be the authors of what those in government say and do, but they determine who the authors shall be or at least who the overseers of the authors shall be."[30]

In this vein, Pettit repeatedly affirms that the people ought to act only as the "indirect" authors of public policy; they may be, in some sense, "enabled" as authors of the law, but only "imperfectly" so.[31] Accordingly, Pettit defines democracy as "a system of government under which those who are governed enjoy a certain control over those who govern them," and he concedes that the idea of "a certain control" is sufficiently "vague" not to imply total or perhaps even a preponderance of control *by* the governed.[32] On such grounds, the republican philosopher commits himself to a form of government where real political control lies not with the people but "is left wholly or mainly to representatives in parliament, or to a government with a parliamentary majority, or to an elected administration."[33] Consequently, representative democracy and electoral politics, according to Pettit, do and should "realize" public preferences in only a highly mediated way.[34]

Elections, in Pettit's estimation, generally communicate to those who make policy what the "popular valuation" concerning the common good is, such that representatives can proceed to govern on that basis.[35] While the people neither formulate policy themselves nor specifically instruct elected officials how to make policy, they do nevertheless give officials a general sense of what their conception of the common good is, such that the representatives can use the wide discretion entailed by electoral politics in genuine efforts to realize that good. Unlike direct democracy, Athenian or plebiscitary, which endeavors to express the collective will of most citizens, Pettit thus espouses a form of indirect democracy, where the public deliberation accompanying electoral contests and the political authorization signaled by electoral results serve to guide policy makers in the performance of their duties:

> The people should control government democratically because that is the only mode of control under which those reasons can be expected to guide government that are recognized *in common deliberation* as the valuations relevant to determining public policy. This conception represents democracy, not as a regime for the expression of the collective will, but rather as *a dispensation* for the empowerment of public valuation.[36]

Pettit initially intimates that the main problem with the idea of a collective will is the unfeasibility of divining or expressing it under complex modern circumstances.[37] However, Pettit does not ultimately reject the "participatory ideal" accompanying the notion of a collective will exclusively, or even primarily, on the grounds that it is "not feasible in the modern world."[38] As we'll observe later in this chapter, Pettit ultimately rejects such conceptions as "scarcely attractive" on normative grounds;[39] that is, he considers the idea that majority rule accurately approximates popular will to be a threat, perhaps even the greatest threat, to liberty within democracies.[40]

It should be noted: Despite Pettit's emphasis on the overall advantages afforded by elections, he does not consider electoral politics to be an entirely unproblematic route to just and efficient government. Even if Pettit, in a faithful Schumpeterian fashion, relies on an incentivist/consumerist model to argue that electoral politics reliably produces candidates who are likely to address the common good,[41] it would be unfair to claim that Pettit fetishizes elections. Indeed, he acknowledges that elected representatives, like popular majorities, can themselves become agents of domination when they pursue their own interests rather than those of everyone else. In this context, Pettit raises the serious problem of keeping elected elites accountable to the electorate such that the former do not behave tyrannically: "Since [elections] only allow for a very loose control of the policies eventually pursued by government, they may fail to stop those elected to power from nurturing policies that fail to answer to particular interests or from pursuing policies in a way that doesn't answer to popular interests. The electorally democratic state may be an elective despotism. . . . "[42]

In light of these remarks, it is somewhat surprising to observe Pettit argue that electoral regimes promote greater accountability than any other type of polity, more so even than those, he states explicitly, such as ancient democracies, in which most offices were distributed through lottery.[43] However, Pettit makes this claim in a somewhat misleading fashion: while, in theory, elections may facilitate accountability in ways that lotteries, considered in isolation, do not, Pettit neglects to mention that, in practice, virtually every popular government that deployed lotteries also subjected officeholders to strict post-tenure public scrutinies where former magistrates gave account of their actions and faced serious punishment for misconduct. There is certainly no reliable evidence available that demonstrates the superiority of election/reelection schemes in securing greater elite accountability for citizenries to those characterized by lottery/scrutiny; in fact there are serious grounds to conclude just the opposite.[44]

Indeed, Pettit himself concedes that representative democracy's inherent indirectness allows magistrates to conduct themselves with a potentially pernicious independence from the public: representation means that "electoral control still allows governmental policy making to be influenced by factors [other than those pertaining to] the common, recognizable interest of people."[45] Pettit lists the following among the arbitrary factors that potentially undermine the efficacy of representative democracy: campaign promises are not often translated into law, policy implementers enjoy wide prerogative in carrying out their tasks, and particular lobbies can wield undue influence over the policy-making process.[46]

To counteract representative democracy's inherent susceptibility to this kind of distortion, Pettit endorses "contestatory" means for challenging the policy outcomes of ordinary electoral politics.[47] Pettit frequently invokes alternative institutions – judiciaries, tribunals, ombudsmen, upper houses, and local boards – through which individuals, specific subsets of the citizenry, and (more ambiguously) even the citizenry itself might variously contest, review, or amend decisions made by elected elites.[48] He calls this the "editorial" dimension of democratic politics that must supplement the "authorial" dimension reflected in electoral procedures.[49] Through the latter, the people articulate the common avowable interests that the state ought to further; through the former, they protest and denounce state policies that do not conform to their estimations of what constitutes interests that can be justified in terms of the commonweal.[50]

However, it must be noted that Pettit understands contestatory procedures to operate in just as indirect and reactive a manner as he does electoral politics: he states unequivocally that the "procedural, consultative, and appellate measures," which constitute the contestatory dimension of his theory of democracy, "give ordinary people *passive* rather than active control of what happens. If the measures work effectively, then they ensure not that ordinary people dictate what policies will be selected and applied but that the policies selected and applied will conform to people's common, recognizable interests."[51] Contestation allows citizens "to raise an effective voice" concerning policies that adversely affect them, but not, Pettit insists, to decide directly on their implementation or revocation.[52]

Pettit argues that, in order to facilitate contestation, however passive, democracies must allow citizens to challenge government policy on at least three grounds: "for its legality under public law; for its substantive merit; and for its general propriety."[53] Within Pettit's framework, judicial review by high or supreme courts ensures that government action affecting citizen interests is legal or constitutional. Pettit would further authorize tribunals that oversee, for instance, land use, immigration, education, and such to address whether substantive dimensions of public policy in these domains track the interests of citizens; such specialized tribunals would hold public hearings, conduct official inquiries, publish their findings, and offer recommendations in "white" or "green papers."[54]

Most intriguing among Pettit's extra-electoral institutions is the figure of the ombudsman, an agent of contestation who, at first glance, functions in a manner reminiscent of the plebeian tribunes in Rome. According to Pettit's stipulations, citizens can appeal to ombudsmen to investigate and report on government "maladministration" in the widest sense: incompetence, neglect, corruption, inattention, malfeasance, delay, arbitrariness, abuse of power, and so on.[55] While Pettit would not grant ombudsmen the "power to enforce a remedy," he understands them to serve as effective instruments for securing compensation for aggrieved parties and as catalysts for changing government practice in ways that better serve members of the public.[56]

However, there are significant differences between these two contestatory magistrates, the Roman tribunes and Pettit's ombudsmen. On the one hand, the former were not merely contestatory officials; the tribunes wielded authority to initiate legislation and formally prosecute prominent public and private citizens, authority that Pettit's ombudsmen obviously lack. On the other, Pettit doesn't attribute to the ombudsmen a group-specific character; that is, the ombudsmen are not, as were the tribunes of the plebs, necessarily members of the very groups whose interests they attempt to protect from governmental encroachment and social domination. (As we'll observe later in this chapter, when Pettit does endorse identity-specific officials, in the case of saved seats for representatives of minority groups, their range of action is severely circumscribed by legislative structures and conventions.)

There are, moreover, two other important differences that I wish to address at greater length. First, Pettit refuses to empower ombudsmen – or, for that matter, any contestatory principal *or* agent – with a veto authority over government policy. Second, Pettit does not conceive of common citizens – that is, the vast majority of citizens who do not belong to the ranks of socioeconomic and political elites – as a discrete group entitled to their own ombudsmen. In Pettit's account, for the most part, ombudsmen contest public policy on behalf of individuals or minority groups who claim that their avowed interests have been violated or disregarded – not on behalf of common citizens as a whole, that is, the plebeians of modern republics.

Vetoing the Veto Authority

On both plausibility and utility grounds, Pettit rejects vetoes that enable parties prospectively affected in adverse ways by particular policies to block the implementation of such policies. The veto, according to Pettit, poses little more "than an abstract, purely academic interest," and today enjoys not "the remotest chance of being instituted."[57] More substantively, he argues that vetoes discourage compromise over public policy: with access to formal vetoes, interested parties need not negotiate outcomes (even those that might include appropriate compensation) through which benefits and costs can be distributed with some semblance of equity throughout society; such parties can simply reject certain inconvenient policies tout court.[58] Pettit observes that "the worst hit," if armed with a veto when confronted with onerous but socially necessary policy proposals, "would be likely to block the initiative in the hope of inducing others to bear the costs."[59] In such circumstances, society as a whole would never benefit from advantages to be gained by, say, progressive tax arrangements, power plants, antipollution legislation, or needle exchange programs.

Pettit insists that contestatory democracy should not enable people "to veto public decisions," but rather "to call them into question" by triggering reviews or appeals.[60] Contestation of this kind is more fair and efficacious than vetoes, Pettit suggests, because "it empowers people in the assertion of their perceived interests but does not set them up as dictators with an individual capacity to negate any public decision."[61] While the republican philosopher certainly has a point in circumstances where minority groups or special interests may self-servingly avail themselves of formalized veto authority, it is not clear why, on the same grounds, he explicitly dismisses the tribunician veto in the Roman Republic.[62] Since the tribunes exercised the veto on behalf of the majority of citizens against senatorial and consular initiatives and measures, it would be hard to claim that the tribunician veto illegitimately displaced burdens throughout society and inappropriately scuttled socially beneficial reforms. Indeed, when the tribunes exercised their veto authority in the following cases, they were ensuring that Rome's senatorial order did not impose or displace undue burdens on the majority of citizens: for instance, when the tribunes prevented consuls from proposing patrician-friendly laws before assemblies like the *comitia centuriata*, where voting would be weighted in favor of the wealthy; or when the tribunes halted the levying of troops for wars initiated by the senate to quell popular protest within the republic rather than to further the latter's collective security vis-à-vis external enemies.

Pettit certainly articulates good reasons for rejecting vetoes exercised by individuals or at a "group-level,"[63] but what if the veto-wielding "group" is the demos, that is, the poor, the many? The class-specific character of the plebeian tribunes and the majoritarian constituency that they served largely obviate these concerns, or at the very least, they require Pettit to qualify his criticisms of Rome's tribunician veto. Pettit's comprehensive concern over the capacities of particular groups to shift burdens and subvert the common good through vetoes ignores a salient fact about republican politics that the Romans, especially the Roman plebeians, knew very well: the disproportionate influence of wealthy citizens and the wide discretion enjoyed by magistrates often constitute a de facto veto on policies that the majority of citizens desire to be enacted in their common interest. The de facto veto that elites exercise in such contexts combined with the disproportionate influence and discretion they enjoy over active policy making necessitates institutions through which the majority qua majority not only authorize public policy ex ante but also veto policies in an ex post fashion.

Pettit clearly rules out the use of vetoes as a form of contestation that should be available to either majorities or minorities. But does he at least afford both minorities *and* majorities other institutional avenues of contestation? Or are the latter exclusively reserved for aggrieved individuals and vulnerable minorities? Pettit often seems to suggest that majorities are generally so well served by conventional electoral politics that only individuals and minorities need recourse to contestatory practices. I now examine Pettit's rationale for this position and the ramifications it poses for liberty as nondomination.

Contestation for Both Majorities and Minorities?

Pettit often equivocates on the nature of contestation within his democratic theory: on the one hand, he states that "a government will represent a form of rule that is controlled by the people to the extent that the people individually *and collectively* enjoy a permanent possibility of contesting what government decides";[64] on the other, he baldly declares that contestation "cannot be exercised collectively."[65] Pettit is clearly caught between two forms of contestation: one, reminiscent of the Roman Republic, where the people, through the tribunes, collectively edited or corrected the decisions made by elected officials, such as consuls, or previously elected officials, such as senators; the other form of contestation, more reminiscent of the countermajoritarian institutions favored by post–eighteenth-century liberal constitutionalists, provides avenues through which government bodies protect minorities against potential abuses of majority rule. The former, Roman type allows majoritarian contestation of the government and of whatever special interests might be hijacking democratic rule in self-serving and dominating ways; the latter, Enlightenment type facilitates minority contestation of domination that majorities purportedly exercise through elected elites, or that public officials, acting unilaterally, exercise themselves.

The preponderance of evidence afforded by Pettit's writings, despite isolated statements to the contrary, suggests that he would put contestatory institutions such as the three just mentioned primarily at the disposal of individuals and minority groups. This implies the following:

- Pettit believes that electoral institutions adequately serve the majority of citizens qua majority – that is, the latter need no extra-electoral means to ensure that government is fulfilling its obligations to track the common interests of the majority of citizens.
- Discriminatory policies that disadvantage religious, ethnic, aboriginal, and other minorities are the most pressing types of domination characteristic of democratic politics that most urgently require contestatory redress; imbalances of political and socioeconomic power that obtain between, on the one hand, common citizens, and, on the other, wealthy citizens and public officials, do not, as such, require contestatory redress.

An important question raised by such assumptions is whether Pettit's model provides so much recourse for individuals and minorities via countermajoritarian institutions, insulated from popular accountability, that it stymies the very possibility of democracy as popular rule in any meaningful sense of the term. Furthermore, are countermajoritarian institutions more likely to serve the interests of privileged, well-resourced, and already insulated minorities rather than those of genuinely vulnerable minorities? The record of such institutions actually protecting vulnerable minorities is, after all, decidedly mixed.[66]

Quite commendably, Pettit has long placed protection of vulnerable minorities at the center of his republican theory of freedom: the "politically avowable, perceived interests" of "relevant minorities," he consistently declares, cannot be "just ignored and flouted" in democratic politics.[67] Even on the electoral, authorial side, as opposed to the contestatory, editorial side of his model, Pettit recommends alternative – that is, not strictly electoral – means of ensuring that governmental policy takes account of social diversity.[68] For instance, Pettit advocates saved parliamentary seats for members of every minority group within society: all groups, he insists, should "achieve representation, not by grace of senatorial spokespersons, but via the presence of some of their members. . . . The reliably inclusive legislature will have to incorporate, in their own right, all the voices of difference that are found within the community."[69] Such inclusions do and should have an impact in policy formation, but there are limits to what they can achieve in this regard.[70]

Pettit, after all, intends for this diversification of voices to affect parliamentary *deliberation* primarily but legislative *decisions* only indirectly: "as the assembly of law-makers debates its way towards decision, it takes account of the considerations that are salient, not just from a restricted set of privileged viewpoints, but from the full range of social perspectives."[71] According to Pettit, while minority voices must be heard and taken into account within this scheme, such voices have no binding affect on legislative outcomes. This scenario is, for instance, a far cry from saved-seating arrangements in the *Signoria* of several incarnations of the Florentine Republic, where middling and lower guildsmen could, in theory, collectively outvote members of the upper guilds if they felt that their interests were being threatened by particular policies favored by the latter. Occupational quotas in this case ensured that perspectives ranging widely across the socioeconomic spectrum of the Florentine citizenry enjoyed not only deliberative but also decisional impact.[72]

If the practice of saved parliamentary seats for members of minority groups does not replicate the empowerment of less privileged corporate groups in republican Florence, neither does it approximate the affirmative action for common citizens facilitated by the plebeian tribunes in republican Rome: in Pettit's proposal, saved parliamentary seats still leave minority representatives outnumbered among other legislators, while a particular tribune was formally answerable only to the veto of his tribunician colleagues and to the opinion of his plebeian constituency. Furthermore, the saved-seat strategy, as Pettit recommends it, is a decidedly elite-filtered affair: party elites would have tremendous prerogative in choosing, for instance, the 40 percent of candidates that

Pettit suggests should be legally mandated for women.[73] On the one hand, the Roman plebeians themselves decided, without any senatorial imprimatur, who from among their own ranks would serve as tribunes;[74] on the other, even the consuls of the Florentine guilds, when compiling lists of potential priors to serve on the Signoria, did so without an eye to who was, in their estimation, "electable," since the names would be subsequently submitted not to a general election but rather to a lottery.[75]

In any case, more important for Pettit than the diversity of any particular political body is the ability of diverse types of citizens to contest the policies that such bodies issue, for instance, by writing to members of parliament (MPs), asking ombudsmen to conduct inquiries, and appealing judicial decisions to higher courts.[76] But the great care with which Pettit discusses representation of minorities stands in notable contrast to his somewhat cursory treatment of traditional identity politics within republics, that is, the issue of class or, as so extensively discussed by Aristotle, material inequality. In marked contrast to his assertive, declarative, and institutionally specific approach to the problem of vulnerable minorities, Pettit addresses the distorting effect of resource inequality on democratic politics in a tentatively interrogative mode. For instance, he asks, without endorsing any specific reforms, whether campaign contributions can be limited and made public, and whether electoral campaigns should be privately funded at all.[77]

This hesitance is all the more striking once Pettit confirms the fact that economic inequality has been a perennial problem for republics and for republicanism, and that this continues to be the case: "The problem of controlling the influence of the economically powerful on politicians, and more generally on government, is at once an age-old issue...and a pressing contemporary problem."[78] Yet the best Pettit himself offers on this admittedly fundamental and persistent problem confronting republicanism is the following: "One of the greatest challenges for republican research must be to identify measures for effectively separating the worlds of government and business."[79] In short, Pettit punts on the issue.

At base, Pettit's theoretical framework only indirectly addresses the principle asymmetry of power, that of wealthy citizens over poorer citizens, that has historically plagued republics. To be sure, Pettit intends for his category of "dominium" to cover this kind of power asymmetry: to minimize the dominium of, for instance, employers over employees, liberty as nondomination justifies instances where elected officials pass laws that ameliorate conditions under which the former may arbitrarily interfere with the lives of the latter. Moreover, Pettit's theory also justifies contestatory avenues through which employees, as individuals or as members of worker organizations, can challenge the efficacy or fairness of government policy pertaining to the circumstances of their employment. Yet this approach places the burden of initiative on individuals or groups, either to mobilize behind favorable electoral candidates or to petition government actors for redress and remedy – and in both cases, to do so in competition with superiorly resourced opponents. Recognizing the disadvantages that such arrangements impose upon average citizens, advocates of traditional democracies and *governi larghi* formally structured government institutions to empower the economically disadvantaged – through lottery, class-specific institutions, and direct popular judgment. On the contrary, representative governments, of the kind that Pettit advocates, effectively privatize the issue of domination by the few over the many; they, intentionally or not, put informal obstacles in the path of popular attempts at ameliorating such power asymmetries – notably by confining collective authorization and contestation to the aggrieved's capacity to elect and unelect public magistrates.

Pettit's relative inattention to wealth inequality, or, more specifically, his failure to address socioeconomic inequality through formal constitutional prescription, compounds the following problem, already mentioned previously: Pettit's extra-electoral, contestatory institutions function much more like the countermajoritarian ones typifying liberal constitutionalism – namely, upper legislative chambers and supreme courts – than they do popularly contestatory ones such as the Roman tribunate or the guild-specific, lottery-based practices characterizing Florentine politics. After all, elite-dominated, countermajoritarian institutions such as upper houses and supreme courts, despite being charged with the protection of minorities, nevertheless have proven notoriously susceptible to capture by or collusion with entrenched, highly resourced interest groups. In the U.S. context, one cannot help but think of the way that such institutions for generations served the interests of, respectively, slaveholders (and their segregationist heirs) and capital. To be sure, eighteenth and post–eighteenth-century aristocratic republicans such as Montesquieu, Tocqueville, and, to a lesser extent, Madison anticipated that such institutions would seriously constrain but not fully thwart the will of soon-to-be or recently enfranchised peoples in Europe and the Americas.[80] In practice, however, instead of safeguarding vulnerable minorities, these countermajoritarian institutions all too often facilitated the wholesale cooptation of important government organs and functions by economic elites.[81]

Depoliticized Institutions

The prominence of countermajoritarian institutions in Pettit's model amplifies the fact that he is not – despite some statements to the contrary, as we'll see – principally worried by the prospect that elected elites will *depart* from the will of the people when the latter request policies that advance the common avowable interests of citizens. On the contrary, Pettit seems more profoundly concerned that elected elites will be *too* responsive to popular majorities when the latter desire policies that supposedly undermine the common good or threaten the interests of minorities. Pettit suggests that there are policy spheres where the opinions of popular majorities, unduly swayed by their passions or "aspirational morality," ought to be only indirectly reflected in policies made by representatives – indeed, reflected *even more indirectly* than such views already are within conventional electoral politics.[82]

For instance, Pettit identifies criminal sentencing and the regulation of prostitution as areas where the people's emotional fervor or moral scruples might interfere with good policy making by elected officials.[83] Pettit worries that when the people confront issues such as sentencing or prostitution, rather than "consider the overall consequences of each arrangement and make a rational choice," they instead take an unreflective "moral stand" and encourage their representatives, via the threat of punitive electoral sanction, to make bad policy.[84] Pettit speculates that, in such circumstances, voters may use the ballot "primarily as a way of expressing their personal, often heartfelt stand on some issue of moral or religious significance"; to his mind, they are likely to "use their vote for the pleasure of expressive satisfaction."[85]

Pettit proposes institutional reforms that he hopes will "depoliticize democracy" in circumstances where popular irrationality or moral fastidiousness translates into deleterious policy outcomes. The republican philosopher suggests that, in cases where the people would choose poorly themselves or might punish representatives unfairly for making sensible policies, elected officials should appoint special commissions to discuss and even effectively decide such issues. These commissions should

> take the decisions away from the direct influence of representatives [and should themselves] make the decisions under conditions where considerations of the common good, and only such considerations, are very likely to rule.... By putting [parliamentary] control at arm's length in such a manner – by retaining only the hands-off sort of control that parliaments have over electoral commissions – [these forums] would serve the cause of deliberative democracy.[86]

Pettit recommends that these "depoliticized forums," empowered to discuss and decide especially sensitive legislative and regulatory issues, "would be able to take a long-term view, informed by sustained monitoring, of the costs and benefits of different overtures."[87] These "autonomous, professionally informed" commissions would be comprised of policy experts and community leaders: representatives "of relevant bodies of expertise and opinion, as well as of the people as a whole";[88] Pettit anticipates that their members would "represent different sectors of popular opinion and professional expertise."[89]

With this markedly senatorial move, Pettit entrusts policy making to wise, impartial, and common good–loving elites who speak for the people, rather than entrusting it to the people themselves – or even to their conventionally elected representatives. Pettit's justifications for such institutions, which assume that the populace is too fickle, uninformed, or influenced by emotion and prejudice to make sound decisions, are strikingly reminiscent of those put forward in favor of senatorial independence by Cicero, Guicciardini, and some of the American founders. Such republicans argued that senators, more experienced, wise, and prudent than common citizens, should deliberate over and set the agenda of a republic's policy with only limited influence from common citizens.[90] Pettit puts an exclamation point on the necessity of independence for his senatorially detached, "depoliticized" commissions in cases where the people's emotional or moral proclivities too assertively come to the fore: in such circumstances, he writes, "contestatory democracy requires that the demos, and the legislative representatives of the demos, generally tie their hands and gag their mouths."[91]

This proposal obviously raises many questions: will elected elites regularly usurp their own authority to appoint commissions that subsequently make policy in their place? Would they appoint truly expert, impartial, virtuous, and "representative" individuals to serve as commissioners? How many such persons can be found? Most importantly: is it really possible to distinguish, on the one hand, policy spheres where the people's malevolent passions and misguided moral intuitions come into play from, on the other, spheres where their beneficial or sound ones are apposite to the issues at hand? What policy spheres, exactly, do *not* potentially fall into the first category? By failing to distinguish these spheres with more conceptual precision, Pettit runs the risk of inflating the former category in an alarmingly antidemocratic way. He principally argues by example in this context, focusing, again, on criminal sentencing, prostitution, and, to a lesser extent, electoral redistricting; he does not finely delineate policy spheres that ought to remain conventionally political from spheres that, in line with this scheme, ought to be depoliticized.

Pettit himself flirts with a creeping expansion of policy spheres that are largely insulated from popular judgment when, in another instance, he identifies public prosecution as a task that ought to be depoliticized.[92] This is, I remind readers, one of the primary spheres over which Machiavelli assigns the people ultimate judgment (D I.7–8). Indeed, in a worryingly unspecified "variety" of cases, Pettit suggests that "popular debate" is the "worst possible" venue for democratic contestation: "In these cases, the requirement of contestatory democracy is that the complaints should be depoliticized and should be heard away from the tumult of popular discussion and away, even, from the theatre of parliamentary debate."[93] The Machiavellian term "tumult" begs a comparison with the Florentine on the precise spheres that should be insulated from public debate and contestation: in the *Discourses*, Machiavelli enumerates military strategy (devised by the Roman senate) and emergency measures (adopted by the Roman dictator) as the only matters, due to the pressing need for secrecy or for expeditious action in such cases, that need ought not be subject to the "tumult" of popular discussion and contestation (D I.55, D II.25, D I.34).

Pettit's attempt to depoliticize a wider range of important policy spheres suggests that he largely subscribes to the traditional philosophical narratives concerning the people's inability to judge political matters dispassionately and impartially that, as we've observed repeatedly, Machiavelli explicitly criticized (e.g., D I.58). Moreover, some of Pettit's justifications for contestatory democracy notwithstanding, he expresses very little worry that small cadres of supposedly expert and public-spirited elites will abuse the policy-making authority that his model grants them to exercise on behalf of entire citizenries.[94]

Elites, the People, and "the Real Danger"

In isolated instances, Pettit entertains the notion that elite prerogative is a greater threat to liberty than the arbitrary decisions of popular majorities. For example, at one point he muses that the people, acting as a majority, will be reluctant to abuse minorities for fear of depopulating the polity: "the collectivity is forced, on pain of suffering mass emigration, to track the common avowable interests of its members."[95] At another, Pettit avers, party competition in mass democracies discourages majority tyranny: entrepreneurial politicians consistently court underrepresented groups of citizens in the hopes of enlarging their constituencies; when they do, they tend to "shame majority supporters into changing their allegiance" in ways that benefit previously vulnerable groups and individuals.[96] In the midst of these reflections that give popular majorities considerable benefit of the doubt, the republican philosopher suggests that a tyranny exercised by a "democratic elite" is "probably" more dangerous to liberty than a tyranny exercised by a "democratic majority."[97] The "probably" in this quote, however, proves to be a telling qualification: while Pettit, as he does here, sometimes gestures to the notion that elite prerogative is the greatest threat posed by contemporary democracy, he usually writes, especially when prescribing institutional reforms, as though majority tyranny is clearly the maximum political danger.

Pettit is generally much more wary of the people than he is of elites, and he frequently goes to great lengths to generate rationales for why elites can be expected to act on behalf of the common good, while he tends to accept as fact the notion that the people simply cannot. Pettit insists that popular judgment is prone to "collective unreason,"[98] and he asserts definitively (i.e., without the softening qualifier "probably") that majoritarian tyranny is "the real danger" posed by democracy.[99] Indeed, to Pettit's mind, majority rule potentially replicates the arbitrary, dominating authority wielded in previous centuries by absolute monarchs: "It is quite possible that the people, understood collectively, should dominate the people, understood severally; the collective people can be as uncontrolled an agency, from the point of view of at least some individuals, as the divinely endorsed king."[100]

Pettit rejects the affinity between popular judgment, on the one hand, and the maximization of liberty, social and individual, on the other, noted by authors as different as Plato (who did so with disapprobation), Aristotle, Machiavelli, and scholars associated with the "wisdom of crowds" literature.[101] While such authors detected an empirical correlation between democracy and liberty, Pettit, speaking analytically, asserts that there is no "definitional connection" between the two.[102] Relying instead on the patrician critique of majority rule, Pettit cites Madison and Montesquieu, and implicitly invokes Tocqueville, when he declares: "The tyranny of the majority gives the lie to any suggestion that the elective mode of democratization is bound fully to ensure the friendliness of government to freedom, in particular to freedom as nondomination."[103]

Given this view of the people, generally, and of majority rule, in particular, it is not surprising that Pettit wishes to keep important decisions away from directly expressed and even indirectly expressed popular influence. Pettit recommends that his fora comprised of experts and opinion leaders should make their "judgments away from the theater of politics"; his depoliticized commissions should deliberate and decide without being "exposed to the glare and pressure of public debate."[104] Democracy, Pettit insists, lives not only in "the oxygen of public debate and participation" but also operates in "professionalized forums in which consultations are offered and negotiated, and appeals of various kinds heard and judged"; it exists and perhaps thrives in spaces "not governed by public will, and, often not opened to the public gaze."[105]

Thus, the republican philosopher resoundingly endorses expert commissions that operate at one step removed from parliamentary politics and two steps removed from the people themselves; an endorsement that presupposes, in Pettit's own words, that "it is possible for certain bodies to be impartial on matters where the population is divided."[106] Pettit expects that the political, professional, and opinion elites who comprise his depoliticized fora will commit themselves strictly to factual concerns and common good considerations: such representatives and experts can, with confidence, be asked "to judge on the factual issue of whether the policy as identified and implemented is supported by common, recognizable interests and only by such interests."[107] These actors will not, as many democrats worry,[108] decide matters to their own advantage, or in favor of some special interest to which they're beholden, nor will they succumb to the same ideological divisions that beset society at large: Pettit thinks it plausible to expect such elites to be "free of self-serving interests and be all the more susceptible to considerations of fair play."[109] As evidence for the capacity of such bodies to generate fair-minded, well-considered, and generally beneficial decisions, Pettit invokes the example of criminal juries.[110] However, juries are, of course, comprised not of expert elites but rather of the same common people that Pettit would like to distance from important policy decisions.[111] I return to this point later in this chapter.

Ultimately, what exactly will keep expert commissioners sufficiently depoliticized, impartial, and attentive to the common good? Pettit's answer is deeply Ciceronian: such commissioners wish to enhance "their reputation," and to satisfy their "desire for esteem."[112] They will behave appropriately, according to Pettit, because they "stand to win the good opinion of most of their fellows only so far as they are seen to discharge their allotted brief."[113] This justification requires further elaboration: if a commissioner seeks reputation and esteem earned via the good opinion of fellow commissioners, then we have no reason to expect any better efforts on behalf of the common good than were afforded by the Roman senate, whose members famously vied with each other for the esteem of the entire body. Furthermore, in such circumstances, the evaluation of whether a commissioner has successfully discharged his or her allotted brief is fully determined by similarly situated colleagues, not by the public itself – hardly a standard either reflective of or, certainly, conducive to the common good.

If, alternatively, the audience from which individual commissioners seek approval is comprised of members of parliament, then Pettit must better specify the relationship between the commissioners and MPs. If we are to comprehend the full impact of parliament's estimation of commissioners, we need to know the following: how truly "autonomous" are the former from the latter? In what sense do they operate "at arm's length" from the latter? What does it mean to say that parliament retains "ultimate control" in these circumstances?[114] Presumably, given the fact that commissioners deliberate and decide outside of public view, Pettit does not mean by "their fellows" the average people who actually are their fellow citizens. If he does, if it is the public's esteem that is meant to keep their conduct in the service of the common good, then his commissioners ought to stand for election.

Republicanism and the Disempowered People

These issues aside, Pettit's use of conventional juries as exemplars of rational and objective decision making – indeed, as models for the way he expects his depoliticized commissions to conduct themselves – is all the more curious since he refuses to consider the use of jury-like institutions in roles that he assigns to his depoliticized commissions. In recent years, a number of scholars and public intellectuals have theorized and even overseen experiments with institutions such as citizen juries, minipublics, peoples' assemblies, and deliberative polls; institutions where randomly selected or demographically representative groups of citizens gather together to discuss and vote on salient public policy issues.[115] In fact, some of these bodies have been empowered to make decisions with legally binding authority over policy within specific jurisdictions.[116] Indeed, such minipublics are reminiscent of the popular juries, comprised of five hundred citizens, that judged political trials in democratic Athens. Pettit speaks favorably of these mini–citizen assemblies but he never entertains the notion of granting them the same political autonomy and decision-making authority that he grants to his purportedly depoliticized commissions.[117]

Perhaps Pettit has good cause to be suspicious of opinions that average people express in conventional polls with no legally binding consequence. He draws on evidence suggesting that, when questioned for such polls, people very often express "frustration or exasperation or malice or something of the kind," since, in such contexts, they know that they are not responsible for their opinions.[118] Recall from Chapter 3 how Machiavelli offers similar observations about informally expressed and legally nonbinding popular opinion (D I.7–8, D I.47). However, Machiavelli suggests that when historians and philosophers criticize the people for allowing their passions and moral intuitions to interfere with their evaluations of policy alternatives, such authors unwittingly or willfully confuse popular *opinion* with popular *judgment*. The people, Machiavelli demonstrates, often claim that they want one thing or another in taverns, in their homes, or on the street; nevertheless, they often choose something quite different when they are formally empowered to deliberate and decide within the bounds of an assembly.

Machiavelli suggests that formal procedures of judgment compel the people to descend from the generalities of their opinions to the particulars of their true preferences (D I.47–8). Within institutions very much like many of the minipublics discussed and implemented in various contemporary contexts, Machiavelli argues that the people successfully distinguish genuine accusations from spurious calumnies when they judge political criminals, and they perceptively consider future benefits and ills when they discuss and formulate law (D I.18, D I.58). It is also worth recalling in this context that Machiavelli criticizes perhaps no one more harshly throughout the *Discourses* than popular leaders who deny the people the opportunity to decide for themselves the most important questions facing republics. We observed him chastise Virginius the centurian, Francesco Valori, and Girolamo Savonarola for circumventing legally authorized popular judgment, either for their own selfish purposes or because they thought they knew what was best for the people (D I.7, D I.44, D I.45).

Pettit himself concedes that average people are capable of arriving at well-considered conclusions when they formally assemble to discuss and decide policy issues. In fact, Pettit acknowledges that groups of common people, when presented with information provided by various sources – especially, information that reflects opposing viewpoints – and when permitted to discuss this information at length, these citizens prove admirably capable of making informed decisions that may be said to advance the common good. However, very much *unlike* Machiavelli, Pettit neglects to take this evidence as a cue to further conceptualize or openly endorse institutions that formally empower the people, or some demographically representative or randomly generated subset of them, to make legally binding decisions. Stopping far short of this, Pettit would employ deliberative opinion polls or the decisions of citizen juries in a strictly consultative capacity: that is, as exemplars whose decisions once publicized might influence and hopefully change broader opinion within the wider citizenry or that might impact the behavior of representatives. But Pettit would *not* assign them any direct policy impact themselves.[119]

Through many episodes we've observed (e.g., Coriolanus and the Roman plebs, Manlius Capitolinus and the Roman senate, Pacuvius and the Capuan Republic), Machiavelli demonstrates how arrangements like minipublics or citizen juries that formally empower the people to make real decisions actually compel the people to clarify their preferences when such preferences are unclear and to moderate their impulses when such impulses are excessive. On the contrary, it seems, it is precisely when the people are completely disempowered, or when their only recourse is to ask intermediaries to act for them, that the people allow themselves to succumb to political confusion and fancy – often demanding that representatives behave more rashly and harshly than they would themselves if formally empowered to judge.[120] If Machiavelli is right about the rationally and morally disciplining effect of formal institutions of deliberation and decision on common people, then Pettit's fears about the negative impact of the people's passions and aspirational morality would seem misplaced – or at least worthy of being put to the test.

If, in Pettit's own estimation, contemporary minipublics and citizen juries are genuinely "deliberative" and can, when suitably diverse and representative, reflect the "predominant" view of a collectivity, why shouldn't Pettit entrust such fora to generate binding policy decisions?[121] Or at least, why shouldn't Pettit grant them as much legislative and administrative authority as he grants to depoliticized commissions?[122] After all, if groups of both elites and common citizens can function in a depoliticized way in certain circumstances, why not choose the latter to exercise judgment, especially if the republican philosopher still understands himself to be operating to *some* extent within an explicitly democratic framework? Indeed, smaller, randomly selected or demographically faithful subsets of the entire citizenry that deliberate over and ultimately decide public policy pose, from a democratic perspective, an attractive alternative to institutions that further empower elites to do so. Ultimately, which is more utopian: to expect such minipublics to make generally good decisions, or to expect elites to behave in a consistently impartial and depoliticized fashion?

As we recall from previous chapters, to Machiavelli's mind, princely and senatorial elites – because of their inherent appetite for oppression, their overall disrespect for laws, and their general inclination toward corruption and collusion, conspiracy and cooptation – are constitutionally incapable, by themselves, of effectively punishing individuals who threaten a republic's liberty and of making laws conducive to the public good. Much more often than any prince or elites similarly empowered, the people, according to Machiavelli, will decide appropriately. Rather than placing sensitive policy decisions at one further step removed from the people, as Pettit recommends, Machiavelli enjoins us to theorize ways to approximate the direct judgment that the citizens of many ancient, medieval, and Renaissance democratic republics and governi larghi exercised in assemblies. Even if we were to agree with Pettit that contemporary democracy is not a regime that expresses the collective will, but rather empowers what he calls popular valuation,[123] there is simply no empirical evidence supporting the claim that representative institutions perform the task of reflecting popular valuation any better than tribunician and/or plebiscitary ones.[124]

In this spirit, Pettit probably dismisses citizen-initiated referenda too casually. They are, he claims, potentially too democratic *and* too undemocratic: they can both facilitate majority mistreatment of minorities and permit "influence by moneyed interest groups" to affect referenda results.[125] Moreover, Pettit suggests that referenda invite arbitrary and self-contradictory outcomes since, from one referendum to another, "the voting collectivity cannot be subjected to a discipline of intertemporal consistency"; and, just as he worried in the case of conventional polling, "participants in a large-scale election are often expressive rather than pragmatic in the way they vote."[126] These are perhaps valid objections to referenda as they are often conducted.[127] But citizen referenda could certainly become more reliable and efficacious if, for instance, they were not held in tandem with elections for public office, and if they were made less vulnerable to influence by publicity generated overwhelmingly through private financing. In any case, one wishes that Pettit would work as strenuously to conceptualize conditions under which the people as a whole, or reproduced in virtuo, could be granted the opportunity to make decisions conducive to the common good – at least as much as he does for the experts and community leaders who comprise his purportedly depoliticized commissions.[128]

Redefining Democracy

Pettit notes correctly that under contemporary representative governments, conventional "avenues of public access provide ordinary people with only very limited consultative resources," such as the capacity to petition legislators.[129] But I've demonstrated that the consultative measures that Pettit grants "ordinary people" within his model of "democracy, electoral and contestatory," are not much more robust. The republican philosopher rightfully acknowledges that "democracy" played but one part within the celebrated mixed regime known as the Roman Republic; but democracy, as practiced either directly through the authorial exercise of popular judgment in Rome's assemblies or indirectly through the contestatory functions of the tribunes of the plebs plays *no role* whatsoever in Pettit's reconstructed model of democracy.[130] Most authors within the republican tradition with which Pettit heartily allies himself made no effort to call a regime that excludes *all* direct forms of popular control a "democracy." Most republicans did not understand themselves to be democrats. Quite the contrary. Pettit, while replicating many of their criticisms of democracy, nevertheless attempts to maintain the name "democracy" for the institutional model he endorses, a model from which he excludes all directly participatory practices that one could rightfully consider democratic.

Justifying this approach, Pettit declares that it is a fallacy to associate "democracy exclusively with the rule of the collective people: the rule of the people en masse; in a word, people power"; and, furthermore, he insists that "it would be a mistake to think that democracy exists only so far as ordinary people actively control things."[131] Yet Pettit muddies rather than clarifies matters when he refuses to render distinct, as Machiavelli does, the likely behavior of a people formally empowered to decide in assembly from what Pettit calls "unconstrained, majority rule," or, quite simply, "ochlocracy."[132] Can one adequately base a genuine theory of democracy on the assumption that the people acting collectively (aside from simply choosing public officials) will inevitably conduct themselves in either a frivolous or rapacious manner? Even if Machiavelli did not use the word democracy, the following definition of democracy proffered by Pettit is incompatible with the Florentine's reconstruction of the Roman Republic as a full-fledged *governo largo* in the *Discourses*:

> Democracy is not inherently a collective matter . . . ; it is not inherently a matter of active control; and it is not inherently the sort of system that confines decision making to sites that are available to public scrutiny and influence. Democracy does not mean the reign of the collective, active will of the public or its representatives. It is a system, rather, in which things are organized so that while the people collectively have enough electoral power to guard against false negatives, the people noncollectively enjoy enough contestatory power to guard against false positives.[133]

On the contrary, Machiavelli thought that the people collectively should guard against false negatives (i.e., ensure that government policies accurately reflect common avowable interests) by exercising legislative judgment themselves *and* that they should guard against false positives (i.e., object to government policies that adversely affect common interests) by directly exercising judicial authority and by quasi-directly exercising contestation through the tribunician veto.

Pettit, despite certain claims to the contrary, seems at base to disagree with Machiavelli on the people's political capabilities, especially their ability to carry out tasks that are positively active (as opposed to merely negatively passive or reactive) and their ability to do so in ways that are conducive to the common good. When explaining why "democratic" contestation ought not to be put in collective hands, Pettit renders sharply irreconcilable, on the one hand, majority decision making and, on the other, the rule of "reason": on Pettit's understanding, "the democratic process is designed to let the requirements of reason materialize and impose themselves; it is not a process that gives any particular place to will."[134]

But the republican philosopher distinguishes analytically what is, quite possibly, a false dichotomy empirically: "reason" seldom materializes self-evidently and rarely imposes itself spontaneously in the midst of political controversy; some person or persons must decide, in such contexts, what is reasonable. In a regime organized for the purpose of minimizing domination and maximizing the common good, the people themselves must ultimately set the standard for what is reasonable. Hence, in any democracy worthy of the name, the people should be institutionally empowered, wherever it is remotely efficacious logistically, to deliberate and decide public policy themselves. As Machiavelli demonstrates so well, citizens come to see their own interests most clearly and manage to avow them most articulately through political practices in which they participate directly (D I.47, I.58) and through institutional arrangements in which they discuss and decide not only the appointment of magistrates but also and especially legislation and public prosecutions (D I.58, D I.7–8).

Machiavelli compels democrats to pose the following question to critics of majoritarianism, such as Pettit, who fixate on the excesses and deficiencies of popular judgment: "excessive and deficient as compared to what?"[135] Pettit's project often seems motivated by the largely unfounded belief that decisions by the few are generally correct, that is, more often than not conducive to the common good, and that they can be rendered, in Pettit's sense, fully "depoliticized."[136] In this sense, Pettit seems to approach this problem from a neo-Platonic or neo-Ciceronian standpoint, a standpoint that presumes that reason most likely resides among an elite few (e.g., a polity's best men, representatives elected by the people, or experts appointed by the latter's representatives). Only such a Platonic perspective, according to which some enlightened, depoliticized few can justly and effectively make decisions for everyone else, could justify Pettit's much too insistent rejection of rule by the many.

As demonstrated in previous chapters and earlier in this one, Machiavelli, when arguing against "all the writers," suggests that such a perspective is woefully misguided. In this light, if Pettit and other neo-republicans wish to formulate a truly comprehensive and practically efficacious theory of liberty as nondomination, I suggest that they reconceive institutional design along Machiavellian rather than traditional republican lines. To be sure, traditional republicans espoused constitutional models that successfully allowed alliances between peoples and elites to end monarchical domination exercised by the likes of Tarquin, Bourbon, and Stuart kings. However, in addition, Machiavelli espoused a model wherein the people could prevent domination by their erstwhile allies in such efforts: the political and socioeconomic elites who hold elected magistracies in republics and/or who sit, either literally or figuratively, in the senatorial bodies of such regimes.

Popular Participation versus Republican Domination

In light of Pettit's narrow conception of democracy, that is, given the minimal role that participation plays in his republican model, I suggest that it is fair to question the extent to which his institutional prescriptions are appropriate for the task of realizing his normative goal of minimizing domination. After all, many "republicans," albeit democratically inclined ones, who quite explicitly spoke Pettit's language of "freedom from domination," specifically criticized as instruments of their own domination institutions very similar to the ones that Pettit endorses as guarantees against this domination. The Roman plebs, Florentines of the middling and lower guilds, and, of course, Machiavelli himself demanded institutions and procedures that provided common citizens with both direct access to policy making and the substantive means of contesting the power of social and political elites, including direct judgment by the citizenry over legislative and judicial matters; class-specific magistracies or assembles; and the tempering of elections through randomization measures.

Thus, when Pettit asserts that the "populist" identification of liberty and democratic participation was a relatively late phenomenon, a "new" development, he speaks exclusively from the perspective of aristocratic philosopher-statesmen and of the *literati* who rather dutifully served the former's interest.[137] This claim ignores the aspirations of common citizens within popular governments – *demoi*, populares, and lower guildsmen – who, until Machiavelli, benefited from the efforts of very few if any intellectual spokesmen of note. In general, Pettit, following the Cambridge School historians on whom he relies, recapitulates the "republicanism" of the philosopher-statesmen, which in many respects is an ideological discourse of "the best men" who supposedly guard the common good. On the contrary, Machiavelli's writings give voice to the aspirations of the politically and socially contentious common citizens who challenged aristocratic republican efforts to oppress them and constrict their political participation. In this light, the work of both Skinner and Pettit compels anyone genuinely interested in the principles and practice of popular government to ask: Whose liberty? Which republicanism?

As mentioned in this book's introduction, Cambridge scholars are generally guilty of ignoring the extent to which "republicanism" facilitated conditions that they themselves would identify as incompatible with a robust, nonliberal notion of liberty; in other words, they neglect the fact that, in both practice and theory, republicanism has legitimated considerable arbitrary intervention by socioeconomic elites into the lives of ordinary citizens. Indeed, Skinner and Pettit never pause to consider the fact that the principal regimes and preeminent spokesmen typifying Italian republicanism (in ancient, medieval, and early Renaissance contexts) entitled and enabled wealthy and prominent citizens to affect the lives of poorer citizens in ways that disregarded the latter's avowed articulations of their interests. Republican political and social relations in such circumstances entailed not merely patrician or noble "interference" with the lives of common citizens, but outright "domination" over them.

The following well-known cases characteristic of prominent Italian republics clearly conform, in particular, to Pettit's definition of dominium: in Rome, creditors threatened to impose debt bondage upon plebeian debtors to whom they lent and from whom they collected money;[138] and in Florence, wool producers obstructed the attempts of woolworkers to improve their miserable working conditions through the formation of their own guild, circumstances that eventually erupted in the Ciompi Revolt.[139] Moreover, Livy and Machiavelli catalogue numerous instances of political domination that fit Pettit's definition of imperium – most especially, the Roman senate's refusal to distribute public lands among the plebeians and its frequent enlistment of the latter in unnecessary wars that enriched the nobility while further impoverishing the plebs. A list of other notable instances of noble domination would include, but would certainly not be confined to, nobles setting the terms under which citizens of lower birth or fewer resources may or may not stand for office, can or cannot choose magistrates, and are or are not permitted to marry outside of their class; their establishment of the conditions for when the rules governing these spheres would be changed; and so forth.[140]

It would be difficult to argue that these examples merely constitute cases where the reality of republicanism fails to live up to its own ideals. After all, at an intellectual level, the republicanisms of Cicero, Bruni, and Guicciardini, in large measure, justified the domination of, respectively, nobles over plebeians in Rome, upper guildsmen over members of Florence's middling and lower guilds, and Florentine *ottimati* over the popolo in the post-1494 republic. Moreover, as mentioned previously, the writings of Italian philosopher-statesmen associated directly with "republicanism" can be situated in close proximity to sustained subversions or outright usurpations of popular governments and to discernible narrowings of popular participation that demonstrably did not advance the commonly avowed interests of most citizens.

Scholars working within Pettit's framework will nevertheless counter that this critique fails to pierce the heart of the neo-republican project; that is, empirical/historical criticisms gain no significant traction against "freedom as nondomination," understood primarily as a philosophical standard. But this view misrepresents Pettit's objectives. As the subtitle of his most influential work indicates, Pettit presents republicanism as "a theory of freedom *and* government"; he consequently devotes as much energy to prescribing institutions that he thinks secure nondomination as he does to articulating the philosophical components of his theory of freedom. Therefore, it is not without consequence for Pettit's theory of freedom that his own institutional prescriptions share so much in common with those of quintessential republicans such as Cicero, Bruni, and Guicciardini and their modern heirs – institutional prescriptions that when adopted quite arguably increased, *not* decreased, the domination of ordinary citizens by economic and political elites. One must challenge the viability of a theoretical-practical model such as Pettit's republicanism if its recommended practices consistently, perhaps even invariably, contravene and undermine its normative aspirations. More specifically, a theory of liberty as historically informed, empirically grounded, and institutionally prescriptive as Pettit's aspires to be simply cannot afford to prioritize the philosophical justification of neo-Roman liberty or of freedom as nondomination over the indispensable means that, in particular, Machiavelli and common citizens thought absolutely necessary to attain it: wide and substantive political participation.

I have reminded readers that the broad republican tradition was for the most part committed to a qualified form of oligarchy where socioeconomic and political elites *dominated*, according to Pettit's own definition, common citizens: the minimizing or narrowing of popular participation advocated by the founders of republican theory such as Cicero, Bruni, and Guicciardini, as well as by prominent English, Dutch, American, and French proponents of republicanism,[141] led to political outcomes that did not, in Pettit's terms, "track" the common good as perceived or avowed by the vast majority of citizens. With this in mind, in conclusion I emphasize three important elements common to the republicanisms of Pettit, Cicero, Bruni, and Guicciardini: (1) each marginalizes or constrains the place of popular participation within the politics of republics; (2) each isolates general election as the principal means of appointing magistrates (that is, they reject or eschew alternatives involving lottery, an election-lottery mixture, class or occupational quotas for offices, etc.); and (3) each confers on a rather senatorial set of elites wide deliberative and decisional prerogative over policy questions concerning the common good, without formulating any clear criteria by which one could ascertain the appropriate limits to be placed upon elite judgment.

On these grounds, I've demonstrated that Pettit's adherence to the principles and, especially, practices of traditional republicanism manifests itself in the democratically stunted and elite-empowering form of "electoral and contestatory democracy" that he subsequently espouses; one in which the people exercise both political authorization *and* extra-electoral contestation *indirectly* through representative and otherwise elite-filtered channels. Through the political prescriptions of Machiavelli – whom, pace the interpretations of scholars such as Pocock, Skinner, and Pettit, I understand to be a self-avowed *dissenter* from the republican tradition[142] – I have suggested the following. Should Pettit and progressively inclined republicans wish to elaborate a more substantive theory of democracy, they ought to qualify their relationship significantly to traditional republicanism, which successfully championed liberty as nondomination when challenging arbitrarily wielded monarchical power, but which exhibited a manifestly poor record in ameliorating domination exercised by socioeconomic and political elites within republics; and further theorize and openly endorse institutions of political authorization and contestation that directly empower the people to decide matters of public policy, such as political trials and legislation.

After all, Machiavelli, whom Pettit and other neo-republicans understand as a comrade in the cause of advancing liberty as nondomination, argues that socioeconomic and political elites, *not* common citizens, constitute the greatest threat to liberty within republics and, furthermore, that the people rather than the few are much more likely to make decisions conducive to the common good. Ultimately, I would beseech Pettit and neorepublicans to choose between democracy and republicanism on these grounds: historically speaking, democracy politically compensates common people for their lack of material resources relative to socioeconomic elites and formally empowers the former to deliberate and decide policy themselves; while republicanism, in general, safeguards elite privilege and prerogative from popular challenge and empowers representatives and purportedly neutral or "depoliticized" experts to decide, not always in good faith, on the people's behalf. Rather than – as republicans from Cicero to Madison and beyond suggest – advocating the empowerment of the people's elected representatives to serve as the filter through which the people's views are "refined and enlarged," Machiavelli insists upon institutional arrangements through which the people themselves refine and enlarge their own opinions.

The paramount issue is not whether we deem Machiavelli's politics republican or democratic. Admittedly, this could degenerate into a largely unhelpful semantic debate. The more substantive point is: while Machiavelli's thinking on liberty coincides in important ways with Pettit's indisputably imposing conceptualization of liberty as nondomination, Machiavelli rejects the popularly marginalizing institutional arrangements characteristic of philosophical republicanism from Plato to Pettit. Machiavelli reminds us that, historically, the vast majority of citizens within republics explicitly denounced electoral and senatorial institutions as vehicles of their own domination by socioeconomic and political elites. If we are to find some semblance of objectivity and love for the common good among anyone in real-world republics, it will not be in a collection of the enlightened few advocated by the philosophers – not among Plato's philosopher kings, Cicero's senatorial best men, or Pettit's depolicticized experts. It will be found, rather, Machiavelli avers, in the body of citizens, institutionally empowered to deliberate and decide for themselves.

7

Post-Electoral Republics and the People's Tribunate Revived

> The grandi's ambition will soon destroy a polity if not subdued in various ways and through various modes. . . . Rome would have become servile much sooner if the plebs had not always checked the nobility's ambition.
>
> Machiavelli, *Discourses* I.37

> In polities like Rome and Athens, the people are princes. . . .
>
> Machiavelli, *Discourses* I.58

James Madison famously redefined republics as regimes characterized by electoral representation and by "the total exclusion of the people in their collective capacity" from the workings of government.[1] Very shortly then before "democracy" would reappear on the Western political horizon, Madison, like most of his fellow eighteenth-century republicans, had already precluded from the democratic agenda prominent features of earlier popular governments or *governi larghi*: class-specific magistracies or assemblies; socio-economically unbiased methods for selecting public officials; and formalized procedures through which citizens directly deliberate over and decide public affairs.[2] Madison's rationale was not quantitative but qualitative: it was not the scale of modern regimes that necessitated representation but rather the assumption that elections conducted over large territories would generally produce the "best" statesmen. Arguably, the aristocratic character of elections and the abandonment of class-specific or directly participatory practices portended the pacification of modern democracy before its triumph.[3]

True enough, Madison was less elitist than most of his American contemporaries,[4] and he would become more politically egalitarian not long after the ratification of the U.S. Constitution, when he helped found the first political party in history to adopt the designation "democratic."[5] Nevertheless, largely at Madison's prompting, democracy, electoral democracy, by forgoing any class-specific or direct expression of the general populace, would arguably allow elites as much or perhaps even more free rein than did traditional republicanism, which often reserved ex ante special offices or tasks for prominent citizens to occupy or perform. In this manner, Madison achieved the de facto elitist results desired by Machiavelli's aristocratic-republican contemporary, Guicciardini, without resorting to the overtly elitist, formal restrictions on the general populace's participation in politics that the latter sometimes considered.[6]

Beyond the American context, early-twentieth-century "elite theorists of democracy" sometimes seemed to relish the persistence of political inequality in the age of mass suffrage.[7] More recent and more avowedly progressive theorists of electoral democracy often appear resigned to it.[8] Yet the republican-inherited "minimalist" criterion of popular government generally agreed upon by both sets of democratic theorists – namely, periodic selection of public officials for specific terms of office by a populace enfranchised with universal adult suffrage – seems less and less sufficient to guarantee citizens' liberty in contemporary democracies.[9] As pointed out previously, an increasing number of critics suggest that the primarily electoral model of popular government fails to keep political elites accountable and responsive to the general public and neglects to counteract the disproportionate influence of the wealthy on the workings of government.[10] This chapter marks an intervention into an ever-widening contemporary debate over reforms that might ameliorate this situation. In keeping with the invocation of Madison at its start, this chapter adopts a largely American perspective: I structure my reform proposal to address the constitutional framework of the United States; however, it could conceivably be adapted fairly easily to institutional arrangements within other polities.

Earlier chapters of this book were primarily historical and interpretive: inspired by Machiavelli's writings, the chapters comprising Part II, in particular, focused on institutional alternatives to modern, election-fixated modes of popular participation and elite accountability drawn from ancient, medieval, and early-modern popular governments. I explicated Machiavelli's – and, in certain cases, Guicciardini's – evaluations of offices and assemblies reserved exclusively for common as opposed to wealthy citizens; their analyses of magistrate appointment procedures combining lottery and election; and their weighing of the appropriate roles of public officials versus the general citizenry in accusing and judging officeholders and/or powerful citizens suspected of political impropriety.

In this chapter, I set out an abstract typology of regimes based on mixtures of lottery and election in nomination and appointment procedures of public officials; and I propose a hypothetical elite-accountability institution to be amended to the U.S. Constitution. The latter, a revived tribunate, combines elements of randomization, wealth-exclusion, and direct plebeian judgment that, as we have observed, were prominent in both certain pre–eighteenth-century republican constitutions and in many reform proposals that were intended to make these polities more popularly inclusive and empowering. In other words, through these endeavors I sketch, respectively, quasi-Florentine and neo-Roman institutional responses to the hegemony of elections in contemporary republics, specifically the United States. The first, the typology of regimes, generates lottery/election mixtures with which reformers might replace strictly electoral schemes of magistrate appointment, and the second outlines a tribunician magistracy reserved for common citizens that, among other things, would make political and socioeconomic elites more accountable than do election-focused methods of reward and sanction.

Unlike authors such as Skinner and Pettit, I argued in earlier chapters that Machiavelli's *democratic* proposals for popular participation and elite control largely elude neo-republican attempts to appropriate his political thought. Yet despite the vigor of Machiavellian Democracy, democratic theorists working outside the civic republican paradigm tend to ignore Machiavelli and generally look elsewhere for intellectual resources in their efforts to address the participatory and accountability deficiencies of contemporary democracies: most notably, they tend to draw upon the modern contract or consent traditions of political thought.[11] One reason for this neglect might be that Machiavelli's approach to these issues, at first blush, seems analytically imprecise: he combines normative prescription, historical description, and textual commentary in a way that often renders his conclusions less than readily transparent. Moreover, Machiavelli's prescriptions, when specified, like many institutions of Mediterranean democracies and *governi larghi*, may not seem in any obvious way transferable to contemporary circumstances.

As an example, perhaps Machiavelli's recommendation for a scheme of public accusations, in which every citizen freely and frequently hurls accusations at the prominent and the powerful, is too unwieldy. Likewise, more generally, the citizen lottery system of democratic Athens may be, at face value, an impractical means of appointing public officials within contemporary democracies. Perhaps these Machiavellian and Athenian schemes of, respectively, sanctioning and appointing magistrates cannot be applied directly in contemporary circumstances. The size and complexity of contemporary commercial societies, and the expertise required to govern them, tend to be exaggerated in considerations of this kind.[12] But, for the sake of argument, let me concede that these considerations rule out, in their original forms, certain features of pre-modern popular governments as useful resources for reform-minded political reflection today.

Nevertheless, other aspects of pre-modern popular governments analyzed by Machiavelli and Guicciardini may inspire deeper reflection on and perhaps offer more applicable lessons for constitutionally enabling citizen participation and control of economic and political elites today. For instance, Machiavelli also recommends procedures of accusation through which class-specific magistrates, the tribunes, criminally indict elites on behalf of common citizens. Moreover, Guicciardini's reflections remind us that lot and election were not always employed in an either/or fashion when republics appointed magistrates. In short, we need not necessarily leave the public fate of suspect elites exclusively in the hands of their official peers and adversaries in government; and, perhaps more importantly, we need not be destined to submit to rule exclusively by those who meet the problematic criterion of "electability." For all its power, Bernard Manin's brilliant account of the "triumph of election over lot," on which I have relied extensively throughout this book, does not exhaust the lessons of magistrate appointment and sanction methods in the political history of the West.[13] In this chapter, I attempt to offer alternative lessons for participation and accountability in contemporary democracy, specifically the United States, on the basis of that broader history.

Lot, Election, and a Typology of Regimes

Clearly, Machiavelli, Guicciardini, and the republics they analyzed were more attentive to the asymmetrical power relations between, on the one hand, magistrates *and* wealthy citizens and, on the other, common citizens, than are most modern republican political theorists and practitioners. In particular, Machiavelli's adaptation of the Roman tribunate in his constitutional proposal for Florence, discussed in Chapter 4, goes much further than either traditional or modern attempts to make offices within republics more fully inclusive and widely representative. Certainly, modern democracies that employ proportional representation or that adopt corporatist or consociationalist arrangements are much better than winner-take-all electoral systems at providing a voice in government to a wider array of social groups – notably, labor and, more recently, environmentalists.[14] However, such arrangements are not immune to the criticism that they facilitate "domination by one's own" – that is, party and union elites enjoy tremendous informational and power advantages over average members of political organizations in such systems.[15] On the contrary, Machiavelli's tribunate cum provostship seems designed precisely to place "rank-and-file" plebs in positions of political authority on a regular basis.

Returning to lottery and election as discrete means of selecting magistrates, each method exhibits "negative" and "positive" attributes. Thus far I have emphasized the negative aspects: lotteries keep socioeconomic elites from monopolizing public offices, and elections supposedly sanction political elites retrospectively. Conceived, alternately, in positive terms, lottery within ancient democracies realized the principle of equitable political participation among citizens; it put into practice the egalitarian standard of "ruling and being ruled in turn" for any citizen who wished to serve in office.[16] For modern advocates of popular government, election positively operationalizes the normative principles of representation: the people do not rule, but they consent to rule by elites whom they choose and who are assumed to act more adeptly in the people's interest than can the people themselves, even when that interest is best served by policies that defy the popular will at any given non-electoral moment.[17] The electorate purportedly deters abuse of a representative's discretionary latitude by reconsidering an official's performance and voting accordingly during the next election.[18] In extreme instances, the threat of removal proceedings from which the public is largely excluded is meant to punish and discourage the potential abuse of discretion endemic to representative systems. This, of course, stylizes the differences between democracies ancient and modern: ancient democracies clearly valued expertise, often assigning important military and financial offices via election; and modern republics value equal participation, if not as much as they do expertise and the norm of "consent" legitimating it.

Ideally, each appointment method offers the following advantages to popular government: lot, via randomization, draws on a wide spectrum of perspectives and talents throughout the citizenry and prevents the wealthy and prominent from monopolizing law and policy making; election purports to fill the government with worthy and competent magistrates and functions as a political authorization mechanism for citizens who themselves cannot or do not wish to hold office. It must be noted that the advantages of lottery are more verifiable than those of election: lot is guaranteed to distribute offices randomly among all citizens willing to serve in office – in fact, given demographics, it is likely to place most magistracies in the hands of less wealthy citizens.[19] On the other hand, no empirical evidence available demonstrates that those who win elections are especially capable of providing good government or are significantly constrained in their behavior by retrospective voting patterns. We can be certain only that those who emerge victorious within electoral systems are good at winning elections. The drawbacks of each method are obvious: the inherent amateurism of politics conducted by magistrates appointed through lottery and the aristocratic biases of electoral regimes.

As the history of Italian peninsular republics and Guicciardini's discussion – if not endorsement – of Florence's electoral reforms circa 1497 confirm, the two appointment methods were often combined in practice. One might expect that various combinations of lottery and election could mitigate the respective disadvantages of each method, maximize their specific beneficial attributes, and possibly satisfy each of the two major social groups that favor them individually. In this spirit, I introduce the following typology of regimes that schematizes lot, election, and their mixture as methods of selecting magistrates.

There are two stages of the process to fill public offices that we observed Guicciardini consider in Chapter 4: identifying candidates and appointing officials. In advance of the two major appointment options, lottery and election, candidates for office may be identified randomly within the citizenry by lot or selected by nominators who themselves may be appointed through sortition, through election, or by the choice of small bodies of elites.

Figure 1 shows a schematic of the alternatives of lot and election and their interaction within regimes that are not principalities.

Democracy: (1, A). The theoretical combination corresponding with (1, A) uses lot to establish a small set of names (say, six to a dozen) drawn from among the citizenry, names that are then subjected to a second lottery, which determines who will assume an open magistracy. Indeed, a nominating sortition has no practical impact on the overall distribution of offices among eligible citizens. It might be used to focus public attention on a narrower group of nominating candidates

| | 1. lot | 2. nominators | | |
| | | *a. lot* | *b. election* | *c. upper assembly* |

A. lot	democracy	popular republic	popular republic	oligarchy
B. election	republic	popular republic	oligarchic republic	oligarchy

appointing

magistrates

democracy:	(1, A)	oligarchic republic:	(2, b, B)
popular republic:	(2, a, A), (2, b, A), (2, a, B)	oligarchy:	(2, c, B), (2, c, A)
a republic:	(1, B)		

FIGURE 1. Typology of Republics

potential magistrates or discarded for a general sortition that fills magistracies from the whole pool of citizens in a one-stage process. In principle, therefore, (1, A) conforms closely with the ancient model that enlists randomization to ensure equitable participation among citizens. For reasons stated previously, one can classify such a regime quite easily as a democracy.

Democratic Republics: *(2, a, A), (2, b, A), (2, a, B)*. Things become somewhat murky with the mixing of lot and election in these cases. If election is an elite-enabling, "aristocratic" device, then how can we classify a regime that deploys it to any extent as a "popular" or "democratic" republic – a *governo largo*? This depends on how lot is used to mitigate election's aristocratic bias. Model (2, a, A) corresponds almost identically with the democratic one discussed in the preceding paragraph, save for the insertion of the nominators' discretion over and choice of candidates between the two moments of sortition. However, because lot determines the nominators themselves, their preferences cannot be predetermined or discerned in advance. Thus, we cannot conclude that such preferences are oligarchic or democratic a priori; sometimes their preferences will be mostly one; other times, mostly the other; and sometimes, mixed. There is sufficient indeterminacy in their nominations that the results drawn from the final lottery can be evaluated as sufficiently random. Hence, such an arrangement possesses a democratic quality because any kind of citizen might hold office as a result. On the other hand, the arrangement enlists the consent and discretion of certain citizens, such that cognitive considerations of quality (notability, competence, virtue, etc.) factor into the selection of candidates.

In (2, b, A), the preferences of the nominators might be determined by the fact that they are elected; hence, the kinds of distinctions that come into play to influence the election of magistrates may operate here: because the nominators are elected by the citizens at large, they may reflect a disproportionately wealthy or otherwise notable segment of the citizenry. There is no reason to suppose, on the basis of evidence provided by Guicciardini and Machiavelli, or the republics that they analyzed, that voters use different criteria to judge nominators, as opposed to candidates. The nominators, in turn, may be expected to select citizens most like themselves as candidates, which would bias the ultimate magistracy selection in an overly oligarchic fashion; after all, the subsequent lottery would mostly draw on a pool of wealthy or wealth-serving candidates. However, recall Guicciardini on the 1497 electoral reforms, whereby slates of candidates were elected in advance of an ultimate lottery that performs the final appointment. If we apply this method to the selection of a whole slate of nominators rather than of only one or a very few individuals, the aristocratic quality of election, in fact, might be minimized in this instance as well. If election of a large slate of individuals (say, half a dozen or more) as opposed to the choice of one specific candidate to fill a well-defined office mitigates the aristocratic effect of elections, then the nominators in this case may also reflect a broader spectrum of political preferences. This diversity might then be expressed in their nominations of candidates, such that the ultimate lottery may yield alternatives to wealthy magistrates.[20]

This would not quite be the case with (2, a, B), which therefore would be the least democratic of the popular republics: while the nominators would be selected through lot such that there is no a priori bias in favor of the wealthy and notable, the nominators must choose candidates in a process that may or may not, as indicated earlier, have an aristocratic effect. More importantly, elections make the final determination on the magistracies, a process that favors candidates of distinction, whether only some or whether most of them are in fact notable and wealthy. But this model remains within the parameters of a democratic republic as a result of the randomization at the beginning of the process, on the one hand, and the indeterminacy over the extent of the aristocratic effect in the intervening nominating stage, on the other.

Republic: *(1, B).* In some sense, (1, B) can be considered the paradigmatic case of a mixed regime, *politeia*, or republic, which is ambiguously democratic and aristocratic, popular and oligarchic. Because lot alone determines candidates, the wealthy do not set the agenda or impose their preferences in advance; all citizens willing to stand for office, rich or poor, have a substantive, not merely formal, chance of holding office. On the other hand, because the final determination over officeholding is secured through election of one or very few magistrates, wealthy and notable individuals within the candidate pool can be confident that they will more often than not attain these offices. This is the regime in the typology that perhaps most closely approximates what Aristotle identified as the most just of realizable governments, and what Manin describes as the most domestically stable. Aristotle deemed such a regime just because different parts of the polity contribute their different positive attributes to it (the excellence and ability of the few versus the many's desire for freedom and its good judgment).[21] Manin deems it stable because neither the oligarchs nor the people can be sure how much they could benefit from any alteration of the constitutional status quo.[22] The few will likely rule as a result of election, but because lot provides the people with candidates from a wide spectrum of the citizenry, they can choose to elect candidates not necessarily of the few, if they so desire. In this way, such a regime differs from contemporary republics, which, without recourse to randomization of any kind, structurally ensure that the few, almost invariably, will be elected. Hence, Manin perhaps too complacently affiliates contemporary, exclusively electoral representative government with the most just version of a mixed constitution.[23] A republic that combines lot and election like (1, B) is perhaps equally stable, is certainly as attainable, and is arguably more just.

The Oligarchic Republic: (2, b, B). A regime where nominators are elected, where they themselves elect a slate of candidates, and where magistracies are filled ultimately through a general election among the citizenry is an oligarchic republic. Universal adult suffrage might justify the designation "popular government" for such a regime, but it cannot legitimately be deemed "democracy." There is no control for the aristocratic effect at any level, and even the softening of this effect that might take place through the selection of a wide slate of candidates at the nominating stage is mitigated by the overall, thoroughly electoral, quality of the framework. One would expect the wealthy or their clients to enjoy disproportionate advantage at gaining office over common citizens. The latter possess no claim on such magistrates besides having "chosen" them and having reserved the option not to reelect them at the appropriate time. A "primary election/convention of notables/general election" sequence conforms well to this abstract model.

Oligarchies: (2, c, B), (2, c, A). The term *oligarchy* is usually reserved for a closed system of rule among a few individuals or families. However, this type of regime may use constitutional arrangements and even enlist some broader segment of the general populace to help sort out appointments that inter-elite rivalry and faction have rendered controversial. Besides excluding lower classes of the regime from a share in government, the oligarchs aspire to confine the list of candidates for office to only those individuals among themselves with which they all can live no matter what the result. The oligarchs may achieve this in two ways that amount to the naming of candidates by an "upper assembly," "council of notables," or "selection committee": by constituting themselves formally as a "senate" that officially names candidates, or by negotiating and agreeing upon a group of *nominators* to select candidates. (If they themselves could agree on *candidates*, there would be little reason to resort to constitutional measures at all.) In circumstances where a small assembly or clique appoints the nominators, the latter presumably know which names are acceptable to all of the wealthy families and leading citizens, and which ones are not. In scheme (2, c, B), the names that the nominators propose are then submitted to the people for an election. But such elections are not aimed at garnering popular consent or encouraging wider participation; rather, they serve the primary function of arbitrating among competing elites.[24] In (2, c, A), lot, the paradigmatic democratic device, serves an oligarchic function because the candidates "in the bag" have already been restricted severely by the preferences of the wealthy through their selection of the members of the nominating body. This is very close to the way lot was used by Venice, an oligarchy calling itself a republic, and, to some extent, by Florence under the Albizzi and Medici regimes.[25]

This Guicciardini-inspired typology puts the constitutions of modern popular governments into some institutional-historical perspective and should inspire more critical analysis of the normative and practical status of magistracy distribution in such regimes today. The most intriguing regimes in the typology, from the standpoint of Machiavellian Democracy, are those that combine lot and election in a popularly empowering way. If, on either empirical ("territorial scale") or normative ("representation") grounds, lot cannot or should not completely supplant election in our time, the randomizing quality of sortition nevertheless might be incorporated fruitfully into broader electoral schemes. Whether lot is used to broaden the range of candidates who may be voted on in an ultimate electoral stage (1, B) or deployed to fill offices after candidates have been identified by nominators themselves elected by the general populace (2, b, A), the results would mitigate the dominance of the privileged over magistracies in most "representative democracies" today (2, b, B).

My intention in prompting such innovations is not to guarantee every citizen a rotating term in office, nor would that result ensue from them. However, those citizens who are willing and able to serve and yet do not possess the resources to make themselves appear "electable" (as do the wealthy and their clients) will actually gain a more reasonable chance to hold office through such reforms. Randomization in these circumstances would not actualize the positive aspiration of the ancient democratic citizen to rule and be ruled in turn, but it might help realize the negative one, namely, the aspiration to keep the wealthy and notable from dominating a popular government's offices and thereby from disproportionately determining the government's policies.

Reviving the Tribunes of the Plebs

When contrasted with Machiavelli's neo-Roman model of popular government and his proposal for reinstituting a republic in Florence, contemporary representative democracy suffers from at least two defects: (1) the absence of extra-electoral means by which the general citizenry renders political elites accountable, especially those exercised through the tribunes and the provosts (vetoes, accusations, and/or plebiscites); and (2) the lack of a quasi-formal distinction between economic-political elites and common citizens (as well as institutions corresponding with this distinction, for example, a senate or a Council of the Commune for patricians, *ottimati*, *grandi*, etc., and a tribunate or *concilium plebis* for the *popolo*, plebeians, multitude, etc.). Previously, I have suggested the following: the aristocratic effect and the privileged access to resources and information enjoyed by magistrates in modern republics render elections inadequate mechanisms of elite accountability and responsiveness; moreover, a sociopolitical definition of "the people" that includes wealthy citizens, rather than one that sets the latter apart from or even opposed to the people, allows the wealthy to dominate common citizens in quasi-anonymous and largely uncontested ways.[26] Again, Ciceronian and Florentine notions of "civic republicanism" or "civic humanism," which emphasized socially holistic rather than class- or guild-contestatory notions of citizenship, to a great extent legitimated oligarchic forms of government.[27]

Political philosophers from Aristotle to Machiavelli assumed, and the many republics they analyzed confirmed, that the primary conflicts within republics would ensue between wealthy and less wealthy citizens. Why then did late– and post–eighteenth-century republicans abandon conceptual and institutional class-specificity while drafting their constitutions? When not in the excessively ochlophobic state of mind mentioned before, perhaps many were heartened by what seemed to be a dawning "pluralist" commercial age when a wide spectrum of social groups, relatively equal in power and influence, might supplant the rich/poor citizen cleavage that prevailed in the republics of previous ages.[28] Note, for instance, how Madison, in *Federalist* no. 10, famously begins with a *sociological* discussion of "faction" described in terms of class and inequitable property relations, but, as the essay progresses, increasingly presents faction in terms of a multiplicity of interests.[29] Certainly, virtually all modern republicans fully subscribed to the recently developed *political* idea of absolute, indivisible, and unitary "sovereignty," transposed in their revolutionary age from monarch to citizenry.[30] This notion of a "sovereign people," and, relatedly, of formal juridical equality, discouraged the imposition of legal distinctions among citizens, particularly those corresponding to socioeconomic status. But whatever the reasons – mobophobic prejudices, sociological presumptions of a newly emerging pluralism, political prescriptions for a more homogeneous citizenry, and so on – modern constitutional framers clearly demurred from designing institutions that acknowledged, addressed, or reflected socioeconomic distinctions.[31]

Perhaps one reason that the American founders failed to provide a formal institutional equivalent of the tribunate is this: their late-eighteenth and early-nineteenth-century faith in the power of a widely proliferating free press operating within an increasingly literate public sphere kept virtually all framers of modern constitutions from seriously considering an institutional watchdog by, of, and for common citizens exclusively. The people, the framers believed, need no formal governmental protection in enlightened societies where information arises from varied interests, expresses multiple social perspectives, and flows unrepressed among an active citizenry engaged in a rich associational life.[32] On this understanding, any abuse of power by political officials or even prominent citizens would be exposed to the public and eventually punished by legal authorities. Certainly, this faith has been vindicated in notable instances in which the press revealed, public opinion recognized, and government officials punished egregiously corrupt and/or treasonous behavior on the part of elites.[33] But as Machiavelli pointed out centuries earlier, magistrates and the wealthy have patented advantages over the control of information in "free" environments that permit unequal resources to develop among citizens, advantages that enable them to set the agenda of public opinion, to disseminate favorable and squelch unflattering facts, and, most effectively, to smear populist partisans attempting to expose grandi domination (D I.5). To be sure, Machiavelli did not think that the constitutionalization of a popular ombudsman would completely insulate tribunician magistrates from efforts by elites to discredit, corrupt, and intimidate them (D III.3); nor does it guarantee that grandi will not successfully manipulate the people on occasion by appealing to religious norms and by initiating unnecessary wars (D I.13). But a "free" flow of information, especially but not only when media ownership is consolidated in increasingly fewer hands, is, by itself, an insufficient popular watchdog.[34]

If the need for class-specific institutions was underestimated in the eighteenth century, one might expect that it would have become apparent in the wake of the Industrial Revolution. While the framers might be indulged for an Enlightenment conceit concerning the eventual evaporation of rich/poor class conflict and the evolving permanence of pluralist interest-based conflict in republics, no such leeway should be granted reformers who witnessed the Industrial Revolution and its still alarmingly relevant sociopolitical effects. Intense concentration of wealth and widening inequality reminiscent of traditional republics reemerged as the "commercial republics" theorized by enlightenment political philosophy became the "capitalist democracies" of historical reality. In such circumstances, critics of democratic deficits in modern popular governments ought to have made better use of the institutional lessons offered by traditional, class-based republics.[35] Why did no one ever propose, for instance, in a U.S. context, the installation of a wealth ceiling on eligibility for the House of Representatives, and a wealth floor in the Senate, such that national collegial bodies better resemble the assemblies of traditional popular governments?

Although seeming to entrench the privilege of the wealthy, such an arrangement may spark, in a Machiavellian spirit, sufficient resentment and class consciousness to ensure a more vigorous surveillance of the upper house and its constituencies by both the lower one and the populace at large. Machiavelli suggests that the inevitable power disparities between grandi and popolo within republics should be arranged institutionally so as to make the latter more, not less, conscious of them, and perhaps in order to motivate them toward more active efforts to minimize such disparities. Separate institutions for wealthy and nonwealthy citizens flatter the grandi and aggravate the popolo, thus fostering the social dispositions necessary for a free and stable republic: a relatively loyal elite and an agitated, anti-elitist citizenry. The unitary notion of a "sovereign people" and the strictly electoral/representative institutional arrangements corresponding with it may be, on the contrary, inducements to elite insularity and popular slumber.[36]

Machiavelli's analysis of traditional republics provokes any number of questions about alternative sociopolitical arrangements within contemporary ones: why, for instance, has no one considered an attempt to buy the wealthy out of the political process altogether? As opposed to disenfranchising the magnates without their consent, as the early Florentine guild republics did with deleterious results, perhaps contemporary republics should offer the wealthy political disenfranchisement in exchange for economic insulation. With "money in politics" an ever more troublesome issue, we might consider whether individuals under present conditions earning more than, say, $150,000 in income, or belonging to households of more than $350,000 in net wealth (income, property, and assets),[37] should be relieved of all tax burdens as compensation for giving up eligibility to vote, to stand for office, or to contribute funds to political campaigns. If fiscally feasible, such measures might reduce the *political* influence of capital without simultaneously endangering its arguably indispensable productive capability within market democracies.[38] Of course, even though Machiavelli insists that the grandi value wealth more than honors and office, the unquenchable appetite to oppress that he ascribes to them – correctly, I think – makes it unlikely that they could resist the temptation to convert their economic privilege into political power, especially in order to use the latter to inflate the former even further.

After the spectacle of the State of California's gubernatorial recall in 2004, popularly judged accusations against sitting magistrates that result in real sanctions may have fallen to a level of ill repute in the United States from which they can never be rehabilitated.[39] Moreover, the results of recent ballot initiatives and referenda in that same state have called into question the wisdom of the people's direct judgment over constitutional and policy matters.[40] But neither recalls nor referenda are beyond constructive reform.[41] Recalls may be reconstituted in ways that avoid two salient deficiencies of the California model: such measures should be insulated from efforts by wealthy citizens or magistrates to bankroll or spearhead the ejection of an incumbent officeholder in order to take his or her place personally or by proxy; and reforms should rule out the perverse possibility that the replacement magistrate garners less popular support than the ousted incumbent.

For instance, no public official who sponsors a recall action, or any of his or her major campaign contributors, should be eligible to serve in the accused magistrate's place. And certainly the same prohibition should apply to anyone who spends a considerable amount of personal funds in the publicity campaign against the sitting magistrate; anyone who spends beyond a certain threshold in the effort to dislodge a sitting official simply must be rendered ineligible for the same position. With such corrections, a popular accusation/sanction procedure may prove less prone to perversity or corruption than magistrate-controlled impeachment proceedings, of which the 1998 impeachment of U.S. President Bill Clinton remains exemplary. Moreover, whether contemporary democracies should provide institutional channels through which popular accusations may be directed against corporate officers or wealthy citizens for attempting to hijack the political process for their own purposes, or simply for defrauding a wide swath of the populace, is an intriguing question opened by Machiavelli's discussion of political punishment in republican Rome.

To return to recent California referenda and initiatives[42] that have revitalized timeless (and timelessly exaggerated) objections to direct popular judgment over public policy: "minipublics," which I mentioned in the previous chapter, may offer wider opportunities for average citizens both to refine their opinions in such cases and to impact public policy in novel, salutary ways. As both abstractly conceived and concretely observed by many contemporary democratic theorists, citizen assemblies, deliberative polls, citizen juries, peoples' houses, and such provide randomly selected or demographically reflective groups of common people occasions to discuss and set the agenda over crucial constitutional and policy questions.[43] Canada, Brazil, Denmark, and even China, among others, have empowered various "minipopuluses" to participate directly in constitutional politics by, for instance, drafting electoral reform proposals, and such countries have voluntarily adopted the policy recommendations of these citizen assemblies on issues such as energy conservation and irradiated foods.[44]

In Machiavellian terms, such small bodies of common citizens, drawn from the broader population, may serve as the modern equivalents of the formal assemblies of earlier ages within which the people, "shackled by law," discussed and decided political matters such that their substantive judgment, rather than their unconsidered opinion, prevailed in policy making. Strong evidence suggests that common citizens, when provided with pertinent, even conflicting, information, and when given the chance to deliberate among themselves in such settings, come to well-informed and consensus-oriented judgments over policy.[45] Consequently, an increasing number of scholars now recommend that more governments – local, regional, national or even supranational – grant such minipublics the authority to initiate or vet, via deliberation, policy proposals that then could be passed on to wider publics – indeed, the entire citizenry – for approval or nullification.[46]

This mode of enlisting popular judgment differs markedly from Guicciardini's preferred model in which senatorial bodies initiate or amend laws that the people, formally assembled, either acclaim or reject. (Obviously, it is an even farther cry from strictly representative systems where the people are completely excluded from direct participation in law and policy making.) On the contrary, proponents of minipublics indicate how democracies that avail themselves of such popularly empowering institutions will more effectively keep lobbies, vested interests, and public officials from unduly influencing the framing, sponsoring, and promotion of policy referenda.[47] Indeed, when a subset of the citizenry plays the predominant role in formulating policy proposals in advance of referenda, one might expect the latter to better reflect common concerns; to be more intelligible to the public at large; and to bear, prospectively, the imprimatur of what the general citizenry as a whole might decide if they were given undistorted information and sufficient time to consider and discuss such matters.[48] Of course, the voting public as a whole retains the ultimate authority to decide, by rejecting such an initiative, that a particular citizen assembly does not in fact judge better than the public at large or that it does not after all speak for the actual people.[49]

The following thought experiment is intended to contribute in a constructive way to this burgeoning literature and practical trend in institutional reform. My contribution differs from the minipublics described in the preceding paragraphs because it not only responds to the insufficiencies of contemporary electoral democracy, but it does so from the perspective of Machiavelli's singularly perspicacious analysis of the political life and constitutional forms of pre-modern republics. Here I sketch an institutional reform that would bring the U.S. Constitution into closer conformity with efforts to enhance citizen participation and facilitate popular control of elites in pre-modern popular governments: I propose the establishment of a People's Tribunate of fifty-one lottery-selected, nonwealthy citizens who would wield powers reminiscent of those entrusted to the Roman tribunes for one-year nonrenewable terms. This is a heuristic proposal intended for critical but not necessarily directly practical purposes; it is meant to be loosely instructive rather than strictly prescriptive. I certainly wish that contemporary democracies would experiment with tribunician institutions, much as, in light of the first section of this chapter, I encourage them to explore combinations of lottery and election when establishing procedures for selecting public officials. But tribunician institutions certainly need not take this exact form.[50]

A contemporary college of tribunes could be organized along the following lines.

Composition and Purpose
a) A group of fifty-one private citizens, selected by lottery, gather for one-year nonrenewable, nonrepeatable terms.
b) They will be compensated fully for a year's salary and guaranteed the return of their jobs, as well as granted added incentives such as free college tuition for their children and/or a full-year's tax immunity, among possible other perquisites.
c) Political and economic elites are excluded from eligibility: that is, anyone who has held a major municipal, state, or federal office, elected or appointed, for two consecutive terms at any time in their life; and anyone whose net household worth equals or exceeds $345,000 (i.e., members of the wealthiest tenth percent of family households as established by the most recent U.S. census data).[51]
d) Citizens must be at least twenty-one years old to qualify for the Tribunate.

e) Besides excluding socioeconomic and political elites, the pool of citizens from which the tribunes are drawn may be adjusted in the following way: given the particular history of the United States, and the kinds of inequality not directly related to class that have plagued the polity, the pool of citizens may be altered to give African American and Native American citizens a greater chance of serving as tribunes than straightforward demographics would otherwise yield.[52]

f) The duties of the tribunes are to study and discuss the business of the federal government, five days per week, six hours per day. The tribunes may invite scholars and policy experts (but *not* sitting officeholders) to present information that they themselves deem pertinent to their deliberations.

Constitutional Powers

g) The tribunes are empowered, upon majority vote, to veto one piece of congressional legislation, one executive order, and one Supreme Court decision in the course of their one-year term. The originating institution may not attempt to take up this action again for one calendar year after the end of the Tribunate's term during which the veto was invoked. The tribunes need not avail themselves of this power.

h) The tribunes may call one national referendum, upon majority vote, over any issue they wish. The referendum will take place without any advertising sponsored by parties or interest groups. A nationally televised debate between two tribune-approved advocates – policy experts, public officials, or private citizens – one in favor of and one opposed to the proposition, will precede the referendum. The referendum, if ratified by a majority of the electorate, will take on the force of federal statute. Only two-thirds votes of both the U.S. Senate and House of Representatives may declare the statute to be unconstitutional. The tribunes need not avail themselves of this power.[53]

i) Upon a minimum three-quarters vote, the tribunes are empowered to initiate impeachment proceedings against one federal official from each of the three branches of government during their term of office. Apart from the initiation of such proceedings by the tribunes, the impeachment will be conducted according to the stipulations of the U.S. Constitution. If convicted, the magistrate may appeal the sentence in a national referendum, to which the stipulations of paragraph (h) apply. The tribunes need not avail themselves of this power.

Sanctioning and Restructuring

j) Tribunes, either individually or collectively, may be indicted, after completion of their term(s) of service, for official misbehavior (e.g., treason, corruption, etc.) by a two-thirds vote in a subsequent People's Tribunate. If so indicted, the tribune(s) will be tried before a jury of five hundred randomly selected citizens who meet the eligibility requirements for serving as tribunes (paragraphs c and d), and will face penalties set by existing federal statutes pertaining to the legally appropriate conduct of other public officials.

k) The powers of the People's Tribunate enumerated in paragraphs g, h, and i may be expanded (but not reduced) by two-thirds votes in both the Tribunate and the U.S. House of Representatives: the number of vetoes, referenda, and impeachments that the Tribunate is entitled to exercise or initiate may be increased (but not reduced) according to this procedure; and the voting thresholds for policy enactment or initiation by the tribunes in paragraphs g, h, and i may be lowered (but not raised) by the same procedure.

l) Qualifications for serving as tribune (paragraphs c and d) may be altered upon a minimum two-thirds favorable vote in the Tribunate that then triggers a national referendum, to which the stipulations of paragraph h apply. Qualifications may be changed in the following ways: the minimum age to serve as tribune may be lowered (but not raised) from twenty-one years old; the tribunate may exclude members of *more* (but not less) than the top ten percent wealthiest households among the citizenry; and restrictions on previous officeholding by prospective tribunes may be tightened (but not relaxed).

The idea of a People's Tribunate resonates with several important strands of contemporary democratic theory. Like minipublics in theory and practice, this model attempts to re-create the citizenry writ small – not merely to "represent" it, but actually to *present* it in a microfunctional form.[54] The neotribunate model also exhibits affinities with work in contestatory democratic theory, specifically with scholarship that has called for the reconsideration of group-specific magistracies, institutions, and, in some cases, the veto.[55] Many now argue that particular groups that suffer disproportionately from specific policies should have the opportunity to formally contest and/or contribute to the formation of such policies. However, in the spirit of a more old-fashioned form of identity politics associated with ancient and medieval class-specific officers and assemblies, the group primarily empowered through the American Tribunate is ordinary citizens – common people as opposed to socioeconomic and political elites.

As mentioned previously, because of the specific prejudices and exclusions that have unfortunately characterized American history, a very strong case can be made that non-elite citizens of African American and Native American descent should have the opportunity (e.g., through greater weighting in the sortition) to serve as tribunes beyond their numbers in the population.[56] This, of course, ought to be decided democratically, and in general such selection adjustments must be used sparingly, lest the randomness of the selection process lose its legitimating force. Randomization, as per Athenian democratic practice, must bear most of the burden of distributing this magistracy among different kinds of non-elite citizens. Of course, inequality between the sexes is addressed directly through demographics and randomization: the People's Tribunate would tend *not* to replicate the disparity between the number of women in the general population, on the one hand, and in prominent political and socioeconomic positions, on the other.

Serious criticisms leveled against "real-world" deliberative bodies such as town hall meetings and juries still obtain against many versions of the minipublics discussed in this chapter: evidence suggests that professional, white males tend to dominate discussions within such fora.[57] The revived People's Tribunate should render deliberative interactions more equitable. The historically inspired exclusion of the wealthy from the Tribunate, and the increased chances for socially and economically disadvantaged citizens to serve as tribunes, potentially ameliorates the extent to which professional, white men will monopolize its proceedings: white male tribunes would tend to be of similar socioeconomic backgrounds as tribunes of color and as female tribunes. The class specificity of the People's Tribunate also addresses some of the perversely inegalitarian implications of veto options that many critics raise against certain forms of contestatory democracy.[58] Vetoes, as discussed in Chapter 6, hold majorities hostage to minorities, especially in cases where the latter benefit unfairly from the status quo. This can effectively insulate structurally empowered minorities against efforts for redress on the part of less privileged majorities. However, when wielded by an institution that excludes socioeconomic elites, or that functions as much as possible beyond their influence (as the Roman tribunes did, and as Machiavelli's provosts certainly would have), a veto exercised by the American Tribunate ought to block oligarchically favorable as opposed to popularly progressive policy initiatives.

Another obvious concern raised by any institution based on the minipublic model, the People's Tribunate included, is the question of expert influence: just how insulated from expert and therefore elite manipulation can such bodies really be? Can deliberative bodies of this sort reliably obtain objective information from "neutral" or "nonpartisan" experts?[59] One might expect that experts will inevitably impart information in a partisan manner and use their influence to set agendas in accord with their own interests and preferences, or in accord with those of more powerful social actors to whom they're beholden. Indeed, scholars who closely observed the workings of British Columbia's Citizens' Assembly justify such suspicions, at least partly: they report that staffers had substantive if definitely not decisive influence over citizen deliberators in British Columbia's minipublic.[60] Given the less than definitive evidence available in this case, it would be hasty to adopt an overly pessimistic perspective on the issue of expert influence.[61] Prudence suggests that such institutions generally should meet the imperfect but quasi-objective standards of citizen-expert interactions in the British Columbia Citizens' Assembly and of information provided by relatively nonpartisan governmental institutions such as the U.S. General Accounting Office (GAO).[62]

Most importantly, an institution like the People's Tribunate would allow common citizens of the United States – "common" initially defined by paragraphs a, c, and e, but eventually determined by the citizens themselves (paragraph l) – to contribute substantively to three crucial aspects of public affairs. The people so defined, heretofore "formally excluded" in Madisonian fashion from direct access to national policy making, would be empowered to block policy outcomes that deleteriously affect the commonweal (g); initiate legislation that governs the republic (h); and sanction public officials who threaten the latter's welfare (i). In the spirit of Machiavelli's praise for the Roman tribunes and his aspirations for the Florentine provosts, the American tribunes would serve as the popularly based "guard of liberty" within the American republic.

Guicciardini complained bitterly how the increasing authority of the tribunes gradually expanded plebeian power in Rome, while Machiavelli more gently intimated that over time the functioning of his provosts would have placed more and more power in the hands of "the universality" of Florence's citizens.[63] Likewise, through stipulations k and l, the American tribunes eventually might see their authority expanded such that they would afford the general citizenry ever-widening opportunities to set the boundaries and determine the content of their common liberty, as well as to constrain the actions of those who would seek to limit or menace it.

To argue that the institutions of modern democracies keep elites accountable and responsive in a less than perfect fashion is not to prove that earlier popular governments actually performed these tasks any better. This is an empirical issue that I don't remotely know how to address. Nonetheless, participants in and analysts of earlier republics, especially plebeians, "lower guildsmen," and Niccolò Machiavelli himself, would have predicted that contemporary popular governments, relying exclusively on general elections, were certain to perform poorly in this regard. Again, in elections, prospective magistrates, usually the wealthy or those best funded by them, try to influence ex ante the people who would select them; and they can and do draw upon considerable resources to exert such influence. Moreover, the most consequential form of sanction against an elected magistrate who betrays the populace is almost hopelessly ex post: the follow-through on a standing threat *not* to reelect an unsatisfactory official is postponed for a considerably extended period of time, specifically, until the end of a magistrate's term. Of course, fulfilling Francesco Guicciardini's intuitions, modern constitutional framers professed and believed that novel economic, social, and/or political conditions rendered the oligarchy emerging from narrowly conducted electoral politics a "natural aristocracy." They might have been reminded that no oligarchy ever considered itself "unnatural."[64] If a popular government or a democratic republic is not to veer dangerously toward rule by an unaccountable oligarchy, natural or not, institutional affirmative action for common citizens, "in various ways and through various modes," is a matter of the highest priority.

In this light, contemporary democracies could do worse than reconsider the extra-electoral practices that earlier democratic republics, their partisans, and their greatest proponent, Machiavelli, thought were crucial to ensure the liberty of citizens and the longevity of such polities. Today's democracies should temper the aristocratic biases of elections with elements of randomization when appointing magistrates; they should reserve for common citizens public magistracies or legislatively empowered assemblies that exclude the wealthiest citizens; and they must enlist the participation of the entire citizenry in accusation/appellate processes that mete out punishment for political crimes. The ramifications of such institutional innovations are not purely procedural. Machiavelli, who considered patricians, not the people, to be the preeminent political problem in republics, intimated that such institutions made elites more careful about undermining these regimes. Just as importantly, he suggested, they inspired more spirited class-consciousness and political contentiousness among common citizens. Such are the seemingly forgotten preconditions of liberty within popular government.

Notes

Introduction

1. Bartels 2008; Frank 2005; Fraser and Gerstle 2005; Jacobs and Skocpol 2007; Krugman 2003; O'Leary 2006; and Phillips 2002.

2. By "republic," I refer to a regime that is not a monarchy or autocracy. A "popular government" is a republic where common citizens, not just socioeconomic elites, participate in government in one of the following ways: by exercising majority rule in large, widely inclusive assemblies and by serving in public offices distributed by lottery (as in ancient democracies such as Athens); through class-specific political institutions, such as magistracies or assemblies that are reserved exclusively for poorer citizens (characteristic of many ancient, medieval, and early-modern Italian republics such as Rome and Florence); or, most minimally, by casting votes for candidates for public office in frequent and genuinely competitive elections under conditions of universal adult suffrage (as in modern representative governments). According to this definition, for example, ancient Sparta, medieval Venice, and early modern Geneva are republics but not popular governments.

3. See Baehr 1998; Butters 1985; Lintott 1982; Martines 1979; Molho, Raaflaub, and Emlen 1991, 251–354; Stephens 1983; and Stone 1989.

4. Even, for instance, in the relatively class-conscious context of the French Republic's founding, formal provisions against the wealthy, as such, were not part of the early constitutions. See Fitzsimmons 1994 and Hunt 1984. On the contrary, upwardly graduated levels of wealth determined the extent to which an individual enjoyed citizenship: increasing amounts of taxable wealth determined a citizen's right to vote, to hold intermediary office, and, ultimately, to hold high office. See Crook 1996, 30–53, especially 35–6. Acts of disenfranchisement targeted not socioeconomic elites per se, but chiefly émigrés who had conspired against or fled the republic (Crook 1996, 140–1).

5. Dawood 2007; Elkin 2006; Farrand 1966, I: 423, II: 203–4; and Nedelsky 1991.

6. See Shapiro 2002 on the lack of empirical evidence supporting the "expropriating demos" thesis.

7. Farrand 1966, I: 146–7; Madison, Hamilton, and Jay [1788] 1998, esp., nos. 10 and 51; and Meyers 1981, 395. On the antipopular and antiparticipatory biases of the English republicans, see Skinner 1998, 31–2; on the aristocratic prejudices of

Dutch republicanism, see van Gelderen 2002, especially, 35, 207; and van Gelderen 2005, especially 204, 213.

8. See, e.g., Bartels 2008; Domhoff 1998; Fraser 1997; Jacobs and Skocpol 2007; Mills 1999; and Phillips 2002. In the last decade, the top 10 percent wealthiest households in the United States (with net worths of at least $345,000) controlled over 70 percent of the country's assets. See Wolff 2001 and 2007. Moreover, the top 10 percent of high-income households earned upward of nearly $150,000 annually (see http://www.census.gov/hhes/www/cpstables/032009/hhinc/new06_000.htm). On this basis, when I speak of "the wealthy" in a contemporary U.S. context, I am thinking of the top 10 percent richest citizens: individuals who earn roughly $150,000 in income or more, or who belong to households worth roughly $350,000 of net wealth (including income, property, and assets) or more – categories that overlap significantly but not completely. Of course, as my subsequent analysis will make plain, I think that the dividing line between "wealthy" and "common citizens" should be determined democratically – that is, by the people themselves. For more details, and updated statistics, see Domhoff 2010 and Wolff 2010.

9. See Goodin 2008, 164–5; Levi et al. 2008; and Przeworski, Stokes, and Manin 1999. On the empirical and conceptual standards of "free and fair" elections, see Beitz 1989; Dahl 1971, and Thompson 2002.

10. See Behn 2000; Bowles, Gintis, and Gustafsson 2008; Dowdle 2006; Lewin 2007; Maravall and Sánchez-Cuenca 2007; and Ziblatt 2006, 2008.

11. According to Bartels (2008), the strongest determinants of public policy affecting inequality in the United States are, firstly, the partisan affiliations of elected officials and, secondly, the preferences of the most affluent members of society.

12. Reforms perhaps even more substantive than contemporary advocates and critics of campaign finance reform imagine; see Hohenstein 2007; Kersh 2003; La Raja 2008; Samples 2006; Smith 2006; and Urofsky 2005.

13. Machiavelli, *Il Principe* [1513], in Corrado Vivanti, ed., *Opere I: I Primi Scritti Politici* (Torino: Einaudi-Gallimard, 1997), 114–92; hereafter cited in the text as P with chapter numbers. Translations are my own, although I regularly consult Mansfield 1998, for clear, consistent, cognate-based renderings of Machiavelli's terminology, and Connell 2005, for sensitivity to Italian verb constructions and intimate familiarity with sixteenth-century idiomatic expressions.

14. Machiavelli, *Discorsi* [c. 1513–19], in Vivanti, ed., *Opere I*, 193–525; hereafter cited in the text as D with book and chapter numbers in parentheses. Translations are my own, although, for the reasons stated in the previous note, I rely on, respectively, Mansfield and Tarcov 1996 and Atkinson and Sices 2002.

15. With this particular emphasis on institutional avenues for promoting popular participation and for securing elite responsiveness, my approach also differs from earlier Marxian treatments of Machiavelli undertaken by, most prominently, Althusser 2001 and Gramsci [1925] 1959. While they rightly emphasized the importance of popular advocacy and anti-elitist class conflict in Machiavelli's work, perhaps bewitched by orthodox Marxist illusions of overcoming elites altogether (and of preserving a role for revolutionary intellectual elites), they did not accentuate the institutional means through which, on Machiavelli's recommendation, the people should control elites. Other traditions of continental social and political thought, such as phenomenology and poststructuralism, have explored the

democratic dimensions of Machiavelli's political thought, but, again, with disappointing inattention to the importance of institutions and the law in the Florentine's writings. See Lefort 2000 and Merleau-Ponty 1990.

16. Only the first instance of specialized foreign words will appear in italics within each chapter; subsequent occurences of such words are presented without italics.

17. See Livy 1919–26, I–X.

18. See Black 1990, 97; de Grazia 1989, 95–6; Gilbert 1965, 172–4; Najemy 1990, 103, 108–13, 117; and Ridolfi 1963, 130–2.

19. See Black 1990, 97; de Grazia 1989, 251; Gilbert 1965 172–4; Najemy 1990, 117; and Ridolfi 1963, 2, 112, 130–2, 257n. 4; 286, n. 18, 20.

20. See Guarini 1990, 20–1.

21. See de Grazia 1989, 140; Najemy 1990, 103, 113, 117; and Ridolfi 1963, 112, 286n. 18, 20.

22. See, especially, Strauss 1958, 134, 169, 250.

23. Machiavelli also uses the term "the people" interchangeably with *popolani, plebe*, ignobles, the multitude, and the universality; he generally understands them to be poorer citizens who are not members of a republic's patrician or wealthy class. See de Grazia 1989, 162. In both Rome and Florence, the people, as citizens, enjoyed civil equality but not necessarily full political rights; for instance, property, tax status, occupation, and ancestry often determined whether or not a citizen could hold particular offices. See Brucker 1962 and 1977. "The people," by both convention and law, excludes noncitizens such as women, slaves, and resident aliens in both the Roman and the Florentine contexts.

24. Most infamously, Machiavelli declares that "one can say the following about men generally: they are ungrateful, fickle, mendacious, and deceptive; they avoid danger and greedily pursue gain" (P 17; cf. D I.3, D I.37). The contributors to Rahe 2005 perhaps most readily accept such declarations as Machiavelli's ultimate view of all human beings.

25. See, e.g., Aristotle 1985, V.3.1131a23–4; Aristotle 1997, III.9.1279a23, V.1.1301b26–9; Cicero 1999, 22–3.

26. Nelson 2004 demonstrates that Greek historians of the Roman Republic, such as Polybius, Plutarch, and Appian, transmitted an ancient "Greek republican" sympathy for economic equality into their accounts of Roman class conflict, keeping this disposition alive for subsequent republicans to revive in the context of the English and American revolutions. This tradition, as Nelson describes it, was, however, in many respects *politically* inegalitarian, that is, opposed to expansive popular participation and contestation in the political realm. As my interpretation of Machiavelli's accounts of the Brothers Gracchus and of Roman agrarian legislation will make plain in Chapters 3 and 4, Machiavelli was egalitarian in *both* of these senses. Machiavelli thought that republics should, on the one hand, "keep the public rich and the citizens poor" (D I.37), and, on the other, enable the plebeians to participate extensively in domestic politics.

27. See Headlem 1933 and Najemy 1982.

28. See Guicciardini [1512] 1998, 122–3; cf. Pocock 1975, 127–31.

29. Although somewhat outdated, the classic studies of Rome's tribunate and assemblies are, respectively, Bleicken 1955 and Botsford [1909] 2005.

30. See Guicciardini [1530] 2002, 391–2; Montesquieu [1734] 1999, 84; and in a more qualified manner, Cicero 1999, 164–7.

31. See Machiavelli, "Discursus on Florentine Affairs" ("Discursus Florentinarum Rerum Post Mortem Iunioris Laurentii Medices") (1519–20), in Vivanti, ed., *Opere I*, 733–45; hereafter cited in the text as DF with chapter numbers.

32. That is, even scholars inclined to recognize Machiavelli's progressive, proplebeian, and protodemocratic stance ignore the central institutional requirement of his conception of democracy or governo largo: the tribunes are notably absent in de Grazia 1989 and Hulliung 1984 and merely treated in passing by Gilbert 1965, 185; the provosts are completely missing at crucial moments of the analyses of Silvano 1990, 56–61 and Viroli 1990, 154–5.

33. This section draws upon arguments more fully elaborated in McCormick 2003.

34. Skinner 1990a, 137.

35. Skinner 1990a, 123.

36. Skinner 1981, 65–6; 1990a, 130, 136. On social conflict in Rome, see Raaflaub 2005.

37. Skinner, 1990a, 137, 140; cf. also Skinner 1981, 25, 36, 64, on Machiavelli as conventionally Ciceronian; and 2002, 207–9, where Skinner suggests that Cicero and Machiavelli fundamentally agree on the substance of justice, even if Machiavelli refrains from using the word.

38. Tuck (1993, 20–1) concedes that Machiavelli jettisoned many important strains of Cicero's thought, especially those that overlapped with Seneca's stoicism. But he insists that the Florentine also retained important Ciceronian elements in his thought, particularly those regarding the security of the republic and the not exclusively moral character of "virtue."

39. Pocock 1975, 212, 232.

40. Pocock 1975, viii, 3. On the existential aspect of Pocock's book, see Palonen 1998.

41. Pocock 1975, 183.

42. Pocock's shortcoming in this regard is prefigured by the writings of the major philosophical inspiration of his book: Hannah Arendt. Arendt's own existential preoccupations, her ambivalence over social (as opposed to political) conflict, and her greater distrust of the many than the few culminate not in the "radical" democratic politics that so many contemporary readers attribute to her, but rather in a fairly traditional aristocratic republicanism. See Arendt 2006, 1–10, 49–105, 207–73, most tellingly at 268. At appropriate points throughout this book, I engage interpretations of both Machiavelli, specifically, and democracy, generally, inspired by the work of Arendt, and, in a similar spirit, Sheldon Wolin (1994, 1996).

43. If Machiavelli had argued that the people are essentially just as ambitious and avaricious as the nobles, in the manner that Skinner suggests, only intransigent, corruption-inducing factional conflict could ensue – a kind of conflict that Machiavelli explicitly criticizes (e.g., D I.7). Cf. Bock 1990; Rosenblum 2008, 64–7, 76–7; and the "Proemio" of Machiavelli's *Florentine Histories*: see Machiavelli, *Istorie Fiorentine* [1532] 1962, Franco Gaeta, ed. (Milano: Feltrinelli, 1962), 68–71; hereafter cited in the text as FH with chapter numbers.

44. See Pettit 1999a, Pocock 1975, Skinner 1998, Viroli 1997 and 1998. While there are subtle differences in these authors' individual understandings of republicanism (see Buttle 2001; Pettit 2002), they all tend to distinguish the republican tradition from a liberal-democratic one. Sympathetic theorists Dagger, Ryan, and Miller (1997) attempt to combine republicanism and liberalism in the cause of a more progressive political theory generally; see Bellamy and Castiglione (1996) in the contemporary context of European integration. On difficulties in distinguishing,

as Skinner and Pocock do, liberalism from republicanism, see Holmes 1995, 5–6; Isaac 1988; Larmore 2001; Larmore 2008, 139–95; Patten 1996; Rogers 2008; and Sunstein 1988.

45. See Pocock 2003, 582; Skinner 1990b, 308–9.
46. Pocock 2003, 582
47. Skinner 1973, 1983, and 1990b, 308–9.
48. Pocock 1975, viii, 3; see McCormick 1993.
49. For an account of Guicciardini's substantial influence on subsequent European political thought, particularly in the reason of state literature, see Tuck 1993, 38–42.
50. Cf., respectively, Plamenatz 2006; Pocock 1975; Strauss 1958.
51. See Gilbert 1965; Manin 1997, 53–4, 70.
52. On the ill-fated efforts of seventeenth- and eighteenth-century democratic republicans in North America and the Caribbean to establish extra-electoral elite accountability measures, such as public scrutinies, in addition to electoral ones, see Maloy 2008. On the victory of more elitist over more democratic republicans during the founding era of the United States, see Wood 1998.
53. See Canovan 2005.
54. See Lintott 1968 and 1999.
55. See Hunt 1984; Morgan 1989. On the modern endorsement of functionally based rather than socially based institutions of mixed government, see Manin 1994. For other crucial distinctions between republicanisms ancient and modern, see Nederman 2000 and Nippel 1994.
56. Rosenblum (2008) defends the necessary, beneficial, and even moral quality of partisan conflict in democratic politics; a defense that draws, albeit tentatively, on Machiavelli (64–67).
57. See Aristotle 1997, IV.4.1291b9, as well as Yack 1993, 209–31. More recently, consult Acemoglu and Robinson 2005; Bartels 2008; Beramendi and Anderson 2008; Boix 2003, 6–16, 47–58.
58. Throughout this book, I consistently use the word "citizen" to refer to the basic political actor within republics, popular governments, and democracies. The use of the word explicitly raises the question of the status of those inhabitants of and contributors to such polities who are not citizens – it necessarily raises the question of inclusion and exclusion. On the idea that modern citizenship within the U.S. and European contexts has been defined more by exclusionary than by inclusionary impulses, see, respectively, Smith 1997 and Zerilli 1994. From a moral perspective, there is no justification for excluding any adult person from fully participating in the formulation of political decisions that directly affect him or her – none. At the empirical level, however, things become more complicated. Some solace is offered by the fact that historically, in many contexts, the universalist logic by which citizens criticize inequitable conditions among themselves are very often employed subsequently to expand the boundaries of inclusion and render the boundaries of citizenries more expansive. On the problem of the in and out of citizenship, generally, see Goodin 2008, 127–54, and Whelan 1983; on the promise that democratic revisibility affords future reform in this regard, see Habermas 2001, 774.
59. See Williams 2000, 4–6, on the danger of balkanizing groups and ossifying the identities of their members through racially, ethnically, or religiously specific policy measures.

60. See FH III.12–17; Najemy 2006, 156–87.
61. See Bachrach 1967; and Bachrach and Botwinick 1992.
62. On the various kinds of citizen activities – whether conventionally considered "political" or not – that many contemporary scholars consider necessary to support civic life within contemporary democracy, see, e.g., Gutmann 1999; Macedo 1994; Meyers 2008; Putnam 2000; Rosenblum 1998; Sandel 1996; Skocpol 2004; and Warren 2000.
63. Urbinati (2006) spiritedly argues that the Madisonian and Schumpeterian defenses of electoral politics do not exhaust the democratic potential of representation as it exists in contemporary representative governments; most notably, she insists that elected representatives serve the interests of electoral minorities in ways that lottery systems and direct forms of democracy do not (1–59). However, by concluding with the exemplary case of Condorcet's constitutional proposal that combines direct and indirect forms of democracy, Urbinati's study unwittingly confirms many of the deficiencies of electoral government as actually practiced in post–eighteenth-century republics (176–222). Rehfeld (2005) provocatively challenges the geographic presuppositions of modern representation and offers institutional proposals for recasting political constituency within contemporary democracies.
64. At various junctures, I criticize highly "philosophic" approaches to Machiavelli and to democracy – not only those of Skinner and Pettit, but also Straussian and poststructuralist approaches – for making the Florentine's political thought inappropriately aristocratic and democracy itself utterly impracticable – indeed, for exacerbating the latter's susceptibility to oligarchic subversion.

Chapter 1.   Peoples, Patricians, and the Prince

1. I elaborate on this point in McCormick 2008a and 2009a.
2. Machiavelli, "Draft of a Letter to Giovan Battista Soderini (September 13–27, 1506)," in Connell 2005, 127.
3. See Tarcov 2003, 2007.
4. In the Ciceronian tradition of rhetoric, onestà, or more precisely, *honestas*, connotes what is honorable, what is good in itself, as opposed to *utilitas*, what is merely expedient, what is only instrumentally or not inherently good. See Cicero 1991. By associating onestà, a word that Cicero associates with nobility of character (if not blood or birth), with the people as opposed to the great, Machiavelli ennobles the vulgar over the nobility. Moreover, by affiliating the outcome-oriented, and hence expediency-concerned, people with the moral characteristic of onestà, Machiavelli fundamentally problematizes the moral-philosophical distinction between honestas and utilitas. For other considerations on Machiavelli's engagement with Cicero, see Colish 1978; Connolly 2007; Cox 1997; Olmsted 2006, 48–62; and Zerba 2004. On Cicero's impact upon Renaissance humanism, generally, see Tuck 1993, 1–30.
5. Aristotle 1997, I.1, 1252a:1–5.
6. See Coby 1999, 81.
7. Considered together, Clearchus, Hiero, and Baglioni cut to pieces or clearly should have, respectively, a city's nobility, a group of *condottieri*, and the prelates of the Roman Catholic Church (D I.16, D I.27; P 13). These are, incidentally, the three kinds of grandi who, when corrupt (that is, when operating beyond ordinary accountability), most viciously oppress the people: oligarchs, captains, and clerics. Machiavelli states that the "people" and "everyone" are satisfied, or would have

been, by the actions of the individual tyrants in at least two of these three episodes. Of course, Machiavelli later shows that the people are capable of taking such matters into their own hands against the grandi, as in Corcyra, to the same "satisfying" effect (D II.2).

8. See Ridolfi 1963, 106–8.
9. See Ridolfi 1963, respectively, 99–100, 129–32.
10. Ridolfi 1963, 22–130, 133–54.
11. See Najemy 1990, 103–7.
12. See Najemy 1990, 117.
13. This is consistently exhibited by Machiavelli's account of Florence's domestic politics in his *Florentine Histories* (FH). See also Hulliung 1984, 76–8.
14. Nippel 1980.
15. Coby deems the characteristic plebeian state to be "at-restness." See Coby 1999, 97. However, Vatter (2000, 91–5), inspired by the work of Arendt (1996) and Wolin (1994, 1996), may go too far in characterizing the plebeian demeanor as the appetite for "no-rule": this collapses the distinction between oppression, which Machiavelli states that the people seek to avoid, and government, which Machiavelli suggests that the people will tolerate and even welcome when conducted through law (D I.4), or, for instance, as experienced in military service (especially as they become aware of the necessity of ordered and legal government for the realization of their desire not to be oppressed).
16. Manin 1997, 47; Wantchekon and Simon 1999.
17. See, e.g., Viroli 1998, and, much more formidably, Coby 1999.
18. On the elusiveness of the concept "rule," especially in a democratic context, see Markell 2006.
19. Here I follow Brennan 2006; Lintott 1999; Loewenstein 1973; Nicolet 1980; and North 2006.
20. How much genuine "representation" entails direct responsiveness to or immediate defiance of popular will is a perennial topic of modern democratic theory. see, e.g., Mansbridge 2003 and Pitkin 1990.
21. See Millar 2001, 2002; and Yakobson 2006.
22. See Adcock 1964; Millar 1998; and Taylor 1990.
23. Livy 1919–26, II.32–3.
24. Aristotle 1997, VI.2, 1317b: 1–5.
25. Indeed, there may have been much more overlap between military and political reciprocity in Rome than even Machiavelli recognized or at least illustrates; see Chrissanthos 2004.
26. Guicciardini knew this quite well. Indeed, while I will consistently use Guicciardini as an oligarchically inclined foil for Machiavelli throughout this book, I completely agree with Pocock's injunction against crudely reading the former as merely a "mouthpiece" for his class. See Pocock 1975, 219. Indeed, Guicciardini's sophisticated defense of elections is designed not only to keep "unworthy" upstarts from ascending to magistracies; he also thinks that assigning the people the function of selecting individual members of the ottimati for office minimizes conflict among the latter that ensues when they try to sort this out themselves. As Pocock writes, Guicciardini "had no illusions whatever about the way [the ottimati] would behave if allowed to monopolize power and office" (219). These same qualifications apply to Cicero, who was by far not the most intransigent exponent of aristocratic ascendancy among Roman senators. See, e.g., Connolly 2007.

27. Notable contributors to this debate include Honig 2007; Michelman 1997, 163, and 1998, 91; Mouffe 2000; and Olson 2006. Moreover, such scholars also often ask: how can political controversies within already democratized regimes be settled democratically when democratic principles and procedures are the precise objects of contention? In doing so, this literature often operates as if contending parties within democracies forsake *all* shared assumptions of a common good or of common interests; they effectively reduce all democratic controversies to situations of anarchy. This exemplifies the pitfalls entailed by accounts that treat democracy principally as a philosophical problem. See, as potential avenues leading away from the dead ends posed by this literature, Geuss 2008; and Meckstroth 2009 and n.d.
28. Acemoglu and Robinson 2005; Boix 2003; and Huntington 1993.
29. See Anderson 1999; O'Donnell and Schmitter 1986; and Rustow 1970.
30. See Eley 2002.
31. On the various ways that democracies have facilitated or prohibited self-revision, see Schwartzberg 2007.

Chapter 2.   Democratic Republics and the Oppressive Appetite of Young Nobles

1. The question of the book's intent was raised almost immediately after it appeared; see Donaldson 1988, 1–29, 87–110. But Baron 1961 certainly framed the issue for contemporary scholarship.
2. See, respectively, Dietz 1986, and Langton 1987, 1277–88.
3. For example, see Skinner 1981, 49–50.
4. However, I take very seriously Coby's caveats regarding the search for subsurface enjoinders to action or attempts at motivating readers in Machiavelli's writings; see Coby 1999, 5–6, 288 n. 33.
5. What do we make of the fact that the specific "potential prince," Hiero of Syracuse, who Machiavelli names as the model for his dedicatees, became a tyrant after establishing a principality? It could be an indication of the harshness, the severity, even the tyrannical quality of Machiavelli's notion of a republic's "free way of life" – its modes and orders, or laws and institutions, as well as the disposition of its citizens and magistrates. See Mansfield and Tarcov's introduction to Machiavelli [1513–19] 1997, xxv–xxvi. But the fact remains that Hiero is a singular prince, an individual tyrant, and is *not* an example of "princes plural," a fact that perhaps foreshadows Machiavelli's argument for the necessity of individual personal authority in the establishment or reformation of a republic (e.g., D I.9, III.30). Princes plural (including the people empowered collectively as "prince," D I.58) normally govern republics, but republics are founded and reformed by singular princely individuals. Nevertheless, the tyrannical or potentially antirepublican quality of the Hiero example is perhaps moderated by the amalgam of Machiavelli's references to the Syracusan in *The Prince* and the *Discourses*: Hiero rises from private citizen to captain, then to prince, and frees his city from dependence on unreliable mercenary forces (P VI; 13); and the institutions that he establishes in Syracuse lay the groundwork for a more popular (D I.58) or free (D II.2) appropriation of them in time. Ultimately, any suggested subordination of republicanism to individual tyranny in the *Discourses'* dedication may be contravened by Machiavelli's eventual revelation that, for all his "virtuous" efforts, Hiero's principality depended on the friendship of the Roman republic for protection (D II.30).

6. Indeed, one of the dedicatees, Rucellai, may have died (in 1519) before Machiavelli finalized the work, in which case Machiavelli decided not to change the dedication. See Mansfield 1979, 22 and 22 n. 5. It will become clear that my interpretation depends less on the specific identities of the dedicatees, which are not unimportant, than the fact that they are plural, young, wealthy, and members of families with distinct oligarchic prejudices who had been Machiavelli's antagonists in the republic of 1494–1512.

7. This is not to say that the *Discourses* would be of no interest or use to princes proper and peoples generally (nor that *The Prince* would be of no use for princes plural or peoples). Strauss alludes to the multiple perspectives that pervade each book; how some predominate and some are subordinate or intermittent; see Strauss 1958, 49; cf. Mansfield and Tarcov 1997, xlii.

8. See Skinner 1981, 49, 50; Viroli 1998, 14, 159; and, e.g., Mansfield 1979, 21. The aristocratic background of the dedicatees is more clearly presented in the historical and biographical literature; see Walker's translation of the *Discourses* (Machiavelli [c. 1513–1517] 1950, 3); and Ridolfi 1963, 168, 170, 174; see also de Grazia 1989, 358, who is especially good on the political and social asymmetries between the author and his addressees.

9. Consult Gilbert's research on the pro-oligarchic/antipopulist preconceptions of the Florentine ottimati in this era, including members of the Rucellai and Buondelmonti families: Gilbert 1957, 187–214; 1968, 442–62; and 1977, 215–46. For a roughly contemporary confirmation of these dispositions in Cosimo's and Zanobi's forebears, see Guicciardini [c. 1508] 1970, 144–5 and 299, respectively.

10. See Butters 1985 and Stephens 1983.

11. In the next two paragraphs, I rely loosely on Butters 1985 and Stephens 1983. See also Najemy 1997.

12. On the ottimati's contempt for Machiavelli, see Black 1990, 71–99, here 97; Gilbert 1965, 172–4; Najemy 1990, 102–17, here 117; and Ridolfi 1963, 130–2.

13. Ridolfi 1963, 99–100.

14. Ridolfi 1963, 80–8.

15. Gilbert 1965 and Najemy 1993.

16. See Hale 1963, 150, and Ridolfi 1963, 174. Zanobi was godfather to one of Machiavelli's children. See de Grazia 1989, 228. On the significance of such relationships in Florentine social life generally, see Kent 2009, McLean 2007, and Padgett 2010.

17. Strauss emphasizes the fact that the dedicatee of *The Prince*, Lorenzo, was Machiavelli's "master." See Strauss and Cropsey 1972, 271–92, here 278 (twice). While Strauss acknowledges that the dedicatees of the *Discourses*, Machiavelli's "two young friends[,] . . . compelled" Machiavelli to write the book, Strauss does not seem to consider the extent to which they too might be Machiavelli's "masters."

18. See the contributions to Hankins 2000a and also Jurdjevic 1999.

19. On the issue of just how "cultivated" an audience of grandi might be, I assume that Machiavelli's dedicatees or readers like them will have a general familiarity with Roman constitutional arrangements and Livy's history of Rome, Machiavelli's ostensible source, but not necessarily that they will be reading Livy along with the *Discourses*, carefully cross-comparing and contrasting the texts and the events described within each of them. On the contrary, Mansfield assumes that a "present-day" noble audience *will* conduct such comparisons while a more popular audience

will not. See Mansfield 1979, 49, 44, respectively. I assume that neither will, but do not rule out the possibility that Machiavelli supposes that some of his readers will do so.

20. It is of course a timeless aristocratic conceit that the few who wield disproportionate authority within most republics do so on the basis of personal qualities that cannot be reduced to material advantage. The Aristotelian and Polybian distinctions between aristocracy and oligarchy address this disposition, while Cicero freely expresses it: "wealth, reputation, or resources, if they are empty of prudence and of a method of living and of ruling over others, are filled with disgrace and insolent pride; and there is no uglier form of state than that in which the richest are thought to be the best" (Cicero 1999, 23). Such authors, however, are notably short on actionable criteria for distinguishing any particular group of genuine aristocrats from mere oligarchs.

21. See Mansfield 1979, 37; Polybius 1979.

22. Livy 1919–26, II.21–4, 27–33.

23. Lintott 1999, 121–8. Machiavelli will emphasize their wielding of public accusations against magistrates and notable citizens (D I.7).

24. Farrar 1993, 17–40; and Ober 1998. For significant qualifications of the grounds for such worries, see Monoson 2000, Ober 1993, and Saxonhouse 1996.

25. See Brucker 1968 and Najemy 1982. The purported excesses of the Ciompians' behavior and demands would play an important role in Florentine humanism's efforts to legitimate both the Albizzi oligarchy and the Medici principality that subsequently ruled the city. See Hankins 2000a, 75–178.

26. See Machiavelli, FH III.12–22.

27. Mansfield 1979, 43.

28. On the cosmological undertones of Machiavelli's use of the term "humors," see Parel 1992 and 2000.

29. Therefore, I disagree with Coby's assertion that Machiavelli distinguishes between the patricians of Rome, on the one hand, and the nobility of medieval and Renaissance Europe, including the ottimati of city-states such as Florence, on the other. See Coby 1999, 65, 304 n. 62. Machiavelli clearly thinks that they are all motivated by the same humor, even if the circumstances in which, and the institutions through which, they express it differ. I do, however, agree with Coby's criticisms of Bonadeo (1969; 1970): Machiavelli does not generally desire the elimination or demise of the grandi, simply because he doesn't think that it brings about circumstances conducive to liberty that are sustainable in the long term. Individuals with a humor to oppress constantly reconstitute themselves within a class of grandi. Although, as mentioned before, there are short-term circumstances where Machiavelli thinks that the elimination of a particular group of grandi might be beneficial (e.g., P 13, D I.16, D I.27, D II.2, FH III.1).

30. Although Machiavelli concedes in P 9 that "libertà," a euphemism for a republic, is one of the possible outcomes of grandi-popular interaction.

31. See Lintott 1999, 44–5, and Mouritsen 2001, 46–7.

32. See Najemy 2006, 63–95, especially 80.

33. Do all grandi have a desire to dominate, and hence do they all owe their wealth and status to this humor alone? No. Surely some gain the latter by inheritance or chance and try to maintain them slothfully, rather than through continued domination. Machiavelli has a word for this subset of grandi, *gentiluomi* or gentlemen, and he explains what tends to happen to them among virtuous people (D I.55). The

implication is that such grandi do not remain great for very long. For a very thorough discussion of the grandi-popolo distinction in the *Discourses*, especially the place of nature and circumstance within it, see Coby 1999, 13, 93, 96.

34. A prince reading the book might ponder why "men" (e.g., P 17) seem to have a different nature than "the people" (e.g., P 9). In the *Discourses*, Machiavelli uses "men," for instance, to stand for a prince at I.29 and for the people or the plebs in I.47.

35. Interestingly, Machiavelli eschews the terms governo largo and stretto in his evaluations of aristocratic and democratic republics. Presumably the terms had become especially inflammatory during the controversies that plagued the 1494–1513 republic, and that culminated in its collapse. Machiavelli instead evaluates regimes according to which group within them should hold the "guard of liberty," the popolo or the grandi, and in terms of which specific republican model should be followed, the Roman versus the Venetian/Spartan one.

36. Consult the imagined conversations between the young ottimati and the low-born but highly accomplished Medici partisan, Bernardo del Nero, in Guicciardini [1524] 1994.

37. Manin 1997, 42–93, 132–60.

38. For representative views of Venice in the Florentine political imagination, see Gilbert 1968 and Guicciardini [1524] 1994. On views of Venice more widely, see Bouwsma 1968 and Haitsma Mulier 1980.

39. Mansfield 1979, 46.

40. For instance, Livy 1919–26, IV.8–9; and, in general, Montesquieu [1734] 1999.

41. Coby astutely notes that I.37 contradicts noble charges entertained by Machiavelli in I.5 regarding the supposed limitlessness of the people's ambition. See Coby 1999, 97.

42. Kapust 2009 shows that republicans from Cicero to Hamilton exclusively identify the volatile interplay of oratory, demagoguery, and redistributive politics as the great threats to republics – almost *never* the oppressive or inequitable circumstances that make such appeals plausible.

43. In a dialogue devoted primarily to military matters and secondarily to domestic politics, Machiavelli places renowned *condottiere* Fabrizio Colonna in conversation with Cosimo and Zanobi. See Machiavelli [1521] 1997, 529–705. In the *Discourses*, with the priorities somewhat reversed, Machiavelli establishes himself as the young grandi's principal interlocutor.

44. In a reading of Aristotle that exhibits more than a slight Machiavellian twist, Yack defines the "political" in terms of the competition that ensues between differing perspectives on justice, domination, and class: see Yack 1993. See also Vatter 2000, especially 108–9.

45. Interestingly, the grandi spokesman invokes Marius, an ultimately unsuccessful populist insurgent, rather than Caesar himself, who actually usurped the liberty of the republic. Perhaps Marius is more hated by the nobles because, unlike Caesar, who is more to be feared, Marius was of notoriously low birth.

46. For extensive discussions on the place of empire in Machiavelli's political thought, see Armitage 2000, 125–45, and Hörnqvist 2004.

47. Indeed, the case of Menenius the plebeian dictator that concludes I.5 seems to indicate that the people and their magistrates will insinuate themselves into the highest levels of domestic politics through their involvement with military and diplomatic affairs.

48. Armitage 2000, 128–32; Coby 1999, 39–41; Kahn 1994, 50–1, 261 n. 13; Mansfield 1979, 45–53, and 1996, 85–92; and Strauss 1958, 110–14.
49. Among Strauss-influenced investigations, Fischer 2000 emphasizes glory in Machiavelli's ostensible endorsement of empire; Coby 1999, 261–8, accentuates greatness; and the contributors to Rahe 2005 prioritize the appetite for acquisition.
50. Prejudice against the Gracchi among Florentine patricians is perhaps best typified by Bruni 1987, 186; and Guicciardini [1530] 2002, 395.
51. Strauss asserts that Machiavelli's nobles are consumed by "the insatiable desire of each for eternal glory in this world." Strauss 1958, 134; cf. 250.
52. Molho, Raaflaub, and Emlen 1991, 33–52, 93–169, 289–354, 565–640; Sealey 1976, 66–133, 238–68; and Waley 1969, 88–157.
53. On the political implications of the quest for glory, see Becker 1973 and Colbourn 1998.
54. Therefore, like Strauss, Mansfield and Tarcov may too easily collapse the grandi appetite to dominate with the appetite for glory: without qualification, they equate "those whose natures insist on [ruling]" with "those who want glory." See Mansfield and Tarcov 1997, xxviii; cf. Mansfield 1996, 238.
55. The aristocratic liberals of the nineteenth century reversed this logic, endorsing empire, in part, as a way of protecting themselves from the plebeians; e.g., John Stuart Mill and Alexis de Tocqueville endorsed imperial projects as a way of channeling outward the domestic threats posed by mass democratization. See Pitts 2005.
56. Read I.12, II.4, II.12, II.16, in light of Machiavelli's exchange with Vettori in Najemy 1993, 156–75.
57. See, e.g., Strauss 1958, 182.
58. See, e.g., P 7, 12, 24. On Florentine debates over imperial expansion, and Machiavelli's place within them, see Ardito 2004.
59. For a fine-grained examination of Machiavelli's estimation of the pros and cons of Swiss military policy, see Coby 1999, 119–20, 138–9.
60. See Brucker 1969, 125–27; Gilbert 1977, 218–22; Ridolfi 1963, 203.

Chapter 3.   The Benefits and Limits of Popular Participation and Judgment

1. See the excerpts from Plato, Thucydides, and Pseudo-Xenophon in Robinson 2004.
2. As Fontana 2003 argues, Machiavelli's pro-plebeian standpoint is partly anticipated by Sallust, who nevertheless is still more evenhanded in his treatment of the nobles and people than is the Florentine.
3. Aristotle 1997, Waldron 1995.
4. Cicero 1999, 22–3: "If a free people chooses the men to whom to entrust itself (and it will choose the best people if it wants to be safe), then surely the safety of the citizens is found in the deliberations of the best men." See Schofield 1999.
5. Guicciardini [1524] 1994; Madison, Hamilton, and Jay [1788] 1998; Schumpeter 1942.
6. See, e.g., Guicciardini [1512] 1998, 123; and [1530] 2002, 390.
7. Guicciardini [1512] 1998; Rousseau 1997; Schmitt 2007.
8. While Machiavelli does not maintain a consistent etymological distinction between opinion and judgment (see, e.g., D II.22), he does maintain a thoroughly consistent conceptual distinction between the two.

9. As does, e.g., Montesquieu [1748] 1989, 203.

10. For recent considerations on this distinction, see O'Leary 2006, 22–6.

11. Machiavelli's description of the Capuans' deliberation includes whistling, shouting, and ridicule – to be sure, not the kind of sober, rationalist, and well-ordered communication generally associated with "deliberative democracy" today; see Benhabib 1996; Gutmann and Thompson 1996 and 2004; Habermas 1996. On the persuasive status of alternative forms of communication, see, e.g., Garsten 2006 and Krause 2008.

12. Contemporary democratic theory emphasizes the benefits of procedures, especially those enlisting popular judgment, that render indeterminate outcomes. In particular, such procedures may forestall political outcomes that merely replicate pre-existing power and resource asymmetries. See Dahl 1971; Przeworski 1991; Tilly 2007.

13. I more fully explore the ramifications of the Capuan episode from Pacuvius's and the nobility's perspectives in McCormick 2008b.

14. On the idea that people attempt to choose quality individuals rather than bearers of particular policies when electing public officials, see Fearon 1999, 55–98.

15. On the significance of talking before voting, see Goodin 2008, 122–4.

16. This insight supports arguments that deliberation in and of itself, and especially if separated from decision-making practices, is not necessarily beneficial for democratic government. See, e.g., Elster 1986, 115; and Goodin 2008. In Machiavelli's examples, deliberation is certainly crucial for the quality of subsequent decisions that the people make; but, conversely, it is the disciplining effect of impending decision that makes popular deliberation "come to particulars."

17. In his comments on Machiavelli's *Discourses*, Guicciardini both confirms the fact that "all who have written about republics" have preferred "a government of the elite to one of the masses," and affirms the elitist preference to be the correct one. See Guicciardini [1530] 2002, 395.

18. See Holmes 2003 on this aspect of Machiavelli's legal theory.

19. This hesitation is curious given how definitively Machiavelli's distinguishes the nature, the "humor," of the people from that of the grandi in *The Prince* and earlier in the *Discourses*. Indeed, we observed how, in the former work, Machiavelli even affiliates the people's nature with a word, *onestà* (honesty, goodness, even honor) that the humanist tradition, following Cicero 1991, reserved for the nobility – albeit, a nobility of character, not necessarily of birth or blood (P 9). This further raises the question of the nature of princes vis-à-vis that of the great; especially, as we noted in the previous chapter, that Machiavelli often refers to members of the grandi as princes plural.

20. Contemporary theorists of "democratic reason" draw upon similar evidence correlating the cognitive diversity of large bodies with the generally optimum decisions they make. See Estlund 2007, Landemore 2007, and Page 2006. For a dissenting view, see Caplan 2007 and, more moderately, Sunstein 2006.

21. Tan 2008 carefully evaluates the democratic character of the Roman contiones; Fontana 2001 discusses their place in Machiavelli's theory of liberty.

22. On the structure of Roman assemblies, see Taylor 1990. Tuck 2008, 39–40, notes how the structure of Roman assemblies avoids the problem of "preference cycling," of "the voting paradox" – i.e., the tendency of majority wishes to conflict with one another.

23. On the prevalence of this practice in Rome, see Taylor 1990; on aristocratic desires for it in Florence, see Pocock 1975, 129, 253, 255.
24. Guicciardini [1512] 1998, 123–24; [1524] 1994, 99–100; [1530] 2002, 390.
25. Guicciardini [1524] 1994, 151; [1530] 2002, 397.
26. Almost singularly among commentators, Urbinati 2002, 65, grasps the novelty of this aspect of Machiavelli's political thought within the republican tradition.
27. Finley 1985, Najemy 2006, and Stone 1989.
28. Again, Machiavelli's views anticipate those of contemporary defenders of "epistemic" democracy, who argue that large bodies of judges are more likely to produce substantively correct decisions than would (a) more narrowly inclusive, elite-comprised alternatives, and (b) the average member of the larger group by him or herself. See Cohen 1986, Estlund 2007, Landemore 2007, Ober 2009, Surowiecki 2004, and especially Page 2006, 197.
29. This episode closely parallels Bartels' findings regarding the knowledge of fiscal and tax policies exhibited by ordinary U.S. citizens. He concludes that they are keenly susceptible to false claims proffered by socioeconomic and political elites; see Bartels 2008, chap. 6. In a broader context, see also Cheibub and Przeworski 1999. Machiavelli's plebeians do, however, show a real capacity to learn from their initial mistakes.
30. Similarly, Thucydides himself neutralizes the extent to which opponents of popular judgment can use the Sicilian expedition against the people: Thucydides the arch-critic of democracy denounced the decision by the Athenian demos; Thucydides the general and military strategist conceded the fact that the latter voted sufficient men and materiel to secure victory, had not unforeseeable factors intervened. See Thucydides 2009, IV.31. See also Finley 1985, 20–3.
31. In particular, Straussian interpreters proceed as if Machiavelli's examples of deference, manipulation, and poor judgment discredit the force of his general claims in favor of the people's good judgment. For instance, with respect to their election of patricians to offices that the people claimed to have wanted for themselves, Strauss suggests, "in defending the virtue of the Roman people against its own opinion, [Machiavelli] questions the wisdom of the Roman people." See Strauss 1958, 137. But Strauss's position assumes that some political actors in Machiavelli's framework are fully enlightened about their own level of enlightenment. On the contrary, Machiavelli shows that, for example, the Roman senate, to which Mansfield insists Machiavelli attributes near omniscience and omnipotence (1996, 235–7), is clearly *not* as wise as it thinks itself to be; for instance, it causes its own usurpation by favoring Octavian over Antony (D I.52), and, most importantly, it causes the destruction of the republic, as a result of greed, by directing imperial conquest beyond the Italian peninsula (D I.37, D III.24). Indeed, Machiavelli demonstrates that even founders such as Romulus, to whom Strauss insists Machiavelli attributes "superhuman" qualities (1958, 127), misunderstand the ultimate ramifications of their own motives and behavior: Romulus intends to found an enduring principality but unwittingly establishes the foundations of a republic (D I.2). It is simply impossible to demonstrate that any actor in the *Discourses* possesses the absolute self-knowledge (qualified "Socratically," to be sure) that Strauss attributes to Machiavelli, to Plato, and to proximate others, as well.
32. See, e.g., Barber 2000, Putnam 2000, and Sandel 1996.
33. Tocqueville [1848] 2000; cf. also Baehr and Richter 2004.

34. The Roman dictatorship was, for most of Rome's history, a temporary emergency institution that ensured the preservation of the republic, not, as it became, an autocratic office of indefinite length (D I.34). On this distinction, see Lazar 2009, McCormick 1998, and Rossiter 1948. Twentieth-century analysts of Roman dictatorship emphasize the extent to which the senate and consuls used it to cow the plebs into submission (Fraenkel 1969, 10, 213; Kirchheimer 1969, 42). This charge must be taken seriously, since the dictator was appointed without the consultation of the popular assemblies and in practice temporarily revoked citizens' right of appeal to the people.

35. This highlights the somewhat misguided nature of theoretical efforts to distinguish negative from positive liberty in the Roman context. Pitkin, for instance, potentially contradicts herself when doing so. She affirms, on the one hand, the "passive," "defensive," and "negative" quality of *libertas* for most Romans: "the Roman plebs struggled not for democracy but for protection, not for public power but for private security." Yet on the other hand, she concedes, "Of course they sought public, institutionalized guarantees of that security" – yet in so seeking these guarantees, they participated actively and extensively in the politics of the polity. See Pitkin 1988, 534–5. In Chapter 6, I raise this issue with respect to Philip Pettit's philosophical efforts to refine a negative conception of republican liberty, a criticism that may be applied to Quentin Skinner's conceptual efforts as well. As a recent wave of historical research shows, the idea that the Roman people were politically passive in aspiration and practice is largely the product of oligarchically biased sources, notably Cicero's writings; see Flaig 2003; Millar 1998, 2002; and Wiseman 2009. On the debate over the extent to which the Roman Republic can be classified a democracy, see Ward 2004.

36. See Livy 1919–26, e.g., IV.49, 51, VI.5, 35; cf. also Plutarch 1921, X.145–241.

37. Baehr 1998, 287ff, details the socioeconomic changes that made Julius Caesar a successful usurper of the republic while the earlier attempts of Cassius, Marius, Appius, and others were failures. The increasing debt and diminishing property shares of the urban and especially rural plebs encouraged them to seek sustenance in military ventures alone. Consistent with Machiavelli, Baehr demonstrates that the ensuing corruption could have been minimized or forestalled by the senate had it adopted programs of debt relief and land distribution which they considered but dismissed (289). The senators continued to serve their own material interest as custodians of the public lands won by the plebs in war and as patrons of the preeminent lenders and landowners in the republic.

38. In the dialogue *The Art of War*, Machiavelli's main speaker, Fabrizio Colonna, impresses on his young patrician interlocutors the need for properly ordered principalities and republics to provide hospitable places at home to which soldiers may return regularly. See Machiavelli [1521] 1997, I.9–11.

39. This undermines Vatter's depiction of Machiavelli as a steadfast opponent of redistributive politics and a severe critic of the deleterious "ennobling" of the plebeians supposedly signified by popular demands for redistribution (e.g., Vatter 2000, 229, 231, n. 30). Furthermore, Machiavelli does not denounce the tribunes, Tiberius and Gaius Gracchus, for pursuing redistribution as such; he merely criticizes the Gracchi for their imprudent *timing* in introducing these laws, "not their intention" in proposing them (D I.37). For a more nuanced interpretation, see Nelson 2004, chap. 2.

40. Aristotle 1997, III.11, 1281b, 34–8.
41. Condorcet 1994, 95, 256.
42. Locke 1989, 406–28.
43. Ackerman 1991 offers a sophisticated account of how constitutions can instantiate knowledge yielded by the long-wave learning curves characteristic of democratic politics. However, Ackerman unabashedly conceives of democratic peoples as homogeneous wholes, which, from a Machiavellian perspective, too easily enables elites to distort expressions of the popular will.
44. On Machiavelli's intimations that "prudence" dictated that the Gracchi should have refounded the republic so as to "keep the public rich and the citizens poor," see McCormick 2009b.

Chapter 4. Elections, Lotteries, and Class-Specific Institutions

1. Manin 1997, 132–60.
2. Manin 1997, 42–93.
3. Hansen 1991, 230–1; Ober 1993, 8, 76–80, 97–103.
4. On the utility and justice of lotteries, sortition, or randomization within a contemporary public policy context, see Bennett 1999, Duxbury 1999, Harcourt 2007, Samaha 2009, and Stone 2007, 2009.
5. Cf. Coby 1999, 25–31, 60; Lintott 1999, 11–15, 121–8, 205–11; Nicolet 1980, 325, 340–59.
6. See Lintott 1999, 43, 53–4, n. 67; and Taylor 1990, 60–4.
7. Lintott 1999, 120.
8. On the persistent problem of domination by one's own entailed by any scheme intended to advance a disadvantaged group through group representation, see Williams 2000, 231.
9. I rely upon Jolowicz 1967, Lintott 1999, Loewenstein 1973, and Nicolet 1980 for legal and institutional details of the Roman Republic not laid out explicitly in Livy or Machiavelli.
10. See, respectively, Taylor 1962 and Marshall 1997.
11. In short, the "negative" check on the grandi provided by the plebeians within Machiavelli's scheme explicitly does *not* preclude active, "positive" governing by the people through legislation proposed via the tribunes or individual citizens and then discussed and voted on by the plebeians or the entire citizenry in their assemblies (D I.18). An aversion to "rule" by the people and to the necessity of institutions for a flourishing democracy characterizes both poststructuralist democratic theory and poststructuralist appropriations of Machiavelli (see, respectively, Laclau and Mouffe 1984, and Vatter 2000, 91–3). However, Machiavelli's own view of what the people should actually do – actively and through legal institutions – was neither so normatively pure nor so practically enfeebled as such "radically democratic" readings suggest (see also Arendt 1996; Ranciere 2007; and Wolin 1994, 1996). While these theorists uphold "no-rule" as a normative political principle, Machiavelli suggests that the best one can hope for from a republic, governo largo, or democracy is an alternation between rule and being ruled among citizens – a dispersal of rule throughout the citizenry, but *not* a dissolution of rule as such. Moreover, he generally understood law as the concrete instantiation of hard-won democratic gains (always necessary, if not permanently sufficient, for liberty), not as the inherent antithesis to democratic vitality. Machiavelli simply did not confuse

popular government with anarchism. He would have guffawed at the notion of "no-rule," and recoiled at the idea that law and liberty, institutions and democracy were incompatible. From a Machiavellian standpoint, such claims neither promote genuine popular participation nor supply an effective avenue for the popular contestation of elites, but rather arguably guarantee the people's subjection to the latter.

12. Manin, Przeworski, and Stokes 1999, 34.

13. Whether or not failure to win reelection is a viable sanction for public officials, there are, to be sure, perils posed by efforts to make punishment *too* stringent: within electoral systems, public officials who are certain to lose their office will often seek rents; in traditional democracies and republics, magistrates facing severe punishment will often launch coups. As Rose-Ackerman (1999, 127) observes, democratic accountability depends on elites who "feel insecure about their prospects, but not too insecure."

14. Cicero (1999, 166) suggests that the tribunes ultimately serve the interests of the nobles: since the people as a whole cannot generally be punished for misbehavior, it is good that they have leaders who can be punished on such occasions, and who therefore have an interest in keeping the people in line. The view that usefulness to the nobility was in fact Machiavelli's ultimate justification for the tribunate is fairly pervasive among Straussian scholars. To the extent that this claim is explicitly postulated in classical sources, not only Cicero but, for instance, Livy (1919–26, VI.19) and others as well, it seems odd that Machiavelli would make this a secret, esoteric teaching – especially since such interpreters understand Machiavelli to be perpetrating a wholesale overturning of the classical tradition. In any case, based on previous discussions and further elaboration in this chapter, I argue that any potential benefit offered to the grandi by the existence of the tribunes is far outweighed by the benefits they provide to common people. This will become clearer in my account of Machiavelli's proposed tribunician office for Florence, the provosts, presented later in this chapter. Moreover, any claim that the tribunes, first and foremost, served patrician interests must confront the following facts: Machiavelli notes how the Roman senate tolerated Appius Claudius's tyranny during the rule of the Ten precisely because the nobles desired the permanent suspension of the tribunate (D I.40); and the conservative revolution affected by Sulla's dictatorship stripped the tribunes of virtually all of their political authority in 82–1 BCE (see Keaveney 2005, 140–2).

15. See, e.g., Livy 1919–26, III.19.

16. Coby 1999, 56, and Millar 2002 complain that Machiavelli isn't more precise in his discussion of the Roman assemblies. But Millar goes too far in his criticisms, especially given his excessively democratic reading of Rousseau's account of Rome's assemblies. See Millar 2002, 71, 75, 113.

17. Guicciardini ([1524] 1994 and [1530] 2002) promoted general election – open eligibility and wide suffrage – precisely because it tended to elevate socioeconomic elites to office. Rousseau (1997, 130) seems to desire a similar outcome when he prescribes more restricted electoral methods, specifically, weighing votes in favor of wealthier citizens. See McCormick 2007a.

18. The historical concilium plebis almost certainly excluded patricians. Lintott suggests that "it would surely have been improper, even repugnant, to include patrician votes in a decision which would be described as 'X . . . plebem rogavit plebesque iure scivit,'" as a law made by and for the plebeians. See Lintott 1999, 54. He

adds a footnote of citations supporting the fact that patricians did not attend the concilium until very late in the republic (54, n. 67), which Taylor (1990, 60–4) corroborates.

19. See Barber 1984; Cohen 2006; Miller 1984; O'Leary 2006, 29; Strong 2002; and Viroli 1988.
20. See McCormick 2007a.
21. See, e.g., Livy 1919–26, II.44.
22. Martines 1979, 34–62.
23. In the *Florentine Histories*, see FH II.37, II.41, III.14, IV.12, VII.26; for a rare beneficial result, see FH II.32.
24. Najemy 1982, 126–65, 217–63.
25. Brucker 1977; Rubinstein 1966.
26. Viroli (1998, 126) overestimates Machiavelli's criticisms of the Florentine people in the *Florentine Histories* (especially, FH III.1). Hulliung (1984, 75–8, 86) grapples much more seriously with Machiavelli's differing depictions of the Roman and the Florentine peoples in the *Discourses* and the *Florentine Histories*; while at times he may overestimate Machiavelli's criticisms of the people, Hulliung still manages to recognize that Machiavelli fundamentally blames the nobles for causing strife in both works and within each republican context (77).
27. See Ardito 2004; Black 1990; and Ridolfi 1963, 80–8.
28. Martines 1979, 48–50; Salvemini 1899, 198–207.
29. Martines 1979, 58–71, 94–110. For Machiavelli's own account of this collusion, see FH III.21.
30. See DF 733–45.
31. Butters 1985, 306–7, 311–12; and Stephens 1983, chaps. 5 and 6.
32. See, especially, Silvano 1990, 56–61, and Viroli 1990, 154–5. Such interpreters apparently ignore Machiavelli's instruction to Pope Leo at the proposal's outset: carefully and completely read through the proposal before ultimately evaluating it (DF 738).
33. While Machiavelli cites the need to mollify the most ambitious, prideful, and conde-scending citizens by establishing a life-tenured "signorial" class, Viroli mistakenly suggests that Machiavelli, in good Ciceronian fashion, wished to accommodate "the wisest and most honoured citizens." See Viroli 1990, 155.
34. More specifically, the one provost in weekly residence may appeal a decision of the ordinary Signoria to the full body of thirty-two signors who are eligible to be priors that year. The latter may not convene without two provosts in attendance; the two provosts together can appeal decisions of the Thirty-Two to the Council of Two Hundred. This "Select" council, in turn, may not convene without six Gonfaloniers of the People's Companies, including two provosts, present, any three of whom could direct policy decided there to the Great Council for approval. Finally, the latter may not sit without twelve Gonfaloniers present, among whom must be three provosts, all of whom, again, have full voting powers in the popular Council.
35. At the conclusion of D I.47, Machiavelli speaks of the beneficial educational effect that holding office in the post-1494 republic had on members of the Florentine popolani, who often spouted misinformed and prejudiced opinions as private indi-viduals but who learned the more complicated realities of politics once they became magistrates. Machiavelli's proposal for provosts would educate an even larger num-ber of common citizens who would be circulated from "the piazza to the palazzo" on a more frequent basis.

36. In the *Florentine Histories*, Machiavelli uses the same phrase to describe the function performed by the traditional Gonfaloniers of the Companies of the People that, in the *Discourses*, he applies to the Roman tribunes: they acted "against the insolence of the great" (FH II.22). In the post-1494 republic, Machiavelli served as secretary to the executive committee, the Ten of Liberty, whose charge, when founded, was "to protect the weak from the strong."

37. Manin 1997, 53–4, 57, and Pocock 1975, 128, 253–5, 485, intimate but do not affirm this.

38. See Guicciardini [1512]1998, 122–3; [1530] 2002, 381–438. Cf. Madison, Hamilton, and Jay [1788] 1998, nos. 10, 37, 39, 57, 60, 63.

39. While these Guicciardinian insights into election's general aristocratic effect were taken up with gusto in the American and French republican contexts, they did not fully take hold in Great Britain until the mid- to late-nineteenth century. At that time, Walter Bagehot, in making the case for an enlarged franchise, argued that the British electorate's "deference" to elites reflected a particular cultural disposition rather than a political fact about the common people everywhere and always. See Bagehot [1867] 2001.

40. Guicciardini [1530] 1965, 76, 123, 125.

41. See, in order of the periods they cover, Najemy 1982; Brucker 1977; Rubinstein 1966 and 1954; Butters 1985; and Stephens 1983; cf. also Bock, Skinner, and Viroli 1990, 1–71.

42. Brucker 1962, and Najemy 1982.

43. Najemy 1982, 51.

44. Najemy admirably conveys the seemingly infinite number of appointment schemes proposed and appointment models adopted during the years 1280–1303: after all, the issue of appointing priors was reopened near the end of every two- then four-month term of the Signoria. See Najemy 1982, 17–78.

45. Guicciardini [c. 1508] 1970, 106.

46. Guicciardini [1512] 1998, 126.

47. Silvano 1990, 41.

48. Guicciardini [1512] 1998, 126–7.

49. Rubinstein 1954, 154.

50. Guicciardini [c. 1508] 1970, 128–9.

51. Butters 1985, 36, challenges Guicciardini's claim that the move to lot at the definitive stage expanded the range of officeholders very much at all. He reports that only one person entered the Signoria who had not been preceded there by another family member at some earlier point in time. But this is a potentially faulty standard, as the Florentine ottimati likely discriminated among family members intergenerationally, deeming some descendents of previous officeholders unworthy of holding office themselves. For instance, while Machiavelli's grandfather and great-grandfather had served in high office, he himself, due to his father's poverty and questionable birth as well as his own modest means and dubious moral reputation, was clearly deemed unsuitable for high office by the city's elite. See Ridolfi, 1963 2, 257n. 4. Thus, if similar "black sheep" members of established families had started to gain access to the magistracies more often than they had previously as a result of the constitutional reforms discussed here, this no doubt would have annoyed ottimati such as Guicciardini. (I heartily thank John Padgett for sharing his data on the Machiavelli family tree, and for providing important contextual information concerning eligibility [formal and informal] for office in the Florentine republics.)

52. Butters 1985, 36.
53. Gilbert 1968, 442–62, and 1977, 215–46; Skinner 2002, 126–30, 138–9, 148.
54. Guicciardini [1512] 1998, 137. One should keep in mind that Guicciardini composed this reform proposal while serving as the Florentine Republic's ambassador to Spain. By including ambassadors here, the young Guicciardini is proposing to make himself a life-termed member of the Florentine senate.
55. Guicciardini [1512] 1998, 137–8.
56. Guicciardini [1512] 1998, 135.
57. Guicciardini [1530] 2002, 391–7.
58. See Cicero 1999, 164–7; Montesquieu [1734] 1999, 84.

Chapter 5. Political Trials and "the Free Way of Life"

1. Dunn 2005, and Finley 1985.
2. Pettit 1999a.
3. Fear of public exposure and censure, as much as exile, imprisonment, and fines, seems to deter political misbehavior in these contexts. See Allen 2000; Elster 1999; Forsdyke 2005; and Kelly 2006.
4. Lintott 1999, 147–62.
5. Because ancient democracies such as Athens distributed most offices through citizenwide lottery, class divisions proved less salient in government institutions, and policies pursued by magistrates could be expected to reflect the common good. Nevertheless, the Athenians could impose harsh punishments through their public scrutiny procedures: all magistrates faced post-term investigations of their conduct (*Euthynai*), which could lead to a formal trial (an *Eisangelia*), on charges of treason, bribery, potential tyranny, and general "injustice against the people" (*prodosia*). See Elster 1999, 253–78.
6. For insightful discussions of Coriolanus in the context of republican politics and Machiavelli's political theory, see Coby 1999, 25–6, 33; and Nelson 2004, 49–86.
7. See Gilbert 1968, 442–62; and 1977, 215–46; and Skinner 2002, 126–30, 138–9, 148.
8. Ridolfi 1963, 99.
9. de Grazia 1989, 140; and Ridolfi 1963, 112, 286n. 18 and 20.
10. Najemy 1990, 102–17, here 108–12; Ridolfi 1963, 99–101. Cf. also Black 1990, 71–99.
11. Ridolfi 1968, 172–206. Also see Guicciardini's self-penned accusatory and exculpatory discourses on his career from this era: Guicciardini [1527] 1993.
12. Guicciardini [1530] 1965, 76, 123, 125; [1530] 2002, 397.
13. See Machiavelli's *Florentine Histories* (FH IV.24–7). Consult Mansfield's especially suggestive discussion of the Giovanni Guicciardini episode: Mansfield 1979, 61–2.
14. Kaplan 1977; and Lintott 1999, 94–6, 109–13.
15. Wantchekon and Nickerson 2000.
16. In McCormick 2007b, I suggest that this case poses a lesson for how populist reformers might counter smear campaigns launched by the nobles, especially in light of Machiavelli's recommendations for how Savonarola, Valori, and Soderini should have tried the aristocratic enemies of the Florentine Republic before the people collected in the Great Council, as discussed at length later in this chapter.
17. Guicciardini [1512] 1998, 133.
18. Guicciardini [1512] 1998, 147.

19. Guicciardini [1512] 1998, 146.
20. Guicciardini [1512] 1998, 144.
21. Guicciardini [1512] 1998, 144.
22. Guicciardini [1512] 1998, 144.
23. Guicciardini [1512] 1998, 131–2.
24. Guicciardini [1512] 1998, 132.
25. Guicciardini [1512] 1998, 146–7.
26. Butters 1985, 306–7, 311–12; and Stephens 1983, chaps. 5 and 6.
27. Livy 1919–26, II. 34–9.
28. In I.40, Machiavelli speaks of the "envy" aroused in the Roman nobility by the people's possession of the tribunate, and, in an implicit contrast with the behavior of Brutus, how they indulged rather than punished the younger nobles' oppression of the plebs and support for Appius Claudius's tyranny.
29. See, e.g., Mansfield 1979, 53–62; 1996, 29, 241–6, 253–4. See also Strauss 1958, 112–13, 169, 206.
30. Guicciardini [c. 1508] 1970, 106; cf. Machiavelli I.45.
31. Guicciardini [c. 1508] 1970, 103–6.
32. Guicciardini [c. 1508] 1970, 132.
33. Guicciardini [c. 1508] 1970, 116, 125, 131.
34. Guicciardini [c. 1508] 1970, 132–3.
35. Guicciardini [c. 1508] 1970, 134–5.
36. Guicciardini [c. 1508] 1970, 135.
37. Guicciardini [c. 1508] 1970, 141.
38. Guicciardini [c. 1508] 1970, 296–7.
39. In this respect, the mistakes of Valori, Savonarola, and Soderini are prefigured in the example of Virginius, a plebeian leader of not inconsiderable spirit and acuity (D I.40, I.44): Machiavelli criticizes him for eschewing popular judgment by denying the deposed tyrant, Appius Claudius, a popular appeal of his death sentence, an appeal to which he was legally entitled (D I.45).
40. On Machiavelli's much more sympathetic depictions of Valori outside of the *Discourses*, see Jurdjevic 2002, 185–206.
41. On the role that the young ottimati played in overthrowing the republic and restoring the Medici, see Butters 1985 and Stephens 1983.
42. Guicciardini [c. 1508] 1970, 295–7.
43. Guicciardini [c. 1508] 1970, 297–303.
44. Guicciardini [c. 1508] 1970, 192, 206–7, 219–21, 248–50; cf. Guicciardini [1512]1998, 132.
45. Machiavelli admits speaking to Duke Valentino and Cardinal Rouen in *The Prince* (P 3, P 7). But he never emphasizes such intimacy with Soderini in the *Discourses* – perhaps due to the political-personal animosity existing between the former Gonfalonier and the families of Machiavelli's dedicatees.
46. Ridolfi 1963, 99.
47. Here Machiavelli parts company with contemporary democratic theorists who endorse the "wisdom of crowds" (e.g., Estlund 2007 and Page 2006). Rather than emphasizing the epistemic correctness of popular judgment, Machiavelli operates with a more conceptually open and politically unbounded type of judgment (see Zerilli 2005). Machiavelli abandons the substantive, objectively evaluable good outcomes (such as the technical guilt or innocence of an accused) generated by popular judgment and instead suggests that the people, acting as a trial body

and using criteria that they set for themselves and that are not imposed on the people externally, by definition, renders good decisions. Furthermore, he accentuates the instrumental benefits that follow from popular judgment so conceived: elimination of a republic's enemies, deterrence of future offenders, and diminished likelihood of retaliation by friends and relatives of those who have been punished.

48. I need to emphasize the following: Just because Machiavelli argues that popular judgment is inherently "ordinary" and that leaders can avoid extraordinary measures by availing themselves of it when dealing with patrician rivals, this does not mean that Machiavelli completely rules out "extraordinary" measures, wielded unilaterally by princely individuals, especially in "corrupt" republics (e.g., D I.17–18). I merely suggest here that ordinary ones, those formally empowering the people to judge, are preferable for Machiavelli, that is, less likely to establish inconvenient precedents or encourage immediate reprisals.

49. Stephens (1983, 203–55) attributes the eventual and permanent demise of the Florence Republic to the ottimati's preference for Medici rule rather than a power-sharing arrangement with the popolo in a governo largo.

Chapter 6. Republicanism and Democracy

1. On Cicero, see Colish 1978, Olmsted 2006, Connolly 2007, and Zerba 2004; on Bruni, see the contributions of Hörnqvist 2000, Najemy 2000, and Hankins 2000b to Hankins 2000a, 75–179.
2. This chapter expands upon McCormick 2010.
3. Dunn 2005, 17; Finley 1985, 28.
4. Cicero 1999, 22–3 (sections I.51–2). Cf. Wood 1988, 22, 169–71, 174–5.
5. Murray 1966; Seager 1972; Wood 1988, 204–5.
6. Plutarch 2005, 323–73.
7. Baron 1966; Najemy 1982.
8. Bruni 1987, 116–26, 171–4; Hankins 2000a, 1–14, 75–178.
9. Najemy 1982.
10. Machiavelli FH IV. 2–4.
11. McCormick n.d.
12. Guicciardini [1512] 1998.
13. See Molho, Raaflaub, and Emlen 1991, 135–354, 565–640. On Cicero and empire, see Cicero 1993, 120; Cicero 1999, 72–4; and Steel 2001; on Bruni in the same regard, see Hankins 2000b and Hörnqvist 2000.
14. Against Skinner's revival of neo-Roman or republican liberty for contemporary progressive purposes, Kapust (2004) and Maddox (2002) emphasize the deeply oligarchic quality of actual Roman politics that severely constrained the liberty of most Roman citizens; however, Maddox emphasizes the extent to which popular participation and the institution of the tribunes mitigated this state of affairs, while Kapust is less sanguine, emphasizing only the negative, obstructionist, and defensive quality of popular and tribunician power. Ando (2010) discredits neo-Roman republican liberty further when he argues that Cambridge and Cambridge-inspired scholars who revive it fail to note that this particular notion of negative liberty was most fully articulated as a justification for the Principate of Augustus Caesar. In a different vein, Springborg (2001) raises serious questions concerning any uncoupling of Roman liberty from its inherently misogynist/androcentric

attributes – questions raised in a similar and even more provocative manner about Machiavelli's own theory of liberty in Pitkin's classic study (1999).

15. See Hörnqvist 2004.
16. Pettit 1999a and 2001.
17. Pettit 1999b, 2000, and 2004.
18. Pettit 2000, 105.
19. On the difficulties entailed by sharply distinguishing liberalism from republicanism, see Holmes 1995, 5–6; Isaac 1988; Larmore 2001; Larmore 2008, 139–95; Patten 1996; and Rogers 2008.
20. Skinner 1998, ix–x; but also see Holmes 1995, 13–41. Shklar's (1989) "liberalism of fear" would seem to be an obvious example of a liberal theory not concerned narrowly with the injustices associated with direct interference, as such; moreover, it is a theory that has proven fruitfully applicable to other contexts of injustice (see, e.g., Levy 2000).
21. Pettit 1999a, 55, 290–2; Pettit 2001, 156–8; or, what he terms elsewhere, "perceived interests" (Pettit 1999b, 165–6, 170, passim).
22. Pettit 1999a, 30; cf. Pettit 1999a, 27. While Pettit states that his theorizing constitutes "a distinctively republican story," he also claims that it does not pursue "slavish fidelity to the republican tradition" (2001, 173).
23. Pettit 1999a, 28.
24. Pettit 1999a, 187; Pettit 1999b, 166.
25. See Pettit 1999a, 182, 210.
26. See Colish 1971; Guarini 1990.
27. Pettit 1999a, 28; Skinner 2002, 198.
28. Pettit 1999a, 30. According to Pettit, a good becomes a common good when "cooperatively admissible considerations support its collective provision" (2001, 156). However, Pettit deliberately provides no list of issues that necessarily constitute democratic commonality – that is, for democratic citizens to decide. He, I think rightly, operates under the presupposition that democracies necessarily enjoy some grounds of commonality (2000, 108).
29. Pettit 1999a, 29.
30. Pettit 1999a, 294.
31. Pettit 2000, 125; Pettit 2001, 161.
32. Pettit 2000, 106, 114. Pettit interprets the traditional standard of the common good – "What touches all ought to be considered and approved by all" – in a decidedly weak democratic sense: "This does not say that what touches all ought to be decided by all, only that what touches all ought to elicit the considered approval of all. And that is to say that what touches all ought to be controlled by all in the passive mode of control, not necessarily in the active" (2000, 140).
33. Pettit 2004, 52.
34. Pettit 1999a, 168.
35. Pettit 2004, 58; cf. Pettit 1999b, 173.
36. Pettit 2004, 58, emphases added.
37. "The core difficulty with the notion of collective will is that it presupposes collective agency, and that the existence conditions for a collective agent are too demanding for a large-scale populace or electorate to satisfy." See Pettit 2004, 60, n. 9.
38. Pettit 1999a, 81.
39. Pettit 1999a, 81.

40. Pettit 1999b, 177. For a more unabashedly antidemocratic exposition of this argument, see Posner 2004.
41. Pettit 2001, 160–1. Again, cf., Posner 2004.
42. Pettit 1999a, 293–4.
43. Pettit 1999b, 173.
44. See Ober 1993; Przeworski, Stokes, and Manin 1999.
45. Pettit 2000, 126.
46. Pettit 2001, 162.
47. Pettit 2001, 154, 174.
48. Pettit 1999a, 292–7; Pettit 2000.
49. Pettit 2001, 160–3.
50. Pettit 2001, 159. Electoral politics performs a "positive search-and-identify" function while contestatory politics performs a "negative scrutinize-and-disavow" function within Pettit's conception of democracy.
51. Pettit 2000, 139–40, emphasis added.
52. Pettit 2001, 174.
53. Pettit 2001, 171.
54. Pettit 2000, 131.
55. Pettit 2000, 172.
56. Pettit 2000, 172; cf. Pettit 2000, 133. Indeed, this is precisely how ombudsman officers function throughout the world; see Gregory and Giddings 2000.
57. Pettit 1999b, 178.
58. Pettit 1999b, 178.
59. Pettit 2000, 118.
60. Pettit 1999b, 178.
61. Pettit 1999b, 180.
62. Pettit 2001, 163.
63. Pettit 2000, 118.
64. Pettit 1999a, 185, emphasis added.
65. Pettit 2001, 163.
66. Dahl 1957; Hirschl 2005 and 2007; Rosenberg 1991.
67. Pettit 1999b, 178.
68. Even if they are not elected, Pettit insists that administrative and judicial bodies must be sociologically diverse, not "statistically dominated" by members "of one religion, one gender, one class, or one ethnicity," and so he advocates "statistical representation for the major stakeholder groupings" of society. Pettit 1999a, 192–3.
69. Pettit 1999a, 191.
70. On the importance of representing diversity in such contexts, see Goodin 2008, 233–54; Phillips 1995; Williams 2000; Young 1990 and 2000.
71. Pettit 1999a, 191.
72. Williams (2000, 222) concedes that, when it comes to impacting policy outcomes, representing groups in contemporary parliamentary contexts can only amplify voices so much.
73. Pettit 1999a, 191.
74. Pettit 1999a, 191. Pettit is more in tune with the spirit of the Roman tribunes when he recommends allotting seats to "representatives" of indigenous peoples, that is, those they choose among themselves.

75. Indeed, when considering the advantages of mixing different types of electoral systems, Pettit mentions majoritarian and proportional procedures, but he never considers incorporating a practice that was quite prevalent in traditional republics, namely, lottery. See Pettit 2000, 135.
76. Pettit 1999a, 193.
77. Pettit 1999a, 194.
78. Pettit 1999a, 194.
79. Pettit 1999a, 194.
80. Madison, Hamilton, and Jay [1788] 1998, nos. 51, 62–3; Tocqueville [1840] 2000, vol. I, chaps. 15–16.
81. See Dahl 2003; Kramer 2004; and Levinson 2006.
82. Pettit 2004, 53, 55.
83. Pettit 2004, 56–7.
84. Pettit 2004, 56–7.
85. Pettit 1999b, 177.
86. Pettit 2004, 53, 55.
87. Pettit 2004, 56–7.
88. Pettit 1999a, 197; Pettit 2004, 53, 56–7.
89. Pettit 2004, 56–7; cf. Pettit 2000, 136.
90. Since all Roman senators previously held an elected post, theoretically, citizens indirectly authorized them to deliberate and set the policy agenda for the public; in the American case, before the direct election of U.S. senators, citizens generally "appointed" senators indirectly through intermediary, elite-comprised bodies such as state legislatures.
91. Pettit 2000, 136.
92. Pettit 2001, 169.
93. Pettit 1999a, 196.
94. Markell (2008) suggests that, in general, Pettit's ambiguous and inconsistent use of the terms/concepts "avowed interests" and "arbitrary" allows him to empower governments to usurp the judgment of individuals whose domination the former are supposed to alleviate.
95. Pettit 2001, 154.
96. Pettit 2000, 117.
97. Pettit 2000, 117; Pettit 2001, 162.
98. Pettit 2001, 154. For a contrary view, see Mackie 2004.
99. Pettit 1999b, 177.
100. Pettit 1999b, 174.
101. Contemporary theorists of "democratic reason" draw upon similar evidence correlating the cognitive diversity of large bodies with the generally optimum decisions they make. See Page 2006, Estlund 2007, and Landemore 2007. For a dissenting view, see Caplan 2007 and, more moderately, Sunstein 2006.
102. Pettit 1999a, 30.
103. Pettit 1999b, 176–7. Curiously, Pettit (1999, 182) cites Machiavelli (D I.58) on the superior judgment of the people, but he never operationalizes this insight within his framework, instead deliberately confining collective decisions with binding force to the electoral realm. In particular, he doesn't trace the institutional implications of this view that sets Machiavelli so far apart from the other republican authors with whom Pettit, like Skinner, groups him. Moreover, Pettit then uses Machiavelli to impose a strict divide between laws and orders such that the latter may be

maintained beyond a popular desire for change. However, Machiavelli gives many examples of the Roman people changing orders as well as laws, for better, in the case of the tribunate, and for worse, in the case of the Decemvirs.

104. Pettit 1999a, 197; Pettit 2000, 136.
105. Pettit 2000, 140. Kapust (2004, 397–8) suggests that, in such moments, Pettit imports the paternalism of Roman senatorial and clientilist politics into his framework.
106. Pettit 2000, 120.
107. Pettit 2000, 120.
108. See, e.g., Dahl 1989, 50–75; and O'Leary 2006, 5.
109. Pettit 1999b, 181.
110. Pettit 1999b, 181.
111. On the democratic ramifications of juries, see Abramson 1993.
112. Pettit 1999b, 181; Pettit 2000, 120.
113. Pettit 2001, 165.
114. Pettit 1999a, 197; Pettit 2004, 53, 55–7.
115. Dahl 1989; Fishkin 1991 and 1997; Goodin 2008; Neblo 2005 and n.d.; O'Leary 2006; Thompson 2008; and Warren and Pearse 2008.
116. See Baiocchi 2001 and 2005; Fung 2003; Fung and Wright 2003; Goodin 2008, 11–37; and Warren and Pearse 2008, xi–xii, 1–16.
117. Goodin (2008, 37) summarizes cases where such minipublics have had more than just the effect of informing public debate: minipublics have been involved in "determining the referendum question on electoral reform in British Columbia, influencing Danish policy on irradiated food, [and] emboldening Texas utilities to invest more heavily in renewable energy even if at slightly higher prices to consumers."
118. Pettit 1999a, 168, citing Brennan and Lomasky 1993.
119. Pettit 1999a, 169.
120. For instance, evidence suggests that electoral competition in the United States results in excessively punitive and racially biased incarceration policies – policies more punitive and biased than the citizenry would choose a priori, whatever their basic views on race or crime. See Murakawa 2007 and 2009.
121. Pettit 2000, 136.
122. Pettit 2004, 57.
123. Pettit 2004, 58.
124. Pettit 2004, 57.
125. Pettit 2000, 134.
126. Pettit 2000, 134. Somewhat inexplicably, Pettit elsewhere condones the possibility of changing electoral rules through popular referenda: Pettit 2001, 161.
127. Although it must be noted that most collective bodies, other than life-termed senates or supreme courts, are open to charges of intertemporal inconsistency.
128. Are there occasions when enlightened and well-meaning elites might better secure conditions of nondomination for common people than can the latter themselves? In theory: of course. But in his disquieting empirical study of electoral representation and political responsiveness in contemporary America, Bartels (2008) provides only one example where this seems to be the case and many others where quite the opposite occurs; that is, elected officials normally discharge their duties in a self-serving manner or in a manner that benefits the socioeconomic elites to whom they're beholden. The possible exception to this state of affairs (that seems to

affirm the rule) is the case of the estate tax: elected officials affiliated with the Democratic Party consistently opposed the repeal of the estate tax in the United States despite its general unpopularity with their constituencies. They seem to assume that the electorate is misinformed about the extent to which repeal of the estate tax would benefit only the most affluent citizens; but Bartels' evidence suggests that the more average people know about the estate tax, the *less* they actually like it. Average people seem to value intergenerational family continuity for citizens of *any* socioeconomic status more than they do general socioeconomic egalitarianism in this instance – which begs the question of whether elites in this case actually are acting in citizens' self-avowed best interests (Bartels 2008, 27, 147–8, 197–221).

129. Pettit 2001, 170.
130. Pettit 1999b, 167.
131. Pettit 2000, 139–40.
132. Pettit 2000, 139.
133. Pettit 2000, 141.
134. Pettit 1999a, 201.
135. Pettit 1999a, 81.
136. Pettit 2004, 59.
137. Pettit 1999a, 30.
138. See Livy 1919–26, VIII.28.1.
139. Cohn 1980; Najemy 2006, 124–76.
140. See Garnsey 1970.
141. Farrand 1966, I.146–7; Madison, Hamilton, and Jay [1788] 1998, especially nos. 10 and 51; and Meyers 1981, 395. On the antipopular and antiparticipatory biases of the English republicans, see Skinner 1998, 31–2; on the aristocratic prejudices of Dutch republicanism, see van Gelderen 2002, especially 35, 207; and van Gelderen 2005, especially 204, 213.
142. See McCormick 2003.

Chapter 7.   Post-Electoral Republics and the People's Tribunate Revived

1. Madison, Hamilton, and Jay [1788] 1998, no. 10 and no. 63, respectively. For several notable objections to my depiction of the U.S. Framers on these issues, see Shea 2006.
2. On the evolution of democratic institutions and theory, see, respectively, Dunn 1993 and Held 1997.
3. Manin 1997.
4. See, e.g., Pocock 1975, 520.
5. Dahl 2003, 24.
6. Guicciardini [1512] 1998, 122–3.
7. See Michels [1911] 1990; Mosca [1896] 1980; Pareto 1987; and Schumpeter 1942.
8. See, e.g., Dahl 1990 and Przeworski 1999.
9. Dahl (1971) went so far as to call elite-dominated electoral regimes "polyarchies," rather than spoil the name "democracy" by associating it with the former. Moreover, Dahl's own theory of popular government has over time incorporated more robust standards for evaluating elections and the social conditions within which they take place (see, respectively, Dahl 1990, 71–6, 84–9; and 1989, 220–4).

Przeworski, for his part, once defined democracy in the very thinnest of terms: specifically, as a scenario where political losers accept the result of *any* procedure – electoral or not – for selecting political elites (e.g., Przeworski 1991, 10–12). With elections now firmly established as his baseline (Przeworski 1999), Przeworski has been exploring the feasibility of extra-electoral devices for the popular control of elites: see Manin, Przeworski, and Stokes 1999.

10. See Bartels 2008; Goodin 2008, 164–5; Levi, Johnson, Knight, and Stokes 2008; and Przeworski, Stokes, and Manin 1999.

11. See Herzog 1989; Pateman 1989, 65, 83; and Waldron 1987 on the limits of contract and consent theory. For a recent, more applied work relevant to these issues, see O'Leary (2006), who is chiefly concerned with the impact of geographic and demographic size on the relationship between citizens and representatives (e.g., 3, 7, 9, 19–22).

12. Somewhat neutralizing such exaggerated claims is, for instance, Urbinati's (2004, 53–75) analysis of the thoroughly modern and infinitely viable institutional compromise between "direct" and "representative" democracy on a nation-state scale proposed by M. J. N. de Condorcet, but never adopted.

13. Manin discusses the combination of lot and election in the ancient Roman and the Renaissance Italian contexts as a way of setting agendas or of mitigating intra-elite factionalism, but never as a means of controlling elites or expanding participation in office. See Manin 1997.

14. On recent trends toward mixing majoritarianism and proportionality in countries such as Israel, Italy, Japan, New Zealand, and Venezuela, see Shugart and Wattenberg 2001. On consociational arrangements, see Grofman and Lijphart 2003; Lijphart 1992.

15. Classically articulated by Michels [1911] 1990.

16. Aristotle 1997, VI.2, 1317b: 1–5.

17. See Pitkin 1990.

18. See Fiorina 1981 and Powell 2000; on the way that "policy switching" problematizes this conception, see Stokes 1999 and 2001.

19. On the various uses of randomization in contemporary public policy making, see Bennett 1999, Duxbury 1999; Harcourt 2007; Samaha 2009; and Stone 2007, 2009.

20. Hence, I do not consider the "scrutinies" that preceded lottery in the Florentine republics to be, as they are often called, "elections," because the process determining eligibility for magistracies often culminated with the placement of over five thousand names into the bags of office (see Brucker 1962, 67; Najemy 1982, 177). As both Guicciardini and earlier civic humanist Leonardo Bruni intuited, judgment about the possible suitability for officeholding of such a large number of persons does not entail the same discrimination as selecting one or two individuals to actually hold a specific, presently available office. See Bruni [1442] 2004, 73.

21. See Aristotle 1997, III.11, 1281b, 34–8 (see also III.13, 15; VI.8; and VIII.2).

22. Manin 1997, 128.

23. Manin 1997, 238.

24. See Wantchekon 2004, 17–34.

25. See Lane 1973, 110, 259. The increasingly wide discretion exercised by the *arroti*, who performed the scrutinies, and the *accoppiatori*, who drew names from the bags of eligibility in the appointment lotteries, allowed the Albizzean oligarchy and Medicician principate to appear republican in form. See Rubinstein 1966, 1–135.

Padgett and Ansell (1993, 1259–1319) suggest that the Medici did not maintain their power in Florence through control of appointment mechanisms alone or even primarily. The depth and extent of the clientage system established by Cosimo de' Medici ensured his family's ascendance by extrapolitical means. On the persistence of clientage in electoral regimes, see Kitschelt and Wilkinson 2007; and Medina and Stokes 2007.

26. For another perspective on the pathologies attendent to notions of sociopolitical holism or homogeneity, see Connolly 1995.

27. See Asmis 2004 and 2005; Hankins 2000a, 75–178; and Jurdjevic 1999.

28. See Wooton 1994.

29. See Hamilton, Madison, and Jay [1788] 1998, no. 10. See Dawood 2007; Elkin 2006; Levinson 2006; and Nedelsky 1991.

30. Morgan 1989.

31. Steeped in knowledge of classical theory and practice, the American Founders (see Richard 1994; Sellers 1994), in particular, considered but rejected such institutions: John Adams ([1790] 1805, 280) floated the idea of a Roman-style senate, arguing that a body reserved for the wealthiest citizens would *minimize* their influence. Madison toyed with the idea of having one legislative branch elected by propertied citizens and the other elected by those without property (Meyers 1981, 398–9). Moreover, he discussed but rejected Pennsylvania's version of the Roman censors (who originally supervised the census, taxation, voting brackets, admission to the senate, and sumptuary regulations; see Lintott 1999, 94–103) to review the constitutionality of legislative and executive actions (Madison, Hamilton, and Jay [1788] 1998, nos. 48 and 50).

32. For discussions of the impact of the press on American democracy, see Levy 2004 and Martin 2001. In the European context, consult Habermas 1989 and van der Zande and Laursen 2003. More generally, see Keane 1991.

33. See, e.g., Bernstein and Woodward, 1987; Rudenstine, 1998.

34. Goodin 2008, 155–85; Janeway 1999; McChesney 1999.

35. Rattan (2001) overdraws the extent to which class conflict in ancient republics and industrial democracies differs when he suggests that the expansion of the citizenry to encompass the working class in the nineteenth century brought more pronounced conflicts of interest that critical discourse could not overcome. Indeed, his description easily could be applied to, for instance, agrarian controversies in Rome.

36. Arnold 1993; Mansbridge 2003.

37. The top 10 percent richest households, measured at approximately $345,000, controlled over 70 percent of wealth in the U.S., according to 2001 statistics: see Wolff 2001 and 2007. These estimates may be conservative: more recent statistics suggest that the wealthiest 20 percent of households own 85 percent of the nation's wealth, which means that the lowest 80 percent of households controlled only 15 percent of overall wealth in the United States. See Domhoff 2010 and Wolff 2010.

38. Przeworski and Wallerstein 1988.

39. See the symposium on the recall and its ramifications in Symposium on the California Recall 2004.

40. Proposition 8, banning gay marriage, passed on November 4, 2008; Propositions 1A and 1B, which would have raised necessary state revenue through higher taxes, failed on May 19, 2009.

41. As O'Leary (2006, 4) states, perhaps too ungenerously, "experiments with direct democracy, such as the initiative and recall, are burlesque caricatures of their original purpose." For a comprehensive normative examination of referenda, see Tierney 2009.
42. See Bowler and Glazer 2008; Ellis 2002; Matsusaka 2008.
43. Dahl 1989; Fishkin 1991 and 1997; Goodin 2008; Neblo 2005 and n.d.; O'Leary 2006; Thompson 2008; and Warren and Pearse 2008.
44. See Baiocchi 2001 and 2005; Fung 2003; and Fung and Wright 2003; and Warren and Pearse 2008, xi–xii, 1–16. For a concise and analytically sharp summary of the functioning of these various minipublics in practice, see Goodin 2008, 11–37.
45. See, especially, Cutler et al. 2008; Fishkin 1991 and 1997; Neblo 2005 and n.d., Ratner 2008; and Warren and Pearse 2008, 16.
46. See Ferejohn 2008; and Warren and Pearse 2008, xii.
47. Observers of the British Columbia Citizens' Assembly (BCCA), which was charged with formulating a new electoral system for the province, suggest that the British Columbia minipublic chose an electoral model much more favorable to voter choice than elected officials themselves, by all indications, would have designed. See Blais, Carty, and Founier 2008.
48. See Goodin 2008, 23–7, 266–7.
49. In fact, the electorate of British Columbia rejected via referendum the electoral system proposed by the BCCA.
50. In other words, it is not intended for direct implementation as are the progressive reforms proposed by Bruce Ackerman, James Fishkin, and/or their protégés. I have not taken the same care, for instance, in exploring the feasibility of the model, calculating its cost, finalizing its details, and so on, as they do in Ackerman and Fishkin 2004.
51. See http://tiger.berkeley.edu/sohrab/politics/wealthdist.html; see also Wolff 2001 and 2007.
52. James (2008) evaluates the mirroring of the province's citizenry within the BCCA in terms of gender, age, and geography; he concludes that aboriginals should have been included in disproportionately larger numbers to ensure that they enjoyed a real and not just token impact on the deliberations of the group.
53. O'Leary (2006, 8) assigns his minipublics an intriguing legislative function: he empowers the local assemblies in his Assembly Reform with a "gate-opening" function. If 50 percent of local assemblies vote in favor, then a bill that is stuck in a House or Senate committee must be brought to the floor for debate and vote. O'Leary suggests that this would successfully counter "intransigent committee chairs and excessive special interest leverage" (125).
54. Dahl 1989 and Fishkin 1991.
55. See Guinier 1995; Williams 2000; and Young 1990, 184–5.
56. On the persistence of racial inequality in American democracy, see Dawson n.d. On the problem of cultural minorities more generally, see Kymlicka 1996 and Parekh 2002.
57. See Sanders 1997. However, evidence from the BCCA suggests that better educated and informed members did not exert disproportionate influence over the assembly's proceedings. See Blais, Carty, and Founier 2008.
58. In addition to Pettit 2000, 105–46, discussed in Chapter 6, see Shapiro 2003, 16–19, 48.
59. See Shapiro 2003, 33.

60. See Lang 2008, and Pearse 2008.
61. Shapiro, for instance, may be too pessimistic in this respect, especially since he does not supply a standard with which to evaluate quasi-objective knowledge of *any* kind: he is as critical of the kind of information that emerges from the adversarial context of competitive elections as he is of the kind of information that experts impart in supposedly nonpolitical contexts. See Shapiro 2003, 30.
62. On interest group influence and referenda generally, see Gerber 1999.
63. Guicciardini [1524] 1994, 151; [1530] 2002, 392; Machiavelli, DF 743–4.
64. See Morgan 1989, 286.

Acknowledgments

A scholar incurs an embarrassing number of debts when he takes too long to write a book. The initial, inchoate ideas for this project emerged while I was a graduate student at the University of Chicago some time ago. Stephen Holmes's and Bernard Manin's courses and scholarship on the history of constitutionalism and representative government were early inspirations, as were Pasquale Pasquino's and Nathan Tarcov's seminars almost entirely devoted to Machiavelli's *Discourses*. These former teachers continue to impact my life and work as interlocutors, as friends, and, in the case of Nathan, as a treasured colleague as well. During those years, I also benefited in myriad ways from Dan Carpenter's rare intellect and from the even rarer friendship we continue to share. The notion of "Machiavellian Democracy" crystallized while I was an assistant professor at Yale, where the "realist" tradition of democratic theory still provokes vibrant debate: Bruce Ackerman, Seyla Benhabib, Bob Dahl, Ian Shapiro, Stephen Skowronek, Rogers Smith, Steven Smith, Allan Stam, and Leonard Wantchekon continually assured me of the project's originality and insisted on its importance for the study of contemporary democracy.

Throughout the years, many people have read the manuscript in part or as a whole and kindly offered sober comments and penetrating criticisms. I cannot possibly thank them all but would like to single out the following: Richard Bellamy, Corey Brettschneider, Barbara Buckinx, Dario Castiglione, Josh Cohen, Bill Connell, Yasmin Dawood, Mary Dietz, John Dunn, David Dyzenhaus, David Estlund, Benedetto Fontana, Rainer Forst, Bryan Garsten, Marco Geuna, Jacqueline Hunsicker, Arthur Jacobson, Mark Jurdjevic, Vicky Kahn, Daniel Kapust, Sharon Krause, Matthias Kumm, Hélène Landemore, Nomi Lazar, Sandy Levinson, Jason Maloy, Robyn Marasco, Kirstie McClure, John Najemy, Michael Neblo, Josh Ober, Alan Patten, Rob Reich, Melvin Rogers, Michel Rosenfeld, Melissa Schwartzberg, Giorgio Scichilone, Jake Soll, Céline Spector, Nadia Urbinati, Miguel Vatter, Leo Walsh, Joseph Weiler, Bernie Yack, and Michelle Zerba. Moreover, Philip Pettit and Quentin Skinner responded to my criticisms of their work with remarkable grace and generosity.

I owe special thanks to my University of Chicago colleagues – both in and out of political science, whether still in Hyde Park or now departed – who have engaged this project so eagerly and earnestly over the years: Danielle Allen, Cliff Ando, Carles Boix, Cathy Cohen, Julie Cooper, Bob Gooding-Williams, Bernard Harcourt, Stathis Kalyvas, Charles Larmore, Brian Leiter, Jacob Levy, Michèle Lowrie, Patchen Markell, Emanuel Mayer, Sankar Muthu, David Nirenberg, John Padgett, Robert Pippin, Alberto Simpser, Dan Slater, Susan Stokes, Lisa Wedeen, Iris Young, Linda Zerilli, and, most especially, Jennifer Pitts. Gregory Conti provided research assistance of such quality (proofreading, completing citations, preparing the index, and so on) that I'm tempted to name him a collaborator. I have learned infinitely more from my Chicago students, like Greg, than they possibly could have from me, and I thank them for their unrivalled intellectual curiosity and intensity, in particular: Gordon Arlen, Emily Brown, Anita Chari, Teresa Davis, Bridget Fahey, Sam Galloway, Loren Goldman, Andrew Hammond, Lindsay Knight, Rita Koganzan, Matt Landauer, Amanda Machin, Amanda Maher, Mara Marin, J. J. McFadden, Chris Meckstroth, Travis Pantin, Natasha Piano, Jacob Schiff, Will Selinger, Ian Storey, and Stephane Wolton.

Earlier versions of sections and chapters from the book appeared in the *American Political Science Review* (2001, 2006); *Political Theory* (2003, 2007); the *International Journal of Constitutional Law* (2010); and *Politics and the Passions, 1500–1850*, V. Kahn et al., eds. (2006). I gratefully acknowledge the publishers of these journals (respectively, Cambridge U.P., Sage Publications, and Oxford U.P.) and the edited collection (Princeton U.P.). Lew Bateman at Cambridge University Press steadfastly supported this project and patiently waited as many deadlines passed before he received the final manuscript. I also thank Eric Crahan, Mark Fox, and Anne Lovering Rounds at Cambridge. Andy Saff meticulousnessly and expediently handled the copyediting and proof correcting responsibilities.

The stimulating and congenial working environment of the Radcliffe Institute for Advanced Study, Harvard University, facilitated the book's completion in 2008–9. I can't express sufficient gratitude to Barbara Grosz, Judy Vichniac, and the entire Radcliffe staff. In October 2009, Harvard's Center for American Political Studies held a symposium on the penultimate draft of the book. Much of the audience in attendance actively participated in the event, and the following faculty commentators carefully read, enthusiastically engaged, and ruthlessly criticized the manuscript, chapter by chapter: David Armitage, Dan Carpenter, Harvey Mansfield, Eric Nelson, Nancy Rosenblum, and Richard Tuck. I am profoundly grateful for their strenuous efforts that I hope helped to transform a respectable manuscript into an infinitely better book. All the remaining shortcomings are, of course, entirely my own responsibility.

For more than fifteen years, Bruce Western has indulged countless conversations over the precarious state of liberty and equality in the contemporary world, conversations without which this book would never have taken shape.

My work has been enriched beyond words by his intelligence, wisdom, passion, and encouragement. My parents, John and Bernice, as ever, provided an unshakeable foundation of stability and confidence. The generosity and hospitality of my "adoptive" parents, Jane and Brandon Qualls, made possible the book's completion, as did the expert and tender childcare provided by Mae Mahinay. Gia Pascarelli unselfishly supported and encouraged me in countless ways during the project's early stages, not least of all by sharing her intimate familiarity with and unbounded enthusiasm for all things Tuscan. Nicoletta Machiavelli sat (for the most part) patiently at my side during much of the book's composition; a constant source of amusement, vexation, and joy, her singular presence is deeply missed.

I would especially like to thank the following for sharing their love, support, and rock-solid judgment during some exceedingly difficult times: my sister, Kara McCormick Lyons; her husband, Michael Lyons; and my dearest friends, Jo McKendry and Bruce Western. The infinitely generous and loving Alyssa Anne Qualls made countless sacrifices that enabled me to revise and then finish the book. Words cannot remotely convey the extent of my debt nor the depth of my gratitude to her. Over the years, this lifelong student has been blessed by an astounding succession of wonderful teachers – both in and out of the academy; among mentors, colleagues, students, and friends. Annabelle Declan McCormick, in such a short span of time, is proving to be the greatest teacher of all. I dedicate this book to her with boundless love and in eager anticipation of further lessons.

Chicago, November 2010

Works Cited

Abramson, Jeffrey. 1993. "The Jury and Democratic Theory." *Journal of Political Philosophy* 1, no. 1: 45–68.

Acemoglu, Daron, and James A Robinson. 2005. *Economic Origins of Dictatorship and Democracy*. Cambridge: Cambridge University Press.

Ackerman, Bruce. 1991. *We the People 1: Foundations*. Cambridge, MA: Harvard University Press.

Ackerman, Bruce, and James Fishkin. 2004. *Deliberation Day*. New Haven: Yale University Press.

Adams, John. [1790] 1805. *Discourses on Davila*. Boston: Russell and Cutler.

Adcock, F. E. 1964. *Roman Political Ideas and Practice*. Ann Arbor: University of Michigan Press.

Allen, Danielle. 2000. *The World of Prometheus: The Politics of Punishing in Democratic Athens*. Princeton, NJ: Princeton University Press.

Althusser, Louis. 2001. *Machiavelli and Us*, ed. Francois Matherson; trans. Gregory Elliott. London: Verso.

Anderson, Lisa, ed. 1999. *Transitions to Democracy*. New York: Columbia University Press.

Ando, Clifford. 2010. "'A Dwelling Beyond Violence': On the Uses and Disadvantages of History for Contemporary Republicans." *History of Political Thought* 31, no. 3: 1–38.

Ardito, Alissa. 2004. *Machiavelli's Madisonian Moment: The Tuscan Territorial State as an Extended Republic*. Ph.D. Dissertation, Political Science, Yale University.

Arendt, Hannah. 2006. *On Revolution*. New York: Penguin.

Aristotle. 1985. *Nicomachean Ethics*, trans. Terence Irwin. Indianapolis, IN: Hackett.

———. 1997. *The Politics*, trans. and ed. Peter Simpson. Chapel Hill: University of North Carolina Press.

Armitage, David. 2000. *The Ideological Origins of the British Empire*. Cambridge: Cambridge University Press.

Arnold, Douglas A. 1993. "Can Inattentive Citizens Control Their Elected Representatives?" In *Congress Reconsidered*, fifth edition, ed. Lawrence C. Dodd and Bruce Ian Oppenheimer. Washington, DC: CQ Press, 401–16.

Asmis, Elizabeth. 2004. "The State as a Partnership: Cicero's Definition of *res publica* in His Work *On the State*." *History of Political Thought* 25: 569–98.

———. 2005. "A New Kind of Model: Cicero's Roman Constitution in *De republica*." *American Journal of Philology* 126: 377–416.

Atkinson James B., and David Sices, ed. and trans. 2002. *The Sweetness of Power: Machiavelli's Discourses and Guicciardini's Considerations*. DeKalb, IL: Northern Illinois University Press.

Bachrach, Peter. 1967. *The Theory of Democratic Elitism: A Critique*. Boston: Little, Brown.

Bachrach, Peter, and Aryeh Botwinick. 1992. *Power and Empowerment: A Radical Theory of Participatory Democracy*. Philadelphia: Temple University Press.

Baehr, Peter. 1998. *Caesar and the Fading of the Roman World: A Study in Republicanism and Caesarism*. London: Transaction.

Baehr, Peter, and Melvin Richter, eds. 2004. *Dictatorship in History and Theory: Bonapartism, Caesarism, and Totalitarianism*. Cambridge: Cambridge University Press.

Bagehot, Walter. [1867] 2001. *The English Constitution*, ed. Paul Smith. Cambridge: Cambridge University Press.

Baiocchi, Gianpaolo. 2001. "Participation, Activism, and Politics: The Porto Alegre Experiment and Deliberative Democratic Theory." *Politics & Society* 29, no. 1: 43–72.

———. 2005. *Militants and Citizens: The Politics of Participatory Democracy in Porto Alegre*. Stanford: Stanford University Press.

Barber, Benjamin R. 1984. *Strong Democracy: Participatory Politics for a New Age*. Berkeley: University of California Press.

———. 2000. "The Crack in the Picture Window: Review of Putnam, Bowling Alone." *The Nation* 271, no. 5: 29–34.

Baron, Hans. 1961. "Machiavelli: The Republican Citizen and Author of *The Prince*." In *In Search of Florentine Civic Humanism*, vol. II. 1988. Princeton, NJ: Princeton University Press, 101–54.

———. 1966. *The Crisis of the Early Italian Renaissance*. Princeton, NJ: Princeton University Press.

Bartels, Larry. 2008. *Unequal Democracy: The Political Economy of the New Gilded Age*. Princeton, NJ: Princeton University Press.

Becker, Ernest. 1973. *The Denial of Death*. New York: Free Press.

Behn, Robert D. 2000. *Rethinking Democratic Accountability*. Washington, DC: Brookings Institution Press.

Beitz, Charles R. 1989. *Political Equality: An Essay in Democratic Theory*. Princeton, NJ: Princeton University Press.

Bellamy, Richard, and Dario Castiglione, eds. 1996. *Constitutionalism in Transformation: European and Theoretical Perspectives*. Oxford: Blackwell.

Benhabib, Seyla, ed. 1996. *Democracy and Difference*. Princeton, NJ: Princeton University Press.

Bennett, Deborah J. 1999. *Randomness*. Cambridge, MA: Harvard University Press.

Beramendi, Pablo, and Christopher J. Anderson, eds. 2008. *Democracy, Inequality and Representation: A Comparative Perspective*. New York: Russell Sage.

Bernstein, Carl, and Bob Woodward. 1987. *All the President's Men*. New York: Simon & Schuster.

Black, Robert. 1990. "Machiavelli, Servant of the Florentine Republic." In *Machiavelli and Republicanism*, ed. Gisela Bock, Quentin Skinner, and Maurizio Viroli. Cambridge: Cambridge University Press, 71–99.

Blais, Andre, R. Kenneth Carty, and Patrick Founier. 2008. "Do Citizens' Assemblies Make Reasoned Choices?" In *Designing Deliberative Democracy: The British Columbia Citizens' Assembly*, ed. Mark E. Warren and Hillary Pearse. Cambridge: Cambridge University Press, 127–44.

Bleicken, Jochen. 1955. *Das Volkstribunat der Klassischen Republik*. Munich: Beck.

Bock, Gisela. 1990. "Civil Discord in Machiavelli's Istorie Fiorentine." In *Machiavelli and Republicanism*, ed. Gisela Bock, Quentin Skinner, and Maurizio Viroli. Cambridge: Cambridge University Press, 181–201.

Bock, Gisela, Quentin Skinner, and Maurizio Viroli, eds. 1990. *Machiavelli and Republicanism*. Cambridge: Cambridge University Press.

Boix, Carles. 2003. *Democracy and Redistribution*. Cambridge: Cambridge University Press.

Bonadeo, Alfredo. 1969. "The Role of the 'Grandi' in the Political World of Machiavelli." *Studies in the Renaissance* 16: 9–30.

———. 1970. "The Role of the People in the Works and Times of Machiavelli." *Bibliothéque d'Humanisme et Renaissance* 32: 351–78.

Botsford, George Willis. [1909] 2005. *The Roman Assemblies from Their Origin to the End of the Republic*. Boston: Adamant.

Bouwsma, William J. 1968. *Venice and the Defense of Republican Liberty: Renaissance Values in the Age of the Counter Reformation*. Berkeley: University of California Press.

Bowler, Sean, and Amihai Glazer. 2008. *Direct Democracy's Impact on American Political Institutions*. New York: Palgrave Macmillan.

Bowles, Samuel, Herbert Gintis, and Bo Gustafsson, eds. 2008. *Markets and Democracy: Participation, Accountability and Efficiency*. Cambridge: Cambridge University Press.

Brennan, Geoffrey, and Loren E. Lomasky, eds. 1993. *Democracy and Decision: The Pure Theory of Electoral Preference*. Cambridge: Cambridge University Press.

Brennan, T. Corey. 2006. "Power and Process under the Republican 'Constitution'." In *The Cambridge Companion to the Roman Republic*, ed. Harriet Flower. Cambridge: Cambridge University Press, 31–64.

Brucker, Gene. 1962. *Florentine Politics and Society, 1343–1378*. Princeton, NJ: Princeton University Press.

———. 1968. "The Revolt of the Ciompi." In *Florentine Studies: Politics and Society in Renaissance Florence*, ed. Nicolai Rubinstein. Evanston, IL: Northwestern University Press, 314–56.

———. 1969. *Renaissance Florence*. Berkeley: University of California Press.

———. 1977. *The Civic World of Early Renaissance Florence*. Princeton, NJ: Princeton University Press.

Bruni, Leonardo. [1442] 2004. *The History of the Florentine People, vol. II*, ed. and trans. James Hankins. Cambridge, MA: Harvard University Press.

———. 1987. *The Humanism of Leonardo Bruni: Selected Texts*, trans. and ed. Gordon Griffiths, James Hankins, and David Thompson. Binghampton, NY: Medieval & Renaissance Texts & Studies.

Butters, H. C. 1985. *Governors and Government in Early Sixteenth Century Florence, 1502–1512*. Oxford: Oxford University Press.

Buttle, Nicholas. 2001. "Republican Constitutionalism: A Roman Ideal." *Journal of Political Philosophy* 9, no. 3: 331–49.

Canovan, Margaret. 2005. *The People*. Cambridge: Polity.

Caplan, Bryan. 2007. *The Myth of the Rational Voter: Why Democracies Choose Bad Policies*. Princeton, NJ: Princeton University Press.

Cheibub, Jose Antonio, and Adam Przeworski. 1999. "Democracy, Elections, and Accountability for Economic Outcomes." In *Democracy, Accountability, and Representation*, ed. Adam Przeworski, Susan C. Stokes, and Bernard Manin. Cambridge: Cambridge University Press, 222–50.

Chrissanthos, Stefan G. 2004. "Freedom of Speech and the Roman Republican Army." In *Free Speech in Classical Antiquity*, ed. Ineke Sluiter and Ralph M. Rosen. Leiden: Brill.

Cicero, Marcus T. 1991. *On Duties*, ed. E. M. Adkins. Cambridge: Cambridge University Press.

———. 1993. "For Murena: When to Sacrifice a Principle." In *On Government*, trans. Michael Grant. London: Penguin: 106–59.

———. 1999. *On the Commonwealth and on the Laws*, ed. James Zetzel. Cambridge: Cambridge University Press.

Coby, Patrick J. 1999. *Machiavelli's Romans: Liberty and Greatness in the Discourses on Livy*. Lanham, MD: Lexington.

Cohen, Josh. 1986. "An Epistemic Conception of Democracy." *Ethics* 97, no. 1: 26–38.

———. 2006. "Reflections on Rousseau: Autonomy and Democracy." *Philosophy and Public Affairs* 15, no. 3: 275–97.

Cohn, Samuel Kline, Jr. 1980. *The Laboring Classes in Renaissance Florence*. New York: Academic Press.

Colbourn, Trevor, ed. 1998. *Fame and the Founding Fathers: Essays by Douglass Adair*. Indianapolis, IN: Liberty Fund.

Colish, Marcia L. 1971. "The Idea of Liberty in Machiavelli." *Journal of the History of Ideas* 32: 323–50.

———. 1978. "Cicero's De officiis and Machiavelli's Prince." *Sixteenth Century Journal* 9: 81–93.

Condorcet, Jean-Antoine-Nicolas de Caritat, Marquis de. 1994. *Foundations of Social Choice and Political Theory*, trans. and ed. I. McLean and F. Hewitt. Aldershot: Elgar.

Connell, William, ed. and trans. 2005. *Machiavelli's The Prince*. Boston: Bedford.

Connolly, Joy. 2007. *The State of Speech: Rhetoric and Political Thought in Ancient Rome*. Princeton, NJ: Princeton University Press.

Connolly, William E. 1995. *The Ethos of Pluralization*. Minneapolis: University of Minnesota Press.

Cox, Virginia. 1997. "Machiavelli and the Rhetorica ad Herennium: Deliberative Rhetoric in *The Prince*." *Sixteenth Century Journal* 28, no. 4: 1109–41.

Crook, Malcolm. 1996. *Elections in the French Revolution: An Apprenticeship in Democracy, 1789–1799*. Cambridge: Cambridge University Press.

Cutler, Fred, Richard Johnston, R. Kenneth Carty, Andre Blais, and Patrick Founier. 2008. "Deliberation, Information and Trust: The British Columbia Citizens' Assembly as Agenda Setter." In *Designing Deliberative Democracy: The British Columbia Citizens' Assembly*, ed. Mark E. Warren and Hillary Pearse. Cambridge: Cambridge University Press, 166–92.

Dagger, Richard, Alan Ryan, and David Miller, eds. 1997. *Civic Virtues: Rights, Citizenship, and Republican Liberalism.* Oxford: Oxford University Press.

Dahl, Robert Alan. 1957. "Decision-Making in a Democracy: The Supreme Court as a National Policy-Maker." *Journal of Public Law* 6: 279–95.

_____. 1971. *Polyarchy: Participation and Opposition.* New Haven: Yale University Press.

_____. 1989. *Democracy and its Critics.* New Haven: Yale University Press.

_____. 1990. *A Preface to Democratic Theory.* Chicago: University of Chicago Press.

_____. 2003. *How Democratic is the American Constitution?* New Haven: Yale University Press.

Dawood, Yasmin. 2007. "The New Inequality: Constitutional Democracy and the Problem of Wealth." *Maryland Law Review* 67: 123–49.

Dawson, Michael C. n.d. *From Katrina to Obama and the Future of Black Politics.* New York: Perseus Press.

de Grazia, Sebastian. 1989. *Machiavelli in Hell.* Princeton, NJ: Princeton University Press.

Dietz, Mary G. 1986. "Trapping *The Prince*: Machiavelli and the Politics of Deception." *American Political Science Review* 80, no. 3: 777–99.

Domhoff, G. William. 1998. *Who Rules America?: Power and Politics in the Year 2000.* Portland, OR: Mayfield.

_____. 2010. "Wealth, Income, and Power in America." http://sociology.ucsc.edu/whorulesamerica/power/wealth.html.

Donaldson, Peter S. 1988. *Machiavelli and Mystery of State.* Cambridge: Cambridge University Press.

Dowdle, Michael W., ed. 2006. *Public Accountability: Designs, Dilemmas and Experiences.* Cambridge: Cambridge University Press.

Dunn, John, ed. 1993. *Democracy: The Unfinished Journey, 508 BC to AD 1993.* Oxford: Oxford University Press.

_____. 2005. *Setting the People Free: The Story of Democracy.* London: Atlantic.

Duxbury, Neil. 1999. *Random Justice: On Lotteries and Legal Decision-Making.* Oxford: Oxford University Press.

Eley, Geoff. 2002. *Forging Democracy: The History of the Left in Europe, 1850–2000.* New York: Oxford University Press.

Elkin, Stephen L. 2006. *Reconstructing the Commercial Republic: Constitutional Design after Madison.* Chicago: University of Chicago Press.

Ellis, Richard J. 2002. *Democratic Delusions: The Initiative Process in America.* Lawrence: University Press of Kansas.

Elster, Jon. 1986. "The Market and the Forum: Three Varieties of Political Theory." In *Foundations of Social Choice Theory*, ed. Jon Elster and Aanund Hylland. Cambridge: Cambridge University Press, 103–32.

_____. 1999. "Accountability in Athenian Politics." In *Democracy, Accountability, and Representation*, ed. Adam Przeworski, Susan C. Stokes, and Bernard Manin. Cambridge: Cambridge University Press, 253–78.

Estlund, David. 2007. *Democratic Authority: A Philosophical Framework.* Princeton, NJ: Princeton University Press.

Farrand, Max, ed. 1966. *The Records of the Federal Convention of 1787, vols. I–III.* New Haven: Yale University Press.

Farrar, Cynthia. 1993. "Ancient Greek Political Theory as a Response to Democracy." In *Democracy: The Unfinished Journey, 508 BC to AD 1993*, ed. John Dunn. Oxford: Oxford University Press, 17–39.

Fearon, James. 1999. "Electoral Accountability and the Control of Politicians: Selecting Good Types versus Sanctioning Poor Performance." In *Democracy, Accountability, and Representation*, ed. Adam Przeworski, Susan C. Stokes, and Bernard Manin. Cambridge: Cambridge University Press, 55–98.

Ferejohn, John. 2008. "The Citizens' Assembly Model." In *Designing Deliberative Democracy: The British Columbia Citizens' Assembly*, ed. Mark E. Warren and Hillary Pearse. Cambridge: Cambridge University Press, 192–213.

Finley, Moses I. 1985. *Democracy Ancient and Modern*, revised edition. New Brunswick, NJ: Rutgers University Press.

Fiorina, Morris P. 1981. *Retrospective Voting in American National Elections*. New Haven: Yale University Press.

Fischer, Markus. 2000. *Well-Ordered License: On the Unity of Machiavelli's Thought*. Lanham, MD: Lexington.

Fishkin, James. 1991. *Democracy and Deliberation: New Directions for Democratic Reform*. New Haven: Yale University Press.

———. 1997. *The Voice of the People: Public Opinion and Democracy*. New Haven: Yale University Press.

Fitzsimmons, Michael P. 1994. *The Remaking of France: The National Assembly and the Constitution of 1791*. Cambridge: Cambridge University Press.

Flaig, Egon. 2003. *Ritualisierte Politik: Zeichen, Gesten und Herrschaft im Alten Rom*. Göttingen: Vandenhoeck & Ruprecht.

Fontana, Benedetto. 2001. "Republican Liberty in the Language and Rhetoric of Machiavelli." Manuscript: Baruch College, CUNY.

———. 2003. "Sallust and the Politics of Machiavelli," *History of Political Thought* 24, no. 1: 86–108.

Forsdyke, Sara. 2005. *Exile, Ostracism, and Democracy: The Politics of Expulsion in Ancient Greece*. Princeton, NJ: Princeton University Press.

Fraenkel, Ernst. 1969. *The Dual State: A Contribution to the Theory of Dictatorship*, trans. E. A. Shils. New York: Octagon.

Frank, Thomas. 2005. *What's the Matter with Kansas? How Conservatives Won the Heart of America*. New York: Holt.

Fraser, Nancy. 1997. *Justice Interruptus: Critical Reflections on the "Postsocialist" Condition*. London: Routledge.

Fraser, Steve, and Gary Gerstle, eds. 2005. *Ruling America: A History of Wealth and Power in a Democracy*. Cambridge, MA: Harvard University Press.

Fung, Archon. 2003. "Recipes for Public Spheres: Eight Institutional Choices and Their Consequences." *Journal of Political Philosophy* 11: 338–67.

Fung, Archon, and Eric Olin Wright, eds. 2003. *Deepening Democracy: Institutional Innovations in Empowered Participatory Governance*. London: Verso.

Garnsey, Peter. 1970. *Social Status and Legal Privilege in the Roman Empire*. Oxford: Clarendon.

Garsten, Bryan. 2006. *Saving Persuasion: A Defense of Rhetoric and Judgment*. Cambridge, MA: Harvard University Press.

Gerber, Elizabeth R. 1999. *The Populist Paradox: Interest Group Influence and the Promise of Direct Legislation*. Princeton, NJ: Princeton University Press.

Geuss, Raymond. 2008. *Philosophy and Real Politics*. Princeton, NJ: Princeton University Press.

Gilbert, Felix. 1957. "Florentine Political Assumptions in the Period of Savonarola and Soderini." *Journal of the Warburg and Courtauld Institutes* 20: 187–214.

———. 1965. *Machiavelli and Guicciardini: Politics and History in Sixteenth-Century Florence*. Princeton, NJ: Princeton University Press.

———. 1968. "The Venetian Constitution in Florentine Political Thought." In *Florentine Studies: Politics and Society in Renaissance Florence*, ed. Nicolai Rubinstein. Evanston, IL: Northwestern University Press, 442–62.

———. 1977. "Bernardo Rucellai and the Orti Oricellari: A Study on the Origin of Modern Political Thought." In *History: Choice and Commitment*, ed. Felix Gilbert. Cambridge, MA: Harvard University Press, 215–46.

Goodin, Robert. 2008. *Innovating Democracy: Democratic Theory and Practice after the Deliberative Turn*. Oxford: Oxford University Press.

Gramsci, Antonio. [1929] 1959. "The Modern Prince: Essays on the Science of Politics in the Modern Age." In *The Modern Prince and Other Writings*, trans. Louis Marks. London: International, 135–88.

Gregory, Roy, and Philip James Giddings, eds. 2000. *Righting Wrongs: The Ombudsman in Six Continents*. Amsterdam: I.O.S. Press.

Grofman, Bernard, and Arend Lijphart, eds. 2003. *Electoral Laws and Their Political Consequences*. New York: Agathon Press.

Guarini, Elena Fasano. 1990. "Machiavelli and the Crisis of the Italian Republics." In *Machiavelli and Republicanism*, ed. Gisela Bock, Quentin Skinner, and Maurizio Viroli. Cambridge: Cambridge University Press, 17–40.

Guicciardini, Francesco. [c. 1508] 1970. *The History of Florence*, trans. M. Domandi. New York: Harper Torchbooks.

———. [1512] 1998. *"Discorso di Logrogno": On Bringing Order to Popular Government*, trans. Athanasios Moulakis. Lanham, MD: Rowman & Littlefield.

———. [1524] 1994. *Dialogue on the Government of Florence*, trans. Alison Brown. Cambridge: Cambridge University Press.

———. [1527] 1993. *Autodifesa di un Politico*. Roma-Bari: Laterza.

———. [1530] 1965. *Maxims and Reflections*, trans. M. Domandi. Philadelphia: University of Pennsylvania Press.

———. [1530] 2002. "Considerations of the Discourses of Niccolò Machiavelli." In *The Sweetness of Power: Machiavelli's Discourses and Guicciardini's Considerations*, ed. and trans. James B. Atkinson and David Sices. DeKalb, IL: Northern Illinois University Press, 381–438.

Guinier, Lani. 1995. *Tyranny of the Majority: Fundamental Fairness in Representative Democracy*. New York: Simon & Schuster.

Gutmann, Amy. 1999. *Democratic Education*. Princeton, NJ: Princeton University Press.

Gutmann, Amy, and Dennis Thompson. 1996. *Democracy and Disagreement*. Cambridge, MA: Harvard Belknap Press.

———. 2004. *Why Deliberative Democracy?* Princeton, NJ: Princeton University Press.

Habermas, Jürgen. 1989. *The Structural Transformation of the Public Sphere: An Inquiry into a Category of Bourgeois Society*, trans. Thomas Burger with Frederick Lawrence. Cambridge, MA: MIT Press.

———. 1996. *Between Facts and Norms: Contributions to a Discourse Theory of Law and Democracy*, trans. William Rehg. Cambridge, MA: MIT Press.

———. 2001. "Constitutional Democracy: A Paradoxical Union of Contradictory Principles?" *Political Theory* 29, no. 6: 766–81.

Haitsma Mulier, Eco O. G. 1980. *The Myth of Venice and Dutch Republican Thought in the Seventeenth Century*, trans. Gerard T. Moran. Assen, Netherlands: Van Gorcum.

Hale, J. R. 1963. *Machiavelli and Renaissance Italy*. New York: Collier.

Hankins, James, ed. 2000a. *Renaissance Civic Humanism: Reappraisals and Reflections*. Cambridge: Cambridge University Press: 143–79.

———. 2000b. "Rhetoric, History, and Ideology: The Civic Panegyrics of Leonardo Bruni." In *Renaissance Civic Humanism: Reappraisals and Reflections*, ed. James Hankins. Cambridge: Cambridge University Press, 143–78.

Hansen, Mogens H. 1991. *The Athenian Democracy in the Age of Demosthenes*. Oxford: Blackwell.

Harcourt, Bernard. 2007. "Post-Modern Meditations on Punishment: On the Limits of Reason and the Virtues of Randomization." *Journal of Social Research* 74, no. 2: 307–46.

Headlem, James Wycliffe. 1933. *Election by Lot at Athens*. Cambridge: Cambridge University Press.

Held, David. 1997. *Models of Democracy*. Stanford: Stanford University Press.

Herzog, Don. 1989. *Happy Slaves: A Critique of Consent Theory*. Chicago: University of Chicago Press.

Hirschl, Ran. 2005. "Constitutionalism, Judicial Review, and Progressive Change." *Texas Law Review* 84: 471–507.

———. 2007. *Towards Juristocracy: The Origins and Consequences of the New Constitutionalism*. Cambridge, MA: Harvard University Press.

Hohenstein, Kurt. 2007. *Coining Corruption: The Making of the American Campaign Finance System*. DeKalb, IL: Northern Illinois University Press.

Holmes, Stephen. 1995. *Passions and Constraint: On the Theory of Liberal Democracy*. Chicago: University of Chicago Press.

———. 2003. "Lineages of the Rule of Law." In *Democracy and the Rule of Law*, ed. Adam Przeworski and José María Maravall. Cambridge: Cambridge University Press, 19–61.

Honig, Bonnie. 2007. "Between Decision and Deliberation: Political Paradox in Democratic Theory." *American Political Science Review* 101, no. 1: 1–17.

Hörnqvist, Mikael. 2000. "The Two Myths of Civic Humanism." In *Renaissance Civic Humanism: Reappraisals and Reflections*, ed. James Hankins. Cambridge: Cambridge University Press, 105–42.

———. 2004. *Machiavelli and Empire*. Cambridge: Cambridge University Press.

Hulliung, Mark. 1984. *Citizen Machiavelli*. Princeton, NJ: Princeton University Press.

Hunt, Lynn. 1984. *Politics, Culture, and Class in the French Revolution*. Berkeley: University of California Press.

Huntington, Samuel. 1993. *The Third Wave: Democratization in the Late Twentieth Century*. Norman: University of Oklahoma Press.

Isaac, Jeffrey C. 1988. "Republicanism vs. Liberalism?: A Reconsideration." *History of Political Thought* 9, no. 2: 349–77.

Jacobs, Lawrence R., and Theda Skocpol, eds. 2007. *Inequality and American Democracy: What We Know and What We Need to Learn*. New York: Russell Sage Foundation.

James, Michael Rabinder. 2008. "Descriptive Representation in the British Columbia Citizens' Assembly." In *Designing Deliberative Democracy: The British Columbia*

Citizens' Assembly, ed. Mark E. Warren and Hillary Pearse. Cambridge: Cambridge University Press, 106–26.

Janeway, Michael. 1999. *Republic of Denial: Press, Politics and Public Life*. New Haven: Yale University Press.

Jolowicz, Herbert F. 1967. *Historical Introduction to the Study of Roman Law*. Cambridge: Cambridge University Press.

Jurdjevic, Mark. 1999. "Civic Humanism and the Rise of the Medici." *Renaissance Quarterly* 52, no. 4: 994–1020.

———. 2002. "Machiavelli's Sketches of Francesco Valori and the Reconstruction of Florentine History." *Journal of the History of Ideas* 63, no. 2: 185–206.

Kahn, Victoria. 1994. *Machiavellian Rhetoric: From the Counter-Reformation to Milton*. Princeton, NJ: Princeton University Press.

Kaplan, Arthur. 1977. *Dictatorships and 'Ultimate' Decrees in the Early Roman Republic, 501–202 BC*. New York: Revisionist Press.

Kapust, Daniel. 2004. "Skinner, Pettit, and Livy: The Conflict of the Orders and the Ambiguity of Republican Liberty." *History of Political Thought* 25, no. 3: 377–401.

———. 2009. *Contesting the Republic: Republicanism, Rhetoric and Roman Historiography*. Book manuscript, Political Science Department, University of Georgia.

Keane, John. 1991. *The Media and Democracy*. Cambridge: Polity Press.

Keaveney, Arthur. 2005. *Sulla, The Last Republican*. London: Routledge.

Kelly, Gordon. 2006. *A History of Exile in the Roman Republic*. Cambridge: Cambridge University Press.

Kent, Dale. 2009. *Friendship, Love, and Trust in Renaissance Florence*. Cambridge, MA: Harvard University Press.

Kersh, Rogan. 2003. "Influencing the State: U.S. Campaign Finance and Its Discontents." *Critical Review* 15, nos. 1–2: 203–20.

Kirchheimer, Otto. 1969. *Politics, Law and Social Change: Selected Essays of Otto Kirchheimer*, ed. F. S. Burin and K. L. Shell. New York: Columbia University Press.

Kitschelt, Herbert, and Steven I. Wilkinson. 2007. "Citizen-Politician Linkages: An Introduction." In *Patrons, Clients and Policies: Patterns of Democratic Accountability and Political Competition*, ed. Herbert Kitschelt and Steven I. Wilkinson. Cambridge: Cambridge University Press, 1–49.

Kramer, Larry D. 2004. *The People Themselves: Popular Constitutionalism and Judicial Review*. New York: Oxford University Press.

Krause, Sharon R. 2008. *Civil Passions: Moral Sentiment and Democratic Deliberation*. Princeton, NJ: Princeton University Press.

Krugman, Paul. 2003. *The Great Unraveling: Losing Our Way in the New Century*. New York: W.W. Norton.

Kymlicka, Will. 1996. *Multicultural Citizenship: A Liberal Theory of Minority Rights*. Oxford: Oxford University Press.

La Raja, Raymond J. 2008. *Small Change: Money, Political Parties, and Campaign Finance Reform*. Ann Arbor: University of Michigan Press.

Laclau, Ernesto, and Chantal Mouffe. 1984. *Hegemony and Socialist Strategy: Towards a Radical Democratic Politics*. London: Verso.

Larmore, Charles. 2001. "A Critique of Philip Pettit's Republicanism." In *Social, Political, and Legal Philosophy: Philosophical Issues 11*, ed. Ernest Sosa and Enrique Villanueva. Oxford: Blackwell, 229–43.

———. 2008. *The Autonomy of Morality*. Cambridge: Cambridge University Press.

Landemore, Hélène. 2007. *Democratic Reason: Politics, Collective Intelligence, and the Rule of the Many*. Dissertation: Government Department, Harvard University.

Lane, Frederic. 1973. *Venice: A Maritime Republic*. Baltimore: Johns Hopkins University Press.

Lang, Amy. 2008. "Agenda Setting in Deliberative Forums." In *Designing Deliberative Democracy: The British Columbia Citizens' Assembly*, ed. Mark E. Warren and Hillary Pearse. Cambridge: Cambridge University Press, 85–105.

Langton, John. 1987. "Machiavelli's Paradox: Trapping or Teaching the Prince." *American Political Science Review* 81, no. 4: 1277–88.

Lazar, Nomi Claire. 2009. *States of Emergency in Liberal Democracies*. Cambridge: Cambridge University Press.

Lefort, Claude. 2000. "Machiavelli and the Verita Effetuale." In *Writing: The Political Test*, trans. David Ames Curtis. Durham, NC: Duke University Press, 109–41.

Levi, Margaret, James Johnson, Jack Knight, and Susan Stokes, eds. 2008. *Designing Democratic Government: Making Institutions Work*. New York: Russell Sage Foundation Press.

Levinson, Sanford. 2006. *Our Undemocratic Constitution: Where the Constitution Goes Wrong (and How We the People Can Correct It)*. New York: Oxford University Press.

Levy, Jacob. 2000. *The Multiculturalism of Fear*. Oxford: Oxford University Press.

Levy, Leonard W. 2004. *Emergence of a Free Press*. Chicago: Ivan R. Dee.

Lewin, Lief. 2007. *Democratic Accountability: Why Choice in Politics Is Both Possible and Necessary*. Cambridge, MA: Harvard University Press.

Lijphart, Arend. 1992. *Democracy in Plural Societies: A Comparative Exploration*. New Haven: Yale University Press.

Lintott, Andrew. 1968. *Violence in Republican Rome*. Oxford: Clarendon.

––––––. 1982. *Violence, Civil Strife, and Revolution in the Classical City, 750–330 B.C.*, London: Croom Helm.

––––––. 1999. *The Constitution of the Roman Republic*. Oxford: Oxford University Press.

Livy, Titus. 1919–26. *History of Rome (Ab Urbe Condita), Books 1–10* (vols. I–IV), trans. B. O. Foster. Cambridge, MA: Harvard University Press (Loeb).

Locke, John. 1989. *Two Treatises of Government*. Cambridge: Cambridge University Press.

Loewenstein, Karl. 1973. *The Governance of Rome*. Amsterdam: Kluwer Academic.

Macedo, Stephen. 1994. *Liberal Virtues: Citizenship, Virtue, and Community in Liberal Constitutionalism*. Oxford: Oxford University Press.

Machiavelli, Niccolò. [1513] 1997. *Il Principe*. In *Opere I: I Primi Scritti Politici*, ed. Corrado Vivanti. Torino: Einaudi-Gallimard, 114–92.

––––––. [c. 1513–1517] 1950. *The Discourses of Niccolò Machiavelli*, ed. and trans. Leslie J. Walker. 2 vols. London: Routledge and Kegan Paul.

––––––. [c. 1513–19] 1997. *Discorsi sopra la prima deca di Tito Livio*. In *Opere I: I Primi Scritti Politici*, ed. Corrado Vivanti. Torino: Einaudi-Gallimard, 193–525.

––––––. [1519–20] 1997. "Discursus Florentinarum rerum post mortem iunioris Laurentii Medicis." In *Opere I: I Primi Scritti Politici*, ed. Corrado Vivanti. Turin: Einaudi-Gallimard, 733–45.

––––––. 1521 [1997]. *Dell'Arte Della Guerra*. In *Opere I: I Primi Scritti Politici*, ed. Corrado Vivanti. Turin: Einaudi-Gallimard, 529–705.

————. [1525] 1988. *Florentine Histories*, trans. Laura F. Banfield and Harvey C. Mansfield. Princeton, NJ: Princeton University Press.

————. [1532] 1962. *Istorie Fiorentine*, ed. Franco Gaeta. Milan: Feltrinelli.

Mackie, Gerry. 2004. *Democracy Defended*. Cambridge: Cambridge University Press.

Maddox, Graham. 2002. "The Limits of Neo-Roman Liberty." *History of Political Thought* 23, no. 3: 418–31.

Madison, James, Alexander Hamilton, and John Jay (as Publius). [1788] 1998. *The Federalist Papers*. New York: Mentor.

Maloy, Jason Stuart. 2008. *The Colonial American Origins of Modern Democratic Thought*. Cambridge: Cambridge University Press.

Manin, Bernard. 1994. "Checks, Balances and Boundaries: The Separation of Powers in the Constitutional Debate of 1787." In *The Invention of the Modern Republic*, ed. Biancamaria Fontana. Cambridge: Cambridge University Press, 172–94.

————. 1997. *The Principles of Representative Government*. Cambridge: Cambridge University Press.

Manin, Bernard, Adam Przeworski, and Susan C. Stokes. 1999. "Elections and Representation." In *Democracy, Accountability, and Representation*, ed. Adam Przeworski, Susan C. Stokes, and Bernard Manin. Cambridge: Cambridge University Press, 29–54.

Mansbridge, Jane. 2003. "Rethinking Representation." *American Political Science Review* 97, no. 4: 515–28.

Mansfield, Harvey C. 1979. *Machiavelli's New Modes and Orders: A Study of the Discourses on Livy*. Ithaca, NY: Cornell University Press.

————. 1996. *Machiavelli's Virtue*. Chicago: University of Chicago Press.

————, ed. and trans. 1998. *Machiavelli's The Prince*. Chicago: University of Chicago Press.

Mansfield, Harvey C., and Nathan Tarcov, ed. and trans. 1997. *Machiavelli's Discourses on Livy*. Chicago: University of Chicago Press.

Maravall, José María, and Ignacio Sánchez-Cuenca, eds. 2007. *Controlling Governments: Voters, Institutions, and Accountability*. Cambridge: Cambridge University Press.

Markell, Patchen. 2006. "The Rule of the People: Arendt, Archê, and Democracy." *American Political Science Review* 100, no. 1: 1–14.

————. 2008. "The Insufficiency of Non-Domination." *Political Theory: An International Journal of Political Philosophy* 36, no. 1: 9–36.

Marshall, Bruce. 1997. "*Libertas Populi*: The Introduction of Secret Ballot at Rome and Its Depiction on Coinage." *Antichthon* 31: 54–73.

Martin, Robert W. 2001. *The Free and Open Press: The Founding of American Democratic Press Liberty*. New York: New York University Press.

Martines, Lauro. 1979. *Power and Imagination: City-States in Renaissance Italy*. New York: Knopf.

Matsusaka, John G. 2008. *For the Many or the Few: The Initiative, Public Policy, and American Democracy*. Chicago: University of Chicago Press.

McChesney, Robert W. 1999. *Rich Media, Poor Democracy: Communication Politics in Dubious Times*. Champaigne-Urbana: University of Illinois Press.

McCormick, John P. 1998. "The Dilemmas of Dictatorship: Toward a Theory of Constitutional Emergency Powers." In *Law as Politics*, ed. David Dyzenhaus. Durham, NC: Duke University Press, 163–87.

———. 2003. "Machiavelli against Republicanism: On the Cambridge School's 'Guicciardinian Moments.'" *Political Theory: An International Journal of Political Philosophy* 31, no. 5: 615–43.

———. 2007a. "Rousseau's Rome and the Repudiation of Republican Populism." *Critical Review of International Social and Political Philosophy (CRISPP)* 10, no. 1: 3–27.

———. 2007b. "Machiavelli's Political Trials and the 'Free Way of Life.'" *Political Theory: An International Journal of Political Philosophy* 35, no. 4: 385–411.

———. 2008a. "Prophetic Statebuilding: Machiavelli and the Passion of the Duke." Paper presented at a Symposium on "Reason of State," at the University of California, Los Angeles, sponsored by the Conference for the Study of Political Thought (April 25).

———. 2008b. "Subdue the Senate: Machiavelli's 'Way of Freedom' or Path to Tyranny?" Paper presented at the conference "Machiavelli: Philosophy, Rhetoric, and History," at the Beinecke Rare Books Library, Yale University (October 17–18).

———. 2009a. "Machiavelli, Weber and Cesare Borgia: The Science of Politics and Exemplary Statebuilding." *Storia e Politica* I, no. 1: 7–34.

———. 2009b. "Machiavelli and the Gracchi: Prudence, Violence and Redistribution." *Global Crime* 10, no. 4: 298–305.

———, ed. n.d. *Civic Liberty and Republican Government. Selected Political Writings of Francesco Guicciardini*. Princeton, NJ: Princeton University Press.

McLean, Paul Douglas. 2007. *The Art of the Network: Strategic Interaction and Patronage in Renaissance Florence*. Durham, NC: Duke University Press.

Meckstroth, Christopher. 2009. "The Struggle for Democracy: Paradox and History in Democratic Progress." *Constellations* 16, no. 3: 410–28

———. n.d. *Democratic Progress: Paradox, Struggle, and Constitutional Change*. Ph.D. Dissertation, Political Science, University of Chicago.

Medina, Luis Fernando, and Susan C. Stokes. 2007. "Monopoly and Monitoring: An Approach to Political Clientelism." In *Patrons, Clients and Policies: Patterns of Democratic Accountability and Political Competition*, ed. Herbert Kitschelt and Steven I. Wilkinson. Cambridge: Cambridge University Press, 68–83.

Merleau-Ponty, Maurice. 1990. "A Note on Machiavelli." In *Signs*, trans. Richard C. McCleary. Evanston, IL: Northwestern University Press, 211–23.

Meyers, Marvin, ed. 1981. *The Mind of the Founder: Sources of the Political Thought of James Madison*. Hanover, NH: University Press of New England.

Meyers, Peter Alexander. 2008. *Civic War and the Corruption of the Citizen*. Chicago: University of Chicago Press.

Michelman, Frank. 1997. "How Can the People Ever Make the Laws? A Critique of Deliberative Democracy." In *Deliberative Democracy: Essays on Reason and Politics*, ed. James Bohman and William Rehg. Cambridge, MA: MIT Press, 145–72.

———. 1998. "Constitutional Authorship." In *Constitutionalism: Philosophical Foundations*, ed. Larry Alexander. Cambridge: Cambridge University Press, 64–98.

Michels, Robert. [1911] 1990. *Political Parties: A Sociological Study of the Oligarchical Tendencies of Modern Democracy*. New Brunswick: Free Press.

Millar, Fergus. 1998. *The Crowd in Rome in the Late Republic*. Ann Arbor: University of Michigan Press.

———. 2001. "The Roman Republic." In *The Roman Republic and the Augustan Revolution*, ed. Fergus Millar, Hannah M. Cotton, and Guy M. Rogers. Chapel Hill: University of North Carolina Press, 85–161.

———. 2002. *The Roman Republic in Political Thought*. Boston: Brandeis University Press.

Miller, James. 1984. *Rousseau: Dreamer of Democracy*. New Haven: Yale University Press.

Mills, C. Wright. 1999. *The Power Elite*. Oxford: Oxford University Press.

Molho, Anthony, Kurt Raaflaub, and Julia Emlen, eds. 1991. *City-States in Classical Antiquity and Medieval Italy*. Ann Arbor: University of Michigan Press.

Monoson, Susan Sara. 2000. *Plato's Democratic Entanglements: Athenian Politics and the Practice of Philosophy*. Princeton, NJ: Princeton University Press.

Montesquieu, C. B. S., baron de [1734] 1999. *Considerations on the Causes of the Greatness of the Romans and Their Decline*, trans. D. Lowenthal. Indianapolis, IN: Hackett.

———. [1748] 1989. *The Spirit of the Laws*, trans. and ed. Anne M. Cohler, Basia Carolyn Miller, and Harold Samuel Stone. Cambridge: Cambridge University Press.

Morgan, Edmund S. 1989. *Inventing the People: The Rise of Popular Sovereignty in England and America*. New York: W.W. Norton.

Mosca, Gaetano. [1896] 1980. *Ruling Class*, ed. Arthur Livingston; trans. H. D. Kahn. Westport, CT: Greenwood.

Mouffe, Chantal. 2000. *The Democratic Paradox*. London: Verso.

Mouritsen, Henrik. 2001. *Plebs and Politics in the Late Roman Republic*. Cambridge: Cambridge University Press.

Murakawa, Naomi. 2007. "The Political Causes and Consequences of Mass Incarceration." *Perspectives on Politics* 5, no. 3: 629–32.

———. 2009. *Electing to Punish: Congress, Race, and the American Criminal Justice State*. Book manuscript, Department of Political Science, University of Washington.

Murray, Robert J. 1966. "Cicero and the Gracchi." *Transactions and Proceedings of the American Philological Association* 97: 291–8.

Najemy, John M. 1982. *Corporatism and Consensus in Florentine Electoral Politics, 1280–1400*. Chapel Hill: University of North Carolina Press.

———. 1990. "The Controversy Surrounding Machiavelli's Service to the Republic." In *Machiavelli and Republicanism*, ed. Gisela Bock, Quentin Skinner, and Maurizio Viroli. Cambridge: Cambridge University Press, 102–17.

———. 1993. *Between Friends: Discourses of Power and Desire in the Machiavelli-Vettori Letters of 1513–1515*. Princeton, NJ: Princeton University Press.

———. 1997. "'Occupare La Tirannide': Machiavelli, the Militia and Guicciardini's Accusation of Tyranny." In *Della Tirannia: Machiavelli con Bartolo*, ed. Jérémie Barthas. Firenze: Leo S. Olschki, 75–107.

———. 2000. "Civic Humanism and Florentine Politics." In *Renaissance Civic Humanism: Reappraisals and Reflections*, ed. James Hankins. Cambridge: Cambridge University Press, 75–104.

———. 2006. *A History of Florence: 1200–1575*. Oxford: Blackwell.

Neblo, Michael. 2005. "Thinking Through Democracy: Between the Theory and Practice of Deliberative Politics." *Acta Politica* 40, no. 2: 1–13.

———. n.d. *Common Voices: The Problems and Promise of a Deliberative Democracy*. Book manuscript.

Nedelsky, Jennifer. 1991. *Private Property and the Limits of American Constitutionalism: The Madisonian Framework and Its Legacy*. Chicago: University of Chicago Press.

Nederman, Cary J. 2000. "Rhetoric, Reason and Republic: Republicanisms – Ancient, Medieval and Modern." In *Renaissance Civic Humanism: Reappraisals and Reflections*, ed. James Hankins. Cambridge: Cambridge University Press, 247–69.

Nelson, Eric. 2004. *The Greek Tradition in Republican Thought*. Cambridge: Cambridge University Press.

Nicolet, Claude. 1980. *The World of the Citizen in Republican Rome*, trans. P. S. Falla. London: Batsford Academic.

Nippel, Wilfried. 1980. *Mischverfassungstheorie und Verfassungsrealität in Antike und früher Neuzeit*. Stuttgart: Klett-Cotta.

———. 1994. "Ancient and Modern Republicanism." In *The Invention of the Modern Republic*, ed. Biancamaria Fontana. Cambridge: Cambridge University Press, 6–26.

North, John A. 2006. "The Constitution of the Roman Republic." In *A Companion to the Roman Republic*, ed. Nathan Stewart Rosenstein and Robert Morstein-Marx. Oxford: Blackwell, 256–77.

Ober, Josiah. 1993. *Mass and Elite Democratic Athens: Rhetoric, Ideology and the Power of the People*. Princeton, NJ: Princeton University Press.

———. 1998. *Political Dissent in Democratic Athens: Intellectual Critics of Popular Rule*. Princeton, NJ: Princeton University Press.

———. 2009. *Democracy and Knowledge*. Princeton, NJ: Princeton University Press.

O'Donnell, Guillermo, and Phillipe C. Schmitter. 1986. *Transitions from Authoritarian Rule: Prospects for Democracy*. Baltimore: Johns Hopkins University Press.

O'Leary, Kevin. 2006. *Saving Democracy: A Plan for Real Representation in America*. Stanford, CA: Stanford University Press.

Olmsted, Wendy. 2006. *Rhetoric: An Historical Introduction*. Oxford: Blackwell.

Olson, Kevin. 2006. *Reflexive Democracy: Political Equality and the Welfare State*. Cambridge, MA: MIT Press.

Padgett, John F. 2010. "Open Elite?: Social Mobility, Marriage, and Family in Florence, 1282–1494." *Renaissance Quarterly* 63: 1–55.

Padgett, John F., and Chris K. Ansell. 1993. "Robust Action and the Rise of the Medici, 1400–1434." *American Journal of Sociology* 98, no. 6: 1259–1319.

Page, Scott. 2006. *The Difference: How the Power of Diversity Creates Better Groups, Firms, Schools, and Societies*. Princeton, NJ: Princeton University Press.

Palonen, Kari. 1998. *Das 'Webersche Moment'. Zur Kontingenz des Politischen*. Wiesbaden: Westdeutscher.

Parekh, Bhikhu C. 2002. *Rethinking Multiculturalism: Cultural Diversity and Political Theory*. Cambridge, MA: Harvard University Press.

Parel, Anthony J. 1992. *The Machiavellian Cosmos*. New Haven: Yale University Press.

———. 2000. "Review of Coby, Machiavelli's Romans." *American Political Science Review* 94, no. 1: 165–6.

Pareto, Vilfredo. 1987. *Political and Historical Theory of the Elites*. London: Classical Reprints.

Pateman, Carol. 1989. *The Disorder of Women: Democracy, Feminism and Political Theory*. New York: Blackwell.

Patten, Alan. 1996. "The Republican Critique of Liberalism." *British Journal of Political Science* 26: 25–44.

Pearse, Hillary. 2008. "Institutional Design and Citizen Deliberation." In *Designing Deliberative Democracy: The British Columbia Citizens' Assembly*, ed. Mark E. Warren and Hillary Pearse. Cambridge: Cambridge University Press, 70–84.

Pettit, Philip. 1999a. *Republicanism: A Theory of Freedom and Government.* Oxford: Oxford University Press.

———. 1999b. "Republican Freedom and Contestatory Democratization." In *Democracy's Value,* ed. Ian Shapiro and Casiano Hacker-Cordon. Cambridge: Cambridge University Press, 163–89.

———. 2000. "Democracy: Electoral and Contestatory." In *Nomos XLII: Designing Democratic Institutions,* ed. Ian Shapiro and Stephen Macedo. New York: New York University Press, 105–46.

———. 2001. *A Theory of Freedom: From the Psychology to the Politics of Agency.* Oxford: Oxford University Press.

———. 2002. "Keeping Republican Freedom Simple: On a Difference with Quentin Skinner." *Political Theory: An International Journal of Political Philosophy 30,* no. 3: 339–56.

———. 2004. "Depoliticizing Democracy." *Ratio Juris* 17, no. 1: 52–65.

Phillips, Anne. 1995. *The Politics of Presence.* Oxford: Oxford University Press.

Phillips, Kevin. 2002. *Wealth and Democracy: A Political History of the American Rich.* New York: Random House.

Pitkin, Hanna F. 1988. "Are Freedom and Liberty Twins?" *Political Theory: An International Journal of Political Philosophy* 16, no. 4: 523–52.

———. 1990. *The Concept of Representation.* Berkeley: University of California Press.

———. 1999. *Fortune Is a Woman: Gender and Politics in the Thought of Niccolò Machiavelli: With a New Afterword.* Chicago: University of Chicago Press.

Pitts, Jennifer. 2005. *A Turn to Empire: The Rise of Imperial Liberalism in Britain and France.* Princeton, NJ: Princeton University Press.

Plamenatz, John. 2006. *Man and Society: Political and Social Theories from Machiavelli to Marx.* London: Longman Press.

Plutarch. 1921. *Lives,* vol. X. New York: Macmillan.

———. 2005. "Cicero." *The Fall of the Roman Republic: Six Lives.* New York: Penguin, 323–73.

Pocock, J. G. A. 1975. *The Machiavellian Moment: Florentine Political Thought and the Atlantic Political Tradition.* Princeton, NJ: Princeton University Press.

———. 2003. "Afterword." In *The Machiavellian Moment,* second edition. Princeton, NJ: Princeton University Press, 553–84.

Polybius. 1979. *The Histories.* New York: Penguin.

Posner, Richard. 2004. *Law, Pragmatism and Democracy.* Cambridge, MA: Harvard University Press.

Powell, G. Bingham. 2000. *Elections as Instruments of Democracy.* New Haven: Yale University Press.

Przeworski, Adam. 1991. *Democracy and the Market.* Cambridge: Cambridge University Press.

———. 1999. "Minimalist Conception of Democracy: A Defense." In *Democracy's Value,* ed. Ian Shapiro and Casiano Hacker-Cordon. Cambridge: Cambridge University Press, 23–55.

Przeworski, Adam, Susan C. Stokes, and Bernard Manin, eds. 1999. *Democracy, Accountability, and Representation.* Cambridge: Cambridge University Press.

Przeworski, Adam, and Michael Wallerstein. 1988. "Structural Dependence of the State on Capital." *American Political Science Review* 82, no. 1: 11–29.

Putnam, Robert. 2000. *Bowling Alone: The Collapse and Revival of American Community.* New York: Simon & Schuster.

Raaflaub, Kurt A., ed. 2005. *Social Struggles in Archaic Rome*. Malden, MA: Wiley-Blackwell.

Rahe, Paul A., ed. 2005. *Machiavelli's Liberal Republican Legacy*. Cambridge: Cambridge University Press.

Ranciere, Jacques. 2007. *Hatred of Democracy*, trans. Steve Corcoran. London: Verso.

Ratner, R. S. 2008. "Communicative Rationality in the Citizens' Assembly and Referendum Processes." In *Designing Deliberative Democracy: The British Columbia Citizens' Assembly*, ed. Mark E. Warren and Hillary Pearse. Cambridge: Cambridge University Press, 145–66.

Rattan, Gurpreet. 2001. "Prospects for a Contemporary Republicanism." *The Monist* 84, no. 1: 113–30.

Rehfeld, Andrew. 2005. *The Concept of Constituency: Political Representation, Democratic Legitimacy, and Institutional Design*. New York: Cambridge University Press.

Richard, Carl J. 1994. *The Founders and the Classics: Greece, Rome, and the American Enlightenment*. Cambridge, MA: Harvard University Press.

Ridolfi, Roberto. 1963. *The Life of Niccolò Machiavelli*, trans. C. Grayson. Chicago: University of Chicago Press.

_____. 1968. *The Life of Francesco Guicciardini*, trans. C. Grayson. New York: Knopf.

Robinson, Eric W., ed. 2004. *Ancient Greek Democracy: Readings and Sources*. Malden, MA: Wiley-Blackwell.

Rogers, Melvin L. 2008. "Republican Confusion and Liberal Clarification." *Philosophy & Social Criticism* 34, no. 7: 799–824.

Rose-Ackerman, Susan. 1999. *Corruption and Government: Causes, Consequences, and Reform*. Cambridge: Cambridge University Press.

Rosenberg, Gerald N. 1991. *The Hollow Hope: Can Courts Bring about Social Change?* Chicago: University of Chicago Press.

Rosenblum, Nancy. 1998. *Membership and Morals: The Personal Uses of Pluralism in America*. Princeton, NJ: Princeton University Press.

_____. 2008. *On the Side of Angels: An Appreciation of Parties and Partisanship*. Princeton, NJ: Princeton University Press.

Rossiter, Clinton. 1948. *Constitutional Dictatorship: Crisis Government in Modern Democracies*. Princeton, NJ: Princeton University Press.

Rousseau, Jean-Jacques. 1997. *The Social Contract and Other Later Political Writings*, ed. Victor Gourevitch. Cambridge: Cambridge University Press.

Rubinstein, Nicolai. 1954. "I primi anni del Consiglio Maggiore di Firenze, 1494–99." *Archivio Storico Italiano* 112: 151–94.

_____. 1966. *The Government of Florence under the Medici, 1434 to 1494*. Oxford: Clarendon.

Rudenstine, David. 1998. *The Day the Presses Stopped: A History of the Pentagon Papers Case*. Berkeley: University of California Press.

Rustow, Dankwart. 1970. "Transitions to Democracy: Toward a Dynamic Model." *Comparative Politics* 2, no. 3: 337–63.

Salvemini, Gaetano. 1899. *Magnati e Popolani in Firenze dal 1280 al 1295*. Florence: Carnesecchi.

Samaha, Adam M. 2009. "Randomization in Adjudication." *William and Mary Law Review* 51, no. 1: 1–86.

Samples, John Curtis. 2006. *The Fallacy of Campaign Finance Reform*. Chicago: University of Chicago Press.

Sandel, Michael J. 1996. *Democracy's Discontent: America in Search of a Public Philosophy*. Cambridge, MA: Harvard University Press.

Sanders, Lynn M. 1997. "Against Deliberation." *Political Theory: An International Journal of Political Philosophy* 25, no. 3: 347–77.

Saxonhouse, Arlene W. 1996. *Athenian Democracy: Modern Mythmakers and Ancient Theorists*. Notre Dame, IN: Notre Dame University Press.

Schmitt, Carl. 2007. *Constitutional Theory*, trans. Jeffrey Seitzer. Durham, NC: Duke University Press.

Schofield, Malcolm. 1999. "Cicero's Definition of Res Publica." In *Cicero the Philosopher: Twelve Papers*, ed. J. G. F. Powell. Oxford: Oxford University Press, 63–84.

Schumpeter, Joseph A. 1942. *Capitalism, Socialism, Democracy*. New York: Harper.

Schwartzberg, Melissa. 2007. *Democracy and Legal Change*. Cambridge: Cambridge University Press.

Seager, Robin. 1972. "Cicero and the Word Popularis." *Classical Quarterly* 22, no. 2: 328–38.

Sealey, Raphael. 1976. *A History of the Greek City-States, 700–338 B.C.* Berkeley: University of California Press.

Sellers, M. N. S. 1994. *American Republicanism: Roman Ideology in the United States Constitution*. New York: New York University Press.

Shapiro, Ian. 2002. "Why the Poor Don't Soak the Rich: Notes on Democracy and Distribution." *Daedalus* 130, no. 4: 118–28.

———. 2003. *The State of Democratic Theory*. Princeton, NJ: Princeton University Press.

Shea, Christopher. 2006. "51 Angry Plebes: What Machiavelli Could Have Taught the Founding Fathers about Democracy." *Boston Globe*, July 9.

Shklar, Judith N. 1989. "The Liberalism of Fear." In *Liberalism and the Moral Life*, ed. Nancy L. Rosenblum. Cambridge, MA: Harvard University Press, 21–38.

Shugart, Matthew Soberg, and Martin P. Wattenberg, eds. 2001. *Mixed-Member Electoral Systems: The Best of Both Worlds*. Oxford: Oxford University Press, 2001.

Silvano, Giovanni. 1990. "Florentine Republicanism in the Early Sixteenth Century." In *Machiavelli and Republicanism*, ed. Gisela Bock, Quentin Skinner, and Maurizio Viroli. Cambridge: Cambridge University Press, 40–70.

Skinner, Quentin. 1973. "The Empirical Theorists of Democracy and Their Critics: A Plague on Both Their Houses." *Political Theory: An International Journal of Political Philosophy* 1, no. 3: 287–305.

———. 1981. *Past Masters: Machiavelli*. New York: Hill and Wang.

———. 1983. "Machiavelli and the Maintenance of Liberty." *Politics* 18, no. 2: 3–15.

———. 1990a. "Machiavelli's Discorsi and the Pre-Humanist Origins of Republican Ideas." In *Machiavelli and Republicanism*, ed. Gisela Bock, Quentin Skinner, and Maurizio Viroli. Cambridge: Cambridge University Press, 121–41.

———. 1990b. "The Republican Ideal of Political Liberty." In *Machiavelli and Republicanism*, ed. Gisela Bock, Quentin Skinner, and Maurizio Viroli. Cambridge: Cambridge University Press, 293–309.

———. 1998. *Liberty before Liberalism*. Cambridge: Cambridge University Press.

———. 2002. *Visions of Politics, Vol. II: Renaissance Virtues*. Cambridge: Cambridge University Press.

Skocpol, Theda. 2004. *Diminished Democracy: From Membership to Management in American Civic Life*. Norman: University of Oklahoma Press.

Smith, Rodney A. 2006. *Money, Power & Elections: How Campaign Finance Reform Subverts American Democracy*. Baton Rouge: Louisiana State University Press.

Smith, Rogers M. 1997. *Civic Ideals: Conflicting Visions of Citizenship in U.S. History*. New Haven: Yale University Press.

Springborg, Patricia. 2001. "Republicanism, Freedom from Domination, and the Cambridge Contextual Historians." *Political Studies* 49: 851–76.

Steel, C. E. W. 2001. *Cicero, Rhetoric, and Empire*. Oxford: Oxford University Press.

Stephens, J. N. 1983. *The Fall of the Florentine Republic, 1512–1530*. Oxford: Oxford University Press.

Stokes, Susan. 1999. "What Do Policy Switches Tell Us about Democracy?" In *Democracy, Accountability, and Representation*, ed. Adam Przeworski, Susan Stokes, and Bernard Manin. Cambridge: Cambridge University Press, 98–130.

———. 2001. *Mandates and Democracy: Neoliberalism by Surprise in Latin America*. Cambridge: Cambridge University Press.

Stone, I. F. 1989. *The Trial of Socrates*. New York: Anchor.

Stone, Peter C. 2007. "Why Lotteries Are Just." *Journal of Political Philosophy* 15, no. 3: 276–95.

———. 2009. "The Logic of Random Selection." *Political Theory* 37, no. 3: 375–97.

Strauss, Leo. 1958. *Thoughts on Machiavelli*. Glencoe, IL: Free Press.

———. 1972. "Niccolo Machiavelli, 1469–1527." In *History of Political Thought*, ed. Leo Strauss and Joseph Cropsey. Chicago: Rand McNally, 271–92.

Strong, Tracy B. 2002. *Jean-Jacques Rousseau and the Politics of the Ordinary*. Lanham, MD: Rowman & Littlefield.

Sunstein, Cass R. 1988. "Beyond the Republican Revival." *Yale Law Journal* 97: 1539–90.

———. 2006. *Infotopia: How Many Minds Produce Knowledge*. Oxford: Oxford University Press.

Surowiecki, James. 2004. *The Wisdom of Crowds*. New York: Doubleday.

Symposium on the California Recall. 2004. *PS: Political Science and Politics* 37, no. 1: 7–32.

Tan, James. 2008. "Contiones in the Age of Cicero." *Classical Antiquity* 27, no 1: 163–201.

Tarcov, Nathan. 2003. "Arms and Politics in Machiavelli's *Prince*." In *Entre Kant et Kosovo: Etudes offertes á Pierre Hassner*, ed. Anne-Marie Le Gloannec and Aleksander Smolar. Paris: Presses de Sciences Po, 109–21.

———. 2007. "Freedom, Republics, and Peoples in Machiavelli's *Prince*." In *Freedom and the Human Person*, ed. Richard Velkley. Washington, DC: Catholic University of America Press, 122–42.

Taylor, Lily Ross. 1962. "Forerunners of the Gracchi." *Journal of Roman Studies* 52, no. 1 & 2: 19–27

———. 1990. *Roman Voting Assemblies*. Ann Arbor: University of Michigan Press.

Thompson, Dennis F. 2002. *Just Elections: Creating a Fair Electoral Process in the United States*. Chicago: University of Chicago Press.

———. 2008. "Who Should Govern Who Governs?: The Role of Citizens in Reforming the Electoral System." In *Designing Deliberative Democracy: The British Columbia Citizens' Assembly*, ed. Mark E. Warren and Hillary Pearse. Cambridge: Cambridge University Press, 20–49.

Thucydides. 2009. *The Peloponnesian War*, trans. Martin Hammond. Oxford: Oxford University Press.

Tierney, Stephen. 2009. "Constitutional Referendums: A Theoretical Enquiry." *Modern Law Review* 72, no. 3: 360–83.

Tilly, Charles. 2007. *Democracy*. Cambridge: Cambridge University Press.

Tocqueville, Alexis de. [1840] 2000. *Democracy in America*, ed. and trans. Harvey Mansfield and Delba Winthrop. Chicago: University of Chicago Press.

Tuck, Richard. 1993. *Philosophy and Government, 1572–1651*. Cambridge: Cambridge University Press.

———. 2008. *Free Riding*. Cambridge, MA: Harvard University Press.

Urbinati, Nadia. 2002. *Mill on Democracy: From the Athenian Polis to Representative Government*. Chicago: University of Chicago Press.

———. 2004. "Condorcet's Democratic Theory of Representative Government." *European Journal of Political Theory: An International Journal of Political Philosophy* 3, no. 1: 53–75.

———. 2006. *Representative Democracy: Principles and Genealogy*. Chicago: University of Chicago Press.

Urofsky, Melvin I. 2005. *Money and Free Speech: Campaign Finance Reform and the Courts*. Lawrence: University Press of Kansas.

van der Zande, Johan, and John Christian Laursen, eds. 2003. *Early French and German Defenses of Freedom of the Press*. Boston: Brill Academic.

van Gelderen, Martin. 2002. *The Political Thought of the Dutch Revolt, 1555–1590*. Cambridge: Cambridge University Press.

———. 2005. "Aristotelians, Monarchomachs and Republicans: Sovereignty and respublica mixta in Dutch and German Political Thought, 1580–1650." In *Republicanism, A Shared European Heritage: Volume 1, Republicanism and Constitutionalism in Early Modern Europe*, ed. Martin van Gelderen and Quentin Skinner. Cambridge: Cambridge University Press, 195–219.

Vatter, Miguel E. 2000. *Between Form and Event: Machiavelli's Theory of Political Freedom*. Amsterdam: Kluwer Academic.

Viroli, Maurizio. 1988. *Jean-Jacques Rousseau and the "Well-Ordered Society,"* trans. Derek Hanson. Cambridge: Cambridge University Press.

———. 1990. "Machiavelli and the Republican Idea of Politics." In *Machiavelli and Republicanism*, ed. Gisela Bock, Quentin Skinner, and Maurizio Viroli. Cambridge: Cambridge University Press, 143–71.

———. 1997. *For Love of Country: An Essay on Patriotism and Nationalism*. Oxford: Oxford University Press.

———. 1998. *Founders: Machiavelli*. Oxford: Oxford University Press.

———. 2000. *Niccolò's Smile: A Biography of Machiavelli*. New York: Farrar, Strauss and Giroux.

Waldron, Jeremy. 1987. "Theoretical Foundations of Liberalism." *Philosophical Quarterly* 37, vol. 147: 127–50.

———. 1995. "The Wisdom of the Multitude: Some Reflections on Book 3, Chapter 11 of Aristotle's *Politics*." *Political Theory: An International Journal of Political Philosophy* 23, no. 4: 563–84.

Waley, Daniel Philip. 1969. *The Italian City-Republics*. London: Longman Press.

Wantchekon, Leonard. 2004. "The Paradox of 'Warlord' Democracy." *American Political Science Review* 98, no. 1: 17–34.

Wantchekon, Leonard, and David Nickerson. 2000. "*Multilateral Intervention Facilitates Post Civil War Democratization.*" Manuscript: Yale University.

Wantchekon, Leonard, and Mario Simon. 1999. "*Democracy as an Arbitration Mechanism.*" Manuscript: Yale University.

Ward, Allen M. 2004. "How Democratic Was the Roman Republic?" *New England Classical Journal* 31, no. 2: 101–19.

Warren, Mark E. 2000. *Democracy and Association.* Princeton, NJ: Princeton University Press.

Warren, Mark E., and Hillary Pearse. 2008. *Designing Deliberative Democracy: The British Columbia Citizens' Assembly.* Cambridge: Cambridge University Press.

Whelan, Frederick G. 1983. "Democratic Theory and the Boundary Problem." In *Liberal Democracy: Nomos XXV*, ed. J. R. Pennock and J. W. Chapman. New York: New York University Press, 13–47.

Williams, Melissa S. 2000. *Voice, Trust, and Memory: Marginalized Groups and the Failings of Liberal Representation.* Princeton, NJ: Princeton University Press.

Wiseman, T. P. 2009. *Remembering the Roman People: Essays on Late-Republican Politics and Literature*, Oxford: Oxford University Press.

Wolff, Edward N. 2001. *Top Heavy: The Increasing Inequality of Wealth in America and What Can Be Done about It.* New York: New Press.

———. 2007. *Recent Trends in Household Wealth in the United States: Rising Debt and the Middle-Class Squeeze.* Annandale-on-Hudson, NY: Levy Economics Institute of Bard College.

———. 2010. "Recent Trends in Household Wealth in the United States – An Update to 2007." *Working Paper No. 589.* Annandale-on-Hudson, NY: Levy Economics Institute of Bard College.

Wolin, Sheldon S. 1994. "Norm and Form: The Constitutionalizing of Democracy." In *Athenian Political Thought and the Reconstruction of American Democracy*, ed. J. Peter Euben, John Wallach, and Josiah Ober. Ithaca, NY: Cornell University Press, 29–58.

———. 1996. "Fugitive Democracy." In *Democracy and Difference: Contesting Boundaries of the Political*, ed. Seyla Benhabib. Princeton, NJ: Princeton University Press, 31–45.

Wood, Gordon S. 1998. *The Creation of the American Republic, 1776–1787.* Chapel Hill: University of North Carolina Press.

Wood, Neal. 1988. *Cicero's Social and Political Thought.* Berkeley: University of California Press.

Wooten, David, ed. 1994. *Republicanism, Liberty, and Commercial Society, 1649–1776.* Stanford, CA: Stanford University Press.

Yack, Bernard. 1993. *Problems of a Political Animal: Community, Justice and Conflict in Aristotelian Political Thought.* Berkeley: University of California Press.

Yakobson, Alexander. 2006. "Popular Power in the Roman Republic." In *A Companion to the Roman Republic*, ed. Nathan Stewart Rosenstein and Robert Morstein-Marx. Oxford: Blackwell, 383–400.

Young, Iris Marion. 1990. *Justice and the Politics of Difference.* Princeton, NJ: Princeton University Press.

———. 2006. *Inclusion and Democracy.* Oxford: Oxford University Press.

Zerba, Michelle Louise. 2004. "The Frauds of Humanism: Cicero, Machiavelli, and the Rhetoric of Imposture." *Rhetorica* 22, no. 3: 215–40.

Zerilli, Linda M. G. 1994. *Signifying Woman: Culture and Chaos in Rousseau, Burke, and Mill.* Ithaca, NY: Cornell University Press.

———. 2005. "'We Feel Our Freedom': Imagination and Judgment in the Thought of Hannah Arendt." *Political Theory* 33, no. 2: 158–88.

Ziblatt, Daniel. 2006. "How Did Europe Democratize?" *World Politics* 58, no. 2: 311–38.

———. 2008. "Does Landholding Inequality Block Democratization?" *World Politics* 60, no. 4: 610–41.

Index